Items should be returned on or before the date shown below. Items
not already requested by other borrowers may be renewed in person,
in writing or by telephone. To renew, please quote the number on the
barcode label. To renew online a PIN is required. This can be requested
at your local library.
Renew online @ **www.dublincitypubliclibraries.ie**
Fines charged for overdue items will include postage incurred in recovery.
Damage to or loss of items will be charged to the borrower.

 Comhairle Cathrach
Bhaile Átha Cliath
Dublin City Council

**Leaeharlanna Poiblí
Chathair Bhaile Átha
Cliath**

Due Date	Due Date	Due Date
Brainse Rátheanaigh
Raheny Branch
Tel: 8315521

10/5/18 | | |

PORTRAITS FROM LIFE

PORTRAITS FROM LIFE

MODERNIST NOVELISTS AND AUTOBIOGRAPHY

JEROME BOYD MAUNSELL

OXFORD
UNIVERSITY PRESS

OXFORD
UNIVERSITY PRESS

Great Clarendon Street, Oxford, OX2 6DP,
United Kingdom

Oxford University Press is a department of the University of Oxford.
It furthers the University's objective of excellence in research, scholarship,
and education by publishing worldwide. Oxford is a registered trade mark of
Oxford University Press in the UK and in certain other countries

© Jerome Boyd Maunsell 2018

The moral rights of the author have been asserted

First Edition published in 2018

Impression: 1

Published in the United States of America by Oxford University Press
198 Madison Avenue, New York, NY 10016, United States of America

British Library Cataloguing in Publication Data
Data available

Library of Congress Control Number: 2017944564

ISBN 978–0–19–878936–9

Printed and bound by
CPI Group (UK) Ltd, Croydon, CR0 4YY

For my mother and father

Contents

List of illustrations

Introduction

There is no such thing as a true portrait. They are all delusions and I never saw any two alike.[1]

Nathaniel Hawthorne

I n his *Lives of the Most Excellent Painters, Sculptors, and Architects* (1550, 1568), Giorgio Vasari briefly tells the story of how the young Francesco Mazzola, also known as Parmigianino, created his *Self-Portrait in a Convex Mirror* (1523–4), to take with him from his home town of Parma to Rome at the outset of his life as an artist. This small image in oil on poplar wood, of the artist in the act of portraying himself, was begun by the painter, Vasari tells us, "in order to investigate the subtleties of art."[2] Seeing the "bizarre effects" produced by a convex barber's mirror when he tried to draw his reflection, Parmigianino "had a ball of wood made by a turner [...] the same size and shape as the mirror."[3] Once his unusual canvas was made, "he set to work to counterfeit on it with supreme art all that he saw in the glass, and particularly his own self, which he did with such lifelike reality as could not be imagined or believed."[4] The resulting painting was an eerie, sphinx-like work which questions the very art of portraiture, and especially of self-portraiture, while looking mysteriously out at us as if it knows some answers that it doesn't want to tell. At the rounded base of the glass, the artist's hand—busy at work, we infer, creating the painting—is stretched hugely out of shape, and is almost larger than his head. Reaching out towards us, it also blocks our view, as if to remind us that however faithful his image might seem, the artist controls exactly what he lets us see.

Other, more searching thoughts might come to us, still caught in the stare of this painting. By making a direct copy of the mirror, the image demonstrates, in what seem to be undeniable terms, how much all portraiture rests on artifice, and illusion—and going further, that the same might be said of the self. The room behind the artist seems to curve and bend around him, and yet he maintains his perfect poise, in the act of making. Watching him, you almost expect him to carry on painting: for the hand to move and add another deft stroke to the image. The painting exists in a stilled and endless present, although it is almost five hundred years old, and its riddles remain unresolved.

In his long poem about the painting, "Self-Portrait in a Convex Mirror" (1973–4), the American poet John Ashbery reaches for the ways that the portrait strains at the edges of the visible, marveling at how "the time of day or the density of the light / Adhering to the face keeps it / Lively and intact in a recurring wave / Of arrival."[5] For Ashbery, the picture shows the artist trying to depict nothing less than the fact

> That the soul is a captive, treated humanely, kept
> In suspension, unable to advance much farther
> Than your look as it intercepts the picture.
> [...] It must move
> As little as possible. This is what the portrait says.[6]

In the pages that follow, I will be looking at self-portraiture in writing, rather than painting, during the first half of the twentieth century. There are obvious differences between visual and literary portraiture; yet the often hidden artificiality behind even the most accurate depiction of a life—so wryly exposed by Parmigianino's self-portrait—should serve us well as a playful warning note. The seemingly lifelike nature of portraiture in literature and in painting makes it appear less artful than it is. This is even more the case in literary portraiture, where any life depicted has to be represented in language. Words can sometimes reveal more than a visual portrait. And yet, in words or images, likenesses are mere likenesses, and the truth of a life, if there is such a thing, remains just out of reach. Literary portraiture offers us achingly close simulacra: lives frozen, reconfigured, remade. "A biography cannot imitate life," as Henry James's biographer Leon Edel writes. "It rearranges its material; it tells a flowing continuous story—something our lives never were."[7]

Autobiography is an impossibility, never quite catching its subject. Gertrude Stein saw it in terms of a detective story, with the fatal hint that it might even kill its subject, substituting it for someone else. But it is an impossibility with almost endless potential. There are multiple versions of the telling of any one life, just as the forms of life-writing are multiple—including autobiographies, biographies, diaries, letters, and memoirs, to name only a few of these forms. Every instance of autobiography is as unique as the life it relates.

*

Portraits from Life focuses on how seven major novelists—Joseph Conrad, Ford Madox Ford, Henry James, Wyndham Lewis, Gertrude Stein, H. G. Wells, and Edith Wharton—depicted their own lives in their memoirs and autobiographies.[8] To clarify one central definition, often taken in slightly different ways: autobiographies broadly take life as a whole and focus on the author, while memoirs are often focused on only a part of a life, or on other people. Both forms are treated equally and interrelatedly in this book, which, to a lesser, subsidiary extent (and generally when they illuminate the memoirs and autobiographies in some way), occasionally also looks at these authors' diaries, letters, notebooks, and autobiographical novels.

In singling out the lives of novelists, in particular, whose very *métier* consists in making things up, this book inevitably sometimes moves into the endlessly contested borderland between supposedly non-fictional autobiographies, and fiction. As we will see, the categories of "fact" and "fiction" are often stretched out of their conventional shapes in novelists' autobiographies, which sometimes flexibly demonstrate the ways in which fictional techniques are inescapable and can even hew closer to the so-called "truth" of a life. Yet most of the time, *Portraits from Life* does at least try to respect the lines between the memoir or autobiography and the novel, as did many writers of this period, even while they played with them.

In the preface to his memoir *Father and Son: A Study of Two Temperaments* (1907), Edmund Gosse declared that his book was "scrupulously true"—something he thought even more "necessary to say" at "the present hour, when fiction takes forms so ingenious and so specious."[9] Virginia Woolf—who went on in her semi-fictional "biographies" *Orlando* (1928) and *Flush* (1933) to experiment with fusions of life-writing and the novel, and who thought and wrote about the aesthetics, potential, and problems of biography and autobiography intermittently throughout her life—also respected, while she tried at times to overcome it, the difference between "the truth of real life and the truth of fiction."[10] Nonetheless, sometimes the only way to discern if a book should be taken as "true," or as fiction, rests on what kind of text the author says it is. But, as I argue, there is a difference—even if an extremely subtle one—between the kind of autobiography we often loosely refer to when we describe a novel as autobiograph*al*, and *an* autobiography. The latter is the main focus of this book.

Portraits from Life spans the period of literary Modernism, from 1900 until just after the Second World War. During these years when fiction was rein-vented (edging ever so close to autobiography in the novels of James Joyce and Marcel Proust), biography was also reshaped and revolutionized, by the work of Lytton Strachey and many others. In her 1927 essay "The New Biography," Woolf made clear that the days of the Victorian biography—a "parti-coloured, hybrid, monstrous birth"[11]—were over. "With the twentieth century," Woolf writes, "a change came over biography, as it came over fiction and poetry. The first and most visible sign of it was in the difference in size. In the first twenty years of the new century biographies must have lost half their weight."[12] Not only that: "the point of view had com-pletely altered."[13] In the 1920s, biographers aspired to be artists rather than mere historians.

Memoirs and autobiographies also changed radically in the Modernist period, sharing an equal shift in status. Many of the writers gathered together in these pages deliberately developed new forms of autobiography, as they wrote and reflected on what had happened in their lives. In doing so, their written lives also evolved a modern sense of self, and what it was possible to say about oneself. Some of these writers dramatically rearranged their lives on paper, playing with chronology and identity, memory and personae. At the same time, the act of remembrance also made them come to terms with the shape of their own lives.

Writing about oneself, as many autobiographers discover, nearly always involves writing about other people. All autobiography is, in this sense, group biography. Woolf, in her fragmentary notes towards an autobiography, "Sketch of the Past" (1939–40), noticed how she could only convey a clear sense of herself through her portrayal of how she was connected to other people, and by extension society in general, through "instincts, affections, passions, attachments":[14]

> It is by such invisible presences that the "subject of this memoir" is tugged this way and that every day of his life; it is they that keep him in position [...] if we cannot analyse these invisible presences, we know very little of the subject of the memoir; and again how futile life-writing becomes. I see myself as a fish in a stream; deflected; held in place; but cannot describe the stream.[15]

Woolf's observation here applies especially to the influence of family, but it is also relevant to friendship. Many of the writers in *Portraits from Life* also knew each other, and wrote about each other in their autobiographies. So we will see the same figures appearing, and disappearing, and reappearing, moving from book to book, page to page, rather like characters in a novel. We will see these writers through their own self-portraits, as well as through the self-portraits of others. Sometimes, the ways in which these writers depicted each other were quite self-conscious, and reciprocal—and they also read each other's memoirs and autobiographies. Art and life overlap strangely and directly in autobiographies, and many of these writers recognized this. Ford Madox Ford dedicated his book *A Mirror to France* (1926) to Gertrude Stein, and in response, Stein gave Ford a mirror. They both appeared in each other's autobiographies a few years later. "Biography," wrote Woolf, "will enlarge its scope by hanging up looking glasses at odd corners."[16] Something of this method also underlies and echoes how many of these writers depicted each other, sometimes merely glancingly, sometimes at great length. Different facets of each of these seven writers appear, and sometimes the same figure is portrayed from very different viewpoints.

So this book is a group portrait, revealing the interactions *between* the seven writers it depicts. Artistic groups are found throughout the story of Modernism, and the narrative traced in *Portraits from Life* touches on several movements, magazines, and alliances: from literary Impressionism, and the group of novelists settled in Kent and East Sussex in the early years of the century—Joseph Conrad, Ford Madox Ford, Henry James, and H. G. Wells—to the wider circles of the *English Review*, *Blast*, and Vorticism in London; and Cubism, Gertrude Stein's salon, *transition*, and the *transatlantic review* in Paris. The overall arrangement of the sequence of the chapters moves generally forward chronologically, with detours and anomalies as we follow these writers' accounts in their autobiographies. The narrative thus cuts a unique line through its period, from the Edwardian years to the First World War, through the 1920s and 30s, concluding on the other side of the Second World War. The main urban hubs throughout are London and Paris, with the focus moving from the south-east of England towards various locations in the South of France. However, a variety of other places are recalled, as these writers freely dart around in time, remembering, and also traveled to other places: above all, America, where several of these novelists (Henry James, Gertrude Stein, and Edith Wharton) were born, and where they often returned.

The seven writers collected here were chosen above all for their performance as autobiographers, as well as for how they interacted with each
other. Memoir-writing was part of the way they placed themselves in
groups, declaring allegiances and affinities. Each writer is connected to
someone else in the book—and in some cases, connected to several others.
While they formed friendships and artistic alliances with each other, they
do not, altogether, form an obvious coterie. But the connections they made
in their reminiscences have been pivotal in piecing together this group
portrait, which draws out their various ties as much as possible.

*

Portraits from Life is, above all, an experiment in biography, and in group
biography, of its own, rather than a critical study. It aims to tell a story, to
craft a narrative; and it owes more to the procedures of biography than of
literary criticism, although it is informed by, and sometimes fuses, both. It
draws primarily on a magisterial tradition of biographical writing about
its subjects. Dealing with many shape-shifting forms of autobiography and
life-writing, *Portraits from Life* is also something of a shape-shifter itself,
altering several crucial aspects of biography—above all chronology—in order
to view its subjects afresh.

The heart of this book lies in focusing on the periods during their lives
when each of these novelists worked on their memoirs and autobiographies.
These periods inform the biographical frame of each individual chapter.
Edmund Gosse, in "The Custom of Biography" (1901), observed how
Victorian biography buried the dead "under the monstrous catafalque of
two volumes (crown octavo)."[17] Autobiographies, however, are always written from the shifting perspective of life, not of death. They depict life as it is
actually happening—and they are often as affected by the present tense of
the circumstances they are written in, as by the past tense of what is being
remembered. Woolf, in her "Sketch of the Past," realized that the present
time of the writing of her memories was just as important as what she was
recalling, and so she used the present as a "platform":

> 2nd May . . . I write the date, because I think that I have discovered a possible form
> for these notes. That is, to make them include the present—at least enough of
> the present to serve as platform to stand upon. It would be interesting to make
> the two people, I now, I then, come out in contrast. And further, this past is
> much affected by the present moment. What I write today I should not write
> in a year's time.[18]

In a similar way, all the novelists in *Portraits from Life* are depicted from the "platform" of the writing of their autobiographies and memoirs, looking back, frequently in middle or old age. In some cases the frame of the period of reminiscence is more distinct and pronounced than others. Ford Madox Ford, for example, wrote autobiographies almost throughout his adult life. Sometimes, to accommodate this, or wherever fresh light can be shed on these authors' creation of their autobiographies or on their portraits of others, the biographical frames of the chapters have been slightly stretched and made more flexible. But the "platform" of the period of composition remains a recurring motif.

One of the strengths of literary biography is the way it can chart artistic process in detail. Yet while biographies of writers often recount how novels were written, they tend to have a blind spot where the writing of autobiographies is concerned. Until quite recently, the actual *writing* of memoirs and autobiographies—frequently a task that took several years, absorbing some of these writers' creative energies obsessively—tended to be presented by biographers as a fait accompli, as if these books somehow wrote themselves.[19] This strange blindness is addressed directly in *Portraits from Life*, which fully utilizes the ways in which the art of biography can illuminate reminiscences— both in reconstructing the act of remembrance, and in helping to put together the "facts" of what is being remembered.

The traditional sense of a split between the life and the work of a writer makes much less sense in the study of autobiography. It is very hard to fully understand any author's autobiography without an understanding of their lives. A biographical approach to autobiography sheds light on the genre in direct, rather than tangential, ways. And as we will see, all of the writers in this book also evolved highly sophisticated theories of their own about biography and autobiography, as they reflected on the enticements and dangers and possibilities they discovered.

*

Ford Madox Ford and Gertrude Stein both wrote literary portraits throughout their life. Ford's "Literary Portraits" were part of his journalism, but they can also be connected with the short forms of the exponents of the "New Biography," especially Lytton Strachey and Harold Nicolson. For Stein, literary portraiture was linked to visual portraiture, and her "portrait-writing" began with her friendships with Henri Matisse and Pablo Picasso, and a desire to respond to the advances of Cubism. Wyndham Lewis, the only one of these seven writers who was also a painter, also drew or painted many portraits of his friends and contemporaries, especially from the 1920s onwards, as well as drawing and painting many self-portraits.

This book, then, as well as a group portrait or group biography, can also be read as a sequence of individual literary portraits, which move between the forms of the essay and the biography, and between narrative and criticism. These portraits do not aim for completeness, as they depict each of these writers through the prism of their reminiscences. To use a phrase chosen as a title by Henry James for a collection of his criticism in 1888, these are all "Partial Portraits." In arranging this material, I have not set out to sketch these writers' whole lives in miniature, so much as to aim to grasp what elements of their own lives each of these writers themselves drew out when they looked back and recounted their experience.

But throughout these pages we will still have to keep looking all the time for the one characteristic of life-writing that is perhaps the hardest to gauge (and which, once again, can only be supplied by biographical knowledge): of what has been left out, of all the omissions, evasions, and revisions. As Hermione Lee says of the art of biography, there will be an infinity of "things that aren't there: absences, gaps, missing evidence."[20] Sometimes, this will be entirely premeditated by these autobiographers, or a matter of discretion— Parmigianino's hand which blocks the viewer now seen again in writers' swerves and dodges. Sometimes, it is due to the workings of memory, as the autobiographer looks back and finds that much is blurred or gone.

In other cases, grasping only a part of a life, or an aspect of character, cannot be helped. There is far too much of life to be contained in any narrative. For this reason, biographers cherish the elusive essences which define characters: the telling glances or moments that reveal a whole person. A character can be caught in a sentence or phrase, or it can be endlessly redrawn over hundreds of pages. Yet can any self be fixed on the page for more than a few moments—or is the truest sense of character caught only on the move?

Susan Sontag wrote in her journal on December 31, 1958, "In the journal I do not just *express* myself more openly than I could to any person; I *create* myself";[21] the same is true for all self-portraiture. At the same time, the search to make sense of one's life leads one endlessly back into the past, sometimes urgently. "We have to rediscover, to reapprehend," writes Proust in the last volume of *A la recherche du temps perdu*, "[...] that reality which it is very easy for us to die without ever having known and which is, quite simply, our life."[22] This is the quest of all autobiography, and part of what we can learn from biography: even if other people's lives (and perhaps even our own) also remain ultimately unknowable. Yet taking heart from Leon Edel's memorable image of the biographer struggling with the multiplicity of "intractable" facts, or the "tons and tons" of materials left behind by many lives, *Portraits from Life* aims to arrive—if only for a moment or two—at that "tiny glowing particle" which contains the "human personality."[23]

Joseph Conrad by H. G. Wells and Jane Wells, *c.* 1900–1905.

Source: Frank Wells, *H. G. Wells: A Pictorial Biography*, London: Jupiter, 1977, p. 36. Reproduced with permission from United Agents LLP.

I

The secret of my life

Joseph Conrad

I am not a personage for an orderly biography either auto or otherwise...[1]

Joseph Conrad

In January 1904, Józef Teodor Konrad Korzeniowski, known to his readers as Joseph Conrad, moved up to London with his wife and five-year-old son from Pent Farm, the house in Kent he had been renting for the last few years from his younger friend and collaborator Ford Madox Hueffer (later Ford Madox Ford). He had turned forty-six in December, after a "disastrous"[2] year which had seen him begin and struggle despairingly with *Nostromo*, whose ending moved further and further away, and whose serialization was imminently to begin in *T.P.'s Weekly*. "It is a sort of desperate move in the game I am playing with the shadow of destruction,"[3] Conrad wrote to his friend John Galsworthy, of the impending relocation, with typically fiendish, apocalyptic humor. The previous year had been marked by mounting debts and ill-health. The temporary move up to London, as well as providing a brief escape from another cold, dark winter at the Pent, was due to Ford's invitation. He was staying three months at his brother's house in Kensington, 10 Airlie Gardens. The Conrads stayed around the corner, in a flat at 17 Gordon Place.

Conrad and Ford had recently published their co-written novel *Romance* (1903), and they had become entangled in a mass of mutual financial, artistic, and domestic dependencies and possibilities since they had started to collaborate in 1898. The collaboration had not yet yielded great results, but there was still hope and promise. *Romance* was far from the complete failure

Conrad seems to have expected. "Neither of us cares for it," Conrad informed George Gissing at St Jean-Pied-de-Port that December of 1903, refraining from sending him a copy of the novel, and indulging in his usual sardonic fatalism. "C'est inepte, inepte—and it has done better than any of my work. Congratulate me!!"[4] To Ford's mother Catherine Hueffer, Conrad also remarked, "I think that Ford and I have no reason to be dissatisfied with the reception of *Romance* [...] For myself the only question is whether the collaboration is good for Ford?"[5]

The two collaborators' friends and neighbors in Kent and East Sussex had their own views on their partnership. Henry James, who had moved to Lamb House in Rye in 1898 at the age of fifty-five, and who, for Conrad, represented an impeccable ideal of what a writer should be, thought the idea was "like a bad dream which one relates at breakfast."[6] H. G. Wells, who lived much closer to the Pent, in Sandgate on the coast, also worried that associating with Conrad wouldn't help Ford's career,[7] as well as ruining Conrad's prose style. For all the qualms of James and Wells, James might have been piqued: he had written to Wells in September and October 1902 suggesting that they, too, collaborate. James offered to be Wells's "faithful finisher,"[8] working on his drafts, but Wells wasn't interested in the idea.[9] And neither of them could have predicted what the duo of Conrad and Ford were to begin working on in London in 1904: a book of dictated reminiscences, in which Conrad—almost unwittingly—made his first approaches to writing his autobiography.

Conrad and Ford were an incongruous pair. Ford was sixteen years younger than his Anglo-Polish co-writer, and although he had published several books, was not yet as well-known. Conrad was gaining a reputation in literary circles, but made little money from his work. Superficially, they didn't match up. Conrad was exaggeratedly formal in gestures and dress-sense, alternating between an extraordinary politeness and an equally extraordinary agitation: as Conrad's wife Jessie wrote, it was an ominous sign of over-excitement if he ever got up without putting on his starched collar (or "boiled rag"),[10] and tie. Ford was more bohemian, known for his drawling manner. Both men were fathers: Ford's two daughters were still very young, the elder just older than Conrad's son. Ford often affected diffidence, especially when he really cared about something. He probably wouldn't have been averse to drying his hat in the oven, or using Conrad's suits as extra blankets in bed, as he supposedly once did, according to Jessie[11]—a notorious source of aggravation between Jessie and Ford, who never got on.

Ford's later descriptions of the older writer in *Joseph Conrad* (1924) portray him fondly as a figure almost from another age, and equally out of place: a "small rather than large" man, "dark in complexion with black hair and a clipped black beard," who "entered a room with his head held high, rather stiffly and with a haughty manner, moving his head once semi-circularly."[12] During their earlier collaboration on novels, most of the material they worked on was written by Ford, although Conrad would despair at its quality, showing Ford how to sharpen his scenes. But perhaps Conrad needed Ford more than Ford needed him, and in the new venture in autobiography their roles would be reversed, with Ford prompting Conrad, and taking notes from his dictation in shorthand. Conrad usually found writing agonizing, and would sit out his writer's block at his desk, unable to even produce a page for weeks at a time, until he found a solution. Ford, however, was often fluently productive. Artistically, each possessed and gave something the other lacked. Ford was already showing his aptitude for finding exactly the right word in a sentence: he would go on to become a virtuoso in the art and tone of prose, balancing each word with utmost care against the next. For all his fluency, he sometimes had difficulties in structuring and sustaining his narratives. Conrad, meanwhile, was a master of building suspense page by page, yet often had trouble with the nuances of English, which was, after all, an adopted tongue for him, his third after Polish and French.

Conrad followed Ford to London partly to raise his own spirits. His illnesses the previous year afflicted his whole writing life, but they had been particularly bad of late—heavy, immobilizing depression, and gout which made his hands swell, so that writing became physically painful. He was well past the date when he had promised to deliver *Nostromo* to his literary agent, James B. Pinker. Yet he was also about to do some of the best work of his life on the novel.

The situation deteriorated rapidly once he was newly installed in London. Within days of the move, Jessie fell in the street and hurt her knee, an injury that almost crippled her, and nearly resulted, at one point, in amputation; then, Conrad's bank failed. In these straitened circumstances, and to generate money for his family and *Nostromo*, Conrad and Ford set to work on the series of autobiographical sea sketches, modeled on Turgenev's *Sportsman's Sketches*, that were initially published as pieces in various journals mainly throughout 1904 and 1905, before being collected in book form in October 1906 as *The Mirror of the Sea: Memories and Impressions*. These told, in a loose, discursive way, of the twenty years Conrad spent at sea between the ages of sixteen and thirty-six, before he became a writer.

*

Autobiography is often seen as introspective, and the act of writing one's own life necessitates self-reflection and shaping of experience. But it can also be one of the most collaborative of literary genres—certainly when the autobiographer is not a professional author, and has to enlist the help of a ghostwriter. It is a literary genre where the distinction between being an author and a writer really counts. As well as searching introspection, autobiography often creates books of structured talk, between the auto-biographer and the listener or ghostwriter. But the ghostwriter is never completely a ghost. The presence of another person in the room always inflects the texture of the autobiographer's talk, even if this inflection is entirely unconscious.

In the case of Conrad and Ford writing the *Mirror*, the ghostwriter, Ford, was also an author, who had collaborated with the autobiographer for several years on novels. And the ghostwriter's presence impacted hugely on the actual talk and writing. The sketches proved to be one of the most successful works of collaboration that the two writers produced, as they colluded in telling the life at sea of that strange creation—almost a fiction—called "Joseph Conrad." Ford was responsible for the initial idea: in a way, acting as Conrad's biographer, Conrad's Boswell, and, through his suggestions, drawing the story out of his subject. In this, the *Mirror* was rather like a book of "table talk," or conversations with an artist or writer, with all the inter-rogator's questions removed. It was also, in some ways, like a series of sittings for a visual portrait. Near the outset of his writing life Ford published a biography of a painter, his grandfather, *Ford Madox Brown* (1896); he was also, around the period of the *Mirror*, an art critic, publishing *Rossetti* in 1902 and *Hans Holbein* in 1905. The experience of helping Conrad with his memoirs had an abiding influence on Ford's own work, which would begin, itself, to move towards reminiscence several years later.

The balance of power between the two writers in the *Mirror* shifted uneasily throughout its course, as it did throughout their literary partner-ship. The first sketches were dictated late in the evenings in London, from 11 p.m. to 1 a.m., as Conrad wrote Wells in February,[13] while *Nostromo* took up the days. They were a revelation in production for Conrad, who realized how much he could get down by talking rather than writing. As he exclaimed to Wells: "I've discovered that I can dictate that sort of bosh without effort at the rate of 3,000 words in four hours. Fact!"[14] To Sidney Colvin, Conrad likewise commented that dictation "is the only way, I discover, to breast the high wave of work which threatens to swallow me up altogether."[15] By the middle of March, the first six sketches were done,[16] although Conrad had to drag Ford down to Deal with him for one of them, when Conrad had to see a doctor there, due to his frayed nerves.[17]

Laconic as he seemed, Ford felt the pressure too. Later that year, perhaps to get away from it, and suffering from alarming spells of dizziness and agoraphobia which persisted throughout the spring and summer, he went to Germany for five months in August, alone, on the advice of a specialist, returning to London in December. Although he might have seemed no more than a literary lackey, Ford arguably, in the early sections of the *Mirror*, helped rewrite whole patches of Conrad's life. He also, single-handedly, prompted Conrad's interest in autobiography, as Conrad went on with the sketches with his new secretary Lilian Hallowes, and on his own, on and off over the next two years, in Kent, London, Capri, and Montpellier, showing a careful interest in the figure he cut on the page. Once Conrad realized that Ford was not well enough to go on with them, he wrote to his collaborator in mysterious terms at the end of May 1904 asking what share of the proceeds to pay him. "A small calculation will fix our proportions; for I suppose we can not finish the whole together. Can we?"[18] What exactly those proportions consisted of is hard to gauge precisely. Certainly, the two were able to mimic each other's styles, and sometimes did so. And at some points in the *Mirror*, Ford might well have done much more than merely transcribe Conrad's talk. Parts of Conrad's self-portrait were not just written down, but quite possibly made up, by Ford.

Conrad's attitude towards autobiography was deeply ambivalent. He always valued his privacy, refusing most requests for personal disclosures; and his excessive formality masked a form of intense shyness. While he was convulsively restless and outspoken in his letters, and energetically inhabited a plethora of personae and alter-egos in his fiction, he was a reluctant autobiographer. Self-revelation was anathema to him, at least in what he saw as an unveiled state. In his life, he always liked to look his best: not out of vanity, so much as insecurity. He notoriously disliked posing for photographs, finding it, as his second son John remembered, "a very real ordeal [...] particularly if he was being photographed by a stranger."[19] He resisted the camera, showing a defiant exterior that gave little away. His first attempt at literary self-portraiture was similar, filled with poise and pride at never presenting himself in a state of undress. Like many autobiographers, he was wary of the "egoism" in such a project. Ford's urgings gave him the excuse to begin without seeming vain or self-obsessed.

In the earliest letters to Pinker about the *Mirror*, Conrad told him of these "essays—impressions, descriptions, reminiscences, anecdotes and typical traits—of the old sailing fleet which passes away for good with the last century."[20] In April, still briefing Pinker, Conrad wrote—characteristically—as though it was all about someone else. "Here is Conrad talking of the events and feelings of his own life as he would talk to a friend."[21] Once the book was published, Conrad proved unusually attached to the *Mirror*. He sent an elaborately inscribed copy to Henry James, who replied that "nothing you have done has more in it."[22] Wells also sent him a letter of praise, commending the sketches for their "delightful (it's the right word) talk of seas and winds and ships. It's talk, good talk [. . .] full of all the admirable calm, a quality that never deserts you [. . .] I see better as I go to and fro."[23]

*

For all Conrad's attachment to it, the *Mirror* was extremely coy about self-revelation. It is unashamedly a book about work; and it is much more about boats and the sea than Conrad and his voyages—to Australia, Africa, Asia, and South America. Covering the period from 1874, when he first became a sailor, until around 1895, when his sea life ended with the publication of his first novel *Almayer's Folly*, it shows its author only in the slightest of glimpses: presenting Conrad as a dutiful, conscientious "English" sailor, glorifying the sea life, and telling us little about his youth in Poland, or his recent experiences as a struggling Edwardian writer. Yet Conrad in his 1919 "Author's Note" to the *Mirror* declared that "the following pages rest like a true confession on matters of fact which to a friendly and charitable person may convey the inner truth of almost a lifetime."[24]

Autobiography crept into the *Mirror* as it progressed. The short sketches on aspects of life at sea, which take up the first half of the self-portrait, gradually span outwards into isolated fragments of memory, forming a series of photographically static tableaux, which are never quite, at first, allowed the animation of sequential narrative. One of the first long trains of reminiscence in the *Mirror*, "The Weight of the Burden," only appears after several more technical opening papers on seafaring, and its content almost mirrors the process of Conrad breathing warmth and life into his memories for the first time. Conrad writes of waiting for days on end in a snowbound Amsterdam in the 1880s, when he was twenty-four, as the cargo for his ship was "frozen up-country,"[25] and of going into town every day to write a letter to his ship-owners in Glasgow. He vividly brings back this tiny, seemingly realistic because unremarkable, fragment of his youth: sitting by the cabin stove, as "the ink froze on the swing-table,"[26] taking the "glazed tramcars" to the café, "lofty and gilt, upholstered in red plush, full of electric lights, and so thoroughly warmed that even the marble tables felt tepid to the touch."[27]

Later in the *Mirror*, the memories last longer, as Conrad recalls other mis-adventures at sea. The gradually self-revealing depictions of Conrad's apprenticeship as a sailor begin to partially explain his lifelong surface formality, which appeared so strikingly over-pronounced to his literary acquaintances, and to his family. (Even Jessie remarked on how Conrad— always "Conrad," not Joseph, to his family—"carried fastidiousness to a degree that bordered on the fantastic.")[28] In the *Mirror*, tragedies and near-tragedies are told in a brusque, affectless way, perhaps necessarily: because the sea life of the period was so overrun with such dangers and such stories. In "Overdue and Missing," Conrad recounts, novelistically through direct conversation, the tale of a drifting steamer lost in Arctic wastes, which nearly killed all the crew. Conrad's friend was second officer.

> "We had three weeks of it," said my friend. "Just think of that!"
> "How did you feel about it?" I asked.
> He waved his hand as much to say: It's all in the day's work. But then, abruptly, as if making up his mind: "I'll tell you. Towards the last I used to shut myself up in my berth and cry."
> "Cry?"
> "Shed tears," he explained, briefly, and rolled up the chart.[29]

The *Mirror* contains many such expressively repressed moments and shards of conversation, evocative of a whole system of thought and feeling which, as Conrad reconstructed himself in these pages as a model sailor, lay at the foundations of his self-image. In the self-portrait, sober constancy was raised to the level of an ideal; yet he found it impossible to hold this pose for ever in the *Mirror*, just as in life. Once he lost the rigid mask, he swung to the other extreme, as though his efforts of suppression increased his subsequent intensity.

As the *Mirror* continues, the static, essay-like sketches give way not only to more prolonged reminiscence, but finally to dramatic, far-fetched episodes.

The nostalgic non-fictional tone eventually becomes excitable, anecdotal, novelistic; tilting and sliding into what is probably outright fiction. The extensive use of dialogue throughout many of the sketches suggests the possibility of their fictionality at a formal or technical level, but as the *Mirror* proceeds it becomes harder not to suspect that the content has also been reshaped. In "Initiation," Conrad rescues people from a sinking boat, never discovered, and embarks on colorful reminiscences of his years in Marseilles in the 1870s. This Marseilles period, when Conrad was a teenager, before he touched English soil for the first time in Lowestoft, is the setting for a series of adventures at the end of the *Mirror*. Conrad writes of gun-running episodes in a probably make-believe balancelle called the *Tremolino*,[30] during a Carlist war which was, in fact, largely over at the time.[31] In a scenario recalling *Nostromo*, Conrad recounts the death of one César Cervoni, killed swiftly by his uncle Dominic after being pushed overboard, weighed down by the gold he had stolen—without acknowledging that a real César Cervoni lived on long past these semi-mythological events.[32]

For all Conrad's later protestations that it rested "on matters of fact," by the end of the *Mirror* he has crossed the line between fact and fiction, though exactly where and when is very hard to pinpoint. Usually the traffic across this line moves from life towards fiction. Here, Conrad went the other way, and turned make-believe into memoir. So the *Mirror* ended by displaying a streak of self-mythology: the trait of the incorrigible storyteller, whose anecdotes and episodes have been polished for effect, perhaps to the point of exaggeration or invention.

There is nothing surprising in this. All autobiographies and memoirs are tinged by distortions, omissions, alterations, selections, impressions, and artful reshapings. But Conrad's relations between fact and fiction were unusual mainly for the way he later tried to manipulate the lines between them. While always privileging fiction, he also came to understand the literary power of factuality, the foundation of veracity on which much of biography and autobiography's force implicitly rests. And he intuited how much of this factuality was often semi-illusory, often resting as much in the mind of the reader—along with the generic framing of a book and what it calls itself— as in the text itself. In the *Mirror*, he experimented with blurring these lines for the first time: it was his first sustained attempt at non-fiction. Later in life, however, he more consciously manipulated generic boundaries.

In 1917, for instance, when his short novel *The Shadow-Line* was published, Conrad tried to frame it as "exact autobiography,"[33] subtitling it

"A Confession," because he was nervous about its quality. He thought that the book would be read more leniently if it were taken as being essentially true.[34] So while the title *The Shadow-Line* refers to that stage in life where someone first grows from youth to maturity, the novel's framing also played deceptively with another liminal shadow-line—which Conrad crosses so flagrantly in the *Mirror*—that thin, indefinable line between what we perceive to be fact and what we perceive to be fiction.

Over the years, Conrad moved back and forth across this shadow-line, as he claimed varying degrees of truthfulness for his books at different points in his life, often describing his novels, almost proudly, as being factually true. His sea novels, especially, often *were* very true to life. He frequently even used the real names of people he had worked with and ships he had sailed on. Sometimes, he tweaked names slightly, so that the Olmeijer he met in real life became the Almayer of *Almayer's Folly*, or a real-life White became Wait. He never wrote a book which did not have some basis, however small, in his experience; although the balance between fact and fiction, between how closely he drew from life, and how much he invented, was to shift. Often, as in the *Mirror*, it even shifted within a single book: sometimes masquerading as something that had really happened to Conrad when it hadn't, and sometimes pretending to be fiction. Sometimes, Conrad's retellings created, through repetition, kaleidoscopic variations on the truth, in life even more than on the page, as Jessie Conrad wrote in her memoir of her husband, *Joseph Conrad as I Knew Him* (1926).

> He lived life as a novel; he exaggerated simple trifles, though quite unconsciously [...] Often and often I have sat and marvelled at the extent to which, in his mouth, the same story varied. Each statement, if the same in the main, would be entirely different in detail. I suppose, with a born novelist, the mixture of fact and fiction in narration does always tend to vary. Dates varied most. I have read and re-read his written reminiscences, and although I am never tired of them, in the printed page I miss those varying arabesques of detail.[35]

When a researcher caught up with Conrad near the end of his life, checking facts, his findings spurred Conrad into making one of the clearest statements he ever formulated about the maze of truths and untruths in his work. In one sense, this serves as a defense of what all novelists do when they work from their own experience and transform it into stories; and interestingly, Conrad steps back from the statement in his 1919 foreword to the *Mirror* that it was a "confession." Here it is not the *Mirror*, but his second autobiography,

A Personal Record, begun in 1908, a few years after the *Mirror*, that he claims to be essentially true.

> I need not point out that I had to *make* material from my own life's incidents arranged, combined, coloured for artistic purposes. I don't think there's any-thing reprehensible in that. After all I *am* a writer of fiction; and it is not what actually happened, but the manner of presenting it that settles the literary and even the moral value of my work. My little vol: of autobiography [*A Personal Record*] of course is absolutely genuine. The rest is more or less close approxi-mation to facts and suggestions. What I claim as true are my mental and emotional reactions to life, to men, to their affairs and their passions as I have seen them. I have in that sense kept always true to myself.[36]

*

Conrad was not straightforwardly truthful in the *Mirror*, but he was true to himself, and to others, in many other ways. If the myths he propagated in his work all focused on his adventurous life at sea, that life came to an end when he began writing full-time in the mid-1890s. In a sense, his life stopped, as he now put everything into his writing, and soon, his burgeoning family. His marriage to Jessie, in 1896, was a mystery to many of his friends—and from the evidence of several letters, an enigma to himself as well—yet the couple stayed together, until Conrad's death, with Jessie giving birth to two sons: Borys in 1898, and John in 1906. In one vital letter written soon after his marriage, Conrad divulged, with less irony than usual, what he wanted out of life. "I confess to you," he wrote, "I dream of peace, a little reputation, and the rest of my life devoted to the service of Art and free from material worries. Now, dear Madame, you have the secret of my life."[37]

To this aim, too, Conrad remained faithful. Yet his dream of modest material ease would stay far out of reach for years. Until late 1907, the Conrads' base in England remained the Pent—as Jessie put it, "a remote, country place, without electric light"[38]—with periods in Europe and London to escape the winters there. *Nostromo* was misunderstood, and did not bring respite from the debts building with Pinker. *The Secret Agent*, published in September 1907, likewise brought little relief. The Conrads moved from the Pent to a farmhouse, Someries, near Luton in Bedfordshire, soon after it appeared. But Conrad disliked Someries, and fairly soon returned to Kent.

The formal collaboration on novels with Ford had ended by this time, but the movements of the two writers still overlapped. Ford had been making a mark with several new books—six volumes in 1905 and 1906 alone—and he had traveled to America on a lecture tour, returning to his cottage in Winchelsea, near Rye, early in 1907, taking a flat in Holland Park in London that summer. In 1908, Ford became more exclusively based in London, launching and becoming the editor of the *English Review*—whose first issue, in December 1908, included contributions from Thomas Hardy, Henry James, John Galsworthy, W. H. Hudson, and H. G. Wells. Conrad contributed "Some Reminiscences"—which would later, with the subsequent instalments in the *English Review*, be collected in book form as *A Personal Record* (1912).

When Conrad embarked on the first of these pieces in 1908, the reminiscences brought the two collaborators back together for a spell, mainly due to Ford. Conrad was deep in the composition of "Razumov," which became *Under Western Eyes* (1911), yet he still found time to start this new project. As he put it, the reminiscences were "the result of a friendly suggestion, and even of a little friendly pressure. I defended myself with some spirit; but, with characteristic tenacity, the friendly voice insisted, 'You know, you really must.' "[39] As well as commissioning the series, Ford once again actively helped in writing the new self-portrait, which was to be, from the start, much closer to an autobiography than the *Mirror*.

Conrad's Polish biographer Zdzisław Najder has suggested that another spur to the reminiscences was Robert Lynd's attack on Conrad in the *Daily News*, a month before Conrad began the reminiscences in 1908, in which Lynd, cruelly, accused Conrad of being a man "without country or language."[40] Lynd could well have been the "gentleman" Conrad mentions in the reminiscences, "who, metaphorically speaking, jumps upon me with both feet."[41] So the new self-portrait might have been a literary self-defense. The *Mirror* had presented Conrad as a perfect "English" sailor; these new reminiscences were to go further into his origins and early years in Poland: to reinvestigate the nationality Lynd said he didn't have. It was also surely significant to Conrad that they would appear in a journal called the *English Review*, whose very title had been Conrad's idea, as Ford tells us.

At the end of August 1908, Conrad moved for a few weeks from Someries to Aldington in Kent, into "rooms in a farmhouse not very far from the Hueffers,"[42] as Conrad told Edward Garnett. Once installed in Aldington, Conrad wrote straightaway to Pinker about his plan for the new reminiscences, informing him that he would dictate them to Ford, "who consents

to hold the pen for me—a proof of friendship and an act of great kind-
ness."[43] Ford much later, in his book of reminiscences *Return to Yesterday*
(1932), recalled the early sessions of dictation for "Some Reminiscences" as
having taken place "on a little terrace [...] high up in the air, with the great
skies over the Romney Marsh below,"[44] with Conrad "rushing feverishly up
and down the terrace!"[45] Writing to Pinker, Conrad was, from the outset,
thinking about how the pieces would make up a book, as he suggested
some possible titles. "These are to be intimate personal autobiographical
things under the general title (for book form perhaps) of the Life and the
Art. They will tell in a measure my own story and as it were the story of my
books [...] these are things which I could not dictate to anyone but a
friend."[46] Other titles Conrad considered were "The Pages and the Years,"[47]
"The Leaves and the Years,"[48] and "The Double Call: an Intimate Note,"[49]
all of which highlight the theme of duality in Conrad's life.

As in the *Mirror*, the burst of collaboration was followed by a protracted
period when Conrad continued alone, and dictating to Lilian Hallowes,
back in Someries until mid-February 1909 before returning to Aldington
for a more settled residence for the rest of that year. And as he worked
on this new self-portrait, Conrad told different people different things
about it. To Wells, he was offhand about the project, and once again wary
of apparent "egoism": "Ford persuaded me to some reminiscences for the
E.R [...] A megalomaniac's stuff but easy to spin out."[50] To Ford, once he
was away from him, he was technical: "the trouble is, what to keep out."[51]
To Pinker, he talked it up: "a mere casual suggestion has grown into a very
absorbing plan [...] it may be, so to speak, *the* chance of a lifetime—coming
neither too soon nor yet too late."[52] He was now fifty years old, about to
turn fifty-one.

He had not wanted to write the *Mirror*. There was a more insistent
psychological need to write *A Personal Record*. He wanted once again to
present his best face. But again, he couldn't maintain the pose for long. He
was only ever able to reconstruct his life in pieces. As he tried to put a public
self together, piece by piece, something else in his life-story always pulled the
other way, revealing the fragility of the edifice. Where the *Mirror* was purely
about his life at sea, *A Personal Record* dealt with his childhood, his nationality,
and his family. It soon revealed the faultlines lying deep within his experience. Once he had started it, he knew it would have to be different in form
from most other autobiographies. "Of course the thing is very far from
conventional in its composition," he wrote to Pinker. "It does not much

resemble other people's reminis^{ces}. Oh dear no!"[53] And to E. V. Lucas, he declared: "I felt I could not proceed in cold blood on the usual lines of an autobiography."[54]

The first problem he faced was how to begin. Of course, no one remembers their first years of life, although most biographies begin obstinately at the beginning. In 1921, in a short piece called "The First Thing I Remember," Conrad wryly commented on this universal void. Stories told by other people, he knew, make up our earliest memories: "one generally is told of them afterwards and then thinks one remembers."[55] In this piece his first memory was of having "part of a cheek and an ear frost-bitten,"[56] but he suspected this "image-memory" was a "later fabrication";[57] something he had been told. His second memory was of his mother at the piano, slowly turning to look at him, and stopping in her playing. He dates it as being from early in 1861 (he was born in 1857).

> This, I rather think, is a genuine instance of the memory of a moment; for I do not remember who opened the door for me nor yet how I came there at all. But I have a very convincing impression of details, such as the oval of her face, the peculiar suavity of her eyes, and of the sudden silence. That last is the most convincing as to the genuineness of its being an experience; for, as to the rest, I have to this day a photograph of her from that very time, which, of course, might have gone to the making up of the "memory".[58]

Conrad knew from experience the extent to which early memories are told by others, or later reconstructed, because when he searched his memory for his own early recollections for *A Personal Record*, there were so many unverifiable gaps. His mother had died when he was seven-and-a-half; his father had died when he was eleven. His family were sent into exile when he was four, several hundred miles north-east of Moscow, after being sentenced by the Russians for revolutionary activities—the part of "Poland" he was born in having been annexed by Russia. When Conrad came to write of his early youth in the reminiscences, he formed the portrait of his mother not from his own few memories of her, but from the two-volume *Memoirs* of his guardian, Tadeusz Bobrowski.[59] His "memories" came from someone else's self-portrait. Where many memoir-writers face ethical questions about how much they should reveal about their family, Conrad lacked knowledge about his mother and father. He also planned the time-scheme of the *Mirror* and *A Personal Record* to ensure no revelations about Jessie, Borys, and John: all of whom, unusually, went on to write memoirs of him after his death.

This touches on the wider problem Conrad faced: as he had put it to Ford, "what to keep out." There were also other things he kept secret. He didn't want to tell, for instance, of how he had attempted suicide in Marseilles by shooting himself in the chest as a young man, not long after he had chosen his own country—the sea—at the age of sixteen, and had first reached the sea through France. This was a secret he had even kept from his family.

*

All autobiography hinges on turning-points, giving shape—even if illusory or retrospectively formed—to a life as it is depicted. Remembrance molds the formless multiplicities of life into patterns which often hinge on crucial pivots. These patterns, and pivots, can be alluring to many autobiographers, searching to make sense of life. It is sometimes a matter of how closely one looks: for each day of life can have a turning of its own. In life-or-death situations, however, such as Conrad's attempted suicide, turning-points become most stark. The suicide was avoided entirely in *A Personal Record*, which attempted not to locate such points in Conrad's life, but to bring the disparate parts of his experience back together. All the phases lay so far apart that Conrad felt he would find no links between them. They teemed with so many turnings and departures that what he felt was lacking was consistency. The reminiscences offered a chance at reparation. As Conrad wrote to Wells, they were "a unique opportunity to pull myself together";[60] to stitch the elements of his life back into a coherent whole.

The way he did so, strangely, was to overturn the foundation on which biography is usually laid: chronology. The idea behind *A Personal Record* was a biographical *jeu d'esprit*—one very suitable for the life-story of a novelist—as Conrad decided to tell only of how he wrote his first book *Almayer's Folly*. The reminiscences tell the story of a manuscript, the story of his formation as a writer; and he intended to cover only the years 1889–1895, when he was at work on this novel. He chose this short span of years with care. It was the only period in his experience when his different lives—as a Pole, a sailor, and a writer—came together simultaneously, since he went back to Poland at this time, and was both a sailor and a writer. Much of *Almayer*, as he went on to tell, was written on board ships.

Conrad was also consciously striving for specific literary effects in his choice of this time-scheme. Memory, he knew, doesn't line the facts out in sequence when we look back at our lives. Our past days don't sit neatly stacked up, to be related in strict order: they interrelate, and strike sparks off each other, constantly shuffled into new associations. Memory, and autobiography, have their own order, their own links and hierarchies. And to the remembering mind, sequential chronology is an utterly artificial construction.

To reflect this, in his novels, along with Ford, Conrad developed the device of the "time-shift"; in which the temporal scheme of events moves back and forth rather than always straight ahead. Similarly, in *Joseph Conrad*, subtitled *A Personal Remembrance*—partially in homage to *A Personal Record*— Ford complained that many novels "went straight forward" chronologically, in a way that was untrue to how one got to know people in real life. Ford added, choosing the one date—the first month of the First World War— when no one would ever forget what they had been doing:

> Life does not say to you: In 1914 my next door neighbour, Mr. Slack, erected a greenhouse and painted it with Cox's green aluminium paint [...] If you think about the matter you will remember, in various unordered pictures, how one day Mr. Slack appeared in his garden and contemplated the wall of his house. You will then try to remember the year of that occurrence and you will fix it as August 1914 [...][61]

Conrad's few pronouncements on the art of biography also showed his mistrust in its conventions. In a preface to Thomas Beer's biography *Stephen Crane* (1923), Conrad stated his disregard for "such things of merely historical importance such as the recollection of dates";[62] and his lack of interest in such matters was notorious. "After hearing from Mr. Beer of his difficulties in fixing certain dates in the history of Stephen Crane's life," Conrad writes, "I discovered that I was unable to remember with any kind of precision the initial date of our friendship. Indeed, life is but a dream—especially for those of us who have never kept a diary or possessed a notebook in our lives."[63] Fiction, Conrad more boldly asserted in an essay on Henry James in 1905, paradoxically stood "on firmer ground [...] nearer truth" than history, which was "based on documents [...] on second-hand impression [...] But let that pass. A historian may be an artist too, and a novelist is a historian, the preserver, the keeper, the expounder, of human experience."[64]

In "A Familiar Preface" to *A Personal Record*, written in 1911 when he was preparing the reminiscences as a book, Conrad emphasizes and defends the unconventional form of his recollections, reporting—with ironic parenthetical asides and nested reported speech that recall the indirect methods of his novels—conversations he had had about his memoirs.

> They [...] have been charged with discursiveness, with disregard of chrono-
> logical order (which is in itself a crime), with unconventionality of form
> (which is an impropriety). I was told severely that the public would view with
> displeasure the informal character of my recollections. "Alas!" I protested
> mildly, "could I begin with the sacramental words, 'I was born on such a date
> in such a place' "?[65]

Conrad here implicitly compares biographical form and chronology to social codes, which he feels he has to break, because of the nature of his life. And in *A Personal Record* he certainly does not begin with the words, "I was born on such a date in such a place," but with the sentence: "Books may be written in all sorts of places."[66] *A Personal Record* goes on to depict, with great virtuosity, the strange texture of the writing life. The autobiography recreates what becoming a writer, for Conrad, during his long apprentice-ship, involved: a dual life, always moving between reality and fiction, and often, from one country to another.

Although he referred to Jean-Jacques Rousseau's *Confessions* (1782) in *A Personal Record*—as an act of untrammeled self-revelation which he did not want to emulate—Conrad lacked exemplars in his attempt to write reminiscences which told of the writing life in a form which broke with the Victorian conventions of biography. But Edmund Gosse's *Father and Son* offered a recent precedent.[67] Writing autobiography piece by piece, as Conrad did, also meant there was an intrinsic fragmentation in the reminiscences, as well as an in-built interruption to the instalments, which, as they appeared in the *English Review*, were all followed by the phrase "(*To be continued*)."

Conrad worked this into the theme of *A Personal Record*, which frequently depicts scenes where he is suddenly shaken out of his literary reveries. The first instalment opens with Conrad writing *Almayer's Folly* on board ship in Rouen in 1893, when he was thirty-five, composing dialogue about the now-distant Malayan isles—"'*It has set at last,' said Nina to her mother* [...]"[68]—and being interrupted in his literary labors by the abrupt entrance of "the third officer, a cheerful and casual youth, coming in with a bang of the door."[69] The progress of the writing of *Almayer's Folly*, as Conrad portrays it in *A Personal Record*, was a story of continual interruptions, as the unfinished manuscript was taken up, and put aside, and taken up again, while Conrad traveled the world as a sailor. "Line by line, rather than page by page, was the growth of *Almayer's Folly*,"[70] as Conrad writes.

Conrad folds many moments from different times and places into the first instalment of the reminiscences. People and scenes open out from his memories like tiny origami figures. Conrad writes of London, and how he came to be in Rouen; of seeing Almayer in "eastern waters"[71] for the first time before writing the novel *Almayer* about him years later in a Pimlico square. Conrad depicts the act of beginning *Almayer* as a kind of ghostly visitation, a hallucination, in which his immediate reality, "writing at that table, situated in a decayed part of Belgravia," dissolved, and fictional and real characters became hard to tell apart. Indeed, writing about Almayer makes him "live again with a vividness and poignancy quite foreign to our former real intercourse":[72]

> I had been treating myself to a long stay on shore, and in the necessity of occupying my mornings, Almayer (that old acquaintance) came nobly to the rescue. Before long, as was only proper, his wife and daughter joined him round my table, and then the rest of that Pantai band came, full of words and gestures [...] They did not clamour aloud for my attention. They came with a silent and irresistible appeal.[73]

Only a few pages later, Conrad remembers pointing at a map of Africa in 1868 as a child and saying "When I grow up I shall go *there*."[74] He moves again between different periods of his life, dream and reality, the writing life and life at sea, as he then recounts nearly losing the manuscript of *Almayer* on "a specially awkward turn of the Congo between Kinchassa and Leopoldville."[75] "I got around the turn more or less alive," Conrad writes, "though I was too sick to care whether I did or not; and, always with *Almayer's Folly* amongst my diminishing baggage [...] At that date there were in existence only seven chapters of *Almayer's Folly*, but the chapter in my history which followed was that of a long, long illness and very dismal convalescence."[76] Once he was recovered, *Almayer*, "like a cask of choice Madeira, got carried for three years to and fro upon the sea [...] the whole MS. acquired a faded look and an ancient, yellowish complexion."[77]

The narrative of *A Personal Record* soon turns to a trip in the 1890s back to Conrad's birthplace in Poland, "or more precisely Ukraine."[78] Still carrying and again nearly losing the MS of *Almayer*, "advanced now to the first words of the ninth chapter,"[79] Conrad takes the train to Berlin, to Warsaw, and to Kiev, before an eight-hour ride by sledge on a journey into his past, wrapped in fur against the cold.

> I saw again the sun setting on the plains as I saw it in the travels of my childhood.
> It set, clear and red, dipping into the snow in full view as if it were setting on

the sea. It was twenty-three years since I had seen the sun set over that land; and we drove on in the darkness which fell swiftly upon the livid expanse of snows till, out of the waste of a white earth joining a bestarred sky, surged up black shapes, the clumps of trees about a village of the Ukrainian plain.[80]

The voyage leads to fragmentary memories of Conrad's mother, in 1864, and of his youth. So at the center of the journey into the past are Conrad's parents. We also appear to approach the interior in his memories as he recalls a tragic farewell scene of youth when he was only "a small boy not quite six years old"[81]—his departure with his mother, back into exile, after a brief stay at home. The scene is composed almost like a photograph, a careful inventory of all that Conrad lost, as servants and relations all gather on the steps to see mother and son off in the carriage—his grandmother, his uncle, his cousin, Mlle. Durand the governess, whose "sobbing voice alone [...] broke the silence with an appeal to me: '*N'oublie pas ton français, mon chéri*'."[82] "Each generation has its memories," Conrad writes, recording and naming the Russian official, Bezak, who gave the order for this departure—the departure to her death—of his mother and his childhood self, back in the 1860s.

The early instalments of *A Personal Record* recreating Conrad's journey into his past mimic the journey in autobiography he was making in this pages—pushing further on into his memories to travel back in time. Many of these memories were troubling, or painful, especially in the first three instalments which deal so largely with his background in Poland.

At the beginning of the fourth instalment, Conrad returns to *Almayer*. Before *Almayer*, Conrad says, he had never really attempted to write anything; and, looping back to the opening episode of the reminiscences, he redramatizes his first day writing the novel in Pimlico. Even this recollection leads once more to dangerous familial ground, as Conrad, slipping the avowed time-scheme of *A Personal Record* again, recounts his early reading of Cervantes, Dickens, Hugo, Trollope, and Shakespeare—and an early memory of sitting at his father's desk. Conrad's father, Apollo Korzeniowski, was a playwright, poet, and translator; and his example no doubt stirred Conrad's own literary strivings.

"These things I remember," Conrad observes, "but what I was reading the day before my writing life began I have forgotten."[83] He remembers the weather on that first day writing *Almayer*, and in another seamlessly managed shift between his waking life and the writing life moves between the account of writing the novel, and another memory of the real-life

Almayer as he saw him on a Bornean river one day. In a fantastical reverie, he imagines talking with Almayer in the after-life, justifying having used his name so freely. All this still chimes with the initial plan of the reminiscences.

But the *Almayer*-motif of *A Personal Record* moves more out of view in the last three instalments, while at the same time, Conrad appears to be struggling more with what he should reveal. "To survey with wonder the changes of one's own self is a fascinating pursuit for idle hours,"[84] he writes in the fifth instalment; yet "the matter in hand [...] is to keep these reminiscences from turning into confessions."[85] Where the *Mirror* managed this ultimately by moving towards fiction, *A Personal Record* likewise succeeds in avoiding confession, mostly by becoming ever more loosely associative and discursive.

The last parts of *A Personal Record* come very close to the present, as Conrad tells of writing *Nostromo*, and again being interrupted, sitting at his desk. Someone comes in and asks the writer, "How do you do?"[86]—and the imaginary landscape of *Nostromo* dissolves before Conrad's eyes, to his despair.

> I had heard nothing—no rustle, no footsteps. I had felt only a moment before a sort of premonition of evil; I had the sense of an inauspicious presence—just that much warning and no more; and then came the sound of the voice and the jar as of a terrible fall from a great height—a fall, let us say, from the highest of the clouds floating in gentle procession over the fields in the faint westerly air of that July afternoon. I picked myself up quickly, of course; in other words, I jumped up from my chair stunned and dazed, every nerve quivering with the pain of being uprooted out of one world and flung down into another—perfectly civil.
>   "Oh! How do you do? Won't you sit down?"[87]

The anecdote, Conrad feels, says more about his life "than a whole volume of confessions *à la* Jean Jacques Rousseau would do"[88]—and seen alongside the interruptions in the writing of *Almayer*, it encapsulates the central theme of the reminiscences: of constant deferral and delay in composition. As with many scenes in *A Personal Record*, little, sharp fragments of dialogue—short enough to be plausibly and faithfully recalled—show the total failure of the outer world, for Conrad, even to hint at the depths of the inner.

As in the *Mirror*, the reminiscences lead out eventually, in the final two instalments, to Marseilles. Conrad closes *A Personal Record* abruptly, sailing for the first time under an English flag, "the symbolic, protecting warm bit of bunting flung wide upon the seas, and destined for so many years to be the only roof over my head."[89] Yet this ending, like this identity, feels a little patched and provisional; it only just holds the whole thing together.

*

Conrad wrote all these reminiscences to deadline for the *English Review*, and the seven instalments originally appeared one by one, with even the last one "(*To be continued*)," between December 1908 and June 1909. In 1909, as Conrad had suspected it might, despite Ford's undoubted skills as an editor, the *Review* had already begun to flounder. Ford was in financial trouble, and his domestic life was even more complicated: his relationship with the novelist Violet Hunt now made him wish to obtain a divorce from his wife Elsie Hueffer, who always refused. Ford, to strengthen his case for a divorce, had invited a young woman called Gertrud Schablowsky to stay in his flat in London.

The very real sense of potential scandal and disarray surrounding Ford's marital affairs made some of his older literary friends wary, if not the younger generation of writers and artists with whom Ford was increasingly spending his time with Hunt at her house South Lodge, between Kensington and Notting Hill, at 80 Campden Hill Road. Henry James, later in 1909, once he heard that Ford's relationship with Violet Hunt was about to enter the divorce courts, wrote to Hunt that this now "compels me to regard all agreeable and unembarrassed communication between us as impossible,"[90] even though they were old friends—perhaps fearing he would become associated with the scandal. When Elsie talked to Conrad in April 1909, Conrad was thrown by his friend's marital crisis, and he also had a severe attack of gout which lasted several months. When he failed to finish the eighth instalment of his reminiscences on time, Ford printed a note in the July issue of the *Review*, much to Conrad's irritation: "We regret that owing to the serious illness of Mr Joseph Conrad we are compelled to postpone the publication of the next instalment of his Reminiscences."[91]

But there never was another instalment. Even though Ford was the only person who ever seemed to lift Conrad out of his depressions, Conrad had been building for a break with him almost since the start of the year, for the confusion he was causing professionally as well as personally. Around the end of April, he had written him a searing, yet still affectionate letter: "it strikes me my dear Ford that of late you have been visiting what might have been faults of tact, or even grave failures of discretion in men who *were* your *admiring* friends with an Olympian severity [...] I have the right to warn you that you will find yourself at forty with only the wrecks of friendships at your feet."[92] When Ford then reproached Conrad in May for not having seen the American writer Willa Cather, who was on a visit to England, Conrad was even more angry, especially since he felt that Ford had abused his trust by sending his "letter written with perfect openness to your wife to a third party [...] Look here my dear Ford—this sort of thing I *won't* stand if you had a million dollars in each hand."[93]

The very public note about his illness in the *English Review* was a final provocation. Conrad wrote to Ford pointedly using his surname, "Dear Hueffer," protesting at Ford's accusation that he had left the reminiscences in a "*ragged condition*" by ending them so abruptly,[94] and insisting that they were finished as they were. "It is another instalment which would make the thing ragged. It would have to begin another period and another phase."[95] Conrad's letter takes the phrase "*ragged condition*" personally, as though his very soul were under question. And it particularly hurt that Ford—"a man with a fine sense of form and a complete understanding, for years, of the way in which my literary intentions work themselves out"[96]—should not have seen that they were finished. He refused to continue with the series for the *English Review*, partly because the new editor was Russian. "The ER I hear is no longer your property and there is I believe another circumstance which for purely personal reason[s] (exceptionally personal I mean) make[s] me unwilling to contribute anything more to the ER. This reason has of course nothing to do with You you understand. It is not a critical reason. A pure matter of feeling."[97]

Were the reminiscences left in a "*ragged condition*"? Conrad denied it vehemently, and never wrote any more of them, seeing *Some Reminiscences* through to publication in book form, initially published under that title in London by Nash in 1912, and as *A Personal Record* in America. Although he never told Ford this, at several points in the following years Conrad did contemplate adding to them. Shortly after the appearance of *A Personal Record* as a book, and perhaps not coincidentally, precisely the same period that Henry James was working on his memoir, *A Small Boy and Others*, Conrad contemplated a sequel. "I was indeed thinking of a 'suite' to my Remces under the general title of Some Portraits family and others," he wrote to the editor of the *English Review*, who was by that stage Austin Harrison, "but that is not possible now."[98] A few years later, however, he did make one further important attempt to depict his Polish experience.

*

In July 1914, without realizing that Europe was on the brink of the First World War, Conrad went with his family back to Poland for a final time. He had found a measure of financial ease with his novel *Chance* in 1913—a central turning-point in what remained of both his writing and his real life. Having spent so many years working continuously, he felt this was a good time to show Jessie and his two sons where he had come from. He wrote about the trip soon afterwards in a short piece called "Poland Revisited." Where *A Personal Record* made the journey back to Poland in memory, this piece recounts a similar trip, in reality. In "A Berlin Chronicle," Walter Benjamin writes: "I have long, indeed for years, played with the idea of setting out the sphere of life—bios—graphically on a map."[99] In this mapping, for Conrad, it is always Poland, not the sea, at the center; yet every time he goes there, he traces disappearances.

Setting out on their journey in 1914, the Conrads took the train up to London from Kent, where since 1910 Conrad had finally settled at Capel House in Orlestone near Ashford; and for Jessie, Borys, and John, it was to be a family holiday. Yet Conrad, in "Poland Revisited," was filled with foreboding. "As we sat together in the same railway carriage, they were looking forward to a voyage in space, whereas I felt more and more plainly that what I had started on was a journey in time, into the past."[100] Arriving at Liverpool Street station, Conrad writes that he also came out of the same station—"Not the same building, but the same spot"[101]—thirty-seven years before, having come down from Lowestoft in September 1878, arriving in England for the first time. As the Conrads took the train to Harwich, for the boat to Hamburg—retracing his very first English train journey all those years before, going in the other direction from Lowestoft to Liverpool Street—Conrad was already overwhelmed by memories.

In Cracow, he wandered the streets at night with Borys, feeling "like a ghost";[102] and he soon found himself wandering helplessly into scenes from his childhood and youth, when he was eleven, those lonely years after his mother died. He remembers walking daily up to a school for day-pupils in the winter of 1868, at eight each morning; and returning home each night at seven, where his father, very ill, lay on his sickbed, tended by two nuns. He remembers, every evening, saying "good-night to the figure prone on the bed"[103] who was speechless and immobile, before going off to bed himself, where he would "often, not always, cry myself into a good sound sleep."[104] And just as *A Personal Record* inexorably led towards a tragic scene of departure into exile, rendered in surreally precise detail, the memories of Cracow lead straight to his father's funeral procession.

> In the moonlight-flooded silence of the old town of glorious tombs and tragic memories, I could see again the small boy of that day following a hearse; a space kept clear in which I walked alone, conscious of an enormous following, the clumsy swaying of the tall black machine, the chanting of the surpliced clergy at the head, the flames of the tapers passing under the low archway of the gate, the rows of bared heads on the pavements with fixed, serious eyes. Half the population had turned out on that fine May afternoon.[105]

The scene is recounted without sentimentality. But Conrad draws a curtain swiftly over it. Not without a sense of tragic irony, "Poland Revisited," in its last, rushed pages, tells how, back in 1914, the Conrads' holiday was interrupted by the outbreak of the First World War, and how, after a forced stay of two months, they finally made it to Vienna, to Genoa, and then to London.

*

Conrad took things hard, throughout his very hard life, and he was always as loyal to his friends as he was to his family. Yet after the reminiscences in 1909, the relationship with Ford, one of his closest friends, and the only person with whom he was ever able to talk fully about his work, was damaged. They had been so close in their partnership that in 1904, when he heard that Ford was ill, in order to raise money for Ford, Conrad had offered to put his name to any piece of scrap writing that Ford had, and sell it to the newspaper which had asked for some of his own early work.[106] In August 1909, Conrad wrote Pinker a "*Private & Confal*" letter about his ex-collaborator, outlining some of the ground for their falling-out that year, mostly concerning the *English Review*. "His conduct is *impossible*," Conrad wrote. "All this will end badly [...] A fierce and exasperated vanity is hidden under his calm manner which misleads people."[107] In December 1909, Conrad wrote to David Meldrum of the breach with Ford. "Another intimate I have seen oftener but I am not likely to see anything of him in the future. He's aggrieved, not I. But that is not worth talking about. Still after eleven years of intimacy one feels the breach."[108]

From 1909 onwards, Conrad dealt with his ex-collaborator warily. And this never really thawed. When Ford published his first volume of reminiscences,

Ancient Lights and Certain New Reflections in 1911, Conrad ordered a copy. But it was Ford who made the subsequent attempts to keep in touch, which became increasingly difficult during and after the First World War, as Ford spent more time in France. When Ford began editing the *transatlantic review* in Paris in 1923, the pair had another exchange of letters, instigated by Ford, who asked Conrad for a contribution along the lines of the *English Review* reminiscences. "If it would amuse you," Ford wrote, "[…] I would come over to a near-by pub & see if we couldn't again evolve something like the original passage of the *Mirror*."[109]

Conrad was getting old—he would be dead in less than a year—and his response was a mixture of nostalgia at the good old, bad old times of the *English Review*, and an acceptance that times had now changed. The old intimacy was still there, somewhere, but it was a thing of the past, only possible through recollection. "I am afraid the source of the *Personal Record* fount is dried up. No longer the same man,"[110] Conrad wrote. "I'd like to do something for the sake of old times—but I daresay I am not worth having now."[111] Yet perhaps he did still have some more things to say. Jessie writes that even the day before he became ill in 1924, and later died, he was contemplating writing a book entitled *Further Reminiscences*.[112]

Henry James in profile, *c.* 1910 by Theodate Pope.
Source: Archives, Hill-Stead Museum, Farmington, CT, USA.

2

A straight dive into the past

Henry James

I move here, indeed, between discretions and disappearances...[1]

Henry James

In the late spring and early summer of 1913, soon after his seventieth birthday, Henry James sat almost a dozen times for a portrait by John Singer Sargent at the painter's studio in Tite Street, Chelsea. The painting was a gift from nearly three hundred of James's friends and admirers; slightly embarrassed, yet no doubt flattered to sit for his old friend, James eventually gave the finished likeness to the National Portrait Gallery. It wasn't the first time he had been to the Tite Street studio as a model: there had also been three sittings only the previous year, between January and March, for a charcoal drawing commissioned by his energetic younger friend Edith Wharton. Neither Sargent nor Wharton was satisfied with the result of this attempt (even though James himself wrote to Wharton that it was a "complete success").[2] Leon Edel describes the charcoal portrait as a "stern heavy-lidded accusing-eyed"[3] James; and the drawing doesn't quite do justice to its subject. It projects his unease, and a look of haunted sadness. Yet this trial run must have informed Sargent in his painting the following year, which gives us a much more grand, portly, settled image of the Master, full of earned and brooding gravity. At closer quarters this portrait still betrays a certain infinite weariness in James's expression—and a tension most surely glimpsed in the awkward clutch of his left hand. But James enjoyed these sessions, only a few streets away from his new flat by the river at 21 Carlyle Mansions, Cheyne Walk, and to which Sargent encouraged him to invite friends to talk to, "to break the spell of a settled gloom in my countenance,"[4] as James put it.

James was always quick to make analogies between painting and writing—he often describes the writer as "the painter of life"[5] or "the painter of character"[6]—and he was intrigued to see a painter of Sargent's stature at work. At the time of both these portraits, he was himself also working on a similar task. During the first sittings for the charcoal drawing early in 1912, James was deep into the dictation of *A Small Boy and Others*; a year later, this had been published, to some acclaim, and he was working on a sequel, *Notes of a Son and Brother* (1914). These two volumes, together with the unfinished, posthumous *The Middle Years* (1917), form his *Autobiography*—a title which was not his, but that of F. W. Dupee, who collected and edited the three books after James's death in 1916.[7] Where the Sargent portrait shows us the social James who dined out endlessly, wrote almost embarrassingly gushing and gracious thank-you letters, and was such an affable guest, his autobiographies present a shy, timid boy, taking his earliest uncertain steps in the world before eventually discovering the path of art. James's avoidance of the title *Autobiography* was surely deliberate, although he does once or twice use the term in correspondence about the books, which cover only a small fragment of his long life, before he really found success as a professional writer.

These are books of youth, written by an old man who had been sick at heart. Yet they seldom deal with disappointments or dismay, preferring instead to reconstruct, in tones of charmed wonder, the American and European worlds of James's childhood and adolescence, which took him backwards and forwards so often across the Atlantic. As a writer whose rallying cry while composing fiction was "Dramatize it! Dramatize it!,"[8] James must have guessed early on that his own externally placid early life would never be the real subject of the books, which end up by realizing the "monstrous" project he had glimpsed a few years before, of writing "the history of the growth of one's imagination."[9] But it took some time for this inner subject to become apparent to James. He began much more humbly, with a slightly distanced little figure of himself, one which had appeared in his work years before, in an essay on his friend George du Maurier. This was the "small American child, who lived in New York and played in Union Square,"[10] who lived and breathed Europe through the pages of English and French periodicals and books.

A Small Boy and Others takes us from James's very earliest beginnings up to 1857, when he was fifteen, ending with his illness from typhoid in Boulogne. *Notes of a Son and Brother* pushes on to 1870, with James turning twenty-seven, ending with the death from consumption of his young cousin Minny Temple. *The Middle Years*, which is really only a fragment, begins by backtracking slightly to James's momentous first solo trip to London in 1869; it then recounts his early London years, before trailing off mid-sentence in a house in Northumberland. By far the shortest, and the weakest of the books, *The Middle Years* also carries the burden of its glumly self-ironizing title. This refers to James's earlier short story of the same name about a dying writer, Dencombe, who realizes too late that he has taken too long to produce his real, best work, and that there will be no "second chance" to make amends. By the time that James was writing this third volume, in the autumn of 1914, the First World War had begun. He seems to have lost heart in the project, if not in writing altogether, as civilization crashed down around him.

James was an unlikely autobiographer. Even in his fiction, he usually claimed to be wary of writing in the first person, a mode which he thought marred the novels of his difficult, "cheeky" friend H. G. Wells. For James, first-person prose was "a form foredoomed to looseness," marred by "the terrible *fluidity* of self-revelation."[11] It is a telling expression: James often imagined art and life as being sealed off from each other. He noted the way that Turgenev "cut the umbilical cord that bound the story to himself";[12] and the recurring complaint he had of Wells's work was its "leak."[13] Writing in the first person, James felt the danger of a "leak" between art and life to be far greater than ever, and for this reason he mostly avoided it. But he had written novels and many stories in this mode, as well as autobiographical non-fiction—not least in the series of prefaces to the ill-fated New York Edition of his novels (1907–1909), which can be seen as an autobiography of his creative life, the "story of his stories." Glancing snatches of autobiography appear throughout his travel sketches and literary essays, where he occasionally draws attention to himself.[14] And privately, in his notebooks (especially in what Edel calls the "American Journals"), James had often written "of all that comes, that goes, that I see, and feel, and observe," so as "to catch and keep something of life."[15]

Strangely, we also catch sight of James throughout his two-volume biography of the American sculptor William Wetmore Story (1903), written largely in the first person, as James used his own memories of Rome and Italy to pad out what he felt to be a terminally mediocre subject. If James was suspicious of first-person prose, he had equally strong reservations and qualms about biography. Much more so than his previous attempt at writing a life, *Hawthorne* (1879), the book about Story uncomfortably enacts his own ambivalence about the whole genre. His early view of literary portraiture, as set down in an essay on Robert Louis Stevenson, was that it should aim for compression and an almost photographic immediacy, trying to "fix a face and a figure [...] seize a literary character," "catch a talent in the fact, follow its line, and put a finger on its essence."[16] This was fine with a writer he admired as much as Hawthorne; but he struggled with Story, producing a book that, page by page, reads like a battle between biographer and subject. This was partly a struggle for dominance, yet there was also a moral dimension. James was aware of the ways that biography could vie with an artist's work, increasing or reducing its power. There was, he knew, something ghostly about biography—not least the obscure pact it made with the death of its subject. And, as he had so memorably suggested in "The Aspern Papers," there was also something deadly in the negotiations biographers had to strike with the keepers of biographical documents. In his short story "The Real Right Thing," James had written of a hapless young biographer, Withermore, who sets up shop in his subject's study, in his subject's house, at the request of his subject's widow. But he is eventually barred from his new workplace by a vision of his subject's ghost, who guards the threshold of his study.

This tale, and this struggle for mastery, hauntingly mirrors the genesis of James's autobiographies. The "germ" or "seed"[17] of the memoirs, like so many of his other books, initially came accidentally, from someone else—in this case sadly prompted by his brother William's death in the summer of 1910, while Henry was staying with him in Chocorua, New Hampshire. After the death, Henry remained at his brother's house in America on and off until the following summer. In an echo of "The Real Right Thing," it was William's widow Alice who suggested to Henry that he write a "Family Book" using William's letters.

This was how the autobiographies began, while Henry stayed on, eerily living in his brother's place. As the English writer W. Somerset Maugham, who dined with Henry in America that winter of 1910, recalled:

> Henry James was troubled in spirit; after dinner the widow left us alone in the dining room, and he told me that he had promised his brother to stay at Cambridge for, I think, six months after his death, so that if he found himself able to make a communication from beyond the grave there would be two sympathetic witnesses on the spot ready to receive it [...] But hitherto no message had come, and the six months were drawing to their end.[18]

Henry had just been through some of the worst years of his life. In October 1908, he had received the first annual royalty statement for the New York Edition, which was crushingly small. Perhaps in imaginative sympathy with his brother's heart condition, Henry felt that he too had problems with his heart, and booked a session with a specialist in February 1909, who seemed to think he was fine, if overweight. In October 1909 came another meager royalty statement for the Edition. Towards the end of the year he had a bonfire in the garden of his house in Rye, East Sussex, in which he burned over forty years' worth of letters and papers. In the New Year, he collapsed, beginning what he would later call "the disaster of my long illness of January 1910,"[19] which manifested itself with gout, an aversion to food, depression, exhaustion, and nausea.

It took some time before he was to define this illness as a kind of nervous breakdown. His young nephew Harry, William's eldest son, came over from America to stay at Lamb House in February 1910, and one evening found the Master in the oak-panelled bedroom in a state of utter despair: "there was nothing to do but to sit by his side and hold his hand while he panted and sobbed for two hours until the Doctor arrived,"[20] as Harry reported back to William. In the Pocket Diaries which James kept for the last years of his life, the entries for 1910 changed nature entirely from the social engagements listed throughout 1909, turning from a record of visits into a grim medical and psychological log. On March 24, 1910, James wrote, "Harry left 1 p.m." to sail the next day; on March 27, Easter Sunday, "Edith Wharton and Teddy called—in motor from Folkestone"; on April 7, "William and Alice arrived 1:30." From then on, many notes were curt and ominous, exclusively health-related. April 10: "Bad day." April 11: "Bad day and night (vertigo from peptonized cocoa)." April 12: "Bad day and night ('grey powder' from Skinner p.m.)." April 14: "Bad day—bad, very, very bad—night."[21]

William and Alice had crossed the Atlantic to look after him, planning that William could take a cure for his heart at Bad Nauheim. After spending some time in Rye, William went on ahead to Switzerland; Henry and Alice joined him in June. By that time, Henry had decided to go back with William and Alice to America, writing to Wharton that "I am wholly unfit to be alone."[22] He needed their company. Later, in Geneva, Alice heard that their brother Robertson James had died of a heart attack. She kept the news to herself for two days, before breaking it to Henry. They all returned to London in July, sailed for Quebec from Liverpool on August 12—and before the end of the month, after reaching his home in New Hampshire, William had died too.

*

The year or so during which Henry remained in America, only returning to England at the end of July 1911, was a fragile, painful, solitary period. Being back in America for the first time in years recharged Henry's memories of his youth, the years before he left so decisively for Europe. He was always prompted into reflective thoughts about his life when he was in America, as he revisited the haunts, and the people, of his past, and memories of place triggered associations. Of all his notebooks, which mostly deal with ideas for novels and stories, the two "American Journals" are the nearest to autobiography. The first, written in 1881–82 when James was thirty-eight, revisiting Boston, took stock of his life so far, and above all the last six years, as, with his fiction temporarily suspended, James tried to persuade himself that he was at least gathering impressions for future work. "Here I am back in America," James wrote in this journal, "[...] after six years of absence [...] I am glad I have come—it was a wise thing to do. I needed to see again *les miens*, to revive my relations with them, and my sense of the consequences that these relations entail. Such relations, such consequences, are a part of one's life, and the best life, the most complete, is the one that takes full account of such things."[23]

The second American Journal, meanwhile, was written in 1904–5, during the trip Henry took to research *The American Scene* (1907), and reads more like sketches in autobiography for that travel book, as James retrod old ground and found memories everywhere around him. He self-consciously knew that he was storing up material for the book he would write back in England. "Everything sinks in," he wrote in this journal in March 1905, "nothing is lost; everything abides and fertilizes and renews its golden promise, making me think with closed eyes of deep and grateful longing when, in the full summer days of L[amb] H[ouse], my long dusty adventure over, I shall be able to [plunge] my hand, my arm, *in*, deep and far, and up to the shoulder—into the heavy bag of remembrance—of suggestion—of imagination—of art—and fish out every little figure and felicity, every little fact and fancy that can be to my purpose."[24]

In 1910–11, staying on with Alice after William's death, Henry once again found himself swamped in possible material—this time, for the projected "Family Book." Now he was the last member of his family left still alive.

William, Robertson, Alice, Wilky: all of his siblings had gone. The past dissolved the present, made it seem like a dream. "Walked with Harry..." Henry wrote sadly, in the usually telegrammatic and brief Pocket Diaries one afternoon, as if overcome by visions of remembrance: "lovely winter day with such hints of spring, such a sunset and such melancholy, tragic hauntings and recalls of the old far-off years."[25]

Yet if this was a difficult and reflective time, he was not entirely reclusive. In New York that October, he stayed at the Hotel Belmont, dining with Edith Wharton, Walter Berry, and Morton Fullerton, the day before Wharton sailed for France; and there were other social events. The Diaries oscillated uneasily between such visits and the ongoing medical log, as if James was not quite able to tell how ill he was. He sought psychoanalytical help. In Boston, he saw James Putnam, a student of Freud, for long talks, which he later acknowledged as being pivotal; in New York, he also began seeing Joseph Collins at the Neurological Institute, every morning at 11 a.m. throughout late March. In July, James stayed with Wharton at her huge house The Mount in Massachusetts for several very hot days, before eventually returning to England and Rye—ending what would be the last of his American sojourns.

What he wanted, of course, was to start writing again. He had not done much work at all for two or three years, since the Edition and his illness. His confidence in producing fiction had been shaken. He was never again to complete a novel, yet he still needed, almost as a matter of psychological survival and recovery, to get back to a major literary task. Work had always played such a large role in his life, that without it, he was completely lost. Now, from his talks with Alice, and with his memories replenished by his recent travels, he had a new project, the "Family Book"; and he was returning with packets of William's letters. But once back at Rye, he couldn't face another lonely winter there. Over the years, he had known many of the other writers who had settled fairly close by for a time—Conrad in Pent Farm, at Aldington, and at Orlestone; Wells at Sandgate; Ford at Winchelsea; Rudyard Kipling in Burwash. G. K. Chesterton had even lived next door to James. But by 1911, life in Lamb House was, as James had partly always wanted it to be, rather solitary, quiet. And it still held associations of his recent illness. So he decided to spend the winter mostly in London, at the Reform Club.

He began the "Family Book" straightaway, once back in England, initially without his typist Theodora Bosanquet. At the end of October, he wrote to her that he needed some rooms in London, "having got back to work and to a very particular job."[26] Bosanquet found two rooms next to her flat at 10 Lawrence Street, Chelsea. This is where *A Small Boy and Others* was written, and initial progress on the project was rapid, impatient. By mid-November, James was writing to Wharton, with a sense of slight triumph and excitement at his resumption of activity.

> I have in any case got back to work—on something that now the more urgently occupies me as the time for me circumstantially to have done it would have been last winter when I was insuperably unfit for it, and that is extremely special, experimental and as yet occult. I apply myself to my effort every morning at a little *repaire* in the depths of Chelsea, a couple of little rooms that I have secured for quiet and concentration—to which a blest taxi whirls me [. . .] every morning at 10 o'clock, and where I meet my amanuensis.[27]

James's letters to Wharton often blend candor, slight mockery, and genuine fear. He called her a "devastating Angel" and a "Firebird," for the way that she would swoop down on him with her lavish lifestyle, her motorcars, her romantic dilemmas, her plans. But it is clear that he relished and looked forward to the hectic times he spent with her. Wharton was a "devastating Angel" because her motor trips, particularly, which James enjoyed so much, threw all his plans for work—and his relatively meager finances—into disarray. In this letter, no doubt to prevent her from distracting him now he was finally working again, he fails to tell her exactly where his "little *repaire*" in Chelsea is, and he shrouds the new project in mystery. Yet the terms he uses for the book he is writing—"extremely special, experimental and as yet occult"—are honest.

At first, Henry didn't know how to deal with the project of the "Family Book"; and he had never written anything along these lines before. What Alice and Henry's nephew Harry might have envisaged, it seems, was something like a Victorian "Life and Letters" biography of William: a biography with long quotes from William's letters, and personal memories by Henry—perhaps bearing in mind how William had edited their father Henry James Senior's *Literary Remains* after his death. What Henry began writing in Chelsea that winter of 1911, however, was quite different.

*

Whenever somebody writes about another member of their family, or writes about themselves in terms of any family relationship, the lines between biography and autobiography become blurred. Some lives—family lives particularly—connect at such essential points that it is often hard to tell where writing about someone else becomes a form of self-disclosure, and writing a portrait of oneself becomes biography of others. This aspect of the projected "Family Book" initially confused Henry. Above all, he wasn't sure, at first, how to work with the documentary material he had been given: the letters. As "The Aspern Papers" showed, Henry knew very well the lengths to which biographers will go to obtain letters, and here he had them at his disposal. But did he really want to write a biography of William based on his letters? In a series of long epistles of his own to Harry and Alice back in Boston—the keepers of William's literary estate, as it were—he began a parallel, evasive correspondence about the progress of the "Family Book." This continued for the next few years, as he told them how he was getting on with it, asked for more family documents to be sent over, reassured them, and requested their unconditional support.

If James's last attempt at biography, about William Wetmore Story, had been a battle between biographer and subject, the "Family Book" was even more so. And, whether because Henry didn't know how best to utilize the documentary materials at hand, or how to write about William so soon after his death, he again found the solution instinctively in writing more about himself than the proposed subject: writing autobiography more than biography. With all his experience in novelistic point of view, he knew he could only write about William from his own vantage point. And, for all their interest, the letters which he had must have appeared fragmentary and piecemeal compared to this rich inner source of potential material. As Henry wrote to Bosanquet, before they set to work, "I find the question of the Letters to be copied or dictated baffles *instant* solution [...] It is a bit complicated, and I may let it wait till I begin to come. I shall rather like to begin with something that goes very straight so as to get the easier back into harness."[28] This proved to be much more about his own life experiences, than about William. Over the following months, as he continued in this vein of autobiography, indeed until the following summer, James tapped into a flood of reminiscence which at first had a wonderfully therapeutic effect. He *was* back at work, finally, and the work made him feel not only mentally better, but even had a corresponding physical effect.

Throughout the dictation of *A Small Boy and Others*, James was improvising; and once he found the source of this recovery through autobiography, it was crucial for him not to stop or interrupt his progress. He was unused to the delicate, close, implicating nature of the subject-matter; yet unlike when composing fiction, he dictated straight off, without notes. At times, the language of the memoir is more like the language of the creative notebooks, where he chases ideas like a butterfly-catcher, following the "tip" of "the tail" of an image, as "vague, dim forms of imperfect conceptions seem to brush across one's face with a blur of suggestion, a flutter of impalpable wings."[29] But in the composition of A Small Boy and Others, James was chasing memories.

*

Each morning, as Bosanquet tells us, after arriving at his "Chelsea cellar"—a "quiet room, long and narrow and rather dark"[30]—James would read over the pages written the previous day. "He would settle down for an hour or so of conscious effort. Then, lifted on a rising tide of inspiration, he would get up and pace up and down the room, sounding out the periods,"[31] while Bosanquet kept up with him on the Remington typewriter. Although the dictation seems to have come freely, without much recourse to notes or reference books to check names and dates and facts, sometimes James did use other props as an aide-mémoire. This, it seems, was the initial use he made of William's letters while writing A Small Boy and Others, rather than quoting from them yet at any length. At other times, he used old photographs to spur his memory.

But it soon became apparent that James was hardly in need of props. The problem—and it did become a problem, eventually—was that he remembered too much, not too little. What he discovered during the experiment of dictating A Small Boy and Others was not only how plentifully stocked the "precious store"[32] of his memory was (as he commented throughout the book), but also how to stir it into action. The process of reflection and imagination that lay behind his fiction—all the hours of dreaming and plotting laid bare in the New York Edition prefaces and the notebooks—could also be placed at the service of memory.

Once started, he found the act of recollection almost embarrassingly easy. During the morning sessions, as his typist tells us, until around 1:45 each day, "a straight dive into the past brought to the surface treasure after treasure."[33] He had been hoarding experiences for his fiction for years: his own, and as a voracious, devouring, "incorrigible collector of 'cases'"[34] and scenarios, those of other people. All the vicarious store of perception that he had collected for fiction—gathered for instance, on long evenings walking the streets in the "great grey Babylon" of London as "possible stories, present-able figures, rise from the thick jungle as the observer moves, fluttering up like startled game"[35]—was also filed away for instant use. The appetite for other people's lives is what fed his fiction, which was able to sustain and nourish itself from the faintest hints and suggestions. This was the secret of his own, outwardly dull life at his desk, even its greatest "joy": the nourishment that art and life gave to each other, "the constant quick flit of associations, to and fro, and through a hundred open doors, between the two great chambers [...] of direct and indirect experience."[36] "Did nothing happen to Henry James except the writing of an extremely long shelf of books?"[37] asks Leon Edel in his five-volume life of James. "Could a man produce so much having, as it is claimed, lived so little?"[38] Yet this endless dance between art and experience was what life to James was all about.

While dictating *A Small Boy and Others*, he seemed only to need the smallest of clues, and like the protagonist John Marcher in his short story "The Beast in the Jungle," he found himself remembering more—"the impression operating like the torch of a lamplighter who touches into flame, one by one, a long row of gas jets."[39] To use another analogy, his memoir revealed the structure of his memory, tangled up as it was with his imagination, as a giant spider's web, made of impossibly intertwined, fragile materials. In James's labyrinthine remembering consciousness, everything was linked and connected to everything else; each memory leads and hangs on to another memory, until "the pages [...] overflow with connections"[40] and it becomes an act of violence to break the threads. His memory worked outwards from shards or fragments of objects or hints of sensations—the taste of peaches, or a piece of clothing, or a billboard on Broadway—and from each fragment, a world reappeared to surround it. Each of the long-gone worlds James remembered was meticulously reconstructed out of small pieces and details, from which he gained a toehold to the next moment of recall.

In the memoir, James presents himself as a child whose education took place on the streets of New York, and with his cousins in Albany, for his first twelve years, until the family made the long-promised trip to Europe in 1855—his first sight of the continent that would become his lifelong home (although Henry claimed, prodigiously, to remember a glimpse of Paris from a visit during his first two years of life, in 1843–45). *A Small Boy and Others* recreates the entire "small warm dusky homogenous New York world of the mid-century,"[41] and the sense and texture of James's early life there; walking alone and with his father along Broadway; going to church and the ice-cream parlor; being tutored by a succession of governesses, before entering a series of creaky educational establishments. In a sequence of disconnected, fragmentary scenes, James traces the gropings for his "earliest aesthetic seeds"[42] in visits to Barnums, or in evenings of watching acrobatics and dancers at Niblo's, before formative trips to the theaters in the Bowery, and adventures deep in the pages of English books.

James wanted to show the earliest nourishments of his perception, in as much detail as he could. Inadvertently, perhaps, the story which emerges from the American youth James recounts is one of repeatedly seeking aesthetic replenishment in a culture which didn't provide it for him. Everywhere, in his portrait of early youth, he emphasizes the ramshackle roughness of New York and Albany, and the improvised unsuitability of his formal education. The undercurrent of the memoir shows how James triumphed over this, and somehow made his own education in art, despite all the humorous and inappropriate efforts of his teachers. If, as a writer, James's watchword had been "Dramatize it! Dramatize it!," here in *A Small Boy and Others*, it was "as if the authors of our being and guardians of our youth had virtually said to us but one thing [...] one word, though constantly repeated: Convert, convert, convert!"[43] Perhaps only in this way, through converting and distilling experience, could they understand and use artistically everything that happened to themselves, however raw or seemingly unsuitable.

Once in Europe, "at last,"[44] in 1855, almost two-thirds of the way through the memoir, James writes of the family's arrival in London, before they traveled to Paris, Lyons, and Geneva—Henry taking in "a larger draught of the wine of perception than any I had ever before."[45] As he recreates it in the pages of *A Small Boy and Others*, it was the London of Dickens and Hogarth, and the immense galleries of the Paris of the Second Empire, rather than America, which served as his sites of artistic enlightenment and self-discovery, as he gradually became aware of his vocation. The self-portrait is of a dawdling, gaping, wondering boy, whose only desire is to look at the spectacle of life and take his fill of the multitudinous scenes and impressions he sees everywhere around him, much more than to actively participate in them. This small boy took some time to see how all these impressions could be transformed, and to find his direction in life, compared to William, who is only glimpsed in these pages.

*

All autobiography has a certain span or reach, which could be defined not as the period covered within its pages, but the distance between what is being remembered, and the present act of recollection. James had written in the New York Edition prefaces how he delighted in what he called "the *visitable* past"—not the past of documents and archives, or even further back, but the past lying within the bounds of personal experience, which "we may reach over to as by making a long arm we grasp an object at the other end of our own table."[46] While working on the memoir, pacing up and down each morning in the dim room to the rhythmic clacking of the Remington, James soon found that he was interested in trying to represent the reach of his memory as much as his memories themselves. This was perhaps one reason why he seldom troubled to consult notes or references while composing the book, instead preferring to court the free play of his recall. He wanted to try and put memory down on the page as it was: in all its inconsistencies, in its lapses and blurrings just as much as its constant astonishments.

For James, forgetting was intrinsic to his autobiography in an unusual way, in that he seemed to remember everything, but with blots and erasures, distortions. Often, he portrays figures not only as they were, but as he sees them while he tries to remember them: such as his uncle Robert Temple, whom he seemed to see standing before him in his regimental uniform "as a person half asleep sees some large object across the room and against the window-light."[47] James later wrote to Harry about that "conception of an *atmosphere* which I invoked, as, artistically speaking, my guiding star."[48] Along with all the "personal and social and subjective (and *objective*) furniture"[49] of the past, James also catches the glowing, glimmering, flickering atmosphere of memory in which its characters now all sit embalmed in his mind. The effect is impressionistic, as James uses blurred daubs of the brush to seize an essence. Sometimes, he seems to slow down time and fuse habitual scenes together—such as when Henry writes of his father that he seems to see him always in the same pose, writing at his desk facing the window, or of his brother that he seems to see him "drawing and drawing, always drawing."[50] The compression of the portraiture freezes many figures in this way, in a startling, telling pose—almost aiming for the effect of a striking visual image.

In *A Small Boy and Others*, as in his novel *What Maisie Knew* (1897), James was also increasingly interested in representing not only what happened to himself when he was a little boy, but in recreating—even reliving—a young child's consciousness. The dual perspective which results in the memoir is accordingly tightly limited at both ends: on the one hand, by James the old autobiographer, working with his avowedly faulty memory, and at the other end of the spectrum, almost being taken in hand by his older self, by the young child whose knowledge of the world was also necessarily partial, blind, and occluded. Perhaps much of James's recovery from his breakdown lay, precisely, in the success with which he managed to live back into his younger self, and his recreation of the times—what he called "the general Eden-like consciousness"[51]—before his sense of the world became fallen and tainted.

The prose in the memoir, because of this, revels in unabashed superabundance. The late style of James's novels, and of the New York Edition, had been notoriously rich and convoluted; these pages—"*late* late James"[52] as Dupee describes this style—are even more glutted with life. The sheer number of people James puts into the book almost makes the memoir feel crowded, like a gallery in which too many pictures have been hung. Discovering the extent to which autobiography can accommodate group biography, or small sketches and portraits of a group, *A Small Boy and Others* is consequently sometimes almost more revealing of the "others" of the title—except William, and other close family members—than of Henry, who often seems a mere observation post. James felt that the wraithlike figures who strayed across his path, as he looked back across his life, all begged for treatment, pleading not to be ignored and abandoned. He felt a moral compulsion to get them all into his pages, even though by doing so, he had to cram them together. He had faced a similar dilemma as a biographer, writing early in his book about Story on

> the appeal, the ghostly claim [...] of [...] a vanished society. Figures innumerable, if we like to recall them, and if, alas! we *can*, pass before us [...] and meet us [...] Boxfuls of old letters and relics are, in fine, boxfuls of ghosts and echoes, a swarm of apparitions and reverberations [...] We desire for them some profit of the brush we have given them to make them a little less dim.[53]

Writing to his nephew Harry the following July of 1912, to tell him how the projected "Family Book" was coming along—James had by this time written well over 100,000 words without having even reached the commentaries for William's letters—he explained to his nephew, perhaps slightly shame-facedly, about the extent to which he had already overwritten in recounting his memories of childhood:

> [...] in doing this book I am led, by the very process and action of my idiosyncrasy, on and on into more evocation and ramification of the old images and connections, more intellectual and moral autobiography (though all

closely and, as I feel it, exquisitely associated and involved), than I shall quite know what to do with—to do with, that is, in this book.[54]

*

The first phase of dictation to Bosanquet had been a miraculous return to health and work for James, written in a sustained creative burst which reassured him that his powers were not failing, despite all he had been through the years before. During this phase of reminiscence, the Pocket Diaries testified to his recovery, and a busy social life despite the rapid productivity in his mornings with Bosanquet. From the winter of 1911 until the summer of 1912, there were frequent journeys between London and Lamb House; several long weekends as a guest at Howard Sturgis's country house Queen's Acre in Windsor; and numerous, sporadic visits to friends in town, among them to two old acquaintances from Kent: to Wells, who was now living in Hampstead,[55] and to Ford, at South Lodge, as James noted, when he briefly "met Violet Hunt and F. M. Hueffer and went home with them for ½ an hour."[56] James was frequently out and about all this time, at lunches and dinners, and trips to go shopping or to the theater.

Wharton came over from Paris at the end of July with her motor, resting at Lamb House before taking James off to Queen's Acre and a stay at Cliveden, above the Thames, of several days, where he had a slight, if worrying, relapse from overdoing things. Yet the work went on. And taking stock that summer of 1912, as James wrote to Harry and to his agent, James B. Pinker, he began to realize that he would need two books, not one, for his family memories. As his material "of brotherly autobiography, & filial autobiography not less"[57] had become increasingly personal and extensive, he decided that a separate book to be based around William's letters would have to come before a memoir based on the long flood of memories which he had just dictated. Then he switched this order around. *A Small Boy and Others*, Henry suddenly realized, should come before, not after, the volume on William's letters. There had been a tension between biography and autobiography in the project from the start—and between William and himself. This change in the running order now put Henry clearly first. If, as Edel suggests, there had always been rivalry between Henry and William, this change in sequence was a significant psychological fact, with the younger brother finally asserting himself.

The titles Henry finally settled on for the two memoirs make a subtle, if clear, demarcation between the various roles his former self plays in each

of them. Arrived at with great care, after much deliberation, these titles
are much more specific than the general label *Autobiography*. In *A Small Boy
and Others*, autobiography had won out, and the small boy is the hero of the
book; in *Notes of a Son and Brother*, as Henry more dutifully implied, biography
would now come first, and he would finally play the more humble family
roles. Where *A Small Boy and Others* only uses the family letters to help
prompt Henry's memory, in *Notes* he now planned to quote from them at
length in the text. Partly because of this, the writing of *Notes of a Son and
Brother* proved to be more difficult, even if some of its material was drawn
from the surplus of the first phase of reminiscence. In October 1912, with
A Small Boy and Others complete and sent off to Scribner's except for
a short concluding section, Henry fell ill again, back at Rye, with "vivid red
welts—sores—blisters"[58] appearing along his left side. Dr. Skinner—the irony
was not lost on James—was called in again from Ashford, and diagnosed
shingles. As James took to his bed, the Diaries resumed their medical log
until just after the move to Carlyle Mansions at the start of 1913, when social
life began again, and the final part of *A Small Boy and Others*—ending, not
coincidentally, with an account of James's illness from typhoid in Boulogne
in 1857 and subsequent loss of consciousness—was also dispatched.

Illnesses recurred throughout 1913, while *Notes of a Son and Brother* was
being written, although James had got over the worst of his shingles by the
spring. But it was uncanny that his physical well-being should also suffer,
now that he was finally writing about his brother and his father. And this
seemed to have something to do with his problems over how to use the letters.
Nephew Harry was now planning his own edition of William's letters—and
he was keeping a watchful eye on Henry, pestering him with queries about
exactly which letters he planned to use, and how he was progressing.
Henry's irritation over these practical questions, as he wrote to his nephew
wrangling over the letters, began to become almost physical. To stem queries,
Henry deployed his shingles, asking his nephew not to push him too far,
hinting that his illnesses were aggravated by the literary restrictions he felt
from the family. "I wish I could persuade you to a little greater confidence,
through all these heavy troubles of mine, in my proceeding with the utmost
consideration," Henry wrote to Harry. "I shall feel this confidence most,"
he continued

> [...] if you won't ask me too much in advance, or at any rate for some time to
> come, to formulate to you the *detail* of my use [...] of your Dad's Letters [...]
> Let me off [...] from any specified assurances now; I am not fit to make them,

and the sense of having so much to report myself is, frankly, oppressive and blighting. Don't *insist*, but trust me as far as you can.[59]

In *Notes of a Son and Brother*, Henry duly tried to take on the self-effacing guise of family chronicler or biographer, with much more success. He picks up the story of the James family's European stay, where *A Small Boy and Others* had tantalizingly left off with Henry's swoon into unconsciousness; but the focus is more directly on William and Henry James Senior. Henry himself is still to be seen, of course, but there is a subtle shift in perspective from the outset, so that he appears slightly more on the periphery of the book than at its true center. And alongside the long excerpts from William's and his father's letters, Henry also uses many letters by his brother Wilky—several of which referred to Henry and saw him in the third person, almost from the outside.

Notes of a Son and Brother tells initially of the family's periods in Geneva, Bonn, and Paris, before they returned to America and Newport, ostensibly so that William could study painting with William Hunt. Hunt's studio in Newport is portrayed as a magical place, as William James practiced drawing from life there—and Henry reached his own realization that if he himself could not draw, like William, then perhaps he could write, and so, in that way, "live by the imagination."[60] The pages remembering the seaside world of Newport throb with revelation, even if Henry insists how he had been marked by his European experience. His literary influences now looked towards Europe, even while he was back in America, as he wrote of how he devoured the pages of the *Revue des Deux Mondes*, and through the influence of John La Farge, discovered Balzac and Browning.

Where *A Small Boy and Others* shows Henry's widening perception, and traces his imagination in that way, the growth of his literary talent throughout the 1860s is depicted more directly in *Notes of a Son and Brother*, if very gradually and in secretive terms, as Henry nurtured it under various other guises. The book never quite comes out and tells how James's actual writing evolved, so much as it implies how it slowly blossomed under adverse conditions, even during Henry's unhappy stint as a Harvard law student in 1862. This growth of Henry's writerly self is the real autobiographical theme of the volume, even though it is told in a submerged way, carrying on beneath the more explicit family events: the move from Newport to Boston in 1864; William's trip to the Amazon in 1865; the Jameses finally settling down in Quincy Street, Cambridge in 1866. By the mid-1860s, Henry's writing becomes a more open theme, as he began to feel more sure of the potential revelations of art and the imagination, cultivated on his own, in such an externally uneventful way. "Seeing further into the figurable world *made* company of persons and places, objects and subjects alike," Henry writes. "It gave them all without exception chances to be somehow or other interesting, and the imaginative ply of finding interest once taken (I think I had by that time got much beyond looking for it), the whole conspiracy of aspects danced around me in a ring."[61]

As Henry quoted extensively from the letters at his disposal in *Notes of a Son and Brother*, he also told the stories of the others in his family in a more impartial way, giving his comments, as it were, in the margins—almost as if he was an editor, more than a writer; detached, if curious, more than personally involved. Many letters were included only as they came to hand, arriving in packets from across the Atlantic as the book was being written. As it moved into the years of the American Civil War, an inevitable narrative began to build through its letters from the front by Wilky, who was fighting in it, as was Bob. The sense Henry referred to, throughout the autobiographies, that "real" life was always elsewhere, and that he was not born to participate, so much as observe it—and ultimately depict it—from afar, intensifies as he remembers the dispatches his two more active brothers sent home; and even more so as Wilky was wounded and brought home on a stretcher. James visited soldiers, as he writes in this second memoir, at Portsmouth Grove, yet he never took part in the conflict. His sense of his own passivity reaches a crisis in the book, as he tells of his non-participation in the war, due to the unspecified, ambiguous "obscure hurt"[62] which he did himself while helping to put out a fire—weirdly, just like his father, who suffered a serious injury in youth while also putting out a blaze. James makes the "obscure hurt" so obscure, in fact, that he almost implies he faked it.

At the climax of the second memoir, James wrote himself even further out of the picture, with his arrangement of a sequence of moving letters between his cousin Minny Temple and her friend, John Chipman Gray, which James had received almost by chance while writing the book. In piecing these letters together to tell the story of Minny's death from tuberculosis in 1870, James again chose to take the vantage point of an observer—even though he had been much more directly involved in these events. Minny, he wrote, "was really to remain [...] the supreme case of a taste for life as life, as personal living"[63] to him—as opposed to Henry's perpetual life-at-one-remove. Her death, he writes in the last line of the book, represented the end of his and William's youth. But the death also symbolized and assisted Henry's own birth as a writer. He went on to redraw, and to give new life, over and again, to versions of Minny in his work, notably in *Daisy Miller* (1878) and *The Portrait of a Lady* (1881). Just as he could only write about his family in his *Autobiography* once they were all dead, Minny's death bequeathed her to his fiction. When he was writing these final pages, Henry dictated with her image "before me as I write":[64] the faded photograph of her taken in September 1869. And this story of physical deterioration— "essentially the record of a rapid illness,"[65] as James writes—was also a form of displaced autobiography of the present, for James the ageing writer, who, as he finished *Notes of a Son and Brother* in Rye in November 1913, had been ill, on and off, all that year.

*

Portraiture in visual art frequently succumbs to the urge to flatter its subject. This has often had to do with the circumstances of a portrait: the way in which a portrait is commissioned or bought by the subject. The painter or photographer, and the subject, often collude in the likeness, and their closeness while the portrait is being made might tempt the portraitist to flatter. Visual *self*-portraiture removes this worldly agency; and the artist is free to employ absolute candor. Where self-portraiture in painting is free to be as honest as it likes, the same doesn't always apply to autobiography, which is often likely to have the same issues with discretion as biography, since autobiographers know their subjects so well, so intimately—and since their subjects are more likely to be alive than in biography.

In *A Small Boy and Others* and *Notes of a Son and Brother*, James was always a flattering autobiographer. This was not so much in his portrait of himself— which was modest and shy to the point of self-negation—but in all his portrayals of everyone else. While writing his memoirs, depicting lost friends and family, James's imagination brought them back to life by his side; and he wanted to portray them all in the best possible light. Where this was not possible, he often simply left things out. He dodged, fudged, blurred, and was discreet. As he had written in the Story biography, he again felt the need to ensure that all the figures in his memoirs would gain from this "profit of the brush we have given them."

This was one reason why, when he finally came to tackle William's and his father's letters, Henry retouched and rewrote these letters as he went along. Perhaps this was also why he changed the content of the family history in the memoirs—condensing two trips to Europe and back into one, for instance, mainly to make his father look less indecisive and prone to acting on a whim. Addicted to retouching the style of his fiction for years, as evidenced by the laborious rewriting of his entire *oeuvre* for the New York Edition, he seems to have found himself unable not to do the same to the family documents. He had such a strong "sense for fusions and interrelations, for framing and encircling,"[66] as he later wrote to his predictably incensed nephew Harry, that he claimed he couldn't help himself. He himself acknowledged that this was a mistake—writing to Harry, he averred that "the sad thing is I think you're right in being offended"[67] and declared that he should never again stray from his "proper work," meaning the writing of fiction, where such attention to form and style was only ever for the best. But there is little doubt that his often very slight and mild doctorings and rewritings of the letters were done with good, if misguided, intentions. The actual changes Henry made, if numerous, were often very small: minor corrections and smoothings out of syntax, grammar, or rhythm.[68] He was, however, also guided by a general tendency to minimize family discords. Henry wrote to Harry about how he wanted so much in the "Family Book"

> to show us all at our best for characteristic expression and colour and variety and everything that would be charming [...] I found myself again in such close relation with your Father, such a revival of relation as I hadn't known since his death, and which was a passion of tenderness for doing the best thing by him that the material allowed, and which I seemed to feel him in the room and at my elbow asking me for as I worked and he listened.[69]

It was quite deliberately a nicely blurred view of the James family that Henry wanted to create in the memoirs; and he trod carefully, scared of offending the ghosts he summoned up. Memory's "snares" and "traps" which Henry referred to throughout the books were not only in its superabundance, but in all the gnarly subject-matter which had to be delicately handled or put aside gently, to bring out this "charming" family portrait.

As Lyndall Gordon writes, Henry's memoirs "of the 'happy working of all our relations, in our family life' blots out the wreckage of three of the five children"[70]—especially the prolonged nervous illness and subsequent death of his sister Alice James. Alice hardly appeared in the autobiographies, other than in glimpses from William's letters. Henry complained that he didn't have enough letters from Alice to use in *Notes of a Son and Brother*. But as he well knew, Alice had also written extensive, brilliant, and quotable diaries, whose existence Henry wanted to keep private.

As for his two other brothers, Wilky and Bob, Henry portrays them falsely as heroes in the Civil War, without dwelling on how their later lives were marked by disappointments. (After great financial troubles, Wilky died young, while Bob was a chronic alcoholic.) Where he couldn't show them as being "charming," he moved on to something else. And the long portrait of his father in *Notes of a Son and Brother* vaguely glosses over the accident which left Henry James Senior lamed and embittered for life, with a cork leg—rather like the Mathew Brady photograph of him, whose frame ended just below the knee. Henry eventually does mention his father's lameness. But at first, he merely writes that his father preferred walking on hard city pavements to being out in the countryside. Discretion tips over into outright evasion: whenever characters couldn't be shown in a good light, they tend to simply disappear from the memoirs. For all that, in the portrait of his father in particular, Henry was still capable of a slyly humorous tone. He lamented that as a devout follower of Swedenborg, for instance, his father never seemed to meet any other fellow Swedenborgians; he noted sadly that his father's writings, which he spent a lifetime slaving over, found so few readers. Henry implied what he knew—the hard fact that his father's life had been a failure in many ways—but he didn't say so outright. Perhaps the only way to transform this material was in the gently comical tone that he took.

With Minny Temple's letters, Henry also rewrote and retouched many phrases, and destroyed the originals, without asking or telling anyone, even though these letters were not his. In doing this, he later claimed success or otherwise on purely aesthetic grounds—ignoring the moral position of a right to privacy which he would have held fiercely if the same thing had happened to him. In the phrase with which he defends the doctoring of both William's and Minny Temple's letters, he saw everything in the autobiographies, even other people's correspondence, as being ultimately all his own truth, "to do what I would with."[71] Obsessive about retaining his own privacy, James dealt with others' differently, as one of Leon Edel's anecdotes implies. Theodora Bosanquet remembered a day at Lamb House in July 1908 when James showed her his neighbor, the "unspeakable Chesterton," from the window of the Garden Room. Edel continues with a scene which can be found in H. G. Wells's reminiscences:

> Chesterton's presence in Rye produced another incident which H. G. Wells remembered. On this occasion it was William James who climbed the gardener's ladder to peep over the wall at Chesterton. Henry apparently felt it all

right to look out of his own window at Chesterton as passer-by, but that it was wrong to invade privacy in William's fashion. They quarrelled about this, Wells remembered, when he arrived in a car to fetch the William Jameses and Peggy for a visit to his home in Sandgate. James appealed to Wells. "It simply wasn't done, emphatically, it wasn't permissible behaviour in England"— this was the gist of the appeal.[72]

Sometimes James hides behind his high aesthetic principles while writing his family portrait, using his avowed attempt to seize and preserve the truth of memory and atmosphere as an excuse for his slight trespasses, and for avoiding or blurring subjects he wanted to avoid. But his alterations and evasions erred on the side of privacy, not prurience. James's use of other people's letters in his autobiographies might have been unorthodox; but his embrace of the randomness with which he came by these letters was entirely consistent with these views on privacy. It was a literary way of not climbing a ladder to look over the wall at someone else.

He had not actively *sought* very much in the nature of documentary materials for the books. He had tended mainly to use whatever came his way circumstantially. If this made him a haphazard autobiographer or family chronicler, then it was likely that he did so quite consciously. He was always a literary passer-by, in his portraits of others, and didn't intrude. Aesthetically, too, James felt it was important that his reach remained limited. In his 1908 Preface to "The Aspern Papers," he even used the image of the wall and ladder in a slightly different way, noting that "the charm of looking over a garden-wall into another garden breaks down when successions of walls appear. The other gardens, those still beyond, may be there, but even by use of our longest ladder we are baffled and bewildered—the view is mainly a view of barriers."[73] As an autobiographer, James sometimes put up those barriers himself. Arguably, destroying Minny's letters—as he had destroyed forty years' worth of his own, from other people, in 1909—was his way of carrying further his beliefs about personal privacy, which he had thought about many times over the years.

*

In his notebooks, James had long ago mused on "the idea of the *responsibility of destruction*—the destruction of papers, letters, records, etc., connected with the private and personal history of some great and honoured name and throwing some very different light on it,"[74] which he turned into the story "Sir Dominick Ferrand." This was primarily an idea for his writing, but it did appear from his own destructive tendencies towards letters that he, personally, actually believed in this *"responsibility."* The reasons behind this belief were subtle and devious. They lay as much in a hope that through such destruction, literary biography would be raised to the level of an art, as in a straightforward desire for the preservation of privacy.

In an 1897 essay on George Sand, James reflects on the ethics of biography and reading other people's letters. This is "the greatest of literary quarrels," James writes, musing on his own enjoyment of the salacious details—and the artistry—that he finds in Sand's letters. It is "the quarrel beside which all others are mild and arrangeable, the eternal dispute between the public and the private, between curiosity and delicacy."[75]

James understood the urge to know every fact about a subject better than anyone—"when we wish to know at all we wish to know everything."[76] But for writers in particular, he found biography denuding, mystery-shedding. Where his own novels and autobiographies shrouded their subjects in a haze of suggestion, the biographical facts did the opposite: stripping subjects remorselessly of their secrets and their magic. More than the moral right to privacy, it was this aesthetic paring down which troubled James. Biography had a leveling effect on a writer's work. With a great writer, the facts served to cut the work down in size: to humanize, demystify, reduce. This leveling also went the other way, generating interest in work which would otherwise be forgotten. (In Sand's case, James writes, her letters had stood the test of time almost better than her fiction.) Style, in the telling, could also redeem the most squalid biographical material, James realized. It was not the squalor of biographical facts that bothered him, so much as the fear of how they might be told, in relation to the work.

But where did this leave the artist, like himself? How could he ensure that he would be biographized with skill and sympathy? James knew it was impossible to avoid biographization altogether after death—that lay completely out of one's hands. What one could do was destroy things, remove the substructure for any future chronicles. By destroying letters, especially, James hoped, he would increase his own unknowability in future incarnations. He would raise the stakes of the biographical enterprise so high that any biographer who wrote of him would be forced to extremes of ingenuity which made their work, effectively, an art, a fiction—and would leave the work intact and impenetrable. James sets all this down in the essay on George

Sand. "The reporter and the reported have duly and equally to understand that they carry their life in their hands," James writes, evolving a metaphor which goes further than the wall and gardener's ladder:

> There are secrets for privacy and silence; let them only be cultivated on the part of the hunted creature with even half the method with which the love of sport— or call it the historic sense—is cultivated on the part of the investigator [...] Then at last the game will be fair [...] Then the cunning of the inquirer, envenomed with resistance, will exceed in subtlety and ferocity anything we to-day conceive, and the pale forewarned victim, with every track covered, every paper burnt and every letter unanswered, will, in the tower of art, the invulnerable granite, stand, without a sally, the siege of all the years.[77]

The extraordinary rhetorical power of this passage suggests how much passionate thought James put into reflecting on what he calls the "game" of biography. If he had been less than completist when using the family letters, and indeed slightly altered them, this all fitted with his scheme; if he had been evasive and sparing with the facts, this was only in tune with his views about privacy. His memoirs cover his family's tracks; and often, in key scenes, make things seem more, not less, mysterious. All this is hardly surprising from a writer whose whole life's work had been spent inventing fictions; and who, in *A Small Boy*, writes that even when young, "what happened all the while [...] was that I imagined things [...] wholly other than as they were, and so carried on in the midst of the actual ones an existence that somehow floated and saved me."[78] The autobiographies themselves reveal how much this very process of imagination made reality bearable for James and was the guiding motivation of his art.

Wells wrote in his own *Experiment in Autobiography* (1934) many years later— long after their quarrel over Wells's satire of James in *Boon* (1915)—that James never "scuffled with Fact."[79] This is not quite fair as an assessment of James's autobiographies, which are saturated with facts and precisely recalled details, and whose reminiscential processes revealed James's growing fascination with the real circumstances of his early life as he grew older. But James was keenly aware of the ways in which facts were also, often, limited and limiting: in an 1893 review of Flaubert's correspondence, he had written persuasively: "Some day or other surely we shall all agree that everything is relative, that facts themselves are often falsifying, and that we pay more for some kinds of knowledge than those particular kinds are worth."[80] When James misremembered names in his autobiographies, as one reader wrote to Scribner's to point out, he initially remained only mildly contrite. It was all true to *him*, and remained so, even if he made a slip. Yet he was more concerned when his error was more serious, and concerned the Civil War.[81]

*

The way an event is remembered by someone seems as true to the person remembering as what actually happened; there are infinite degrees and shadings of truth; yet at extremes of experience we should never deny the existence of fact. Rather than as a factual record, James's autobiographies are uniquely successful, above all, in representing what memory feels like. They capture memory's textures, its failings, its distortions, its atmospheres, its accretions, its revelations. Few books come close in this attempt—although when the first volume of Proust's immense novel appeared in 1913, an English reviewer compared it to *A Small Boy and Others*.[82] Readers immediately sensed just how much James was pushing at the boundaries of the form of autobiography in this venture into the world of his past, and his explorations of the span or reach of memory.

There is another way the reach of any autobiography can be measured, other than the span between the act of recollection and the memories recounted. This is looking forwards, not backwards—towards the final span between the writing of autobiography, and the writer's eventual death. The ill-health which had plagued James throughout 1913 was a foretaste of future ailments. He perhaps knew that he didn't have long to live. When *Notes of a Son and Brother* was published in March 1914, he was again encouraged by good reviews, writing to Harry that "If I am myself able to live on and work a while longer I probably *shall* perpetrate a certain number more passages of retrospect and reminiscence."[83]

Passages, not volumes—although, with *Notes of a Son and Brother*, James had only reached 1870. At roughly the same rate of progress, the *Autobiography* as a projected whole would perhaps have had another four volumes: one for each decade of his life until 1914. As it is, we are left with a huge gap in the middle of how James might have seen his life, just as he was, in the memoirs, becoming a writer. As Wells wrote, again, in his *Experiment*, it was "a great loss to the science of criticism" that James died before he finished "his slowly unfolding autobiography."[84] James did work on *The Middle Years* in the autumn of 1914, before putting it aside, perhaps to try and progress further with his fiction. He had two unfinished novels to complete, *The Ivory Tower*, and *The Sense of the Past*. But he was to finish no more books before, on February 28, 1916, he died.

Ford Madox Ford, *c.*late 1920s.

3

For facts a most profound contempt

Ford Madox Ford

I never have written a book that has not by someone or other been called autobiography...[1]

Ford Madox Ford

For any novelist, the first—indeed, the only resource that can be consistently and absolutely trusted—is his or her own first-hand experience of life. This holds true even when writing a book heavily dependent on research: a historical novel, for instance; or equally, about any other time or place or person that appears to bear no relation to the writer's own background. This is why so much fictional writing is labeled as "autobiographical." Every writer is affected by their own point of view and the texture of their own experience, whether consciously or not. Life, then, invariably finds its way into the transformations of fiction: but these transformations, these transmutations of the raw material, are where the art of fiction lies. What is perhaps less easily and frequently acknowledged, is that a writer's life also has a tendency to seep into supposedly non-fictional, factual writing. No matter how high we raise the barricades—and many of the conventions of non-fiction writing can sometimes seem like flood-barriers or city walls—language tends to drift towards fictionality. Names, dates, and events stated as clearly as possible can be verified as unarguably true. Nearly everything else—even when written in the most objective of third-person narratives—is affected by the writer's point of view.

The line between fiction and fact is a matter more of ratios and degrees than absolute cut-off points. Originally, a fact was "something done," coming from a Latin verb meaning to make or do; while fiction was "a fashioning or feigning," from a Latin verb meaning to shape, form, devise, or feign—originally, to knead out of clay. At some points these two definitions come close to each other: they touch. Factual writing steels itself against the taint of inaccuracy or fictionality, as though against a disease. The image of infection is, precisely, the right one. All it takes is a chink of hearsay or a slip of the pen for the edifice of literary fact to be called into question. But the importance of defending the line between fact and fiction, at the most critical points (say, in a court of law) should not prevent us from marking out the gradations found all along it.

With the term "autobiographical" there is a similar lack of distinctions; it could be applied to works found at almost any point along the line. In its widest sense, it crosses seamlessly from the literature of fact, to the literature of fiction—the boundary does not affect it. Novels are routinely called autobiographical; works of factual witness are often autobiographical; there is a form of autobiography in diaries and letters; even biographies are often autobiographical. The "I," the writer's point of view, is always there, even when suppressed or disguised; and everything comes from the writer's self. Yet all these kinds of works reveal very different selves.

In the immense body of work produced by Ford Madox Ford—the name Hueffer adopted in June 1919, at the age of forty-five, after his demobilization from the army in January that year—we can find autobiographical writing of many kinds. But much rests on what we mean by this loose term *autobiographical*. The eighty or so books Ford published in his lifetime span an improbable variety of recognized genres, and invent some genres too. He wrote across so many forms, for so many publishers, that his versatility was even a difficulty, since he was constantly being judged on only one, partial, aspect of his talent. Misjudged throughout his life, as a man and as a writer, his changeability encouraged misconceptions. One of his greatest themes became how people are misunderstood. Yet how are we to understand Ford? From his first published book (of fairy tales) in 1891, to his final book (of criticism) in 1938, the year before he died, he wrote poetry, biography, criticism, journalism, reminiscence, propaganda, travel books, novels, and books which mix several of these elements. The novels themselves move between several very different genres.

In one sense, as Ford's biographer Max Saunders suggests, just as Ford notes—with foxingly paradoxical logic—that "Conrad was Conrad because he was his books,"[2] it is all Ford's books together which "make up his own autobiography."[3] True of all writers, as writers, this is especially valid for the two collaborators, whose names were self-fashioned constructs: almost, but not quite, pseudonyms. Ford believed in a writer's "literary personality" as something apart from his corporeal existence. Just as "Joseph Conrad" was a rebirth, a new life on the page for the man who was born Korzeniowski, "Ford Madox Ford" was a post-war symbolic rebirth for the man, and for the writer, who had once been Hueffer. It was another chance.

Varied aspects of autobiography appear across Ford's many books. Often, he revealed himself obliquely, writing in the first person in his journalism, for instance, or in travel books, where the focus is really on something else, and the "I" is just a sidelight. Then there is, of course, his fiction, where, as with many novelists, it is tempting to reach through all the adopted veils and masks to point up likenesses with the life. Of different types, and closenesses to life, this novelistic autobiography—what we tend to mean when we loosely use the term *autobiographical*—frequently reveals the unconscious self of a writer, much more than the biographical recounting of the facts of their life often does. If we were to imagine the self as having different layers which can be unwrapped, this form of novelistic autobiography can, sometimes surprisingly, take us close to a core, away from the surface; and this frequently occurs in Ford. (One image of the self, used by the Portuguese poet Fernando Pessoa, is a ball of string.[4] Of course, the self doesn't have to be imagined in ways that oppose surface and depth.)

Then, there is the subgenre of novels popular among his contemporaries, and also practiced by Ford—the *roman à clef*. Here the relationship between life and novels is explored, as in a game, and the thinness of the veil and the masks separating fictional and real characters is an essential part of the fun. The glimpses of real people are tantalizingly close to life. In his satires such as *The Simple Life Limited* (1911), under the pseudonym Daniel Chaucer, and *The New Humpty-Dumpty* (1912), Ford played with this novelistic subgenre, putting his many writer friends and enemies in between the covers, in disguise. Many, such as his antagonistic friend H. G. Wells, poked fun back, in similar novels like *Boon* and *The Bulpington of Blup* (1933). The masks give the writer freedom, with the defense that what was written was fiction always remaining applicable. As Violet Hunt wrote of Ford's *The New*

Humpty-Dumpty (which savaged Wells with its thinly-veiled character Herbert Pett): "When a literature-picture of a total personality is put together it is non-libellous in effect, being a mere blend—an action of A's, a speech of D's, a look of C, the hair or eyes of F. Surely such a preparation or composite of aliens cannot possibly be dubbed a description of Z."[5]

Whatever genre he wrote, a key part of Ford's literary personality was a celebration—rather than a wary defense—of the thin line between fact and fiction, between novels and life. He didn't only take people from life and put them on the page. He often loved to pretend that fictional characters could step out of their boundaries on the page into reality. He often insisted that he *was* certain fictional characters in other people's books, and did so by making such claims in his own books. Take one of the most celebrated (and disputed) examples: Ford's repeated pride in his claim that Henry James modeled Merton Densher in *The Wings of the Dove* (1902) on himself. Even as a (large) old man, Ford was very fond of quoting a passage on Densher, the "longish, leanish [alas! alas!], fairish young Englishman, not unamenable on certain sides to classification."[6] In his loving critical book-length study *Henry James* (1914)—which James told Archibald Marshall he "wouldn't touch [...] with a ten-foot pole"[7]—Ford indulged in an extended, extraordinary setpiece where he imagines meeting James's fictional characters (of which he thinks there must be around one thousand) at a huge garden-party

in the very center of the London season [...] one of the great garden-parties of the year. There is a band playing in the square [...] But whilst we are waiting in the crowd of new arrivals for our names to be announced, we perceive Madame de Bellegarde talking to Milly Strether [...] Quite on the other side of the garden Newman is talking to Princess Casamassima [...] The author of Beltraffio is proving extremely boring to Miss Kate Croy, who can't keep her eyes off Morton [*sic*] Densher [...] what an immense party it is! [...] an immense concourse of real people, whose histories we just dimly remember to have heard something about [...] Real! Why they are just as exactly real as anybody we have ever met. The fictitious Prince von Vogelstein is just as actual a person to us as Prince von Metternich who was at the German Embassy only the other day, and Milly Strether is just as real as the poor dear little American cousin Hattina who faded away out of life twenty years or so ago.[8]

Ford ended this homage with the proud confession that he had taken a character, Valentin de Bellegarde, from James's novel *The American* (1877) and put him into one of his own novels—unawares, since he seemed so real to him that he thought he had met him. As with much of Ford's work, the humor in this is self-evident, but he's also making serious, usually unmade points about how the boundaries of life and fiction interact and overlap. The passage is about how little we know the people we meet in real life; how the portrayals of characters in fiction affect our perception of even those closest to us; how we can somehow almost get to know those fictional characters better than anyone real, through the magic of art.

Look at this picture of James's garden-party from another angle, and one begins to see what Ford was doing with the line between factual and fictional characters in his volumes of memoir and reminiscence: *Ancient Lights and Certain New Reflections: Being the Memories of a Young Man* (1911), *Thus to Revisit: Some Reminiscences* (1921), *Joseph Conrad: A Personal Remembrance* (1924), *Return to Yesterday: Reminiscences 1894–1914* (1931), and *It Was the Nightingale* (1934). Collectively, these books were all close to being non-fictional autobiographies, and they all chronicled the doings of real people Ford knew during the course of his life. Yet in writing his life, Ford added a quotient of imagination to all these books. In doing so, as another biographer, Arthur Mizener, has observed, he "practically invented a form of fictional reminiscence."[9] Only the last of the books, *It Was the Nightingale*, was explicitly described by Ford as "autobiography," while the others were "reminiscences": the difference being the shift in focus from the portraits of others in the earlier series of books more onto himself. He also called several of them novels. What's most unnerving, and unusual about all of these books is the uneasy mixture of fact and fiction that Ford creates: so much *is* real, that you can't always tell what has been made up. To the unsuspecting reader, the aura of factuality is strong enough to deceive. But the books are full of inventions: seamlessly crossing the shadow-line from fact to fiction, without telling us where.

Ford viewed reminiscence primarily as a vehicle for portraying his contemporaries. And he chose to portray them over and over again, painting and repainting their figures in stories that repeat with slight variations. We all repeat stories about our friends and family over the years—many anecdotes often exaggerated over time, to draw out the maximum humor and effect. Ford turned this into an art, sensing that repetition is intrinsic to autobiography. Memories are not fixed: they change constantly. Memories are multiple. Each time we recall our memories of events, we tend to reinvent them: the memory is never quite the same every time. Memory and imagination often fuse, in such rewritings. Ford explored this phenomenon in his reminiscences relentlessly, embroidering as he went along, creating multiplications of the truth.

The basic facts of a life remain the same—the story only happens once—although there are infinite tellings. In life-writing, we often read elements of the same story, in different forms, from different points of view: first, say, in a letter or journal; then slightly remade in a novel; then told in an autobiography; then seen from one side in a memoir; then told in several biographies. Ford, the self-avowed exponent of literary Impressionism, provides many of the different angles himself. As portraiture, the effect this creates is an overlay, a multiple exposure, where each character is grasped simultaneously from different sides. Though always rooted in some truth, the reminiscences stray, adding or changing the details to get their effects. It's an art of embellishment or improvement, not pure creation, which can nonetheless take us a long way from what might have really happened.

It's also an art of caricature, as Ford knew. The reminiscences can be traced back to his journalism, beginning with his series of "Literary Portraits" of writers appearing anonymously in the *Daily Mail* in 1907, and then continued, this time signed by Ford, in the *Tribune* until 1908. (The series was taken up again for the *Outlook* in 1913 and continued until 1915.) Ford wrote to his agent James B. Pinker—who took Ford on partly through Conrad's persuasions—in an undated letter about the very first portrait series, saying that "I want to make the Lit. Portraits I'm writing for the Mail, into a book with Max's [Beerbohm's] caricatures."[10] From the start, he wanted to make them deliberately over-the-top and exaggerated. Ford returned to literary portraiture throughout his life. Even decades later, in his series of articles for *The American Mercury*, from June 1935 to April 1937, Ford was still writing literary portraits of people he had known and loved, many of whom were, by that time, dead. It was a kind of compulsion.

The initial weekly "Literary Portraits" for the *Mail* in 1907 were often flamboyant, fusing reminiscence and imaginings with an account of each writer's latest book. When the "Literary Portraits" moved to the *Tribune*, Ford changed the format slightly, offering more depth and critical comment. While Ford often used anecdotes, he always made sure that his observations resonated with each writer's "literary personality," as he saw it. In a "Literary Portrait" of 1907, "Authors' Likenesses and a Caricaturist," discussing Beerbohm's caricatures and the artist Daniel Maclise's visual portraits of writers, Ford wrote: "I am inclined to shrink from looking at portraits of literary men. For the writer is expressed by his books, and within the four-square of them his whole personality is contained."[11] Yet Ford's piece here was positive about Beerbohm's caricature of Henry James in his *A Book of Caricatures* (1907)—which also included caricatures of Wells, Sargent, Chesterton, and others. And despite his avowal that a writer's books expressed his or her entire literary personality, Ford also, very often, used elements of biography in his own sketches of others. His attitude to biography was profoundly double-edged.

*

When Ford began writing "Literary Portraits" in 1907, he was about to make what would become a significant step in his break with his first wife Elsie Hueffer, by taking a flat above a poulterer's and fishmonger's shop, at 84 Holland Park Avenue,[12] which would become the premises of the *English Review*. Ford was thirty-three years old, and had spent a large part of his twenties in the countryside, with Elsie, after marrying young and having two children with her: Christina in 1897, and Katharine in 1900. The couple had settled in Kent near the Romney Marsh in Bonnington, before buying Pent Farm, where they lived for two years before moving to Limpsfield in Surrey and letting the Pent to Conrad. From 1901 onwards, the Hueffers had mainly been based in a cottage, The Bungalow, in Winchelsea, near Rye.

Later in life, in *Return to Yesterday*, Ford made Winchelsea, Rye, and the Pent—the respective abodes of his younger self, James, and Conrad—sound like the center of the literary universe, but elsewhere he describes these rural years as fearfully isolating, in artistic terms. Ford had a premature birth as a writer, pushed on by the enthusiasm of his grandfather, who helped him get his first book of fairy tales published in 1891, and whose biography Ford wrote in an uncharacteristically staid, formal style, appearing as *Ford Madox Brown: A Record of his Life and Work* (1896), when Ford was twenty-three. The years with Conrad had been an apprenticeship. Conrad depended on him, yet the fact that Ford was so many years his junior was constantly reflected in the role he was forced to play in the collaboration.

When Ford moved up to Holland Park Avenue in 1907, writing his weekly "Literary Portraits" alongside a plethora of other books around this time, he was beginning to assert his own creative identity much more forcefully. Once he began working on the *English Review*, throughout 1908 and 1909, he was also increasingly involved with other writers in London, although this sometimes led to spectacular fallings-out—with Conrad, over "Some Reminiscences," and with Wells, partly over whether or not *Tono-Bungay* (1909) was to be described as autobiographical. In *Return to Yesterday*, Ford portrayed himself around this time as full of swagger. He has almost become someone else, from the lank, affectedly nonchalant youth who spent his twenties writing in Kent.

> You are to think of me then as rather a dandy. I was going through that phase. It lasted perhaps eight years—until Armageddon made one dress otherwise. Every morning about eleven you would see me issue from the door of my apartment. I should be wearing a very long morning coat, a perfectly immaculate high hat, lavender trousers, a near-Gladstone collar and a black satin stock. As often as not, at one period, I should be followed by a Great Dane [. . .] I carried a malacca cane with a gold knob.[13]

By 1910, however, the year Ford wrote his first volume of reminiscences *Ancient Lights*, it was getting hard to maintain such a swagger through town, mainly because of his relationship with Violet Hunt, who had recently finished an affair with H. G. Wells. In a "Literary Portrait" of Hunt in the *Outlook*, Ford recounted one of his early meetings with her. "I was walking up Bedford Street when our author suddenly jumped out at me from the door of No. 32, and exclaimed: 'I say: Mr. H . . . .n, the publisher, says that you have made the fortune of So-and-So by writing a Literary Portrait of him. Why don't you do one of me?'"[14] Hunt herself, in her memoir *The Flurried Years* (1926), also describes meeting Ford at the *English Review*, sent there at Wells's suggestion in October 1908.[15] Throughout 1909 their affair became more of a reality, and in January 1910, it became a very public matter, as Ford's attempt to divorce Elsie was reported in the newspapers and the court ordered Ford to return to his wife: "MR. HUEFFER TO GO BACK IN FOURTEEN DAYS."[16] Refusing, Ford got ten days in Brixton Gaol. While he was in prison, Hunt moved his things out of 84 Holland Park Avenue to her Victorian villa, South Lodge, nearby, where Ford would be based for the next few years.

During this tumultuous period, *Ancient Lights* began as a series of articles on the Pre-Raphaelites for *Harper's*, with the first appearing in February 1910; it was also based on articles in the *Fortnightly*.[17] In the summer of 1910, Ford went with Hunt to Germany, hoping to be naturalized as a German citizen and get a divorce there. In September, the idea for *Ancient Lights* as a book came closer to Ford when he learned of the death of the painter Holman Hunt, in a train near Neuheim. As Violet Hunt recalled in *The Flurried Years,* Ford dictated the end of *Ancient Lights* to her in Marburg that same September as she lay ill in bed.[18] The naturalization scheme was to backfire, resulting in a marital situation close to bigamy—Elsie would not grant Ford a divorce, yet it appears that Ford and Hunt went through some kind of marriage ceremony in France or Germany, and even if they didn't, behaved as if they had.[19] In *The Flurried Years*, which revolves almost entirely around her relationship with Ford, Hunt deals with the "marriage" with a floating paragraph ending her "Part One": "There is a lacuna here and I may not fill it lest it should be said that I am representing myself to be what I then considered I was in law—his wife. I have been taught since that it was not so—that I never did become his legal wife."[20] In early 1911, after *Ancient Lights* was published in March, Ford was stranded in Giessen, no nearer to becoming German.[21] Eventually, again, he was to return to London.

In all his reminiscences, Ford used techniques more common in fiction than in what he called the "Serious book": passages of dialogue, scenes as well as narration, reported speech mimicked in the vernacular, the time-shift. *Ancient Lights* is less novelistic than the later reminiscences—Ford became increasingly inventive as he got older—but it carries a trademark dedicatory preface. Character, Ford knew, could hardly be conveyed with factual, archival truth—the husks of circumstantial data which fuel biography. He introduced his portraiture at the outset of *Ancient Lights* by satirizing the pedantry of fact-checkers with an exaggerated, mocking, absurdist precision:

> [...] this book is a book of impressions. My impression is that there have been six thousand four hundred and seventy-two books written to give the facts about the Pre-Raphaelite movement. My impression is that I myself have written more than 17,000,000 wearisome and dull words as to the facts about the Pre-Raphaelite movement [...] [But no one has] attempted to get the atmosphere of these twenty-five years. This book, in short, is full of inaccuracies as to facts, but its accuracy as to impressions is absolute [...] I don't really deal in facts, I have for facts a most profound contempt.[22]

This dedication to *Ancient Lights* also, characteristically, takes the form of a letter—a device Ford would use frequently in later works, in a fusion of public and private modes of life-writing. The dedicatory letter of *Ancient Lights* is addressed to Ford's two daughters with Elsie, "My Dear Kids,"[23] the elder of whom was now a teenager. In this open letter, Ford tells his children "the earliest thing that I can remember," "and the odd thing is that, as I remember it, I seem to be looking at myself from outside."[24] He recounts an unsettling anecdote about "looking into the breeding-box of some

Barbary ring-doves that my grandmother kept in the window of the huge studio in Fitzroy Square"[25] in his grandfather Ford Madox Brown's house:

> The window itself appears to me to be as high as a house and I myself as small as a doorstep, so that I stand on tiptoe, and just manage to get my eyes and nose over the edge of the box whilst my long curls fall forward and tickle my nose. And then I perceive greyish and almost shapeless objects with, upon them, little speckles, like the very short spines of hedgehogs, and I stand with the first surprise of my life and with the first wonder of my life. I ask myself: can these be doves?—these unrecognizable, panting morsels of flesh. And then, very soon, my grandmother comes in and is angry. She tells me that if the mother dove is disturbed she will eat her young [...] for many days afterwards I thought I had destroyed life and that I was exceedingly sinful.[26]

Set within the context of Ford's split from Elsie, framed as a letter to his daughters from that marriage, the anecdote conveys Ford's sense of baffled guilt, transgression, and danger hovering over the realm of sexuality, as well as his sense of fear at female wrath. In the anecdote, he recounts how he seems to be looking at himself looking at the breeding doves, whose appearance surprises and shocks him. Motherhood and rage are twinned in the reminiscence. Because of his grandmother's anger, Ford's "first conscious conviction was one of great sin, of a deep criminality."[27] His father, Francis Hueffer, Ford also tells us, always called him "'the patient but extremely stupid donkey'. And so I went through life until only just the other day with the conviction of extreme sinfulness and of extreme stupidity."[28] Ford wishes that his daughters might be spared the "moral tortures"[29] which all this instilled in him. He declares that he is writing these reminiscences because he realized that he was already "forgetting my own childhood":[30] "I find that my impressions of the early and rather noteworthy persons amongst whom my childhood was passed—that these impressions are beginning to grow a little dim. So I have tried to rescue them before they go out of my mind altogether."[31]

Ancient Lights is a self-portrait of Ford's childhood, and a literary group portrait of the Pre-Raphaelites. It was entitled *Memories and Impressions* in America, echoing the subtitle of Conrad's *The Mirror of the Sea*—and Ford constantly plays with words to describe the kind of Impressionism it enacts. In *Ancient Lights*, Ford, as a literary Impressionist, aims to create impressions in the minds of his readers, not with dry facts but with daubs of gesture and anecdote, experimenting with the effects of words in a way that echoes how the Impressionist painters of the preceding decades in France experimented with the effects of paint. Ford also *does* verbal impressions of the speech of many of the people he portrays; and he notes how oppressively impressive these people were, and how "they impressed themselves upon me."[32] The memoir shows Ford, right from his earliest memories, as being not quite his own person, enacting a struggle with his artistic inheritance. *Ancient Lights* opens with a resonant image: a frontispiece of the funeral urn above the doorway of Madox Brown's house in Fitzroy Square, resting precariously, as Ford writes, on a piece of stone "about the size and shape of a folio book," which he always imagined "might fall upon me and crush me entirely out of existence."[33] The second image at the opening of the book is a portrait of Ford as a child, "Tell's Son," painted by Madox Brown. Even from the beginning he was made into a little Pre-Raphaelite.

Ancient Lights is a catalogue of embarrassments, as the young Ford, in preposterous clothes, "a very little boy in a velveteen coat with gold buttons and long golden ringlets"[34] manages consistently to make a fool of himself, and to inadvertently transgress (as he was still transgressing, so publicly, in the divorce courts). Meanwhile the Pre-Raphaelites take the foreground— Ford reproduces a caricature by Madox Brown of Rossetti lying on the sofa early on, possibly to hint at the equally caricatured literary style he is aiming for[35]—in a slapstick sequence of squabbles and domestic quarrels. Slowly, the mood turns towards a reflection on the passing of fashions and eras, as Ford clears the ground for his own work. He mentions his own departure to the countryside in the 1890s, where he "remained for thirteen years, thus losing almost all touch with intellectual or artistic life."[36] A recollection from these Kent days interlocks with a later memoir Ford wrote, as the reminiscences move back and forth.

> I can very well remember coming up by a slow train from Hythe and attempting at one and the same time to read the volume of stories containing *Only a Subaltern* [Kipling] and to make a single pipe of shag last the whole of that long journey. And I can remember that when I came at almost the same moment to Charing Cross and the death of the subaltern I was crying so hard that a friendly ticket collector asked me if I was very ill [...][37]

Ford's own recent fallings-out with his family and friends in 1910 lie somewhat codedly and obscurely beneath the intrigues he depicts in *Ancient Lights*, so comically—"Dear Brown, if P— says that I said that Gabriel was in the habit of..., P— lies."[38] This, Ford implies, is what being part of an artistic milieu entails: his contemporaries were no less touchy than the

Victorian group of the previous century. The Victorians, Ford writes—in a sentence which applies very keenly to himself—knew exactly how "to paint pictures, to write poems, to make tables, to decorate pianos, rooms, or churches. But as to the conduct of life they were a little sketchy, a little romantic, perhaps a little careless."[39] Their "bickerings" could seem "unreasonably ferocious," Ford writes, but "in spite of them the unions were very close."[40] And for all his own disagreements with other artists, the importance of being part of an artistic group never left Ford. His reminiscences always bring people together, even here when he writes of his childhood.

Ford didn't only depict the famous writers and artists he knew. In *Ancient Lights*, he was almost as interested in the maids at Madox Brown's house in Fitzroy Square, and the cabmen, as in the painters and poets who came through the doors. In his later reminiscences, he depicted the rural poor in Kent, mimicking them at length, threading them into his life-story. In January 1911, Ford proposed an idea to Pinker for a book of "Reminiscences of undistinguished people I have met in the course of my varied career."[41] This became *Women & Men* (1923), parts of which were incorporated into *Return to Yesterday*. Like his grandfather, whose great painting *Work* (1852–65) depicts Carlyle alongside navvies digging the road in Hampstead, beer sellers, sandwich-board carriers, and pastry-cook's assistants, Ford saw all people as equally worthy of portrayal.

By the end of *Ancient Lights*, Ford is very much his own man, the author of thirty-seven books "of all shapes and sizes"[42] (he was thirty-seven years old), declaring "I may humbly write myself down a man getting on for forty, a little mad about good letters."[43] Yet even this phrase, "a little mad," shows how he was still tied to his family, echoing a phrase in his grandfather's diaries, which Ford possessed, when the painter declared himself in years of hardship to be "intensely miserable very hard up & a little mad."[44]

As *Ancient Lights* proceeds, however, Ford increasingly sounds the elegiac note for the passing Victorian world of his youth, implying how his own literary Impressionism had now superseded the fashions of the Pre-Raphaelites. At the same time, through the pages of the *English Review*, Ford saw the rising new generation, and felt his relative age and impending obsolescence. In the visual arts in London, Impressionism had moved towards Post-Impressionism precisely around the time of *Ancient Lights*, with Roger Fry's exhibition "Manet and the Post-Impressionists" in November 1910, and the "Second Post-Impressionist Exhibition" in 1912. Ford was aware of the new artistic currents going on around this time. But sometimes his championing of the new made him always feel old. An abiding tension throughout *Ancient Lights* is how Ford keeps returning to the way the new succeeds the old, in a book which simultaneously asserts Ford's modernity and his extremely deep roots in tradition and the Victorian age.

At South Lodge in the years from 1910 until the war, Ford and Violet Hunt played host to a crowd of writers, old and new, and in many ways were at the center of the rising avant-garde in London. As Ford told it in *Return to Yesterday*, the summer of 1914 before the war, when he was out in London nearly every night, crescendoed with new destructive, artistic movements and "isms": Vorticism, Imagism, the rallying cries of *Blast*. In a "Literary Portrait" in the *Outlook* in 1914, "Mr. Wyndham Lewis and 'Blast'," Ford puffed *Blast*, in which an excerpt of his own novel, *The Good Soldier* (1915), appeared (as "The Saddest Story"). But he also revealed his feelings of being under attack from the new manifesto-filled periodical. "Vorticism, Cubism, Imagism—and Blastism—," Ford writes, "may well sweep away anything for which I have stood or fought."[45] Ford gives a satirically hyperbolic sketch of *Blast*'s editor, Wyndham Lewis, whom as Ford pointedly relates, he was the first to publish, in the *English Review*:

> In the luxuriously appointed office stood an individual whom with his unerring eye the editor at once took took to be a Russian moujik. The long overcoat descending to the feet, the black wrappings to the throat, the black hair, the pallid face, the dark and defiant eyes—all, all indicated the Slav... Slowly and with an air of doom the stranger began to draw out manuscripts—from his coat-pockets, from his trouser-pockets, from his breast-pockets, from the lining of his conspirator's hat. The dark stranger uttered no words; his eyes remained fixed on the editor's face so that that official quailed [...] his unwilling eye descended on the pages.[46]

This literary portrait of Wyndham Lewis by Ford appeared on July 4, 1914. Ford would reprise it, and improvise on it, and portray Lewis again, many times throughout his career. As this portrait shows, Ford saw himself as Lewis's elder (he was nine years older), as well as his sometime mentor and first editor. Yet he also felt threatened by him—although hardly threatened enough to refrain from portraying him in outrageously exaggerated and humorous, lavishly visual, terms. Soon after this sketch of Lewis, the First World War was declared, and Ford's "Literary Portraits," in response, became far more concerned with war than writing. By August 8, 1914, Ford uses his space in the *Outlook* to muse on the very point of writing: "And what is the good of writing about literature [...] There will not be a soul that will want to read about literature for years and years. We go out. We writers go out. And, when the world again has leisure to think about letters the whole world will have changed."[47]

At the end of 1913, Ford had turned forty. He had supposedly sat down on that birthday to begin what he called in 1927 his "last book,"[48] *The Good Soldier*. In July 1915, at forty-one, he enlisted in the army. Soon, as he later portrayed it in "Footsloggers," he was heading rapidly who knows where.

*

> [...] in the 1.10 train,
> Running between the green and the grain,
> Something like the peace of God
> Descended over the hum and the drone
> Of the wheels and the wine and the buzz of the talk,
> And one thought:
> "In two days' time we enter the Unknown,
> And this is what we die for!"[49]

The war fell across the center of Ford's life like a dividing line, a partial death. There is no reason to think that he didn't fully expect to die. After the war, he felt like a ghost, and for years after, if not forever, he was a changed person. During the battle of the Somme, in the summer of 1916, as he later recalled in *It Was the Nightingale*, Ford was "blown into the air by something [...] falling on my face."[50] In the same autobiography he notes that "from some date in August till about the 17th September [...] I had completely lost my memory, so that [...] three weeks of my life are completely dead to me."[51] This is how he remembered, or failed to remember, his war trauma in the early 1930s. But closer to the events, Ford's letters trace a similar lacuna. In 1920, Ford wrote to F. S. Flint about the same incident, saying how he was still trying to recover lost shreds of his memory, and how "for thirty-six hours I did not even know my name. It is, as I have said, coming slowly back; in patches it comes quite vividly."[52] Ford mostly kept the war out of his reminiscences—leaving a looming blank in the middle of his life. *Return to Yesterday* ends with the outbreak of war in 1914, while *It Was the Nightingale* picks up Ford's story after peace was declared. Ford may have felt, by the time of these two books, that he had already explored the war in his fiction, in the four volumes of *Parade's End* (1924–28); or perhaps there were deeper psychological reasons for its omission in his reminiscences.

When he was demobilized in 1919, Ford came back to London, but he no longer fitted in. He was estranged from Violet Hunt by then, having started a romance with the Australian painter Stella Bowen. The self-portrait of this time in *It Was the Nightingale* is of a spectral figure just returned from the apocalypse, haunting a London which seems like one vast hallucination. The encounters Ford has are disturbed and unreal. His mind reels. Stripped almost of all earthly possessions, Ford leaves the city, and makes his way down to the laborer's cottage of Red Ford in Sussex, where he slowly begins—after a few life-or-death decisions—to put himself back together. As he tells it, he was almost completely forgotten as a writer. He resurrected an old persona, of the agricultural small-holder, tending his small plot of land, and slowly repaired the half-derelict cottage where he now planned to begin once again.

Ford's first post-war book was another volume of reminiscences. This was *Thus to Revisit* (1921), whose title alludes to the ghost in *Hamlet*, emphasizing how Ford felt himself to be haunting his old country, more than half-dead. By the summer of 1920, Bowen had joined him in Sussex, and was pregnant, giving birth to Esther Julia on November 29. But just as Ford's memory was still only coming back in patches, his writing at the time was also off-kilter, slightly unhinged.

The war is completely avoided in *Thus to Revisit*, which started, like *Ancient Lights*, as a series of articles, this time for the *English Review* and *The Dial*, begun in 1920. Ford subtitled the book *Some Reminiscences*, recalling Conrad's reminiscences for the *Review* over ten years earlier; and he wrote that he saw it as a "continuation of my *Ancient Lights*."[53] Yet the "reminiscences" tag is slightly misleading, as *Thus to Revisit* is closer to literary criticism than memories. But it is, like *Ancient Lights*, a kind of group portrait, giving an account of English literature from the *Yellow Book* to the *English Review*. It is unsteady, but formally inventive, almost novelistic. Playing with the conventions of fact, the index includes imaginary figures—Professors Bauch, Hauch, and Wauch, Mr. P., Mr. X., Mr. Y., and "George Crumb (imaginary Poet)"—alongside real people like Conrad, W. H. Hudson, Henry James, and Stephen Crane. Early on in *Thus to Revisit*, Ford complains about how hard it is to write about the living, rather than the dead.[54] Reflecting on the ethics of biography, Ford evolves his own standpoint, which reflects his ingrained discretion while allowing himself a crucial loophole: "To report details of private history, affections or intimacies is usually infamous—unless, like Boswell, you should be paying public tribute to a figure whom you have much loved."[55]

The two main figures Ford portrays in *Thus to Revisit* are Conrad and James, although they are surrounded by a host of other writers. Ford, now in the English countryside once again, looks back nostalgically to the long period of collaboration with Conrad, when they devoted themselves to questions of literary technique—"buried deep in rural greennesses we used to ask each other how, exactly, such and such an effect of light and shade should be reproduced in very simple words."[56] Conrad is portrayed as a fellow craftsman, all the more heroic for his struggles with English and deep knowledge of French literature. Perhaps because of the depth of their unquestioned prior friendship, or perhaps because of their quarrel, Ford is reticent about Conrad's life, devoting most of his discussion of his friend to his work. Ford's comments about Conrad are nearly all positive, even when discussing potential defects such as Conrad's often-perceived inability to portray women credibly.

Writing of Henry James, meanwhile, Ford makes it clear that the relationship was more formal. Yet it was there nonetheless: in some ways the opposite of Ford's friendship with Conrad, so concerned with intricate creative and technical matters. "I think I will, after reflection, lay claim to a very considerable degree of intimacy with Henry James," Ford notes, hesitantly yet firmly. "It was a winter, and a wholly non-literary intimacy. That is to say, during the summers we saw little of each other. He had his friends and I mine."[57] James, Ford writes, was happier talking with him about writers' personalities than about their books. "I could, I think, put down on one page all that he ever said to me of books."[58]

Now that James was dead, Ford drew him more mischievously, impersonating him at length, and declaring that underneath a placid, even bumbling exterior, James was tough, and even cruel. "He loved to appear in the character of a sort of Mr. Pickwick—," Ford writes, "with the rather superficial benevolences, and the mannerisms of which he was perfectly aware. But below that protective mask was undoubtedly a plane of nervous cruelty. I have heard him be—to simple and quite unpretentious people—more diabolically blighting than it was quite decent for a man to be."[59] Ford, going further into the realms of exaggeration, even hints at a strain of occult malevolence in James: "My own servants used to say that his eyes looked you through and through until you could feel your own backbone within you, and it was held in Rye that he practised black magic behind the high walls of Lamb House."[60]

Thus to Revisit, unlike the other reminiscences, has no dedicatory letter explaining its truth to impressions rather than facts. It hardly needs one, since the whole book is an extended tirade against the tyranny of fact. Fact, argues Ford, is often antithetical to great writing; works of fact often become literature only by virtue of their factual inaccuracies. "Facts are of no importance, a dwelling on facts leads at best to death—at worst to barbarism,"[61] Ford declares, picking up on arguments also traced in his war-time books of propaganda *When Blood is Their Argument* (1915) and *Between St. Dennis and St. George* (1915). A set of diagrams towards the end of *Thus to Revisit* shows Ford's division of literary genres from "Pure Factual" Prose to "Propagandist" Verse at opposite sides.[62] For Ford, here, the facts distorted literature, diverting it from real writing, whose effort was primarily creative, imaginative.

Years later, in *It Was the Nightingale*, Ford wrote of *Thus to Revisit* that "I should imagine it was not a very good book [...] it must have been written in some bitterness [...] No doubt it was even a little mad. I was still bitter about the treatment of any ex-comrades in arms."[63] The war appeared much more centrally—if elliptically—in another book inadvertently taking shape in the summer of 1920, in Ford's "English Country" essays in the *New Statesman*. These became, after a long delay, *No Enemy: A Tale of Reconstruction* (1929): a book of reminiscences "of active service under a thinly disguised veil of fiction [...] part of it having been actually written in the lines."[64] Even more than *Thus to Revisit*, *No Enemy*—which was never published in England in Ford's lifetime, only in America—resonates with psychic shock. This divided, almost schizoid book, compiled from a medley of writings from different times, was "a Tale of Reconstruction" in the textual as well as the psychological sense. It is perhaps Ford's most unclassifiable book, and he wasn't even sure what it was himself, telling Pinker, who spoke of it as a novel, that he saw it more as a "serious book": "I suppose it is really betwixt & between."[65]

No Enemy inhabits a unique no-man's-land in Ford's work. It reads like a book of non-fictional reminiscences forced into a fictional frame. Its ratio of fact and fiction is odd. The way the material is poured into a new form is intriguingly skewed and off-balance. A certain poet, "Gringoire," tells "your Compiler" (who tells us) about his experiences of the war, in a long monologue, with interruptions, organizing his memories around the few times during the conflict when he was able to notice and appreciate the landscape around him. The Compiler—as Ford did for Conrad in *The Mirror of the Sea* and *A Personal Record*—takes down his dictation in shorthand.

This framing gradually collapses, as the Compiler tires of the paraphernalia he uses to present Gringoire's monologues, and lets Gringoire speak more for himself, after warning us not to be shocked. At one point, the two argue over what "the stuff of war-reminiscences"[66] should be—the Compiler often having put his pencil down and stopped transcribing when Gringoire strays too far from the point. They undermine each other in sniping footnotes, sometimes by Gringoire, sometimes by the Compiler. Eventually, the thin mask blurs further and slips off altogether, the last vestiges of the framing crumble, and it's hard to know who's supposed to be talking—Gringoire, the Compiler, or, indeed, Ford.

Beneath this bizarrely framed tussle, the war appears in fragments, and flashes. Memory in the book is maimed and fragmentary, as though parts have been torn out or damaged. "I remember," says Gringoire, "—and I say 'I remember' advisedly, since such an immense number of things blotted themselves out and only crop up in suddenly vivid pictures [...] where it was a duty to notice, one noticed—railway stations in their sequence, streams, contours [...]"[67] The narrative seems to have missing parts, no record of how Ford, or Gringoire, gets from A to B. Or he knows how he gets there, without knowing where "there" will be. *No Enemy* is full of interstices—what might serve as linking passages or narrative corridors in another novel—with nothing at either end. There's a disturbing sense that traumatized memories will suddenly emerge, from all the broken pieces. Figures appear inexplicably, frozen at odd moments, stripped of causality, sequence, time, or place, disembodied talking heads surrounded by erasures. Of a certain Lt. Morgan, Ford writes, "we took together a long railway journey—but I don't remember why or where—probably because I spent it listening to the story of his life. I remember his tired movements as he took his knapsack down from the rack whilst the train was running into some terminus."[68] This is impressionism of a different order from elsewhere in Ford's books: the effect, the impression, becoming all that remains.

*

The greatest of Ford's creative friendships ended on August 3, 1924, when Conrad died. For well over a decade the friendship had been rather one-sided. They didn't see each other much, especially after Ford moved to France with Bowen in 1922, decamping for good from the cold and mud of Sussex, and arriving in Paris around the time of Proust's funeral in November, before going south for the winter and spring. They returned to Paris in the autumn of 1923. Conrad, still in England, became a half-imaginary character for Ford by this stage of their lives. But he was never that far from Ford's mind. From the lines of the war, Ford wrote Conrad letters about the sounds of the shelling and the planes overhead; he worried, in May 1924 on the boat to Plymouth, en route to America for a business trip, that he might never see Conrad again.[69] In the last decade of his life, as he had his success with *Chance*, Conrad grew increasingly distant from Ford, who after the war had to start again almost from scratch—and who never really stopped writing about him, and to him.

In Paris in late 1923, Ford had decided to launch a new review. As he tells it in *It Was the Nightingale*, "a dozen times I was stopped on the Boulevards and told that what was needed was another *English Review*."[70] The *transatlantic review*—which was initially going to be called the *Paris Review*—was based at first in Ford's brother's cottage at 65 Boulevard Arago, where Ford and Stella were staying, before an office was found on 29 quai d'Anjou, on the Ile Saint-Louis.[71] Running throughout 1924, the magazine published work by Hemingway, Joyce, Pound, and Stein—as well as by Ford himself, and many others. Launching the review reinvigorated Ford. As he wrote to Wells in 1923 from 65 Boulevard Arago, "I've got over the nerve tangle of the war and feel able at last really to write again—which I never thought I should do [...] Also Mrs. Ford [...] has more commissions for portraits than she has time for; (She hasn't *much* time)."[72]

As he was launching the new venture, Ford seemed to hope that his slightly broken relationship with Conrad could be taken up and patched over, wondering if Conrad could resume the semi-interrupted autobiography he wrote for him in the *English Review* years before—"Could you possibly write for me about 5,000 words—of Personal Record? [...] I know what a beastly thing it is to ask—I know it fully. But if you took the line of least resistance & just wrote down—even in the form of a letter to me—a personal note as to how the original Personal Record came into being it would be all that I would ask."[73] Conrad declined the proposal to pick up the reminiscences, but he did write a brief note to Ford.

After Conrad's death, Ford wrote *Joseph Conrad: A Personal Remembrance* (1924) in two months, and Conrad's letter to him was reproduced at the beginning in facsimile. Ford's portrait of Conrad is tender, emphasizing the Pole's weird absurdism, reimagining him as an Elizabethan, a larger-than-life, piratical figure. It is full of factual untruths—but all the effects Ford uses serve to commemorate his friend, or to make us laugh. He depicts himself and Conrad with knockabout humor, taking pot-shots at rats outside the Pent with a Flobert rifle. He mimicks Conrad's famously odd accent—"my dear *faller*"[74]—and satirizes his own ineptitude. He pays homage to Conrad's *A Personal Record* with his subtitle, and also by following a similar conceit, structuring *Joseph Conrad* around the writing of their collaboration *Romance*, just as Conrad's reminiscences were framed around the writing of *Almayer's Folly*. Partly due to this conceit, *Joseph Conrad* is also a brilliant "how" of the novel, as much of Ford's non-fiction writing was, describing how collaboration worked, step by step. Ford's preface, dated "Guermantes, Seine et Marne, August" to "Bruges, October 5th, 1924," also displays the extent to which Ford had thought about the form and potential of biography. Despite the "very great aversion from the usual official biography for men of letters whose lives are generally uneventful" which Ford says he shared with Conrad, he frames his own book as a fusion of elements of biography, portraiture, and fiction simultaneously:

> This then is a novel, not a monograph; a portrait, not a narration: for what it shall prove to be worth, a work of art, not a compilation. It is conducted exactly along the lines laid down by us, both for the novel which is biography and for the biography which is a novel. It is the rendering of an affair intended first of all to make you see the subject in his scenery. It contains no documentation at all; for it no dates have been looked up, even all the quotations but two have been left unverified, coming from the writer's memory. It is the writer's impression of a writer who avowed himself impressionist.[75]

Joseph Conrad is as much about Ford as about Conrad—and often, as when Ford describes how Conrad told and retold his stories, always slightly changing the facts,[76] or when he describes Conrad's mythologizing, associative turn of mind[77]—we would be right to detect a self-portrait. At points, very transparently, "as to biography [...] the writer becomes hazy"[78]—partly because "Conrad himself wished to throw a haze"[79] over parts of his own life. Ford tells how he took down "the episode of the *Tremolino* in the *Mirror of the Sea* [...] from Conrad's dictation,"[80] noticing how "Conrad sensibly modified aspects and facts of his word of mouth narrations."[81] He captures the odd formality of their working relationship, and their mutual inability to talk about feelings: "the writer never in his life uttered one word of personal affection towards Conrad. What his affection was or was not here appears. And Conrad never uttered one word of affection towards the writer."[82]

Other figures from the Kent period also inevitably appear in *Joseph Conrad*, among them, fairly briefly, H. G. Wells, who had written to the *English Review* in 1920 to complain about Ford's "imaginative reminiscences"[83] when he had been parodied, in the first instalment of what became *Thus to Revisit*, as an "Eminent novelist." In *Joseph Conrad*, Ford writes of visiting Wells in Sandgate with Conrad to announce—on Conrad's insistence—their collaboration;[84] and how the following day Wells bicycled to Aldington to persuade Ford not to work with Conrad. Ford refuses gently. Wells had been one of the few to stand by Ford when his marriage to Elsie fell apart. But Wells did not mean the phrase "imaginative reminiscences" to be a compliment, as he was displeased and bemused at Ford's embroiderings. All the same, perhaps Ford took the phrase as a creative hint, judging from the highly and unapologetically imaginative scenes in *Joseph Conrad*. Ford, settled in France throughout the 1920s, living mostly in Paris and Toulon in the winters, as well as going on several trips alone to America, was now entering into his greatest phase as an incorrigible fictional autobiographer.

*

> In the long, light, gently swaying carriages
> As the miles flash by,
> And fields and flowers
> Flash by[85]

If memory, in Henry James's autobiographies, could be consciously stimulated—as the writer swings through vast caverns opening and blooming before him—in Ford's late reminiscences its central motif is the zigzag or criss-cross. Memories move along abruptly changing tracks, like trains. In the dedicatory letter to *Return to Yesterday*, written on July 14, 1931 in Cap Brun, near Toulon, Ford told how he came up with the form of the book while sitting with a bandaged foot staring up at the "criss-cross of beams"[86] in the roof of a friend's studio in New York. Henry James, he says, was born close by. The patterns of life, Ford suggests, like the patterns of volumes of memories, are deceptively formless: "Life meanders, jumps back and forwards, draws netted patterns like those on the musk melon."[87] Ford writes that the only excuse for "setting down one's life on paper" is "that one should give a picture of one's time."[88] With this in mind, Ford declares that he has tried to keep himself out of these reminiscences, although he knows that complete self-effacement is impossible. "Being a novelist, it is possible that I romance," he also warns us, and describes *Return to Yesterday* as a novel: "The accuracies I deal in are the accuracies of my impressions."[89] Then in the first chapter the intricate criss-cross begins, as Ford thinks of James, thinks of his young days near Rye, then in New York takes down a book of Kipling stories from the shelves:

> I was eighteen when I first read those words. My train was running into Rye station and I had knocked out the ashes of my first pipe of shag tobacco [. . .] My first book had just been published. I was going courting [. . .] The story was Mr. Kipling's *Only a Subaltern*. The next station would be Winchelsea where I was to descend.[90]

This is the same book he was reading in *Ancient Lights*, still smoking shag tobacco, as the train went the other way, coming into Charing Cross. Ford leaps fifteen years on, walking up the narrow street in Rye to James's house, where he bumps into Kipling coming down. Ford had come to Rye from Winchelsea with Conrad to hire a car. A few pages on, James is coming to visit Ford in Winchelsea in the middle of winter, having walked across the flats with his dog:

> I can still see his sturdy form as arrayed in a pea-jacket which nobly enhanced his bulk, wearing one of his innumerable cricket-caps, emphasising his steps and the cadences of his conversation by digging his cane into the road he stumped under the arch of the sea-gate up the hill into Winchelsea, lugging behind him on a ten yard leather lead his highly varnished dachshund, Maximilian. The dog would gyrate round his master. Mr. James would roll his eyes [. . .][91]

Return to Yesterday weaves with a serpentine movement through Ford's past, with a series of portraits. It is mainly a book about Kent and London, from the 1890s to the 1910s, although it covers Ford's breakdown in 1904 and his attempted cures in Germany, as well as the trip he made to America in 1906, before returning to his subsequent years in London and the *English Review*, moving up to the eve of the war. According to the dates at the end of the book—November 4, 1930 to August 8, 1931—it was conceived in New York, and largely written in France, but parts were written before, and appeared elsewhere, in passages in *Ancient Lights* and *Thus to Revisit* as well as other articles.[92] To that extent, like the "Compiler" in *No Enemy*, Ford's role in making *Return to Yesterday* was one of selection and arrangement, as much as writing and remembering.

Ford was fifty-seven years old in 1930, and he had begun his last, perhaps happiest relationship, with the painter Janice Biala, having met her in Paris on May Day that year, after his shared life with Stella Bowen had broken down, painfully but amicably, by 1928. There was now an immense distance between the world Ford was writing about in these reminiscences, and his new life in France, which gave his memories even more warmth. The portrait he gives of his time in Kent, in particular, has the glow of personal mythology and nostalgia. But it is a comic nostalgia, in which Ford, as so often, plays a blundering role—while securing his place in the pantheon of literature at the turn of the century, as he redrew it.

He was not physically well, to say the least, as he wrote these long-gone memories. At the end of 1930, he had a heart attack. Yet in some letters at this time, as in *Return to Yesterday*, he tried to seem undaunted. In January 1931, Ford went to Toulon with Janice, and by March they had settled in to the Villa Paul in Cap Brun, as Ford wrote to Hugh Walpole soon after:

> a very simple place where we live a life of a frugality which would astonish and for all I know appal you [. . .] [With] an immense view of the Mediterranean and agricultural labours that begin at dawn and end after sunset, I have recovered a good deal of the vitality that I thought had gone for ever with my heart attack last December. And indeed I have got back into complete writing form and have made immense strides with my book so that even if another heart attack *did* carry me off Gollancz would have at least *a* book, for Reminiscences don't need either beginnings or ends.[93]

This was the brave face Ford put on quite often in the 1930s, refusing to be beaten down by his straitened financial circumstances, and his difficulties in getting his books published, made even worse by the Depression. Even though parts of *Return to Yesterday* were compiled from earlier writings, the book's lightness of spirit, considering Ford's ailing health at the time, is astonishing, suggesting a rare inner contentment.

Some of this lightness is achieved by avoiding difficult subject-matter, such as his failure to obtain a divorce from Elsie. Indeed, the erasure of Elsie Hueffer, Violet Hunt, and Stella Bowen from *Return to Yesterday* (and Ford's other autobiographies) is almost total; while the marital intrigues that so defined his life are played out endlessly in his fiction. Partly, this might have been due to the legal complications which would no doubt have arisen if Ford had chosen to write about Elsie—as ever since the breakdown of their marriage, it had been a matter for the courts. Violet Hunt, however, had devoted most of *The Flurried Years*, fairly recently published in 1926, to depicting Ford—who did not retaliate in kind. Whether this was a moral, practical, or artistic decision is hard to say; yet in his reminiscences Ford clearly wished

to avoid details of his private life and his affairs. There was also the delicate
fact to consider that nearly every time Ford began a phase of autobiography,
he was in a new relationship: with Violet Hunt when he wrote *Ancient Lights*;
with Stella Bowen when he wrote *Thus to Revisit*; and with Janice Biala
when he wrote *Return to Yesterday* and *It Was the Nightingale*.

Ford, in his reminiscences, defines his life around his work; and the work
of writing about his work and other writers seemed to help Ford sustain his
idea of himself and his own literary identity. In *Return to Yesterday*, even
facing the dark days of his collapse in 1904, Ford remains oddly blithe. He
lets himself go with his portraiture of other writers, inventing and extem-
porizing freely. In the past, Ford says, he had been "afraid of hurting feelings":[94] these versions are closer to the truth. But he must mean the truth of
impressions. There are stories where the embellishments flag themselves up,
yet still retain a fidelity to what happened. Exaggerations, when pointed in
the right direction, can serve to increase the truth. Yet some of the inventions point to things which only happened in Ford's head—especially when
he once again writes at length of Henry James.

James clearly meant more to Ford than Ford meant to James. Yet in *Return
to Yesterday*, while exaggerating, say, the number of times James came to have
tea in Winchelsea with him, Ford was also quite honest about James's lack
of respect for him. Where so many portraits of James capture his stately elo-
quence, Ford's James again reaches under what he implies is a mere veneer.
The Master is lovingly mocked and impersonated for his verbosity, but Ford
hints again at a demonic side to James, as well as being clear about his desperate attachment to social niceties. Physically, Ford always brings us close
to James's eyes, seemingly fascinated by their oiliness, in a passage which also
appeared in *Thus to Revisit*, now transposed to *Return to Yesterday*: "the brown
face with the dark eyes rolling in the whites, the compact, strong figure, the
stick raised so as to be dug violently into the road."[95] He again emphasizes
a simmering toughness in James: "At times he was unreasonably cruel—and
that to the point of vindictiveness when his nerves were set on edge."[96]
"Occasionally he would burst out at me with furious irritation [...] 'Don't
talk such *damnable* nonsense!' He really shouted these words with a male
fury."[97] Ford writes of his relationship with James that "I do not think that,
till the end of his days, he regarded me as a serious writer."[98]

The portrait of Conrad is far more affectionate, though full of nervous
tetchiness. Ford highlights Conrad's convulsive, spasmodic movements, his

feverishness when in the throes of composition. Like James's irritation, Conrad's "furies would be sudden, violent, blasting and incomprehensible to his victim."[99] As in *Ancient Lights*, Ford, in his portrait of Conrad and James, is someone who draws down the wrath of others, without knowing why. But Ford depicts his first meeting with Conrad in a way that also emphasizes Conrad's formality and excessive politeness, as he sees Ford at the Pent, visiting with Edward Garnett. "I was very untidy in my working clothes," Ford writes. "I said: 'I'm Hueffer.' He had taken me for the gardener [...] 'My dear faller...Delighted...Ench...anté!' He added: '*What* conditions to work in... Your admirable cottage... Your adorable view...' "[100] Soon afterwards, they were collaborating: "I suppose that for seven or eight years we hardly passed a day and certainly not a month without meeting and discussing our joint and several works":[101]

> That was how it went, day in day out, for years—the despair, the lamentations continuing for hours, and then the sudden desperate attack on the work—the attack that would become the fabulous engrossment. We would write for whole days, for half nights, for half the day, or all the night. We would jot down passages on scraps of paper or on the margins of books, handing them one to the other or exchanging them. We would roar with laughter over passages that would have struck no other soul as humorous.[102]

While Conrad is the central figure in *Return to Yesterday*, Ford makes sure to include everyone else of note that he has met, and to sketch their milieus. As with *Ancient Lights*, Ford also pointedly weaves in portraits of less distinguished people, and the country folk he met in Kent, giving "some peasant biographies"[103] in *Return to Yesterday*, which form a counterweight to the depictions elsewhere in the reminiscences of eminent politicians and royalty.

Return to Yesterday ends with another incomprehensibly irate attack, which signals another artistic death for Ford. The coda begins on June 1914, just before the war, with the author surveying London as he stands on the curb in Piccadilly Circus, unawares that he would soon be gone. As Ford strolls out with Ezra Pound one day, he is accosted by Wyndham Lewis, disguised in this book as a "Mr. D. Z.," who addresses him in a "vitriolic murmur": "*Tu sais, tu es foûtu! Foûtu!* Finished! Exploded! Done for! Blasted in fact. Your generation has gone. What is the sense of you and Conrad and Impressionism? [...] Get a move on. Get out or get under."[104] "You and Conrad had the idea of concealing yourself when you wrote," Lewis says to Ford. "I display myself all over the page. In every word. I...I...I..."[105]

Once again Ford is under attack from Lewis, who seems to find the self-effacement of Ford's Impressionism pointless.

At the very end of *Return to Yesterday*, Ford writes of the outbreak of war, which was declared just after he went up to Berwickshire to a house party. The hostess of the party, Mary Borden Turner, Ford writes, let Ford choose some of the guests. "So Mr D. Z. was there, and Ezra was to have come, and the turf of the Scottish lawns was like close fine carpeting and the soft Scottish sunshine and the soft Scottish showers did the heart good."[106] This was the last moment of peace for Ford before the war. "We sat on the lawns in the sunlight and people read aloud—which I like very much. D. Z. had brought the proofs from *Blast* of my one novel. I read that."[107] Sauntering up to the brink of war in this way, *Return to Yesterday* concludes, nonchalantly dangling over the very edge of the abyss.

*

It Was the Nightingale, begun in Paris on January 12, 1933 and finished in Toulon on June 11, the same year, also presents an intricate criss-cross of memory. The period and places covered in the book were closer to the present than *Return to Yesterday*: beginning with Ford's experiences after the war and his time in Sussex, up to editing the *transatlantic review* in Paris. Originally titled *Towards Tomorrow*,[108] and largely written by hand at the Villa Paul, it was much more of an original composition than the previous reminiscences, much less of a compilation. It was also a stylistic departure. While Ford saw *Return to Yesterday* not as autobiography but as reminiscences—"in that form the narrator shall be a mirror not any kind of actor"[109]—the dedicatory letter of *It Was the Nightingale* declares that for the first time in his life, Ford is now writing his autobiography ("a form I have never tried—mainly for the fear of the charge of vanity. I have written reminiscences of which the main features were found in the lives of other people and in which, as well as I could, I obscured myself").[110] Although *It Was the Nightingale* does contain portraits of others, inevitably, it is more about Ford himself than the other reminiscences. We can almost predict the next declaration in the dedicatory letter: that this book is also "a novel."[111] "I have employed every wile known to me as novelist—the timeshift, the *progression d'effet*, the adaptation of rhythms to the pace of the action,"[112] Ford writes, telling us that he had planned to continue up to the Great Depression in 1929. "But I found that subsequent events are too vivid in my mind. Moreover, it is inexpedient to write of living people in their too near presents"[113]—partly because they will be more aggrieved at the portrait, Ford says, in comparison to depictions of things that happened further in the past.

In *It Was the Nightingale*, Ford achieves his ideal of the tone of good prose, which as well as being unobtrusive, as he says, is close to a quiet speaking voice, speaking to someone he loved very much. The tone is so controlled that it carries the weight of the book almost by itself. At the opening, Ford pictures himself "on the day of my release from service in His Britannic Majesty's army—in early 1919":[114] back in London, a ghost in a city of ghosts, slightly shell-shocked. Ford leaves himself standing on the curb in 1919, near John Galsworthy's house "at the corner of the Campden Hill Waterworks,"[115] for almost a hundred pages, sidetracking back and forth over different years and memories triggered by chance associations. The digressions drift, as, his foot still paused half off the ground, Ford decides to recount, say, a lunch with Theodore Dreiser in 1923—until he suddenly returns to the point, as he then sits in a café later in Paris, "where I sat all alone and read that Galsworthy was dead."[116]

He always cuts back to the curb eventually, until he finally decides to leave London, with almost identical words to Lewis's pre-war attack on him in Piccadilly: "as far as London was concerned there was nothing to do but to get out or go under!"[117] Ford extemporizes wildly on his period in Sussex at Red Ford, almost seeming to enjoy the dramatic effects of emphasizing his destitution after the war. As in *Return to Yesterday*, he manages to turn difficult and even desperate material into comedy. Yet there is also incomprehension and bitterness as he writes of how many of the people he had known and liked in London before the war had been killed, or were now impoverished, while other acquaintances "had prospered unbelievably," becoming "war-rich."[118] "We who had returned [...] were like wanderers coming back to our own shores to find our settlements occupied by a vindictive and savage tribe."[119] Seen in this light, Ford's period in Sussex— where, as Stella Bowen's memoir *Drawn from Life* (1941) makes clear, he endured very real poverty—was a painfully forced retreat from a society that no longer had any use for whatever Ford had done or suffered in the service of his country.

As *It Was the Nightingale* progresses, Ford takes the digressive method further, pushing the circles of association away harder each time, tacking back and forth across wider gaps in years, so that the autobiography slips its stated time-scheme unpredictably: sometimes, albeit only briefly, narrating things that happened before and during the war. Writing of his move to the south of France in 1922 with Stella Bowen (who, as with all Ford's treatment of his women in his autobiographies, is quite invisible), Ford changes tracks in time and place once again:

> It was six years since I had seen the Mediterranean, going back to the line from the Red Cross hospital at Mentone [. . .] The Red Cross train had stopped for an hour, at midnight, at Tarascon [. . .] I desperately disliked going back to the line. My lungs were in a terrible condition still [. . .][120]

The chain of memories, as here, continues to move unpredictably, as Ford refers constantly and freely back and forth to other moments in his life throughout It Was the Nightingale. As in all Ford's autobiographies, there are also many glimpses of other writers. Gertrude Stein appears in a typically brief and disconnected snapshot of Paris, as "years ago—I should say in 1913—I was on top of a bus in front of the Bon Marché. I saw Gertrude Stein driving with a snail-like precision her Ford car."[121] The height of the car above the road, Ford writes, "gave to Miss Stein, driving, the air of awfulness of Pope or Pharaoh, borne aloft and swaying on their golden thrones."[122] Ford, due to leave Paris that afternoon, jumps down off his bus to pursue this vision: "I trotted on, keeping that procession in sight for quite a number of blocks," but "she outdistanced me."[123]

Stein's biographer James Mellow writes that Ford must have the dating of this memorable vision of Stein wrong, as at this period Stein had no car and did not drive.[124] What is more important is the impression of Ford's simultaneously grandiose and comic depiction of the queenly Stein here, and his sense of his humility. Stein's own The Autobiography of Alice B. Toklas was beginning to be serialized in The Atlantic Monthly in May 1933, precisely around the time when Ford was finishing It Was the Nightingale. Stein was more an acquaintance than a close friend; and Ford writes in It Was the Nightingale, slightly perplexingly, "I have had so many and such long arguments with that old friend—or enemy—that they seem to fuse, the one into the other in an unbroken chain of battle."[125] But as Stella Bowen notes, Stein often saw Ford and herself in Paris in the 1920s, coming to their parties and inviting them back. Bowen recalled her visits to Stein and Toklas, as the three women "would sit beneath the Picassos and the rest of the collection and discuss methods of dealing with one's concierge, or where to buy linen for sheets, or how to enjoy French provincial life."[126] Both Ford and Stein made sure to provide glimpses of each other in their autobiographies—but they remained glimpses, almost as if they were hailing each other from a distance.

Towards the end of *It Was the Nightingale*, Ford is on a train, between Calais and Paris, when, by chance, he strikes on the principal character for *Some Do Not* (1924), through something someone says that reminds him of his and Conrad's friend Arthur Marwood. His thoughts once again change track suddenly, to another time, another place: "I was in a railway-carriage—not in a French one running down through France, but in a first-class carriage running from Ashford in Kent to Winchelsea in Sussex."[127] So suddenly, he's back in the much earlier time of the *English Review*. Describing the genesis of *Some Do Not* in this way, Ford also recalls the novel's first scene, as the two main characters, two young men, sit "in the perfectly appointed railway carriage"[128] rushing through the Kent countryside.

The associative structure of *It Was the Nightingale* is managed so well that Ford even digresses at length about his method of digression—without seeming to stray from the point. He talks about anything that comes to mind. The thoughts spiral out, reined in by the central pull which holds the book together. It is a centrifugal motion. Moving away from the story, Ford writes, say, about his mother's skill at finding burglar-proof hiding places, or the pain he feels holding a pen, or whether or not he ever used real characters in his novels. ("I never [...] used a character from actual life for purposes of fiction—or never without concealing their attributes very carefully.")[129] It all connects. Frequently, Ford cuts to the scene of the book's composition, in the Villa Paul, "in a room that looks over the Mediterranean,"[130] moving right up to the present tense, in passages more like a journal or diary:

> I was lying this morning before dawn, looking at the Mediterranean framed in a tall oblong by the pillars of the terrace [...] As abruptly as if a conductor had raised his bâton the chorus of small birds began [...] A greyness is there and a single, agonising note infinitely prolonged. Instantly the chorus of small ones ceases [...] The lights of St. M — — die; the sea is like listening, grey satin. The lighthouse turns more slowly, so as to miss no note. It is the nightingale [...][131]

There is a healing quality to *It Was the Nightingale*, both in its dramatizing of Ford's "reconstruction" after the trauma of the war, and in its mood, which suggests that even if he had little worldly wealth by the 1930s, Ford had found happiness with Biala, and their life in France. The pages are suffused with Mediterranean clarity and light. And their echoes reverberate with all his other reminiscences. Writing of how he allows his thoughts to circle out in wide flights, before trying "in the end to let them come home,"[132] like birds around a dove-cote, Ford brings us right back to the opening of *Ancient Lights*, where he saw himself "in a long blue pinafore" looking at the box of ring-doves in Fitzroy Square and incurring his grandmother's anger.

Ford's unique art of reminiscence caused him many public troubles. It was just as misunderstood as he was. But he kept at it nearly until his death in 1939, with his final volume of literary portraits for *The American Mercury* from 1935 to 1937, collected as *Mightier Than the Sword* in England and *Portraits from Life* in America. When Wells denigratingly referred to Ford's "imaginative reminiscences" he was worried—as many of the subjects of the reminiscences might well have been worried—about the effect all Ford's tall stories would have. Reinventing the facts, as Ford did, is dangerous. His books tried to explain themselves in their prefaces. Yet the peculiarity—the originality—of the form he was concocting, compelled many of his subjects to point out, publicly, what was true, and what wasn't. The reminiscences were true enough, close enough to the facts, to seem real, even when they weren't. In their repetitions, they also aimed to create a shifting multiplicity, not a final authority. As Stella Bowen wrote in *Drawn from Life*, Ford "could show you two sides simultaneously of any human affair, and the double picture made the subject come alive, and stand out in a third dimensional way that was very exciting."[133] Bowen also wrote perceptively of Ford's Impressionism:

> All his art was built on his temperamental sensitiveness to atmosphere, to the angle from which you looked, to relative, never absolute values. When he said, "It is necessary to be precise", I used to think that he meant—precisely truthful. Of course, what he really meant was that you must use precision in order to create an effect of authenticity, whatever the subject of your utterance, in the same way as the precision of a brushstroke gives authenticity to an image on canvas, and need have no relation to anything seen in fact. Words to Ford were simply the material of his art, and he never used them in any other way. This created confusion in his everyday life, for words are not like dabs of paint. They are less innocent, being the current coin in use in daily life.[134]

Ford's improvements to fact in his reminiscences were made in the service of story and character, to bring them to life. The reminiscences' power, and their closeness to fact, has meant that the stories Ford tells about the people he knew have indeed infected all their biographies. Once heard, these stories are hard to forget. They are often treated with caution by the writers who quote them—yet they are quoted, all the same, since they bring Ford's era back to life more effectively than many other sources. In Ford's reminiscences, he never quite lets us know when he's pulling our leg, so we treat everything he says with a suspect alertness. We can never be sure when he's telling the truth; we can never be sure when to doubt him.[135] The entire literature of fact, Ford shows, should always be treated with the same caution.

Edith Wharton, *c.* 1936.

Source: Edith Wharton Collection, Beinecke Rare Book and Manuscript Library, Yale University. Reproduced in Cynthia Griffin Wolff, *A Feast of Words: The Triumph of Edith Wharton*, Oxford University Press, 1977, p. 338, and published with permission of the estate of Edith Wharton and the Watkins/ Loomis Agency.

4

The life apart

Edith Wharton

Remember it's not *me*, though I thought it was when I was writing it...[1]

Edith Wharton

Edith Wharton emerged from the First World War almost as a new woman, still charged with plans for reinvention at the age of fifty-six. She was tired—even when young, she had suffered for years from exhaustion—but immediately set about reorganizing her life. In some ways, the war reinforced her commitment to France. She had been swept up in the patriotic fervor and the courage she witnessed during her charity work in Paris, and during her dispatches from the front-lines collected in her book of reportage, *Fighting France* (1915). Before her divorce in 1913, she had swung between France and America rhythmically—one of many nicknames her friend Henry James gave her was "the pendulum-woman"[2] because of this trait—most often between her apartment in the Rue de Varenne in Paris, and her American residence, The Mount in Lenox, Massachusetts. But after the armistice, she gave up America. The two new houses she moved into in 1919 and 1920—the beautifully enclosed Pavillon Colombe outside Paris in the forest of St-Brice, and the Château Sainte-Claire, in Hyères near Toulon, on a rocky promontory with views "south, east & west, 'miles & miles'"[3] out over the Mediterranean towards the Ile de Porquerolles—were to provide the frame for the last seventeen years of her life. She tended to go south to Hyères in December, often staying until June, before motoring back to Paris. Swinging between these two stately residences, surrounded by parks, gardens, pools, and the sea, she entered a late phase of work that was astonishingly sustained, prolific, and profitable.

She was now her own person entirely, free from the marriage endured for twenty-eight years. And she ordered her existence more than ever before. This new life was peaceful, secure, and sheltered; to some extent it was also a retreat from life, after the tumults of the war years. People came to stay with her, as they always had done. She gardened, spent long hours reading, and occasionally still traveled. Yet she kept her most private hours for work.

Each morning, she wrote from very early in bed, by hand, in black ink on blue paper, until lunch, when she would appear to any guests. The pages would be gathered up and typed with the assistance of her secretary Jeanne Duprat, and then revised again, until Wharton was satisfied. In this fashion, the chapters of book after book accumulated throughout the 1920s—novels, novellas, short stories, poetry, travel—beginning with *The Age of Innocence* (1920), started as soon as Wharton moved into the Pavillon Colombe. The subject of the novel, feeding on her memories of the Old New York world of her youth, offered a way around the difficulties of making sense of what she felt to be the incomprehensible rupture of tradition caused by the war. The book gave her a refuge in the distant past, meticulously recalled in fantastic detail. It was not reminiscence so much as reimagining, tapping deep wells of memory to recreate its setting. The novel also led indirectly to an ongoing project of the 1920s and early 1930s, as Wharton began to think seriously about writing her memoirs.

The great success of *The Age of Innocence* prompted a request from *McCall's Magazine* in early 1923. This was for Wharton to write six articles on her recollections of New York Society. In a letter to her editor Rutger Jewett, Wharton replied that she did not want to write the articles, but that the proposal reminded her of a plan "vaguely floating through my mind for some time: namely, the writing of my own early memories, from 1865 to 1885 or 1890."[4] Her initial intention, she informed Jewett, had been to "jot down these remembrances, and put them away."[5] They were to have been a purely private enterprise, not for public consumption; and she only considered the project "to avoid having it inaccurately done by some one else after my death"[6] should her books attract future biographers. But now, "as they would be concerned only with the picture of my family life as a child and young girl," she saw "no particular reason in keeping them back."[7] Even so, the "remembrances" would only be a sideline, done "in the intervals of my novel writing."[8]

Autobiography, she hints, was not a priority; and her memoirs were indeed done only in asides from other work. It would be ten years before her autobiography, *A Backward Glance* (1934), was finished and published, during which time Wharton wrote many other books. But was the long gestation due to indifference, or to an excess of care? Wharton was an avid reader of lives and letters, with a lifelong penchant for certain biographies. She loved Wladimir Karénine's multivolume life of George Sand, which she sent in instalments to Henry James, and later, enthused over the biographical experiments of Lytton Strachey.[9] In one of her only explicit declarations on the art of biography, however, she declared: "Biography makes strange bedfellows."[10] The pairing of biographer and subject—especially seen from the subject's point of view—is in some ways akin to a marriage. But the dead subject has no choice in who writes his or her biography. Wharton was haunted by this, and well knew the value of her memoirs as source material for biographers. This went hand in hand with a slight timidity, if not modesty, about the project.

It was hard for her to even gauge the most appropriate stance to take towards herself. In two fragmentary self-portraits unpublished at her death, Wharton tested her reflection on the page. Both these short texts were put away privately, as she initially envisaged her "remembrances" would be. The *Quaderno dello studente* was begun in Salso, Italy, in 1924, and was kept up for the next decade. On the inside cover of this Italian notebook, Wharton wrote, "If ever I have a biographer, it is in these notes that he will find the gist of me."[11] In these pages, in a series of intermittent notes, she collected the "floating scraps of experience that have lurked for years in the corners of my mind. And gradually [...] I may even be able to jot down a sketch of myself—my own growth and history."[12] The observations in this semi-private place are spurred on at first by motives that have little to do with self-analysis or self-interest. They are merely a pre-emptive strike against future biographers. "When I get glimpses, in books and reviews, of the things people are going to assert about me after I am dead, I feel I must have the courage and perseverance, some day, to forestall them."[13]

Biographers have found the *Quaderno* to be far from revelatory. R. W. B. Lewis describes it as "disappointingly sparse";[14] Hermione Lee says its entries "amounted only to a few stray thoughts and reflections [...] a few melancholy notes [...] on her feelings about animals, solitude, the death of friends, being reviewed, beauty, loss, and happiness."[15] While the *Quaderno* shows little more than Wharton's desire to get her life-story into pre-emptive shape before any biographers, "Life & I," also unpublished until after Wharton's death, gives a fuller portrait. In fact, although it only runs up to the early

1880s, this short three-chapter sketch of Edith as a little girl is far more revealing than her much longer *Backward Glance*, for which it probably served as an unfinished early draft.[16] If it was indeed written before the formal memoir, it can be seen as a dress rehearsal, giving the inner history that the memoir covers up.

Extraordinarily direct and honest, "Life & I" has the close scrutiny of a psychoanalytic case study. Relating Wharton's earliest memories to when she was roughly nineteen, it is a story of gradual psychic strengthening: of how a timid little girl overcame irrationalities. It tells us things found nowhere else in her writing, and does so clearly, unequivocally, sometimes almost as though she was writing purely for herself. There is very little about externals, as the psychic drama of Wharton purging herself of mental aberrations takes the foreground. The text obeys the urge towards secret-sharing of all autobiography. Sometimes, it is even about this, as if Wharton realized, in this uncontrolled attempt at self-portraiture, that one of the deep subjects of autobiography is the very idea of telling the truth. The page becomes a substitute for the psychoanalyst's couch or the Roman Catholic confessional. But how much should be told? In "Life & I," Wharton recalls the "chronic moral malady"[17] which paralyzed her as a child. She always somehow felt a duty to tell the absolute truth, on pain of punishment by God. And yet she also saw how much this could cause mischief. "Nothing I have suffered since," she writes, "has equalled the darkness of horror that weighed on my childhood in respect to this vexed problem of truth-telling, & the impossibility of reconciling 'God's' standard of truthfulness with the conventional obligation to be 'polite' & not hurt any one's feelings."[18]

Ugliness provides Wharton with her first quandary on this score, prompting reflections that she knew it would be "'naughty' to say, or even to think."[19] If, as she writes, the desire "to look pretty"[20] was one of her deepest-seated instincts, this was accompanied by "feeling for ugly people an abhorrence, a kind of cold cruel hate, that I have never been able to overcome."[21] And not just people: "I remember *hating* certain rooms."[22] She fell ill at nine with typhoid while the family were in the Black Forest. She recalls this as the ending of this phase of moral torment over truth-telling, ushering in a new era of more terrifying psychic disturbance.

> I had been naturally a fearless child; now I lived in a state of chronic fear. Fear of *what*? I cannot say [...] It was like some dark undefinable menace, forever dogging my steps, lurking, & threatening; I was conscious of it wherever

I went by day, & at night it made sleep impossible [...] But, whatever it was, it was most formidable & pressing when I was returning from my daily walk [...] During the last few yards, & while I waited on the door-step for the door to be opened, I could feel it behind me, upon me; & if there was any delay in the opening of the door I was seized by a choking agony of terror [...] This species of hallucination lasted seven or eight years.[23]

Wharton was to become a connoisseur of homes and interiors: her first published book of prose, a study on *The Decoration of Houses* (1897), shows the same obsessive love of order and neat enclosure as her *Italian Villas and Their Gardens* (1904). In "Life & I," what seems strange is that she feels this omnipresent dread most intensely at the door of the house: that it is precisely at the threshold between outer and inner worlds that this abstract fear bears down. The door opens into a place of safety and enclosure; it is a shield and barrier as much as a gateway. Wharton stands at the doorstep, terrified. Only behind the door does she know she will be safe. Passing through the threshold, perhaps hearing the key turn in the lock once inside, offers a moment of respite after climactic terror. But only a moment.

In "Life & I," Wharton presents her childhood fear as a mere phase. The self-portrait traces a neat and orderly progression through these various states of unrest; and her fear is replaced by a third, supposedly final neurosis: an obsession with the sufferings and the cruelties done to animals. "This lasted for years, & was the last stage of imaginative misery that I passed through before reaching a completely normal & balanced state of mind."[24] Yet all her life, the fear at the door lingered and metamorphosed. She always saw herself as someone pursued by unabating "Furies." At the same time, she was also scared of freedom, repeatedly seeking sanctuary and secrecy— while aware that such safety was illusory and momentary. Like the concern over truth-telling, the image of respite on the threshold of the door also offers an image of the anxious autobiographer, zealously guarding her privacy: putting up screens and bolting doors, while suspecting they will eventually be prised open. In writing her own life, Wharton became increasingly adept at marking such boundaries, yet did so with an odd awareness of how ultimately permeable they would prove. She became a devotee of the sealed packet, and the supposedly private manuscript left in the archive, as "Life & I" was. (It was first published in 1990.)

One reason that Wharton ultimately settled on a semi-private resting-place for "Life & I" was its candid treatment of sexuality, as well as its account of fears and desires. Opening with a kiss on Fifth Avenue in New York, before she was four years old, "Life & I" tells of her early loves, her childish crush on one of the Rutherfurd boys in Newport, her later flirtations and courtships. It also gives the simple, brave statement, "I did not fall in love till I was twenty-one."[25] Wharton writes that her mother's repeated refusals to enlighten her about the realities of sex ("It was 'not nice' to enquire into such matters")[26] "did more than anything else to falsify & misdirect my whole life."[27] She knew nothing about "the processes of generation till I had been married for several weeks."[28] Yet the short self-portrait—as so much of her writing does, under very tightly controlled formal parameters—pulses with the passion of what she calls "Life."

> And all the while Life, real Life, was ringing in my ears, humming in my blood, flushing my cheeks & waving in my hair—sending me messages & signals from every beautiful face & musical voice, & running over me in vague tremors when I rode my poney, or swam through the short bright ripples of the bay, or raced & danced & tumbled with "the boys". And I didn't know—& if, by any chance, I came across the shadow of a reality, & asked my mother "What does it mean?" I was always told [...] "It's not nice to ask about such things."[29]

Wharton cut off the narrative of "Life & I" around 1881, at a moment in her life-story when she was in Europe with her parents, months before the unmentioned death of her father in Cannes in 1882. Why did she stop writing this version of her life? And why did she stop at exactly this point? If her sense of the dangers of truth-telling, and her fear at the door, were unconscious expressions of a deeper unease about self-revelation, then it is hardly surprising that she was unable to continue the candid vein of "Life & I"—although it is tempting to imagine what the account, if it had been continued up until the time of the writing, would have revealed. It may merely be that "Life & I" fulfilled her initial idea, outlined to Jewett, of writing her life only in its early phases, although it didn't even reach up to 1885 or 1890, as she had first planned in that letter. But something about the candor of the narrative made her uneasy. Perhaps she felt that she had not grasped her subject as firmly as she grasped her characters in novels. When she portrayed herself in *A Backward Glance*, she showed a much more public face, and wrote about the adventures of the same little girl with a novelist's sense of distance. The portrait is more poised, reserved, and veiled. Wharton may have bitterly resented her mother's inhibitions, and the damaging effect they had on her own love life, but in the full autobiography she is very much her mother's daughter, retaining a self-consciously old-fashioned sense of propriety, and what it was "nice" to discuss—courteously, silently, cordoning off entire zones of experience.

*

On October 12, 1927, Wharton's lifelong friend Walter Berry died. Hearing of Berry's first stroke, Wharton had rushed to the Hôtel Crillon in Paris from the Pavillon Colombe to be close to him. She was a witness to his last days, and the death affected her profoundly. She would eventually ask to be buried next to Berry: he was her dearest friend, and sometimes, potentially, the greatest unrequited love throughout her life. She had married Teddy Wharton in 1885, two years after meeting Berry. Early biographers, and many friends, thought she had a later affair with Berry, although it appears they were mistaken. In the aftermath of Berry's death in 1927, Wharton burned all the letters she had written him—the only person she did this for—and assembled a packet labeled "For My Biographer." (This packet, writes R. W. B. Lewis, was mostly about "her husband's various illnesses and her divorce from him.")[30] Then Teddy died in February 1928. That year, no doubt influenced by these two deaths, Wharton signed a contract to write her memoirs.

She was still busy writing fiction. Her novel *The Children* was serialized throughout 1928, appearing as a book that autumn. Then she set to a novel delayed for many years: *Hudson River Bracketed* (1929), based on an unfinished manuscript begun in 1914 called "Literature," stalled during the war. It was the story of the growth of a writer, Vance Weston. This itself was a form of autobiography, using elements from her writing life: Weston, with his name so close to Wharton, was an alter-ego, even though his sex, his background, and his much younger age distanced him from her. Wharton labored over his life during 1928 and 1929, continuing with a sequel, *The Gods Arrive*, which occupied her until 1932, when it was published in September. She probably wrote parts of *A Backward Glance* alongside these two novels. But she only really turned to it exclusively once *The Gods Arrive* was done. In the early 1930s, the autobiography loomed closer, as did other biographical endeavors by or about Wharton's friends, which intensified her anxieties about how other people would write her life, when she died.

In a letter to the art historian Bernard Berenson in February 1931, Wharton wrote, vis-à-vis a proposed life of Walter Berry by a young Leon Edel, "as you know I am trying to get together material for some reminiscences,

& I am perfectly willing, in order to block Mr. Edel, to say that I *may* write a life of Walter myself."[31] (Of course she planned to do no such thing.)[32] By June 1932, Wharton was giving Mary Berenson—who sent her the manuscript of a Life of Bernard Berenson she was working on, which was never finished or published—advice on how to spice up the narrative. She asked Mary for comments in turn. "And now, *please* send me 'by return' some advice as to how to write my own 'Life', for I'm hopelessly stuck, & feel how much easier it wd have been if I'd lived in Florence with picturesque people instead of stodging in New York!"[33] Stuck or not, she worked rapidly throughout 1932. By March the next year she wrote Gaillard Lapsley from Hyères that "My 'Apologia' is on its last lap,"[34] asking about Henry James's last words, so that she would get them right in her self-portrait. She posted the last chapters of what was then called *Retrospect* to Jewett on March 15, 1933, and struck on the title *A Backward Glance* on July 20.[35] It soon began to be serialized in the *Ladies' Home Journal*, appearing in full in 1934 as a lavishly illustrated book.

The autobiography opens with a disclaimer, after briefly reflecting on sorrow and old age, and thoughts that came to Wharton "in the course of sorting and setting down these memories."[36] Carefully, Wharton raises the theme of truth-telling, mentioning reviews of "a recently published autobiography" praised "on the score that here at last was an autobiographer who was not afraid to tell the truth! And what gave the book this air of truthfulness? Simply the fact that the memorialist 'spared no one', set down in detail every defect and absurdity in others, and every resentment in the writer."[37] This is not the kind of autobiography she has written, Wharton warns us. Her self-portrait, she implies firmly at the outset, will only deal with pleasant memories.

A Backward Glance stretches back across Wharton's whole life. It gives the histories of the prior generations of her family, and the romance of her parents, sketching the New York world she remembered before she was four, when the family set off for six years in Europe, traveling through Italy and Spain, with long sojourns in Paris and Florence, before returning to America when she was ten. As in "Life & I," Wharton writes of dancing lessons in Paris with Mlle Michelet; reading in her father's library; "*making up*" stories by holding books in front of her and pretending to read them, while inventing entirely new tales. She tells of life as a *débutante* in New York society, her fearsome "coming-out" party, and her summers spent in Newport by the sea. Where "Life & I" ended in 1881, *A Backward Glance* continues towards the twentieth century, with the regular travels in Europe which began soon after her marriage; her yachting trip of 1888 in the Mediterranean on the "Vanadis"; setting up a house in Newport, and then in Lenox. Step by step, Wharton recalls the stages of her writing career, and her literary friendships; trips to Italy, France, and England; her time at The Mount and among the Parisian literary world of the Faubourg Saint-Germain; her friendship with Henry James and the circle at Queen's Acre in Windsor; her war-time charity work in Paris. Then she briefly touches on the life she rebuilt afterwards.

For all this fullness of scope, the autobiography is notoriously discreet. "Glance" is an apt word for what Wharton does whenever faced with telling things she doesn't want to—she slides around them. Of course, there is omission and evasion. But the most cunningly deployed and persistent technique is deflection. To delight and distract herself, and the reader, Wharton piles up extraneous surface impressions. She wraps layers of drapery around herself, carefully smothering the inner story.

The story proper begins with a kiss on Fifth Avenue, like "Life & I." "The little girl who eventually became me, but as yet was neither me nor anybody else in particular"[38] is walking with her father. But in this telling, Wharton writes about "the little girl" in the third person, initially, with ostentatious control. She lingers over externals, lavishly detailing all the layers of her dress: the white satin bonnet, "patterned with a pink and green plaid in raised velvet," with "a *bavolet* in the neck to keep out the cold, and thick ruffles of silky *blonde* lace under the brim in front."[39] It is a symbolic adjustment, this fixation on clothes, done with a sleight-of-hand typifying the autobiography's glancing method. Wharton lovingly recreates the outer surfaces of her youth. She excavates, like an "assiduous relic-hunter,"[40] the society which formed her. As she performs this archaeological retrieval with one hand, she simultaneously scoops out and places elsewhere all the material about her inner psychic disturbances, her fears, desires, and loves.

The same events from "Life & I" prompt very different responses. While Mlle Michelet's ugly mother cues the dilemma over truth in the frag-mentary text, here she is dressed up—"in a cap turreted with loops of purple ribbon"[41]—and her ugliness glossed over. In place of the throbbing sensations of "Life," and the prim prohibitions about sex by Edith's mother, the full self-portrait gives an anecdote about the disgrace of Edith's cousin George Alfred. "'But, Mamma, *what did he do?*'" Edith asks. "'Some woman'—my mother muttered"[42]—and her ominous omission and lack of specificity reveal the same weight of scorn, but glancingly and indirectly. Edith's love for the Rutherfurd boy goes unmentioned; the narrative instead reflects on the costume of the Newport "archery club meetings," and the hidden faces of their young and beautiful participants, their "heavy veils flung back only at the moment of aiming": "veils as thick as curtains."[43] The haunting fear of the Newport years is absent; instead Wharton depicts the parade of fashionable ladies on their "Ocean Drive," painting in their elaborate attire with an intricate excess of brushstrokes: their "brocaded or satin-striped" dresses, "powerfully whale-boned"; their "flower-trimmed" bonnets "tied with a large tulle bow under the chin."[44]

Beneath all the deflection and drapery, however, is still the same fearful soul depicted in "Life & I." She is simply harder to find. At first the center of the portrait remains one of a lost and lonely girl, whose isolation—as to what really interested her—was extreme. And what really interested her was literature, always depicted with an aura of secrecy. Wharton maintained this secrecy her entire life, as though protecting something priceless. The autobiography traces this secrecy back to her childhood encounters with literature. "There was in me a secret retreat where I wished no one to intrude, or at least no one whom I had yet encountered,"[45] Wharton says of her literary yearnings. The early account of discovering books and "*making up*" in *A Backward Glance* is very similar to "Life & I." Originally, the pages were part of the manuscript of her 1914 novel "Literature," but were then moved by Wharton from fiction to fact: from her novel about a writer's growth into her autobiographies.[46]

"*Making up*," in all its senses of creativity, compensation, and cosmetics, was what Wharton did all her life, through literature. She made up stories which made up for the deficiencies of reality. Through such making up, she built up a personality. The full self-portrait is another tale of strengthening, as Edith progressed from "the same insignificant *I* that I had always known"[47] into the person she wanted to be. Initially, reading books was the key, and was fruitful, if solitary. Early travels in Europe were also important. Later, encounters and friendships with other writers became pivotal. And Edith's life-story, begun as a tale of loneliness, soon becomes a much more social portrait. Like many autobiographies, its later structure becomes "people I have known."

*

Self-portraiture, while often being seen as solipsistic, frequently becomes a story about how other people, often met by chance, have influenced oneself.

Character is relative; it depends on situation. "What is one's personality, detached from that of the friends with whom fate happens to have linked one?"[48] Wharton asks, pointing to the ways in which personality and self-hood depend on and are nourished by friendship and influence. She only talks of friendship here, where choice intervenes as much as chance; rather than of families, where the sense of fate and lack of choice is so much stronger. And tellingly, she doesn't mention love, where other people's impact can prove indissoluble from oneself.

The relativity of personality—the ways in which we adapt our personalities in reaction to other people—also has an aesthetic dimension in the life and work of any writer. Mutual influence and friendship in "real" life between writers or artists has a corresponding effect, if only in reaction, on their work. It is often as important as the mutual influence exerted by writers purely on the page. Biography and autobiography consistently expose these circumstantial elements. This is frequently seen as one of the irremediable trivialities of life-writing: the way that dwelling on circumstantialities leads to the banal, or worse, to plain gossip. Yet many artists' work is nourished by such links.

In her autobiography, Wharton was incredibly selective about who to portray. She knew that such portrayals also related to her self. Certain characters were rubbed out from the portrait; others were raised on plinths. This was not always due to the influence they exerted on her life, or work, or both. Sometimes the most intimate figures were shielded, with the same protective privacy Wharton displayed in all her writing life. But she did most often celebrate those who helped her to connect the two sides of her outer daily existence and her secret writing self. In the early stages of her life, such figures were random and sparse: Walter Berry; Egerton Winthrop; the French writer Paul Bourget and his wife Minnie; Wharton's early editors Edward Burlingame and William Brownell. She eventually met more influential figures; but it took years.

Wharton reserves the most extended, loving portrait in the autobiography for Henry James, whom she first met in Paris at the house of the watercolorist Edward Boit (a good friend of Sargent's) and then later in Venice "in 1889 or 1890."[49] The great man failed to notice her on both of these occasions, even though, as Wharton says, she dressed up to look her prettiest: first in "my newest Doucet dress," then with "*a beautiful new hat!*"[50] But they finally became such good friends, after meeting again in 1903, that their literary fates became intertwined. Their meetings often occurred in very different places. During his American tour of 1904–5, for example, James had stayed with Wharton; and he visited her in Paris in 1907.

Part of their friendship, strangely, in later years, was an almost obsessive urge on Wharton's part to make James sit for his portrait. During another of James's visits to Paris, in 1908, Wharton persuaded James to sit for Jacques-Emile Blanche (which resulted in what she later thought the only extant portrait of James "*as he really was*");[51] in 1912 she commissioned Sargent's charcoal drawing of James, and in 1913, the Sargent portrait for James's seventieth birthday. In a corresponding memorial act, Wharton took full control of the opportunity to portray James in words. And almost possessively, she portrayed sides of him that no one else had seen. As she wrote after James's death, to Lapsley, referring to the inner circle of James's friends at Queen's Acre—"we had a Henry that *no one* else knew; and it was *the* Henry we had!"[52]

Wharton's James is, above all, seen as an equal. Financially operating in realms of which James was in awe, Wharton even sometimes almost seems sorry for James. She portrays him, gently, as a spendthrift, seeming genuinely shocked at the meager fare served and re-served at Lamb House, noting how he was always prepared to "take advantage, to the last drop of petrol"[53] of her car—without ever getting a motor himself. She draws out his sense of fun and playfulness, differing from many portraits, which imply that James was only unintentionally funny. She sees his malice and his humor as being interlinked, his "elaborate hesitancies" as being full of comic timing: "one knew that silver-footed ironies, veiled jokes, tiptoe malices, were stealing to explode a huge laugh at one's feet."[54] She delights in "the quality of fun—often of sheer abstract 'fooling'—that was the delicious surprise of his talk";[55] his dementedly endless humorous allusions, "as four-dimensional as that of the Looking Glass, or the Land where the Jumblies live"; his "heaped-up pyramidal jokes, huge cairns of hoarded nonsense."[56]

Nowhere, perhaps, was this spirit of nonsense more alive in their relationship than in all the names he gave her. "One could make an amusing list," writes Millicent Bell, "of the epithets he created for 'the most *remuante* of women'—the Princess Lointaine, the whirling princess, the great and glorious pendulum, the gyrator, the devil-dancer, the golden eagle, the Fire Bird, the Shining One, the angel of desolation or of devastation, the historic ravager [...] each more hilarious than the last."[57] Wharton's enormous energy and wealth terrified and amused James; if at first he could not take her entirely seriously, he soon, semi-secretly, saw her as a threat, for all their camaraderie. The sales of her books were phenomenal, while his New York Edition flopped. He could not but respect her artistry, even if his criticisms were fierce. The slight tone of mockery in his letters to her changed over time to one of heartfelt sympathy; it switched decisively during the war, when he had nothing but admiration for the way she threw herself into action. She wrote him long descriptive letters from the front-lines, which he devoured.

Wharton's respect for James throughout her autobiography is self-evident; yet she celebrates him slightly more as a man than as a writer. She presents the convivial James, giving glimpses of him amid the literary milieu at Queen's Acre, or motoring together—James accompanied her on her *Motor-Flight Through France* (1908) though not mentioned by name—or visiting the Faubourg Saint-Germain. She depicts him on his trips back to America in 1904 and 1911. She describes him reading poetry aloud, noting that he read very few contemporary novels except Wells's—because, as James told her, "'everything he writes is so alive and kicking'"[58]—"and a few of Conrad's."[59] Wharton's mimicry of James's circumlocutions forms several hilarious set-pieces, most often when James consistently gets them lost motoring, by insisting on offering directions to Cook, the chauffeur. Metaphorically, Wharton subtly implies, much more softly than Wells did in *Boon*, that James's late style was a wrong turning artistically. "This—this, my dear Cook, yes... this certainly is the right corner. But no; stay! A moment longer, please—in this light it's so difficult [...] It may be... yes! I think it *is* the next turn... 'a little farther lend thy guiding hand'... that is, drive on; but slowly, please, my dear Cook; *very* slowly."[60] Yet Wharton, beyond all her playful imitations, is also keen to capture the inspirational quality of James's talk and conversations. She portrays him as a miraculous autobiographer, whose winding syntax and parentheses brought people back to life. She recalls one summer evening in 1911, during James's visit to The Mount, as they were sitting out late on the terrace, when in his improvised verbal memories she glimpsed the stirrings of his autobiographies *A Small Boy and Others* and *Notes of a Son and Brother*.

One of us suddenly said to him (in response to some chance allusion to his Albany relations): "And now tell us about the Emmets—tell us all about them." [...] for a moment he stood there brooding in the darkness, murmuring over to himself, "Ah, my dear, the Emmets—ah, the Emmets!" Then he began, forgetting us, forgetting the place, forgetting everything but the vision of his lost youth that the question had evoked, the long train of ghosts flung with his enchanter's wand across the wide stage of the summer night. Ghostlike indeed at first, wavering and indistinct, they glimmered at us through a series of disconnected ejaculations, epithets, allusions, parenthetical rectifications and restatements, till not only our brains but the clear night itself seemed filled with a palpable fog; and then, suddenly, by some miracle of shifted lights and accumulated strokes, there they stood before us as they lived, drawn with a million filament-like lines, yet sharp as an Ingres, dense as a Rembrandt; or, to call upon his own art for an analogy, minute and massive as the people of Balzac.[61]

Wharton shows how James's spoken verbal Impressionism worked almost magically through blurs, auras, half-glimpsed essences, suddenly, mysteriously, cohering: as, at unpredictable moments, the sinuous verbal haze shifts to reveal a needle-sharp focus. She emphasizes how close James's art as an autobiographer was to his normal talk and conversation, giving a glimpse of exactly how its portraits of others were achieved through dictation, as James paced up and down, remembering, adding stroke after stroke to an image or idea. In a later passage in her self-portrait, Wharton recalls James doing the same at Queen's Acre, as he plunged "into reminiscences of the Paris or London of his youth, or into some slowly elaborated literary disquisition, perhaps on the art of fiction or the theater, on Balzac, on Tolstoy, or, better still, on one of his own contemporaries. I remember, especially, one afternoon when the question: 'And Meredith—?' suddenly freed a 'full-length' of that master which, I imagine, still hangs in the mental picture-galleries of all who heard him."[62]

In such instances, Wharton again crosses the lines between autobiography and normal talk, showing how close they can be. Yet her own autobiography remains considered, careful, intensely *written*: anything but freely discursive. She hints at James's sensitivities, and his inability to take criticism, for all the quietly devastating critiques and advice he gave others on their work. But she keeps her knowledge of his depression out of the portrait. She had seen this at first hand, and had been terrified by her glimpse of its abysses. But there is nothing of this in *A Backward Glance*. It is only in her private letters. She visited James early one afternoon in March 1910, as James's Pocket Diaries also record, and wrote to Morton Fullerton about the encounter.

I was told to come after luncheon; & when I entered, there lay a prone motionless James, with a stony stricken face, who just turned his tragic eyes toward me—the eyes of a man who has looked on the Medusa! [...] I sat down beside the sofa, & for a terrible hour looked into the black depths over which he is hanging [...] I could hardly believe it was the same James who

cried out to me his fear, his despair, his craving for the "cessation of consciousness", & all his unspeakable loneliness & need of comfort, & inability to be
comforted! "Not to wake—not to wake—" that was his refrain; "& then one
does wake, & one looks again into the blackness of life, & everything ministers
to it—all one reads & sees & hears" […] Don't think I am exaggerating: it was
all this & more—with cries, with tears, & a sudden effondrement at the end,
when, after pleading with me to stay—"Don't go, my child, don't go—think
of my awful loneliness!"—he wanted me no more, & could hardly wait for me
to be out of the door![63]

That spring of 1910, Wharton had serious problems of her own. Teddy
Wharton's mental illness had by then become uncontrollable. There was talk
of putting him in a sanatorium. His ups made him behave manically (he
boasted of having had affairs in Boston with chorus girls in a flat he had
bought); his downs left him sobbing and needy. All this is only glimpsed in
the autobiography, as is the rest of their tragically inappropriate union. It is
a glaring omission: there isn't even a photograph of Teddy in the book.
But it is not a complete omission. Teddy makes a few appearances, but only
namelessly as "my husband," and only rarely. The effect of such glances and
rubbings-out is similar to Wharton's mother's exclamation "Some woman!"—
making us aware of something that is not being said.

Omission in autobiography needs to be total for it to work fully;
otherwise it draws attention to itself. Yet Wharton tries not to stimulate any
curiosity with her few dry mentions of Teddy. The marriage is announced
obliquely, then ignored. "At the end of my second winter in New York I was
married; and thenceforth my thirst for travel was to be gratified,"[64] Wharton
writes. "An intriguing *non sequitur!*"[65] exclaims one biographer, Grace Kellogg.
(Although this sentence resonates oddly—unconsciously?—with Wharton's
observation in "Life & I" that for many years, "I still thought that persons
who had 'committed adultery' had to *pay higher rates in travelling* […] because
I had seen somewhere, in a train or ferry-boat, the notice: '*Adults* 50 cents,
children 25 cents'.")[66] Wharton erased Teddy from her life as she wrote it.
She talks around his "neurasthenia" only in one neutrally worded, extremely
guarded paragraph, towards the end. The hole in the narrative highlights the
defensive hand of the writer, shielding the facts.

There are other gaps and absences in the group portrait which *A Backward
Glance* becomes. The depictions of Paris in the early decades of the twentieth
century, and the French Riviera in the 20s and 30s, reveal the extent to
which Wharton kept herself to herself: socializing mainly with the privil-
eged sets of the Queen's Acre circle in England, and Rosa de Fitz-James's

salon in France. Wharton never met Proust, although she read the instalments of *A la recherche du temps perdu* as they appeared. She frequented the
same Faubourg milieu as Proust, and was in Paris, on and off, the whole
time he was writing the novel. Her autobiography is, in its social scenes of
Paris, almost like a chapter of the *Recherche*, depicting a similar world, but
from the angle of an American; and Wharton possibly found encouragement
to depict a writing life—as she also did from 1914 onwards in her books
about Vance Weston—from reading Proust. Walter Berry dined regularly
with Proust. But there was no meeting between Marcel and Wharton, apart
from the literary and intimate encounter of her reading him, and possibly,
him reading her—the *Motor-Flight*, especially, has many Impressionist passages
like the later descriptions of motoring in the *Recherche*.

Wharton also never met Gertrude Stein or any of the habitués of the rue
de Fleurus, later so sharply rendered by Stein in *The Autobiography of Alice B.
Toklas*. Indeed, Wharton avoided the Parisian bohemian world outside the
confines of the elite Faubourg; and her Riviera life was similarly sheltered.
Her social life was entirely different from that of the *ateliers* of modernist
Paris, and of the Nice and Monte Carlo of the young expatriates. The dil-
ettante-type to which Wharton was attracted, and with whom she made the
best of her long-standing friendships, perhaps reveals her old shyness and
reserve, as well as the ingrained habit of living at an elevated social and
financial level: a prerequisite for many of her friendships. James was the only
great writer she came to know well; this is no doubt why she gave him
pride of place in her autobiography.

Wharton also knew, all too well, how meetings between novelists are
often as deflating as they are inspiring. In *A Backward Glance*, on meeting
Thomas Hardy in England on one of her visits, she noted how she found
him "remote and uncommunicative [...] completely enclosed in his own
creative dream."[67] On meeting the "shining galaxy" of talent at weekend
parties near St Albans, Wharton writes, in an image which captures the
effect of banal talk with a writer whose books one has read, "meeting them
in such circumstances was like seeing their garments hung up in a row, with
nobody inside."[68] Yet "good talk" in real life passed into her mind with
"a gradual nutritive force sometimes felt only long afterward."[69] This slow
percolation of talk—sometimes distilling the gist of what was said more
than the exact words—was, Wharton felt, one of the characteristics of her
memory. On meeting Henri Bergson at a dinner, she quizzed him on a theme
closely related to this, asking about the "the odd holes"[70] in her memory,

and why she often forgot great poetry while remembering pointless things and trivia. Bergson's cryptic answer was: "*Mais c'est précisément parce que vous êtes éblouie* (It's just because you are dazzled)."[71]

Near the end of the autobiography, Wharton again recalled Bergson's words, as she stood on July 14, 1919 on a balcony high above the Champs Elysées, watching the procession of the Victory Parade down in the streets below. The occasion was too overwhelming—and still too near—for her to fully depict or grasp. The glare of certain memories makes it hard to look straight at them; and the present also has a Bergsonian "dazzle" or glow.

Many autobiographers feel the change in the texture of their material as their story approaches the time of the writing. Wharton's reaction to this in *A Backward Glance* was to remember and record less and less of her recent past. Even in telling of her war experiences, Wharton is startlingly brief, recounting how she set up workshops for seamstresses in Paris, and also founded hospitals for tubercular children, although she does also mention some trips that she made to the front. In her treatment of the post-war period, Wharton even seemed to feel she had little worth remembering, as her fire in later years was fed only "with the dry wood of more old memories."[72]

She might have felt—as she writes of the war, which she had covered in *Fighting France*—that she had already depicted the same material elsewhere. She might have felt—as she says about her cruise on the "Osprey" in 1926— that she might yet still write about the same material in a future book. But as *A Backward Glance* closes, there is an increasing sense of compartmentalization, and of areas to which we are not allowed access.

*

Wharton always maintained meticulous levels of self-control and self-arrangement. She kept certain pieces of herself out of view, so that many people who met her never saw her private self, only a prickly, even intimidating, public *façade*. And she did a similar thing in her writing. The compartmentalization in her work is so thorough that her books are unusually easy to categorize, and to place in different drawers or genres. Her travel books, for instance, do not feel like autobiography, although they recount segments of her life, because they keep so rigorously to the account of her travels. Her criticism is similarly focused, and has little self-revelation. (She took James's New York Edition prefaces to task for blending reminiscence and criticism, declaring that the technical maxims should be extracted and compiled in another book.) Her fiction—sometimes extremely close to her life—never seems autobiographical, because its elements are so carefully transposed.

To write fiction, she insisted, took so much more than self-confession. You had to simultaneously stand inside and outside your life.[73] When people saw real people in novels, they were missing the point. "It would be insincere," writes Wharton of her characters, "to deny that there are bits of Aunt Eliza in this one, of Mrs. X in that," since "no 'character' can be made out of nothing."[74] But the fictional process uses such characteristics only as elements. "Experience, observation, the looks and ways and words of 'real people', all melted and fused in the white heat of the creative fires—such is the mingled stuff which the novelist pours into the firm mould of his narrative."[75] The liquid image recalls James's fear of writing in the first person: its "*fluidity*"[76] and the danger of a "leak."[77] Wharton also mostly used the third person in her fiction: part of her obsessive making sure she always had her "firm mould."

If the writing of fiction was a hot, dangerous process at root, another image of self and character which Wharton used was cool and controlled. This was from her story "The Fullness of Life," of "a woman's nature" as a "great house full of rooms":

> there is the hall, through which everyone passes in going in and out; the drawing room, where one receives formal visits; the sitting room, where the members of the family come and go as they list; but beyond that, far beyond, are other rooms, the handles of whose doors are never turned; no one knows the way to them, no one knows whither they lead; and in the innermost room, the holy of holies, the soul sits alone and waits for a footstep that never comes.[78]

Unusually, this self-image is not quite an image of surface versus depth. It is more intricately three-dimensional, dependent on the presence of others. Different people have the keys to certain rooms, only used when they discover them. (There was an accompanying fear, for Wharton, of becoming lost and alone in the vast house of one's own soul.)

The same image of the self as a house can also be seen in terms of literary compartmentalization, and the way that we file different kinds of texts in different genres. In life-writing, the layout of the rooms is dictated not only by their literary form (diaries, letters, and notebooks especially) but also by the role of each piece of writing and its level of privacy. Of course, Wharton was very neat and careful when arranging the biographical drawers to be opened and inspected after her death; and they all form different pieces of her archival autobiography. If we were to continue the house metaphor, *A Backward Glance* would be the drawing room; "Life & I" a small, locked sitting-room; the *Quaderno* a closed book within that room. Closer to the bedroom would be Wharton's poetry, recording the adventures of her frail, unpublic soul. But the room most precious to the secret of her whole life— as she liked to arrange it—also kept carefully locked, was the Love Diary she wrote for Morton Fullerton in 1907 and 1908. It was only one of two diaries which she kept at this pivotal period of her life. Whereas one diary, as Hermione Lee writes, was "a record of social engagements and the weather,"[79] the Love Diary, tucked away separately, recorded the affair Wharton had with Fullerton over this period, mainly in Paris.

Suggesting that she saw it as a literary work in its own right, Wharton gave the Love Diary a title: "The Life Apart. (*L'âme close.*)" The French phrase more literally means The Closed or Shut-in Soul. It is written directly to an unspecified "you," which is perhaps why early biographers mistook this "you" for Walter Berry, rather than Fullerton: a bisexual, amorous journalist who was for many years the Paris correspondent of the London *Times*. The diary covers seven months in their affair, and like all diaries, hinges on suggestive gaps and absences. Wharton began it at The Mount, on October 29, 1907, resolving to go further than she had before in "one or two spasmodic attempts to keep a diary. For I had no one but myself to talk to, & it is absurd to write down what one says to one's self; but now I shall have the illusion that I am talking to you, & that [...] something of what I say will somehow reach you."[80] She eventually gave the diary to Fullerton, who read it and returned it. Its early pages have been torn out. Almost, in places, a graph-like tracing of emotions hitherto unexperienced by Wharton, who was forty-four when she met Fullerton in 1907, it records her descent into the love affair.

Where her other autobiographies omit the affair in its entirety, and even at their most loose, display various degrees of personal control, the emotions charted in the Love Diary are recounted with intensity. Wharton partitioned off this segment of her experience between these covers. She seems to have regarded it as the central event in what *A Backward Glance* calls her "uneventful"[81] life. The biographer Cynthia Griffin Wolff writes that Wharton "knew that the Love Diary was bad literature, and she allowed it to be so."[82] Yet the fast curve of the short narrative, the terrain it charts, is exhilarating. The story is a tragedy, enacted in swift strokes, written close to the present; the pacing is theatrical, with vertigo-inducing peaks and troughs.

Wharton makes full use of the gaps of the journal, forming a narrative through inferences and silences.

The Love Diary pulses with the discovery of what Wharton called "Life," much more so than in "Life & I." It makes clear how much Wharton enshrined it as the thing most worth knowing, the most precious vial of all experience. And what she means by Life is often love, or sex. On May 3, 1908, Wharton dreams of going "off with you for twenty-four hours to a little inn in the country, in the depths of a green wood," deciding "*I will go with him once before we separate* [...] It would hurt no one—it would give me my first, last, draught of life."[83] The illicit couple had a "perfect day" a week or so later at Senlis. "Alone in the train returning to Paris, we watched the full moon rise."[84] By May 21: "I have drunk of the wine of life at last [...] Oh, Life, Life, how I give thanks to you for this!"[85] The following day in the diary is entitled "The Last Day," as Wharton packs for America, and, like Lily Bart in *The House of Mirth* (1905), lays out in her room "the dresses, cloaks, hats, tea-gowns, I have worn these last six months"[86]—an actress surveying her past roles. At The Mount in 1908, Wharton felt stifled, thinking of "you who have given me the only moments of real life I have ever known,"[87] in his absence. The diary closes as Wharton recalls what she wrote about Senlis— "One such hour ought to irradiate a whole life"[88]—realizing it isn't enough: "the human heart is insatiable."[89]

The affair went beyond the short period of the diary, into 1909, reaching another moment of union when Wharton and Fullerton stayed in London in June, in Suite 92 of the Charing Cross Hotel. Wharton assiduously recorded and preserved this event in another deliberately only half-locked archival room: the Whitmanesque poem called "Terminus," first published in 1975 by R. W. B. Lewis in his biography. In the poem, Wharton thinks of all the previous encounters in Suite 92, and is at one with them.

> Secret and fast in the heart of the whirlwind of travel,
> The shaking and shrieking of trains, the night-long shudder of traffic;
> Thus, like us they have lain and felt, breast to breast in the dark,
> The fiery rain of possession descend on their limbs while outside
> The black rain of midnight pelted the roof of the station.[90]

Wharton was heading off the next day with Henry James via Queen's Acre to Lamb House in Rye ("a harbourless wind-bitten shore, where a dull town moulders and shrinks, / And its roofs fall in").[91] Fullerton was off to America and "the wide flare of cities."[92] But if the lovers' meeting of

"Terminus" was as close to life as Wharton ever got, it is surely significant that, as Lewis tells us, when Fullerton left her in the morning, he saw Wharton "propped up in bed with a writing board across her knees, scribbling the first words."[93]

The whole affair, as well as being the most intense amorous adventure of Wharton's life, was intrinsically literary from the beginning. Wharton even had the affair in the first place (and justified it to herself) partly as an experiment in life and love which would feed her creativity. She wrote to Fullerton on August 26, 1908, "You told me once I should write better for this experience of loving. I felt it to be so."[94] And Wharton did indeed use her experience from the affair each time she wrote of sexual passion in the future. While the affair was taking place, there was a literary dimension in the exchange of love letters, which delighted Wharton. She describes savoring Fullerton's letters to her, enjoying the experience of reading about their affair as much as the "real" thing.

But it was more than a literary game. The pulverization of the self which Wharton records in the Love Diary was disorienting, even frightening. She lost all sense of who she was. Love was the ultimate, undeniable proof of how the self changes under the influence of others. "Nothing else lives in me now but *you*—I have no conscious existence outside the thought of you, the feeling of you. I, who dominated life, stood aside from it so, how I am humbled, absorbed, without a shred of will or identity left!"[95] Oddly, the language Wharton uses recalls the language she uses writing of fiction: "I am a little humbled, a little ashamed, to find how poor a thing I am, how the personality I had moulded into such strong firm lines has crumbled to a pinch of ashes in this flame!"[96] The letters tell the same story, more force-fully. On May 20, 1908, Wharton wrote, "I am mad about you [...] in the whole universe I see but one thing, am conscious of but one thing, you, and our love for each other."[97] This shattering of the self reached its apotheosis as Wharton, at The Mount in June 1908, hears of a car crash, and "felt the wish that I had been in it, & smashed with it, & nothing left of all this disquiet."[98]

Wharton gave herself to Fullerton on the page much more easily than she gave herself to him in life. The circumstances of the affair were prohibitive. But beyond that, she was too timid, too careful, too cautious a soul to live with such risk and dissolution of her own idea of herself. Even while it was happening, she lived it most fully in the Love Diary. Fullerton, meanwhile, was no lover to trust; all this time he was engaged in several other trysts and complications. Wharton withdrew before the possibility of a fatal smash, having tasted what it would feel like. She rebuilt herself, just as in her later autobiographies, she covered herself with a "carapace."[99] And even while she was doing this, she was frightened that by locking the door to herself, she would lose herself.

She knew this would happen long before it did. She almost luxuriated in its happening. In the Love Diary, Wharton scattered lush and antiquated images of her own decaying soul throughout the text, as her "poor 'âme close' barred its shutters & bolted its doors again, & the dust gathered & the cobwebs thickened in the empty rooms, where for a moment I had heard an echo."[100] And in the poem "Ame close" within the pages of the Diary, Wharton again used the metaphor of her self as a house: but here it was a crumbling ruin, in terminal disrepair.

> Thick ivy loops the rusted door-latch tie [...]
> And flowers turned weed down the bare paths decay [...]
> Yet one stray passer, at the shut of day,
> Sees a light tremble in a casement high [...]
> Yet enter not, lest, as it flits ahead,
> You see the hand that carries it is dead.[101]

This brief taste of life was jaundiced before it began. Wharton protected herself; but the self-protection was self-destructive. Her fear of ruining what was most dear to her held her back from having it. This was the tragedy the Life Apart told. Wharton's reaction to the affair, as she charted it in her letters to Fullerton and in the diary, was a later variation of her early fear at the door. Obeying the dictates of society, and her sense of self-preservation, she went back into the "black box"[102] of her marriage and suffocated. She almost got used to it. To Sara Norton, in November 1908, she wrote, "the change & movement carry me along, help to form an *outer surface*. But the mortal desolation is there, will always be there."[103]

If the present has a glow or "dazzle," diaries and letters often come closest to capturing it, of all the forms of life-writing. The Love Diary, in its sustained second-person address, was also like a letter, with all the inimitable specificity of tone—almost as nuanced as talk—which comes from texts written directly to a certain person. If Wharton had written of the Fullerton affair in her autobiographies—and perhaps she would have done if she had continued "Life & I"—it would have presented itself to her quite differently: certainly with less precision in charting the flickering passage of emotions.

She would have caught the penumbra of the affair, not exactly how it felt. Events gain shape over time, compacting into patterns.

The Love Diary revels in flux and confusion: its passages of waiting bring the present tense so near that it crawls forward inch by inch. Yet compared to the letters of the same period—which plot the course of the affair even more immediately—it is also clear how much of a deliberately fashioned and consciously literary artefact the diary remains, with its interwoven poems, deletions, hesitations, and rehearsals of emotion. It occupies a unique space in Wharton's life-writings as a whole, partly because of the precision with which it has been kept "Apart." It is the piece of the jigsaw that brings the other self-portraits into focus, yet it also contradicts them. Wharton could never have written as desperately as this, as recklessly as this, in her later years. She would not *publish* like this. But she never forgot what happened over this period with Fullerton. She got back in touch with him in later years, yet the two former lovers, exchanging letters, merely resumed a tentative, courteous friendship.

*

In the first months of 1937, the last year of her life, Wharton began another autobiography, with an article, "A Little Girl's New York," first conceived as the opening part of a sequel to *A Backward Glance* called *Further Memories*.[104] By March 17, 1937 Wharton had already abandoned this idea of "a second volume of Reminiscences," feeling that she had "not enough material left."[105] "A Little Girl's New York" was as far as she got. Some autobiographers become more and more frank and self-exposing the more they write their lives. Wharton's reaction, as evidenced by the article, and the decision to abandon the sequel, was the opposite. She built up the carapace further, and wrapped herself up in even more external details. This defensive building-up is the overall movement of her formal autobiographies, from "Life & I" to *A Backward Glance* to "A Little Girl's New York." Wharton is really nowhere to be found in this last article, which focuses, much more even than *A Backward Glance*, exclusively on the outer layers of the New York world of her youth: its houses, its clothes, its customs, its dances, its trips to church, the theater, the opera. The motive for "beginning my old story over again," Wharton writes, was one purely of archival preservation, fixing all these relics as though in aspic, to save them from the darkening world of the late 1930s.

Everything that used to form the fabric of our daily life has been torn in shreds, trampled on, destroyed; and hundreds of little incidents, habits, traditions which, when I began to record my past, seemed too insignificant to set down, have acquired the historical importance of fragments of dress and furniture dug up in a Babylonian tomb. It is these fragments that I should like to assemble and make into a little memorial like the boxes formed of exotic shells which sailors used to fabricate between voyages.[106]

Just as Wharton formed a "carapace" for herself in *A Backward Glance*, "A Little Girl's New York" goes further, being explicitly made of "shells." This "little memorial" was the final resting-place of her "shut-in soul." It was full of bric-à-brac, with Wharton hidden amid the antique lumber, behind the heavy veils of the brownstone houses of the 1870s and 80s, whose "tall windows were hung with three layers of curtains: sash-curtains through which no eye from the street could possibly penetrate."[107]

Wharton, now seventy-five, knew there was not much time left. After a mild stroke on April 11, 1935, losing some sight in her left eye, she had written the following year to her friend from the war-years, Elisina Tyler, with "instructions after my death" and funeral arrangements, telling her that "personal papers are [...] to be found in a small locked portfolio, marked E. W."[108] Perhaps this ill-health, not a lack of material, prevented her further reminiscences. But she enjoyed her last days of life, safely away from the vicissitudes of her middle years. Old age, she had written to Minnie Jones in 1932, was better than people said it was, with its own "quiet radiance [...] in that light I discover many enchanting details which the midday dazzle obscured."[109]

As an old woman, the steely Wharton of the carapace, whose outer shell could sometimes seem so intimidating to people she didn't know, and who mistook her painful shyness and solitariness for toughness, shrank from view and mellowed, even while the encrustations of her life as she wrote it increased. And away from life, finally, she savored it all the more, feeding on her memories and her imaginations without fear. On October 11, 1936, Wharton wrote to Mary Berenson, "I wish I knew what people mean when they say they find 'emptiness' in this wonderful adventure of living, which seems to me to pile up its glories like an horizon-wide sunset as the light declines."[110] "An incorrigible life-lover and life-wonderer,"[111] she was lying next to Walter Berry within a year.

H. G. Wells photographing Ethel Merman in New York on January 14, 1936.
Source: Keystone–France/Getty Images.

5

Alive and kicking

H. G. Wells

No books of mine are autobiographical though of course I use all my experiences...[1]

H. G. Wells

Soon after he moved to Sandgate in Kent, first renting No. 2 Beach Cottages in 1898, and then building Spade House by the sea in 1900, Herbert George Wells launched out in several fresh directions from the journalism and extraordinary science fiction tales which had made his name as a writer. In *Love and Mr. Lewisham* (1900) and *Kipps* (1905), he struck a new, equally brilliant Dickensian vein of social realism and comedy which came much harder to him than the propulsive imaginative stories of science and survival in *The Time Machine* (1895), *The Island of Doctor Moreau* (1896), and *The Invisible Man* (1897). There were autobiographical elements in all his science fiction which brought it down to earth—quite literally in *The First Men in the Moon* (1901) where the narrator, Bedford, returns from his lunar adventures, landing on the Kent coast at Littlestone-on-Sea, not so far from Sandgate. But in his more realistic mode, Wells drew more fully and widely from life, setting free the increasingly unpredictable and volatile elements of novelistic autobiography. Sometimes, these elements had unwanted repercussions in the real world. Nonetheless, Wells was to write more and more books like this over the years.

While Henry James was vampiric in his use of autobiographical elements to vivify his fiction, grasping pieces of other lives here and there to feed into his own work; and while Joseph Conrad redramatized experiences which were safely disconnected in the past, Wells increasingly used things—and people—very close to his present existence. In such moments, his writing became a way of working through—thinking through—his personal situations and dilemmas. When the dilemmas became acute, and social issues and politics also began to outweigh his interest in novels, especially after he moved from Kent to Hampstead in 1909, Wells often became frustrated with the falsity of the fictional enterprise, and its masks. Mid-novel, he can be seen pushing his characters off the page, impatient to get on and air his own views.

He could be very quick to denounce any such autobiographical traces in his novels. Indeed, he often seemed enraged by such hints, showing flashes of hot temper. In 1900, after a review of *Love and Mr. Lewisham* conflated the details of the novel and his life, Wells wrote a letter to the editor, quashing the "insinuation that the book is a thinly veiled autobiography"—"there is no sort of parallelism or coincidence between my private life and the story I have invented."[2] In 1908, after similar claims were made about *Tono-Bungay*, Wells was more irate. "Please trace the *Fool* who started this to his lair & cut his obscene throat,"[3] he wrote to Ford, who was more unperturbed, if still sometimes cautious, about such links being made between himself and his own novels. Wells was deeply uneasy with the autobiographical slants of his fiction. He wanted his life and art to be separate. He knew that comparisons between the two spheres denied his novels their status as fully finished art, implying that he always had one foot in the picture, that he wasn't concerned to entertain or invent. Equally, he resented his private life being revealed or decoded through his work. So such comments by reviewers were a *bête noire*, countered in numerous prefaces where Wells protests that the book you are about to read is a novel, not autobiography.

But part of his fury at these remarks lay in his recognition of their essential truth. If he didn't wish to be seen undisguised in his books, he made few efforts to disguise the other real people he portrays. In *The New Machiavelli* (1911), he included fictionalized portraits of the Fabians Sidney and Beatrice Webb, so close to provoke justified fears of libel. In a letter to Macmillans marked "OBVIOUSLY PRIVATE" Wells is unpenitently forthright about the resemblances. "Are the Baileys a libellous picture of the Webbs? That is quite right."[4] Later in life, he even wished he had put the Webbs in under their real names.[5] Only as he aged, did he become more open about such matters. By the time of his *Experiment in Autobiography* (1934), he unashamedly points to the real events in his novels.[6]

Real-life depictions such as those of the Webbs reflect the "cheek" James saw in Wells: his irreverent, satirical urge to debunk. Close caricature lies at the heart of his creative spirit, which is gleefully mischievous, sprite-like. But even James complained that Wells's tendency to draw so closely from life, from things which had only just happened to him, allowed Wells to stop creating—and inhabiting—fully fictional characters. The Master wrote to H. G. from Boston in 1911 after reading *The New Machiavelli*, gently deploring the lack of "detachment" and "chemical transmutation" in such "autobiography brought [. . .] up to date."[7] It was the same old charge, put with greater subtlety. James hinted at insufficiencies in Wells's fictional process, implying that the materials which he transformed from life into his fiction were too near to him, and were only partially being modified in their journey from life to the page. Breathing the new air of art, characters formed in this way might fail to survive. To keep them alive, more inner vision and transformation—the very lifeblood of fiction—was required.

In *Boon* (1915), however, Wells notoriously brought his depictions of real people closer still, including a merciless, prolonged, undisguised portrait of James, among other contemporaries. With savagely playful mimicry, Wells ridiculed James's art of the novel—revealing how much his own childish humor could taunt and wound. James, Wells wrote, built his novels on an avoidance of reality: he "sets himself to pick the straws out of the hair of Life before he paints her. But without the straws she is no longer the mad woman we love."[8] Wells picks James's plots apart and can't see anything there: "people in the novels of Henry James do not do things in the inattentive, offhand, rather confused, and partial way of reality: they bring enormous brains to bear upon the minutest particulars of existence."[9] "Upon the desert his selection has made," Wells notes, "Henry James erects palatial metaphors [. . .] The chief fun, the only exercise, in reading Henry James is this clambering over vast metaphors."[10]

In *Boon*, Wells also spoke through his thinly-veiled characters more than ever, as he argued in cartoon-like skits about where the novel as artform was heading. Described as the posthumous papers of George Boon, prepared for publication by Reginald Bliss, with an introduction by H. G. Wells (and Wells insisted publicly that Boon and Bliss were the authors),[11] *Boon* was a celebration of heterogeneity—a ragbag of loose odds and ends—deliriously performed by Wells's own splinter-selves. After mocking James, it rushes via a Special Train to Bâle—crammed with writers, with Ford "wandering to and fro up and down"[12] the corridors—for a "World Conference on the Mind of the Race." Wells's pseudo-selves soon splinter off, until Bliss is complaining how hard it is to follow Boon as Boon "goes on with the topic of Hallery again";[13] until Boon is explaining that he "invented Hallery to get rid of myself, but, after all, Hallery is really no more than the shadow of myself."[14]

After many later experiments with dialogue-novels, Wells eventually found another way to speak his mind over or through his characters, in *The World of William Clissold* (1926). Here, playing with generic conventions, he turned to the forms of life-writing, framing the book as the autobiography of a wealthy industrialist, William Clissold, who looked back on his life as he turned sixty, as Wells did around that time. *The World of William Clissold* became a diffuse, three-volume canvas on which Wells discovered, like Proust, that free from fiction's demands of plot and suspension of disbelief, he could talk about whatever he wanted to. He relished the inclusiveness and elasticity of the autobiographical form. But he wanted to keep the mask half off, half on, making elaborately transparent declarations that William Clissold is William Clissold and H. G. Wells is H. G. Wells—just as he wrote at the outset of *Boon* that "Bliss is Bliss and Wells is Wells. And Bliss can write all sorts of things that Wells could not do."[15] In his lengthy "A Note Before the Title Page" of *William Clissold*, Wells states pre-emptively (echoing Ford's *Joseph Conrad*) that "this book, then [...] is a novel,"[16] not an autobiography. He begs us not to peer through Clissold's world back to Wells, as "this is not a *roman à clé* [sic]. It is a work of fiction, purely and completely." Yet "one thing which is something of an innovation has to be noted. A great number of real people are actually named in this story."[17] But the fictitiously named characters, Wells writes, are fictitious. Drawing attention to the multiplicity of the characters he has created throughout his writing life, Wells implies that it would surely be impossible for him to be all these different people.

> It would be a great kindness [if] William Clissold could be treated as William Clissold, and if Mr. Wells could be spared the standard charge of having changed his views afresh [...] because William Clissold sees many things from a different angle than did Mr. Polly, George Ponderevo, Susan Ponderevo, Mr. Preemby, Dr. Devizes, Dr. Martineau, Remington, Kipps, the artilleryman in *The War of the Worlds*, Uncle Nobby, Benham, Billy Prothero, and the many other characters who have been identified as mouthpieces [...] it is a point worth considering in this period of successful personal memoirs that if the author had wanted to write a mental autobiography instead of a novel, there is no conceivable reason why he should not have done so.[18]

Wells is so defensive that he draws attention to his vulnerabilities.[19] Insisting that *William Clissold* is a full-dress novel, he also argues in this preface that all novels have to be drawn from life. He makes the same points in the preface to *The New Machiavelli*—that "it is only by giving from his own life and feeling that a writer gives life to a character"[20]—likewise concluding: "why on earth if one wants to write an autobiography should one write a novel?"[21]

There are many reasons, as Wells knew. His earlier experiences with writing biography, and his libel wranglings over *The New Machiavelli*, made him intensely aware of the contingencies of all non-fictional life-writing, and the protective coverings of fiction. In the Christmas of 1903, Wells had been much shaken when he traveled to St.-Jean-Pied-de-Port, to his friend George Gissing's deathbed. After Gissing's death, on his return to Sandgate, Wells began a preface for Gissing's unfinished novel *Veranilda*, but during his researches discovered more about his friend than he wanted to know. In March 1904, he wrote to Edward Clodd, "There are things [...] that must not come out,"[22] and he had also written in January to Elizabeth Healey, asking her to destroy any old letters of his own. He was shocked how Gissing's old papers were turning up secrets after death. He wrote an evasive preface, withdrawn by the Gissings[23] and replaced by an even more sanitized introduction by Frederic Harrison.[24] It was a crash-course in the pitfalls of biography, from both ends: revealing the dangers both for the subject and the writer. Wells never again attempted anything similar, until the death of F. W. Sanderson, the headmaster of Oundle, where he sent his two boys Gip and Frank. Wells's *The Story of a Great Schoolmaster* (1924) was his only full-length attempt at biography; yet it too brought to mind the all-too-earthly contingencies of writing about real people, being undertaken after his initial compilation of a memoir on Sanderson ran into problems with his widow.[25]

Biography is a blind art, shaped from all sides by circumstances. And autobiography, where it touches on other people—as all autobiography, as soon as the writer tries to depict anything outside his or her own self must do—is equally contingent, in ways that a novel is not. Biography and autobiography, as two different methods of writing about real and not invented people, share an intrinsic sociality and relationality. But they stand on opposing sides from their main subject. "Biographers," as Janice Biala told Ford's biographer Alan Judd, "are like blind men with their sticks."[26] The source material, even when overwhelming, is always fragmentary—more letters, friends, or diaries can always surface—and so the biographer is always working in the dark, from a viewpoint of eternally partial knowledge. Yet autobiographers also work in the dark at times, filling in the gaps and blanks of memory; and curiously, as Hermione Lee remarks, "biographers are supposed to know their subjects as well as or better than they knew themselves,"[27] even if their knowledge is completely different in texture, built up from facts, intuitions, and deductions, rather than the sensoria of lived experience. The relationship between biographer and subject—or between biographer and autobiographer—resembles that between the lawyer and the witness, or the detective and the suspect, with each side guessing what the other side might know.

When Wells, after years of writing autobiographical fiction, set out to write his autobiography, it was partly because he had been biographized by "Geoffrey West,"[28] in *H. G. Wells: A Sketch for a Portrait*, which appeared in 1930. As West wrote, Wells was an "ideal biographee,"[29] proving generously unobstructive; Wells, meanwhile, wrote that he "kept nothing back of any importance"[30] from West, and would read the book to correct it, but only "for any slip in the facts."[31] Wells's interests in education and science meant that he saw biography, from a factual point of view, as scientific. He learned more about himself, as West's researches dug up old letters and associations, many of which he had forgotten. Wells likewise saw that to set the record in the future as he wished, he would have to write his own version of his life. His autobiography eventually became a trilogy—but he had no idea at the outset that it would.

*

Wells wrote the first pages of the *Experiment in Autobiography* in the spring of 1932. He was sixty-five, and had led more lives—sometimes simultaneously—than are usually squeezed into one earthly existence. A superhuman energy, vigor, and ability to bury his emotions lay beneath what he always felt was his rather unassuming physique: he was small, with tiny feet, piercing blue eyes, and a squeaky, high-pitched voice. What he called his "*Drive*"[32] had propelled him, just as his early fictions propelled their narrators far beyond the everyday, irrevocably out of the successive orbits of his life, which was by then largely split between a London flat at 47 Chiltern Court near Baker Street, and the villa, Lou Pidou, he built at Saint Mathieu near Grasse in Provence, with his lover Odette Keun. In recent years, other people had been falling away from him. His second wife, Amy Catherine, or "Jane" as he called her, had died in 1927 from cancer; after her death, he had sold the house, Easton Glebe in Essex, where his family had lived since 1912. His first wife Isabel died in 1931, as did his close friend Arnold Bennett. Another friend, Frank Swinnerton, recalled seeing H. G. in 1931, and finding him crying as he read Bennett's obituary in the newspapers.[33] This glimpse of an emotional outpouring, giving way to sorrow, is remarkable precisely because it is so rare and "out of character."

His solution to emotion was work. He pushed hard that year on *The Work, Wealth and Happiness of Mankind*, the last part of his trilogy on history, biology, and economics. By the early months of 1932, wintering at Lou Pidou, he was also writing a novel, *The Bulpington of Blup: Adventures, Poses, Stresses, Conflicts, and Disaster in a Contemporary Brain*. Finished quickly, that July, it lampooned his old friend Ford Madox Ford under the veneer of its central character, Theodore Bulpington, a "liar in a world of lies"[34]—a deluded coward and self-mythologizer who shapes his life, "past and future, just as I please."[35] It seems an odd time for this attack; Wells was very likely prompted by Ford's recent reminiscences in *Return to Yesterday*, published around the same period. In the novel, Wells skewers the discrepancy between Theodore, and his self-conception or ideal self—a gulf which widens horribly, as Theodore's tragicomic life comes to nothing, and he preserves his own delusions. All his life, Wells was suspicious of people who "romanced" their existence, people who pretended, as he clearly thought Ford did. All his life, Wells was obsessed with facing facts. His view of life and character was more direct and "scientific." Even during the war, as he wrote his journalism, propaganda, and novels, split mostly between London and Essex, Wells had tried to remain pragmatic to the last degree. He never allowed things to fester. He never got stuck in a rut. This was a huge factor in his success.

But by the 1930s, he was beginning to face obstacles which even he found insurmountable. Facing facts is easier when the facts being faced can be changed or at least understood; and over these years, Wells would learn, first-hand, the refuge in a protective self-ideal. In the *Experiment in Autobiography*—subtitled *Discoveries and Conclusions of a Very Ordinary Brain (Since 1866)*—he began with a passage written "one wakeful night [...] between two and five in the early morning"[36] that spring of 1932. His disquiet, anguish, and impatience are palpable, if mysteriously offstage, as he sketches out his character at this point in time: what he goes on to elaborate, via Jung, as his *persona*.

> I need freedom of mind. I want peace for work. I am distressed by immediate circumstances. My thoughts and work are encumbered by claims and vexations and I cannot see any hope of release from them; any hope of a period of serene and beneficent activity, before I am overtaken altogether by infirmity and death [...] I am putting even the pretence of other work aside in an

attempt to deal with this situation. I am writing a report about it—to myself.
I want to get these discontents clear because I have a feeling that as they
become clear they will either cease from troubling me or become manageable
and controllable.[37]

In the *Experiment*, continued throughout 1933 and 1934, Wells tried to write
and think his way out of the situation which brought about this state of
mind. (Note how many times the word "work" is mentioned in that opening
paragraph.) The book was an experiment not only with the form and content
of autobiography, but with its effect on the writer. It was a performance
staged in real time, enacted for the sake of his own healing. He wanted it to
be a "dissection": an almost scientific analysis of his brain and its impulses,
motives, and sensations, as one sample specimen of humanity. He often
refers to this lump of grey matter—"that organized mass of phosphorized
fat and connective tissue which is, so to speak, the hero of the piece"[38]—as
"it" in the third person, as if "it" didn't quite belong to him. Autobiography,
for Wells, was biology, as much as psychology. It was an empirical investigation
into the nature of character, and human behavior, using the only material he
had to hand: himself. The *Experiment* was a close act of self-scrutiny, during
which he professed to heal himself, and to make discoveries about his own
and others' nature.

As an autobiographer, Wells showed an unusual awareness—a disarming
frankness—about the problems and temptations of the genre. He laid them
openly out in full view: the lost zones of memory, the limitations of viewpoint, the constant urge to avoid or omit. "You will discover a great deal of
evasion and refusal in my story,"[39] he writes early on. Such barefaced admission
creates the impression of absolute honesty. He also points to places where
he has been tempted to skip: "a few tactful omissions would smooth out the
record beautifully."[40] As for memory's tricks, he displays none of the sensuous
amazement of Henry James in his autobiographies. He treats his brain as a
piece of hardware, which forgets when there are no connecting links between
memories, or when a memory has not been revisited for long stretches of
time. There is no psychological reason for forgetting or remembering, Wells
writes, disavowing subconscious suppressions. When he forgets, "it is merely
that the links are feeble and the printing of the impressions bad. It is a
case of second-rate brain fabric [...] If my mental paths are not frequently
traversed and refreshed they are obstructed."[41]

Wells saw his duty as an autobiographer to be absolutely frank. Yet
from the start, he fell prey to the pattern-forming impulse inherent in all

life-writing. He was always strong on the outlines of his books, often preferring the stage when he planned and mapped out his plots, to the phase of actual writing. His motto, when seeing the very different compositional methods of Rebecca West, was "Construct, Construct";[42] and the skeletons of even his weakest books are so strong they stand up straight regardless of the prose. From the outset of the *Experiment*, Wells knew what the overall narrative arc would be. It was to depict a gradually broadening outlook, as the hero moved from the lowly surroundings of his Victorian upbringing "in a shabby bedroom over the china shop that was called Atlas House in High Street, Bromley, Kent,"[43] to his eventual status as a citizen of the world. It was to glide from the particular to the general, with Wells a mere part in a wider social frame, as he stumbled "from a backyard to Cosmopolis; from Atlas House to the burthen of Atlas"[44]—with struggles and adventures along the way.

By his own admission, his own development as a novelist had made him more interested in the "splintering frame"[45] of the society surrounding his characters, than in the characters themselves. He knew he could make full use of this in the autobiography, using this angle to deflect the intrinsic egotism of the genre; and also giving a wider portrait of the era. "An autobiography," Wells writes, "is the story of the contacts of a mind and a world."[46] And his own trajectory, progressing from poverty, through the British scientific, educational, journalistic, and political worlds of the early twentieth century, took in an unusually diverse array of spheres. It connected the invisible cultural and political lines reaching from the Socialism of William Morris and the Pre-Raphaelites, to the Fabians and the rise of Marxist sympathy on the Left with Russia, while also tracing the shifting grounds of art and science through this seminal period.

Wells likewise had a strong sense of the *persona* he wanted to reflect. His *persona*, he writes, is a frame of mind in which he can work uninterruptedly towards his aim of service to the World-State. (This ever-elusive utopian dream was much—perhaps too much—in Wells's mind after the First World War.)[47] It is a vision of work unencumbered by life: in a resonant image of the split between life and art, he compares himself to a toad, with the crystal of an idea. Wells took the term *persona* from Jung, adapting it slightly, and using it variably, noting that all *personas* fluctuate. Yet the main divergence from Jung, Michael Draper argues, lies in Wells's idea of the *persona* as something desirable, where Jung sees it more in negative, delusory terms.[48] In *The Bulpington of Blup*, Wells extensively mocked the strain of wishful self-delusion he saw in Ford; yet in his own autobiography, he built the entire structure of the narrative around his own equally abstract self-ideal. Oddly, he believed in it, almost religiously, and enshrined it in his life-story, while retaining an awareness that it was a self-deluding fiction.

If this *persona* represented an end or vanishing point towards which Wells saw the autobiography as heading—even from its conception—he also soon became aware that there would be hurdles in his account of how he got there. The tone of the *Experiment* from its very opening is unforgiving, brutally honest and self-analytical. But he could only apply such total frankness to himself, and it was in his depictions of others that he thought he would face his greatest obstacles. In early phases of the writing, he planned to cut the story of his life short at 1900. Most of his letters in 1932 were unusually discreet, if not downright secretive about the autobiography, as he mentioned other ongoing projects such as *The Shape of Things to Come* and his subsequent work on the film *Things to Come* with Alexander Korda. But Wells did write in January 1933 to S. S. Koteliansky, doubting that the autobiography at this stage could go on further than 1900, "because that would involve an intimate discussion of quite a number of living people."[49]

How was he to get from 1900 to his *persona*? Wells did find an answer to this initially central problem of the autobiography. But his first solution was to draw out the early part of the book, and the years before his birth, turning the courtship of his parents—Sarah the lady's-maid in the country house at Up Park,[50] and Joseph the gardener at the estate—into something like a mini-novel. So, after the early passages of analysis, the mode of static, dissection-like self-disclosure gives way to narrative, as Wells turned his early years into a rattling story: a mixture of Jane Austen, say, and one of his own social realist comedies. His childhood, as he portrays it once he enters this tale in Atlas House, is a sustained attempt to escape from his upbringing by two servants-turned-shopkeepers. His progress is a series of "fugitive impulses";[51] and the only initial escape is illness, or broken limbs.

A fall on a tent peg at a cricket match (his father was a talented cricketer) breaks H. G.'s tibia at "seven or eight"[52]—the accident is seen as a stroke of luck, which gave him time to read.[53] A later smashed kidney and the onset of tuberculosis is likewise recast, as a chance to write. Wells recounts, with some humor, all his false "starts in life":[54] apprenticeship at fourteen as a draper with Rodgers and Denyer in Windsor; a spell with the chemist Samuel Cowap; another draper's apprenticeship at Southsea; Grammar School in Midhurst; a scholarship to study science at South Kensington.

Like his early fiction, it is a story of survival, with Wells only falteringly finding his feet. And the self-portrait gives both the history of his brain, and of his body. He provides a verbal sketch of his anatomy at twenty, still marked by early poverty, showing "what sort of body it was that carried this brain about and supplied it with blood":[55]

> By 1887, it had become a scandalously skinny body. I was five foot five and always I weighed less than eight stone. My proper weight should have been 9 st. 11 lbs., but I was generally nearer to seven, and that in my clothes. And they were exceedingly shabby clothes [...] I would survey my naked body, so far as my bedroom looking-glass permitted, with extreme distaste [...] There were hollows under the clavicles, the ribs showed.[56]

This forms the prelude to his first, failed marriage, to his cousin Isabel; and a new series of fugitive impulses and false starts which dominate his life, while he became a teacher, and then a journalist and writer. Wells's two marriages, to Isabel, then to "Jane," start to occupy the center of the frame— in conflict with his self-avowed *persona*. Wells was fascinated, even obsessed, by the irrationality he had shown in his romantic attachments; and as the *Experiment* progressed, he set to a much closer investigation of this behavior. The closer he looked at his romantic and sexual life, however—the more he analyzed emotions and feelings, through kept letters, that were fixed at one point in a now distant present—the more he felt bafflement and intrigue.

*

H. G. Wells's autobiography suggests that we are strangers to our later selves. Letters, often written shortly before and after the time of the things they relate, provide glimpses of evidence that surprise autobiographers, whose tone is always affected by the amount of time separating them from the self they depict. In writing his *Experiment*, Wells shifted between passages about the present of the writing, and recollections of more distant events. But his *persona* only cohered when he stood further away from it. The image of the self he discovered was pointillist, or like an Impressionist painting. It made perfect sense from far away, but dissolved when examined up close. Indeed, it even depended on a lack of close scrutiny.

Wells easily turned the story of his parents' marriage into a novelistic narrative, since it occurred so long ago, before he was even born. But revisiting old letters, photographs, and shards of passions from thirty or forty years earlier, he could not quite make sense of them, was bemused by his own inconsistencies. His self, as it emerged, was a swarming constellation of impulses, tangled, protean, in flux, contradicting each other under the microscope. To depict it, in the opening of the second volume of the *Experiment*, Wells paused, rewound the narrative slightly, raking back over his relations with Isabel and "Jane," both now dead, "as though I were a portrait painter taking a fresh canvas and beginning over again."[57] Breaking the flow of his progress from student to teacher to writer, he told of anomalies disrupting that life-story. He recounts how he made love with his wife's assistant one day after he was married to Isabel; how he still wanted Isabel after their divorce, when he was settled at Spade House with "Jane." So his fugitive impulses returned, in new forms.

For "Jane," there was not only the evidence of letters, but of "picshuas": the pen-and-ink cartoons Wells drew for her over the years. He reproduced some "picshuas" in the *Experiment*, using them to tell the inner domestic life of their long marriage. They skew the portrait of their relationship, as he wanted, emphasizing its foundation in companionship, humor, and tolerance, rather than great sexual passion. He calls these off-the-cuff self-caricatures, of which hundreds "accumulated in boxes,"[58] "a sort of burlesque diary of our lives."[59] Fixed in the present tense of their drawing (many were done in an instant, ending up in the wastepaper basket), the "picshuas" reveal Wells's swiftness and economy of line as a caricaturist, along with his comical role-playing and nicknaming. They show the sense of fun which balanced his "*Drive*." Spontaneous, exuberant, and relentless, they are also evidence of an overproduction of selves.

As the *Experiment* begins to show, Wells had many names, and he always gave nicknames to others around him. To his family, he was the "Buzzwhacker" or "Buss" or "Bussums" as well as "Bertie." With Isabel, he was "Buzzums" to her "Izzums." In the "picshuas," Wells was "Bins" or "Mr. Bins"—a Cockney contraction he derived from "Husbinder" or "'Usbinder," shortened to "Mr. Binder" and eventually "Bins."[60] "Jane" became "Bits or Miss Bits or Snitch or It, with variations."[61] One of the many slightly unhinged, madcap "Pomes" or poems in the *Experiment* showed how much Jane, as Wells writes with dry humor, "was being, to use Henry James's word 'treated', for mental assimilation":[62]

CHANSON

> It *was* called names
> Miss Furry Boots and Nicketty and Bits,
> And P.C.B., and Snitterlings and Snits,
> It was called names.

Such names as no one but a perfect 'Orror
Could ever fink or find or beg or borror
Names out of books or names made up to fit it
In wild array
It never knew when some new name might hit it
From day to day
Some names it's written down and some it 'as forgotten
Some names was nice and some was simply ROTTEN [...]
It was called names.[63]

Such skits were more than a joke. Deciphering these exhibits and "picshuas" in the *Experiment*, Wells describes them as deflating self-dramatizations. Like *Boon* in spirit—and *Boon* was his only other book published with "picshuas" in it—they also had their serious side, offering psychological insights in comical form. Sometimes, the picshuas were completely explicit about their role in the circuits of self-delusion and self-portraiture: one "Satirical Picshua" in the *Experiment* centered on the discrepancy between "Bits as she *finks* she is," and on another page, "The real Bits."[64] Another, done in 1910 at a time of crisis in the marriage, as Gene and Margaret Rinkel write, was entitled "Bits Under the Microscope," showing "the biologist, Bins, in his lab coat," while he "examines a highly magnified image of little Bits."[65]

For all the humor in the picshuas, skits, and "pomes" to Jane, Wells's portrayal of their marriage in the *Experiment* became as frank as he thought he could make it. He writes of the arrangement they came to, whereby she granted him freedom to seek sexual gratification elsewhere; he also says that, much as this arrangement worked, it had its imperfections. Wells's portrait of "Jane" is precisely that: a portrait of her as she was with the name he gave her. Amy Catherine remains an elusive figure. We never discover how she coped with the constraints her life with Wells put on her. Although Wells writes of her self-sacrifice, something appears to be missing in his perception, in his emotions. The two-dimensionality of the "picshuas" hints at deeper patterns of thought and feeling in his many dissimilar selves.

If, as Janet Malcolm writes of biography, recalling E. M. Forster's distinction in *Aspects of the Novel* (1927), there are always "flat characters"[66] in the background, all the characters in the "picshuas" are quintessentially "flat." Just as Wells sometimes found it hard to inhabit and see right through to his characters in fiction, the recurrent playfulness and superficiality of the portraiture in the *Experiment*—which by its second half is a gallery of the people Wells knew—suggests that he sometimes failed to fully appreciate or understand other characters in life. His perception is comic, sharp, unemotional. The portraits of Gissing, Bennett, and Stephen Crane, among others, are vivid, but without nuance. As Wells reflected on James's critique of his novel *Marriage* (1912), perhaps he, H. G., "had not cared enough about these individualities."[67]

Wells draws attention to this lack. It underlies his account of his gradual rift with James, Conrad, and Ford, all of whom he saw fairly often while living in Kent from 1898–1909. Wells's divergence from these Impressionists—which evolved into a skepticism about being a novelist at all—was rooted not only in his belief in content over style, but in the very way he saw things. Throughout the *Experiment*, Wells often wonders if his own senses are not somehow less strong than those of many people he knew. At one point, he recalls sitting on the beach at Sandgate, next to Conrad, as they argue about how to depict the boat they are both looking at.

> How, he demanded, would I describe how that boat out there, sat or rode or danced or quivered on the water? I said that in nineteen cases out of twenty I would just let the boat be there in the commonest phrases possible [. . .] But it was all against Conrad's over-sensitized receptivity that a boat could ever be just a boat. He wanted to see it with a definite vividness of its own.[68]

The anecdote pinpoints the different prose styles of the two writers; but it goes further, spilling over into their lives. Wells suggests that the "strength of reception"[69] of his own brain was more matter-of-fact than "these vivid writers" with "their abundant, luminous impressions."[70] And indeed in the *Experiment*, Wells depicts Conrad with a certain comic shallowness, as if his Polishness and seriousness were just a role or pose. Wells saw none of the absurd laughter in Conrad that Ford understood; Wells's portrait of Conrad in the *Experiment* laughs at his expense. Conrad, Wells writes, had "acquired an incurable tendency to pronounce the last *e* in these and those. He would say, '*Wat* shall we do with *thesa* things?'"[71]

He finds Conrad's prose over-wrought; he says he agrees with Conrad's own judgment of *The Mirror of the Sea* as his favorite book. "At first he impressed me," writes Wells of Conrad, "as he impressed Henry James, as the strangest of creatures. He was rather short and round-shouldered with his head as it were sunken into his body. He had a dark retreating face with a very carefully trimmed and pointed beard, a trouble-wrinkled forehead and very troubled dark eyes."[72] Wells recalls that he first met Conrad at the Pent, "and my first impression [. . .] was of a swarthy face peering out and up through the little window panes [. . .] We never really 'got on' together."[73]

As for Ford, Wells thinks he is under-rated, but says his recent autobiography *It Was the Nightingale* shows his "extraordinary drift towards self-dramatization"[74] since he changed his name after the war. He depicts Ford, in words that apply much more to himself, as "a great system of assumed personas and dramatized selves."[75]

The most sustained portrait of a writer-acquaintance in the *Experiment* is of Henry James, whose presence hovers over Wells whenever he turns his thoughts towards the art of the novel. But Wells cannot resist the impulse to have some laughs at James's expense—his account of seeing *Guy Domville* (1895) on his first night as a theater reviewer shows more relish than it should in its impersonation of the stilted dialogue: "Be keynd to Her . . . *Be* keynd to Her."[76] Wells's James is a curiosity, "a strange unnatural human being, a sensitive man lost in an immensely abundant brain."[77] He is an over-elaborate phenomenon, beside whom Wells feels uncouthly direct. But the reverence is clear, as James's very mention leads Wells in the *Experiment* into a prolonged justification of his own "*scamped*"[78] or rushed work.

James, along with the other Impressionist writers, forces Wells to consider what he thinks about the aesthetics of the novel—and ultimately leads him to his self-definition as a journalist, the label he defiantly gave himself when he parted ways with these artistic types. ("I write as I walk because I want to get somewhere and I write as straight as I can, just as I walk as straight as I can, because that is the best way to get there."[79]) And Wells also argues defensively that there are more kinds of novels and stories to tell, than the Jamesian method of depicting "deep and round and solid" characters—a method which "no more exhausts the possibilities of the novel, than the art of Velasquez exhausts the possibilities of the painted picture."[80] For the literary study of character, Wells writes, perhaps the forms of biography and autobiography are ultimately more suitable than the novel.

> Who would read a novel if we were permitted to write biography—all out? Here in this autobiography I am experimenting—though still very mildly, with biographical and auto-biographical matter. Although it has many restraints, which are from the artistic point of view vexatious, I still find it so much more real and interesting and satisfying that I doubt if I shall ever again turn back towards The Novel.[81]

However, Wells was partly to "scamp" the *Experiment*, too. He even tells us that he is rushing the book, as though he cannot slow down. After 1900, the building of Spade House with the architect C. F. A. Voysey—documented by photographs in the original edition—is not followed in the same key as the earlier pages. The last quarter of the autobiography swerves away from the in-depth frankness of the previous sections, as Wells leaves much of the action from 1900–34 offstage, moving doggedly towards his *persona* and the World-State.[82] Precisely at the point where his life became problematic and implicatory as regards other people, Wells made the *Experiment* a study of his work.

Partly, this was a matter of the "restraints" of autobiography. He recounts his increasing turn towards politics, propaganda, and polemical journalism during and after the war, and the evolution of his World-State ideal; yet the shadow of the personal stories submerged in the background spreads under all these discussions. The timeframe sweeps forward, leaving inexplicable gaps, until Wells reaches his climax: the interviews he conducted with Franklin D. Roosevelt and Joseph Stalin in 1934. The narrative ends as a travelogue. Wells visits America, and later flies to Russia with his son Gip on July 21, 1934, "reaching Moscow before dark on the evening of the 22nd."[83] By now, the book is a "psycho-political autobiography,"[84] with the two world leaders as prime exhibits. After an unsatisfying meeting with Stalin, Wells flies to Tallinn. "I am finishing this autobiography," he writes, "in a friendly and restful house beside a little lake in Esthonia...."[85] The *Experiment*, having caught up with the present again, is deemed a success.

> I began this autobiography primarily to reassure myself during a phase of fatigue, restlessness and vexation, and it has achieved its purpose of reassurance. I wrote myself out of that mood of discontent and forgot myself and a mosquito swarm of bothers in writing about my sustaining ideas. My ruffled *persona* has been restored and the statement of the idea of the modern world-state has reduced my personal and passing irritations and distractions to their proper insignificance. So long as one lives as an individual, vanities, lassitudes, lapses and inconsistencies will hover about and creep back into the picture, but I find nevertheless that this faith and service of constructive world revolution does hold together my mind.[86]

This *persona*, however, was more of a refuge for Wells than a true destination. It was not that Wells's politics and *persona* were not central to his later sense of himself—the entire second half of his life was concerned with them—but that they have somehow come adrift from reality. He mouths the words, here at the close of the autobiography, sleepwalking almost. Something much closer to home still appears to be bothering him.

*

When he began the *Experiment* in 1932, Wells was still a huge success. One biographer, Lovat Dickson, describes seeing Wells around this time, and his celebrity surrounds the portrayal like a spotlight. The biographer sees him instantly as the unmistakable figure that "the cartoonists had made familiar to us [...] Hardly a week passed when he was not in the news."[87] The finale of the two volumes of the *Experiment* offered a suitable self-portrait for this great public figure. And the two volumes were well-received, clearly fulfilling their public role as portraiture. But Wells was not satisfied for his *Experiment* to be left where it was.

Ever since Jane's death in 1927—even though they had lived apart for years, as Wells spent more and more time with Odette Keun in France through the 1920s—his personal life had been unraveling with alarming speed. Without Jane to be unfaithful to, Wells tried to install Odette in her place, as a satellite around which to orbit. But Odette was not keen to play such a subsidiary role; nor was she so suitable. Wells only spent time in France with her; he never saw her in London. By 1932, Odette's volatility was also becoming unbearable to Wells, who seems, for all his desperation, to have conducted the affair for many years in the spirit of farce. When he began to transfer his emotions, rather confusedly, to Moura Budberg, whom he had met years earlier on another Russian trip, Odette became vehemently jealous. There are many conflicting accounts of the eventual rift. Ultimately, Anthony West writes, Odette threw Wells out of Lou Pidou.[88] By 1932–3, while he was working things out in the *Experiment*, H. G. was, he thought, now fully with Moura. He wanted marriage: but she didn't. Early in 1934, with the autobiography coming closer to its premature end, they stayed together in Bournemouth for almost a month. And by July that year, Wells set off with Gip to Russia, for his interview with Stalin. He said goodbye to Moura at Croydon airport. She was going to Estonia, where they agreed to meet soon at Kallijärv—where Wells, as he says, finished the autobiography.

If the *Experiment*'s ending felt scamped and evasive, this was largely due to what was going on in Wells's life at the time of the writing. Wells made a discovery in Moscow, which had nothing to do with his *persona* or the World-State. At Maxim Gorky's house, a stray remark by his interpreter revealed to him that Moura had just been in Moscow, at Gorky's very house, days earlier, without telling him. She had, it seemed, also been to Russia several other times that year—also without telling him.

In Estonia, he confronted Moura as to the truth. She lied, then wouldn't give him a straight answer. To this day, Moura remains a biographer's—and autobiographer's—sphinx. She was a spy, although it remains unclear for how many sides. Some of the men in her life before Wells included Gorky and the British agent Robert Bruce Lockhart, and indeed she had been seeing both men during all her time with Wells, and her relationships with both of them went deeper than her feelings for Wells.[89] Contemporaries all agreed on one thing: her serenity—yet this serenity came out of danger. Potential exposure was always imminent. Andrea Lynn writes that Nina Berberova, in her biography of Moura, "alleged that in Moscow, Moura was thought to be a secret agent for England; in Estonia, a Soviet spy; in France, Russian émigrés believed that she worked for Germany; and in England, she was regarded as an agent for Moscow."[90] If the tangles of Wells's love life in later years, as we will see, reached an innate profusion, he had met his match in Moura, who was possibly planted on him. The calmness at the end of the *Experiment* was feigned. He was on deadline to finish the text. His *persona* was far more scattered than when he had begun. He kept on at Moura in Kallijärv to tell him the truth, but it appears she never did. His distress in the second half of 1934 became frighteningly real. As Gip writes, the shock of disillusion with Moura "was followed by a deep, nearly suicidal depression. Slowly he worked himself out of it. The self analysis involved in the writing of the Postscript, which he then undertook, played a major part in his recovery."[91] Autobiography, once again, was the cure.

The *Experiment* was published in its two volumes that autumn; Wells now set to writing his life all over again in a "Postscript" to that text: this time recounting the things that were left out. He had reached right up to the present in the *Experiment*, but that didn't mean he couldn't retell his life-story. This Postscript forms the central part of H. G.'s new autobiography, which he knew would have to be published after his death—and after the deaths of the other people he now wished to include. The resulting text was edited and published in 1984 by Gip with the title *H. G. Wells in Love*. Gip writes in his introduction that this book was assembled from a mass of papers left unpublished at Wells's death in 1946. It is a compilation, consisting of Wells's elegiac introduction to *The Book of Catherine Wells* (1927), and the two main sections of the Postscript: "On Loves and the Lover-Shadow" and "The Last Phase." Gip also tells us that the Postscript was begun in late 1934. Wells drew a characteristically strong outline, then wrote the text "straight through [...] until he got to the words THE END, and doubly underlined them, on May 2nd, 1935."[92] Wells rewrote the text "a dozen times in eighteen months until, on September 18th, 1936, he wrote THE END for the last time, accompanied by a note, later deleted, 'On which date I am strongly disposed to write Finis to it all'."[93]

Yet as the dates strewn throughout the text in *H. G. Wells in Love* indi-
cate, this Postscript remained constantly in revision even later through
the 1930s—Wells kept on reviewing these pages obsessively, almost to
atone for his scamping of the *Experiment*. As this process went on—as
Andrea Lynn writes, with H. G. fussing "over his personal love history,
writing and rewriting it intermittently over a period of eight years—and
in his tiny, often illegible handwriting, to what must have been the horror
of his secretary and daughter-in-law, Marjorie Wells [Gip's wife], who typed
his manuscripts"[94]—a mass of extra material, placed in folders marked
"rejected" or "deleted" or "discarded" was generated. And there was also
much material in the final version which Gip was forced to cut, mainly due
to concerns over libel.[95]

In one phrase from these deleted pages, Wells defines his project thus:
"Let me, to make sure that no one misses my point, repeat that this Postscript
is not full autobiography; it is autobiography strictly below the belt."[96] He
wanted it to be published and bound together with the two volumes of the
Experiment, turning the whole into a trilogy. But where the *Experiment* tells
the story of his two marriages and his *persona*, the tale which Wells unveils
in the Postscript is of his "Lover-Shadow": the force which constantly pulls
the other way from his *persona*, settling on one object of sexual desire after
another. The Postscript takes up the story of Wells's life once again from
1900, restructuring it as a search for fulfilment with a succession of different
women. First is Jane, given pride of place, as Wells tries to see her now as
Amy Catherine. Then come affairs with Violet Hunt, Dorothy Richardson,
Amber Reeves or "Dusa," Elizabeth von Arnim or "Little e," Rebecca West,
Odette Keun, and Moura Budberg. This series is itself a tidy simplification
of the *passades* and encounters which occurred in Wells's life. As Andrea Lynn
writes, following hints in David C. Smith's biography, there were also at least
two major later passions: Constance Coolidge and Martha Gellhorn—the
latter tantalizingly glimpsed in *H. G. Wells in Love* as *****. In his "Note
about the Publication of this Postscript," Wells gives his instructions for the
posthumous assembly, suggesting a delay until "Moura and Dusa are either
dead or consenting,"[97] for "***** won't mind."[98] ("She did"[99] writes Gip.)[100]

It's easy to dismiss Wells's conception of his "Lover-Shadow," as some
critics have, as a woolly self-justification for bad behavior, or a scramble of
notions from Freud and Jung.[101] But in *H. G. Wells in Love*, it is very effectively
portrayed not so much as a theoretical abstraction, but a semi-visible metaphor
for sexual desire—almost a character of its own. And it fits into a larger scheme

of imagery. Like Proust's *madeleine*, the "Lover-Shadow" is primarily a novelistic idea, which works through association; it is always in flux, and is not a fixed concept.

Everywhere in these pages, love is seen as a game or performance. Wells writes about the games of charades and role-playing that used to go on at Spade House and Easton Glebe: little plays or shadow shows—"freakish quaint affairs, into which people threw themselves with astonishing zest."[102] Jane loved "dressing up,"[103] Wells recalls, as he tries to glimpse more of her ever-changing "facets": she excelled at these burlesques. His tone as he writes of them is playful, sinister, soft, like a pantomime. Sexuality and personality are glimpsed as a series of poses, selves, and disguises. All this prefigures the idea of the "Lover-Shadow." Trying to give a more searching portrait of Jane, Wells clutches at the successive outer layers of her dress, before he portrays the other self glimpsed in her writings. Character, Wells implies, is, like the self, most clearly glimpsed as an outline or shadow. Just as the self dissolves under the microscope, sexual attraction and the Lover-Shadow—in all their endless clothes and performances—become a baffling series of intermittent impulses, as Wells recounts the affairs which occurred during his marriage to Jane, all excised from his earlier self-portrait.

These appear to begin harmlessly enough, as Wells is keen to insist, retelling the story of the *Experiment* after 1900, making his *passades* and amorous adventures seem like mere sport. Writing of his relationship with Violet Hunt, for example—who was relatively unrevealing about Wells in *The Flurried Years*—Wells makes everything sound cool and rational:

> I met Violet Hunt, a young woman a little older than myself, who had already written and published several quite successful novels. She had a nervous lively wit laced with threads of French [...] We talked of social questions, literary work, and the discomforts and restlessness of spinsterhood [...] we came to an understanding, and among other things she taught me were the mysteries of Soho and Pimlico. We explored the world of convenient little restaurants with private rooms upstairs [...] we lunched and dined together and found great satisfaction in each other's embraces.[104]

But even by the time he writes of the fiascos beneath his tangles with the Fabian Society, and the birth of his child with Amber Reeves, the willed impression of a carefree lack of consequences becomes harder to sustain.[105] With Rebecca West—with whom H. G. had another child, Anthony, born "on a memorable date, August 4th, 1914,"[106] and who would also much later write his father's biography—part of the tint on her portrait came from the raw pain on his side, as he underplays a relationship which had only fizzled out in the 1920s. West, Wells writes, became pregnant very early in their affair: "It was entirely unpremeditated. Nothing of the sort was our intention [...] and when we found ourselves linked by this living tie, we knew hardly anything of each other. We were all, Jane included, taken by surprise [...] We came to like each other extremely and to be extremely exasperated with each other and antagonistic."[107]

The Lover-Shadow continues its relentless role, but H. G.'s portrayal of love as a pantomimic charade or shadow-show—an affair of endlessly, playfully shifting silhouettes and poses—eventually puts the narrative, and his own life, under severe strain. A woman in the 1920s tried to commit suicide in his room, as he tells, with an ostentatious frankness. And his experience of betrayal with Moura is agony.

In wanting to bind this third layer of autobiography to the earlier two volumes of the *Experiment*, Wells was aiming at a particular aesthetic effect: a "stereoscopic self-portrait,"[108] depicting the several sides of his life simultaneously. But this stereoscopic effect, while increasing our vision, makes large parts of the *Experiment* feel like a sham, as the three parts of the whole rub together. As a trilogy, the third volume radically exposes the fraudulence, omission, and evasion in the first two books. Retelling events which appeared before in different guises, as Wells runs over the same patch of ground from new angles, induces a kind of vertigo. It opens up the void beneath all biography and autobiography, if not beneath all lives, and invites us to peer in. It is like the moment in a marriage where the so-called truth comes pouring out, after years of mutual silence. Wells has not been withholding one secret, but a whole sequence of affairs which, as they multiply, show nothing so much as their own essential profligacy. He wants to be frank as an autobiographer—writing, for instance, in his account of his relationship with Rosamund Bland, that "I would rather I had not to tell of it,"[109] before going ahead and telling. He makes us keenly aware of his autobiographical duty to tell all. The more he tells, however, the more one merely suspects the double bluff. His honesty has the duplicitous effect of revealing earlier gaps and lies. This opens up an insatiable craving for truth, an insatiable doubt. Can anyone tell all? At what point would one stop?

Where the climax of the *Experiment* lies in Wells's reassertion of his *persona* and the World-State, the narrative climax of the Postscript is the revelation of Moura's duplicity. As the story reaches Russia once again, the Moscow crisis is told with verve: pages of fevered dialogue and anxious soliloquy which seem torn from a spy romance. This is the point towards which the Lover-Shadow narrative has been heading with a terrible inevitability: Wells giving everything, all his emotions, to a woman whose job it might be to deceive him. After all the affairs and *passades,* the story has the classic arc of tragedy: an almost fatal comeuppance for hubris.

> I was wounded as I had never been wounded by any human being before. It was unbelievable. I lay in bed and wept like a disappointed child. Or I prowled about in my sitting-room and planned what I should do with the rest of my life, that I had hoped so surely to spend with her. I realized to the utmost that I had become a companionless man.[110]

Wells's terrifying dream of Moura as a hollow shell, which he recounts in the Postscript, is also an inevitable realization of his drama of the Lover-Shadow. The excavations of the self and of love which Wells performs throughout the *Experiment* and *H. G. Wells in Love* pull tighter and tighter in their interest, precisely at the speed at which the narratives on which they are built begin to unspool. The movement of this story—learning less and less about someone at exactly the same time as one learns more; knowing less and less about someone, the closer one comes in intimacy and even love—gave no points of traction for Wells's endless "*Drive*" to get at. His despair during the 1930s, and the intellectual and emotional impatience which also gave rise to his strange book *The Anatomy of Frustration* (1936), and later, to the thesis collected in *'42 to '44: a Contemporary Memoir* (1944)—in which the self is depicted as so unstable as to be an almost total illusion[111]—probably came from the impossibility of finding a solution to the *impasse* to which his late life and loves had brought him.

As his biographer David C. Smith writes, Wells's obsessive interest in his own sexual passions and love life has been misunderstood: "Most biographies of HGW skate fairly quickly over his personal and sexual life, often exhibiting distaste."[112] Yet Wells wanted to bind it into his own life-story. In doing so, he was, on one level, merely pursuing the biological slant which he asserted as one of his main purposes as an autobiographer, and also defining his self in keeping with his interest in Freud, Jung, and psychoanalysis. But the need to understand the essence of his fugitive sexual impulses was also more compulsive, multiple, unstoppable.

In the autobiographies, Wells tried to understand how he came to his *impasse*, and how to get out of it. The Postscript also became an attempt to confirm his self-image after betrayal by Moura, and a search for motives, as his jealousy over Moura tormented him. The text itself recounts how he worked himself out of jealousy: one day, he says, after he had also cured himself through further infidelity, Moura's spell just evaporated. He shows this process at work even before this magical moment, recounting his affair with an "American widow."[113]

At the end of 1934, despite their disagreements, H. G. and Moura planned to fly to Sicily for a winter holiday; due to bad weather, they landed in Marseilles, and ended up spending Christmas week with Somerset Maugham at his Villa Mauresque in the South of France. That winter, after Moura went back to England, and Wells stayed in France, he began this other affair. When Moura returned, "the three of us met, and we got on extremely well together. We made excursions; we lunched and dined together and went over to Maugham's to lunch. To the vivid interest of Maugham."[114] Wells has almost regained equilibrium. But the account of Moura in the Postscript continues in asides and dated notes in the text, implying that they kept up an off-on relationship, which meant more to him than to her, throughout H. G.'s last years. Much as Wells deplored self-delusion, once he saw that Moura wouldn't tell him who she was, he seems to have wanted to remain on the surface and to delude himself in his relations with her. In the last, cantankerous years of his life, he appears to have been forced to accept this. This is one subtext of *H. G. Wells in Love*. "We both had a very clear sense of the incurable complexity of individual life; its sustaining pretences and false simplifications,"[115] Wells writes in the Postscript. "The invincible ego lies below mask after mask, even hiding from itself [...] Why go down to that? Why doubt that a woman has a heart until you have torn it out?"[116]

Wells was left with surfaces. This was a logical progression for a self whose very depths consisted of a series of two-dimensional poses; the final destination of a notion of love which was essentially a series of sexual encounters. In late life, he had moved so far beyond his roots, that he didn't know what else to do, but to keep on spinning further away from them. This often looked like evasion—as G. K. Chesterton said, "whenever I met H. G. he always seemed to be coming from somewhere rather than going anywhere"[117]—but it was also part of his endless attempt to face facts. He found solace in writing. He used the autobiographies to shed and commune with earlier selves, and with earlier lives. Just as in his fiction, he drew close to the present, using his pages to help work things through, often almost while they were happening. This allowed Wells, as in a pivotal scene in *William*

Clissold—where the hero talks aloud to himself in the "swaying, jangling, creaking compartment"[118] of a hurtling train across Europe from Geneva to Paris—to "Get it plain. Write it down. Get it plain. Write it down."[119] But it was also a lonely solution.

*

In his essay "How Do Diaries End?," Philippe Lejeune argues that auto-biographies, unlike diaries, always have a fixed end point, in the time of their writing. "An autobiography," writes Lejeune, "is virtually finished as soon as it begins, since the story that you begin must end at the moment that you are writing it. You know the end point of the story, because you have reached it, and everything you write will lead up to this point, explaining how you got there."[120] Autobiographies have moments where the past catches up with the present: the two tenses touch, and bring the story of one's life up to date with the story of the writing. Often, these crossing-points signal that the text is near its end. In H. G.'s case, however, his autobiographies are strewn throughout with crossing-points: especially in the revisions of the Postscript, which interlace the past and present, in a constellation of reflections from different places in his life.

In their rewritings, the autobiographies proved essentially unfinishable: retelling over and over again, before finally entering the present like a diary. In "The Last Phase" of the Postscript, the compulsiveness of Wells's autobiographical impulse meant that even after having finished and refin-ished his posthumous passages on the Lover-Shadow, he still has things about himself he wants to say. The writing edges closer to a journal. As this "Looseleaf Diary" appears in *H. G. Wells in Love*, it runs to a little over twenty pages, with short entries separated by greater ellipses and gaps of time, as Wells kept it more and more sporadically. There is over half a decade compressed in these notes, which offer a chronicle of the ever-shortening distance before death, with the notes crossing over through the present to look ahead to the approaching end. Time appears to be speeding up, as entries dealing with *The Anatomy of Frustration* and Korda's film of *Things to Come* slip away and segue into entries from the end of the 1930s. The marks become a log of old age and ailments—a medical diary—with increasing noting of dates as Wells crawls towards the finish line, now living in his last house at Hanover Terrace, seeing in the Second World War in his seven-ties. The last entry is dated April 28, 1942; and the "Looseleaf Diary" ends with a space left by Wells for someone else to write his obituary, in a "Note by Another Hand."

Wells drew out his endings. He couldn't quite let go. He had exhausted the subject of himself, he thought. Yet he kept on thinking about it. And he kept on thinking about Moura. "I doubt if there is any other woman now for me in the world [...] at least that is how I feel now. I have, I realize, still to master this last phase of life [...] I feel the work I am doing now is worth while,"[121] he wrote in 1935. But Moura came and went as she pleased, an essential mystery. And he kept on writing, making journal entries for his posthumous book. There were various endings drafted for the Postscript, as Andrea Lynn tells us. One discarded ending, now lying in the Wells Archive at Illinois, was dedicated to a posthumous Lover-Shadow. By now, Wells was writing almost purely for the company of writing. By now, he was all on his own.

> I happen to be most damnably lonely to-night. I cannot sleep and I lack the vitality to turn my mind to other work. So I scribble here on and on and I shall wander about my flat and lie down and get up and scribble a bit more and so worry through the night. And the morning will come in due course and bring a sort of healing distraction with it. Even this night cannot last for ever. I shall shave and bath when the day comes [...] And it helps me a great deal, posthumous Lover-Shadow, to think that some day you will read what I am writing.[122]

Gertrude Stein and Alice B. Toklas, 5, rue Christine, 1945 by Cecil Beaton.
Source: © The Cecil Beaton Studio Archive at Sotheby's.

6

You are never yourself to yourself

Gertrude Stein

When I am I am I I.[1]

Gertrude Stein

In the winter of 1905 and the spring of 1906, Gertrude Stein sat eighty or ninety times for a portrait by the young Pablo Picasso in his studio at the ramshackle Bateau Lavoir in Montmartre. Each day she posed for the twenty-four-year-old painter, she left the atelier she shared with her older brother Leo in the rue de Fleurus in the afternoon. She was to turn thirty-two that February, and had only recently settled on her vocation as a writer, usually working alone at the table in the high-walled atelier after everyone had gone to bed, from the small hours of the morning until dawn. The sittings with Picasso were crucially formative to her burgeoning sense of herself as an artist. As the young Spaniard put down her portrait on the canvas, he not only gave her a new self-image, but provided a model of how an artist worked, a model which she studied day by day. The sittings were a two-way exchange: she modeled for him, while able to observe him, too. They were also the crucible for a close friendship between them which would last, on and off, the rest of their lives.

Years later in *The Autobiography of Alice B. Toklas* (1933), written during the summer of 1932, Stein mythologized the sittings, providing the only first-hand account of them, apart from her own other tellings.[2] She recalled the disorder of the studio during the first session, as she sat in a "large broken armchair,"[3] while Picasso "sat very tight on his chair and very close to his canvas."[4] His girlfriend Fernande Olivier read out from La Fontaine. During these repeated sessions, Stein, who was writing the story of Melanctha Herbert in what would be her first published book, *Three Lives* (1909), "meditated and made sentences,"[5] which she would muse on as she walked back to the rue de Fleurus. "She had come to like posing," she would write, "the long still hours followed by a long dark walk."[6]

In the *Autobiography*, Stein tells of Picasso's struggle with the portrait alongside the story of her own literary growth. As she writes, Picasso one day suddenly painted out her head—"I can't see you any longer when I look, he said irritably."[7] The portrait was headless all that summer of 1906 while Picasso was away, at Gósol in Spain, until on the day of his return to Paris, on the threshold of Cubism, he "sat down and out of his head painted the head in"[8] from memory, without any further sittings. Picasso's verdict on the portrait is given early in the *Autobiography*: "everybody says that she does not look like it but that does not make any difference, she will, he said."[9] Stein emphasizes how, when it was finished, she was also under way as a writer— *Three Lives* was also finished by then, she asserts, and she had begun *The Making of Americans*, which would occupy her for several years, not being published as a whole until 1925.

In the *Portrait of Gertrude Stein*, Picasso bestowed his own identity on Stein as much as hers. The head painted from memory was like Stein, but it was also a self-portrait of Picasso. The painter captured Stein's physical composure and poise: her large, settled presence and loose clothes which gave a statuesque interior balance and calm. Some of the expression is hers, betraying her ambition and resolute will; yet the sharpness and angularity of the lines, the urgency and fierce keenness of the pose, also call Picasso to mind. His prediction, as she told it, was correct. Stein did come to look like this, until as a historical figure, her image is tied to the portrait. In *Picasso* (1938), Stein retold the story of the sittings, concluding: "I was and I still am satisfied with my portrait, for me, it is I, and it is the only reproduction of me which is always I, for me."[10] She forged much of who she was from the painting, and was emotionally attached to it. She became its historian, the maker of the myths about its origins.

Portraiture is always a reciprocal, two-way process, although what is recorded is deceptively one-sided. The final painting presents the sum of all the exchanges between the painter and the model.[11] As Stein realized, the experience of sitting for a portrait is enclosed by psychological undercurrents on both sides. Before she left America for Paris in 1903, Stein had trained

at Harvard under William James in psychology, before continuing at Johns
Hopkins University in Baltimore. Her laboratory experiments in automatic
writing and habits of attention often involved a first-hand scrutiny of live
subjects—frequently, close friends or acquaintances who had volunteered
themselves—not unlike the scrutiny of models by painters. Stein's lifelong
interest in portraiture was underpinned by its closeness to her psychological
training. Where Leo, who had shared her interest in psychology, went on in
later life to have an obsessive interest in Freud, and self-analysis, Gertrude
abruptly abandoned science when she arrived in Paris. But she never tired
of portraiture, which mixed her fascination with people with her interest in
art. She would spend all her years in France collecting paintings, as well as
collecting people.

   Whenever Stein sat for a portrait, she watched the artist just as closely as
the artist watched her. Over the years, as the *Autobiography* tells, she modeled
for a long series of portraits: paintings, sculptures, and photographs by Cecil
Beaton, Eugene Berman, Alvin Langdon Coburn, Jo Davidson, Jacques
Lipchitz, Man Ray, Francis Rose, Felix Valloton, and others.[12] As with the
Picasso portrait, the *Autobiography* catalogs the making of all these works,
describing Stein sitting for them. It also traces the eventual development
of Stein's own art of "portrait-writing," as she often wrote word portraits of
the artists in return.

   Literary portraits became one of Stein's favorite genres. Over the years,
she wrote portraits of nearly everyone she knew, beginning—if one follows
the legend of the birth of "portrait-writing" as told in the *Autobiography*—
with "Ada," of her partner Alice B. Toklas, in 1910, before she wrote portraits of Matisse and Picasso. She wrote portraits of all her close friends, and
her family, as well as of people she encountered more briefly. Sometimes, as
with Matisse and Picasso, and her good friend Carl Van Vechten, Stein later
wrote a second portrait, which was really of a different person, as they had
changed over time. Sometimes, as in "Two," she wrote portraits whose subject
was the relationship between people. Sometimes, as in "Men," she wrote
portraits of small groups, or in "Many Many Women," much larger clusters
of people she knew; sometimes, as in "Italians," she even wrote portraits of
crowds or nations.

   Her early portraits drew on the discoveries Stein made about human
nature in the notebooks she initially kept for *The Making of Americans*. In
these notebooks, now at Yale, she gathered reams of material on character,
improvising and adopting working methods like those of a psychologist,

portrait painter, and biographer all at once. She developed a taste for documentary life-writings, as part of this interest in characterology, asking friends to send her eighteenth-century memoirs, letters, and biographies,[13] and to give her whatever contemporary letters—by anyone—they could get hold of, for her to study. She also used people as live specimens. One friend, Annette Rosenshine, used to visit Stein at the rue de Fleurus, as Diana Souhami writes, "at four every afternoon for psychotherapy sessions of an unorthodox sort. She said she felt like a case study. In these sessions she showed Gertrude all letters from family and friends"[14]—as Stein had instructed her to. All of these gleanings went into the notebooks, also filled with insights into Stein's friends and family. Character, in the abstract, was her quarry, which she conceptualized in terms of essences or types; and in her writings at this time, she experimented with mixing one type or trait with another, as though they were colors or paint.

Though seeming to contemporaries as startlingly modern as Picasso's brusque distortions in *Les Demoiselles d'Avignon* (1909) or Matisse's swathes of color in his portrait of Madame Matisse *The Green Line* (1905), Stein's portraits also recalled much older traditions of literary portraiture. In her studies of people, Stein was always searching for what she called their "bottom nature": the driving inner self. Early brief literary lives did the same, excavating what Alexander Pope termed the "ruling passion"—the secret key which unlocked any human heart,[15] and which it was the literary portraitist's task to uncover. Where biography relies on accumulations of traces heaped up by the passage of time, the early literary portrait, because of its enclosure and brevity, tends towards elementals. Stein's literary portraits were to do this, almost naturally. In *The Principles of Psychology* (1890), William James formulated a distinction which also throws light on Stein's art of portraiture, as well as the older traditions of biography. For any man, James writes:

> *Me is the sum total of all that he CAN call his*, not only his body and his psychic powers, but his clothes and his house, his wife and children, his ancestors and friends, his reputation and works, his lands and horses, and yacht and bank-account [...] I [is] that which at any given moment *is* conscious, whereas the Me is only one of the things which it is conscious *of.*[16]

Biography, excluded from the "I" without the factually suspect access of imagination, is often left with the husks of the "Me." Stein's portraits tried to get the "I" of their subjects. Disregarding externals, they mimicked a character's speech or words, not what someone looked like—for as Wendy Steiner notes, "speech is one of those processes which the written word can imitate truly."[17] Stein's portraits went in search of the "rhythm of personality," which Stein believed showed itself in the repetitions of a person's speech and language, and they avoided the outer self, at least initially—although later, as she conceded in the *Autobiography*, she did also experiment with "mixing the outside with the inside."[18]

Memory was also discarded. Picasso's portraits, Stein wrote, searched for what no one had ever tried to express: "things seen not as one knows them but as they are when one sees them without remembering having looked at them."[19] Her own portraits, likewise, banished all sense of a subject's past, to concentrate intently on their present and potential. Memory, for Stein, shrouded the inner self of a character. It made it hard to see a self for what it really was. It resurrected old, false images. Remembering was a form of repetition, Stein thought, obstructing the truth of the present. The early portraits, like *The Making of Americans*, were written in a language of eternal becoming: a rolling, repetitive "continuous present" portraying the slow shifts of self over time. Excluding the past, they formed a record of a subject's present, pointing continually on to the future. They tell what these people *will* be, as much as what they are. Stella Bowen, in her memoir *Drawn From Life*, wrote how what she wanted to capture in her painting was a pose showing "*all* the moments"[20] of a subject's life. Stein perhaps wanted something like this in her literary portraits, which became records of present and future being. They were repetitive, catching the rhythm of personality, yet the repetitions were never exactly the same. Take one early portrait, for instance, of the painter Harry Phelan Gibb:

> He is suffering, he is hoping, he is succeeding in saying that anything is something. He is suffering, he is hoping, he is succeeding in saying that something is something. He is hoping that he is succeeding in hoping that something is something. He is hoping that he is succeeding in saying that he is succeeding in hoping that something is something. He is hoping that he is succeeding in saying that something is something.[21]

Throughout the 1910s and 1920s, Stein experimented with other techniques. As though walking around her subject with each line she set down—just as the Cubist painters broke with the single viewpoint of painting to give a multiplicity of angles—she wrote portraits made of fragmentary shards and associations. Stein went on to move yet further away from literal meaning, eventually formulating a style which closed off all approaches from which it could be conventionally understood. Sometimes it approached pure song. In "Susie Asado," with its melodic opening and closing lines—"Sweet sweet sweet sweet sweet tea"[22]—Stein's abstraction squeezed the essence of its subject out of sound as much as sense. A later, final phase of portraiture, however, embraced narrative. A 1941 portrait of Sherwood Anderson, "Sherwood's Sweetness," squeezed the same essence from its subject as did "Susie Asado," but through the use of anecdote: "I always connect Sherwood with sweet fruits," Stein wrote after hearing of his death. "I remember in New Orleans when he came into the room he had a bag of oranges, twenty-five for twenty-five cents, and he and we ate all the twenty-five oranges; they were orange sweet."[23] In the 1930s and 40s, this new phase of narrative portraiture was seen most sustainedly in her autobiographies. Often seen—as she saw them at first—as an easy step back from her avant-garde advances, the autobiographies actually solved many of the problems Stein faced all her writing life.[24]

Stein had always been an extremely autobiographical writer. She didn't invent things. Her work, in that sense, was not fiction. Her portraits, novels, plays, and poems were filled with cryptic, homely autobiography and references to daily life, so close and personal that only those who shared it could recognize them. The entire body of her work, as Ulla Dydo says, forms a "single spiritual autobiography whose vocabulary is generated by the daily life."[25] Yet the *Autobiography* was different, her first ever "formal" self-portrait. Stein surprised herself, embracing extended narrative and memory for the first time in her writing. The book's superficially simple and direct style appeared such a radical break with all her previous work, however, that it called into question exactly how, why—and even, if—Stein wrote it.

*

By 1932, when she wrote the *Autobiography*, Stein was fifty-eight years old. Every summer, as she had done for a few years, she went with Toklas from the rue de Fleurus, where the couple lived in the winter, to a house in the hamlet of Bilignin, near Belley, in the Rhône valley. Throughout the 1920s, the pair had spent many summers nearby in the Hotel Pernollet. Friends had repeatedly suggested to Stein that she write her memoirs; many figures from her Paris acquaintance had already done so.[26] Stein, as she says on the last page of the *Autobiography*, "always replied, not possibly."[27] So what made her do it in 1932?

One answer was a thirst for acclaim, and a more practical need for remuneration. There's no doubt Stein wanted some success, after years of working steadily, and for little reward. She had hardly ever made any real money out of writing, although she had kept at it, with Toklas's constant support and encouragement, for several decades. She needed this support from Toklas. Even in the early 1930s, the bulk of her work still remained unpublished and unread; and she writes in the *Autobiography* itself that she sometimes felt "a little bitter, all her unpublished manuscripts, and no hope of publication or serious recognition."[28] Writing was always what was most important to Stein, and she organized her entire life with Toklas around it. Yet she was also vulnerable, and often had spells of dejection.

Recently, she had begun self-publishing in the "Plain Edition" with Toklas's help. Through Ford Madox Ford, she had also found an agent, William Aspenwall Bradley. The Depression had taken hold, and the fairly modest family income Stein had relied on all her life seemed insecure. She had her paintings—the Plain Edition was funded by the sale of a Blue period Picasso, the *Woman With a Fan*. Nonetheless she still felt worried about money. When Stein later told the story of how she came to write the *Autobiography*, she always wryly emphasized its mercenary aspects. At the end of the *Autobiography*, Stein tells, in Alice's voice, how she told Alice to write her autobiography: "Just think, she would say, what a lot of money you would make."[29] In a short piece written soon afterwards, in early 1933, "The Story of a Book," Stein was already mythologizing the writing of the *Autobiography* as a gift, an immaculate conception, once again bearing the promise of success.

> If there had not been a beautiful and unusual dry October at Bilignin in France in 1932 followed by an unusually dry and beautiful first two weeks of November would the autobiography of Alice B. Toklas have been written? Possibly but probably not then. Every day during those beautiful six weeks of unusually dry and sunny days, in the morning and in the afternoon, I sat and on a little double decked table as near the sunny wall as I could get I wrote about five hours a day [...] and in six weeks the autobiography was done. I did not write to anybody about the autobiography, I usually do [...] but only to Bernard Faÿ and [Louis] Bromfield I mentioned that I was doing something [...] When it was all done I said to Alice B. Toklas, do you think it is going to be a best seller, I would love to write a best seller. She said, wait until I typewrite it and then I will tell you.[30]

That summer in Bilignin—"a nice summer, a nice quiet summer,"[31] as she wrote to Carl Van Vechten's wife Fania Marinoff in August—Stein also wrote possibly her most difficult, hermetic composition to date, the *Stanzas in Meditation*, in some ways the culmination of her experimental style. Towards the end of the *Autobiography*, the *Stanzas* are mentioned as the last thing Stein has done: just finished, being typed by Toklas. Encouraged by the cryptic mentions of "autobiography" throughout the *Stanzas*, many critics have thought they form an alternative autobiography—"this is her autobiography one of two,"[32] the *Stanzas* say—written by Stein during the evenings for pleasure while the "official" book was written in the day. Put side by side with the *Autobiography* they reveal a mighty split in her two styles.

The *Stanzas* might be autobiography, but if so, they are autobiography of an unprecedentedly elusive and abstract kind. Line by line, word by word, the *Stanzas* calculatedly shut out logic and representation, for a riddling, enigmatic steady song, beyond meaning. Reflecting an ongoing tension between an unspecified "I," "she," and "they," the *Stanzas* always tempt the reader to take the "I" as Stein, and the "she" as Toklas, but never give enough clues for one to do so.

Perhaps because she could not reconcile the split in styles, Stein mythologized how easily she wrote the *Autobiography*—almost to discount it as a serious work. The magic figure of the six weeks to write it seems talismanic; it's likely it took longer than Stein claims. In the manuscript at Yale, in fifteen *cahiers* of the type Stein always used for writing, the conclusion, also telling of the six week gestation, has "two months," crossed out.[33] Yet even the manuscript—whose first page is reproduced in facsimile at the end of the *Autobiography* like a piece of evidence—could have been deceptive. The writing probably began earlier that summer, in May.[34] The myth of quick composition chimes with Stein's keenness—in the *Autobiography* itself, too—to denigrate it, make it seem not only mercenary, as all autobiography is often seen, but thrown off merely for fun.

The other question which has long surrounded the *Autobiography* is whether Stein was really its author. The book's conceit—that it was the autobiography of Toklas, rather than Stein, revealed as the author only on the final page—threw the question of its authorship into play from the start. In a 1946 interview, Stein declared that the book's clipped, unSteinlike style came to her from a revelation that occurred to her while translating some poems just before.

> I was asked to write a biography, and I said "No". And then as a joke I began
> to write the *Autobiography of Alice B. Toklas* [...] A young French poet had

begun to write, and I was asked to translate his poems, and there I made a rather startling discovery that other people's words are quite different from one's own [...] They have a totally different sense than when they are your own words [...] and so I did a tour de force with the *Autobiography of Alice B. Toklas*, and when I sent the first half to the agent, they sent back a telegram to see which one of us had written it! But still I had done what I saw, what you do in translation or in a narrative. I had recreated the point of view of somebody else. Therefore the words ran with a certain smoothness.[35]

Through the experience of translating someone else's work, Stein made the technical breakthrough in voice which enabled the *Autobiography* to mimic Alice so fluently—and to be written in a style unlike anything she had ever done before. Yet Stein also raises the suspicion that Toklas might have helped her in this other form of "translation." In the manuscript *cahiers*, the entire text of the *Autobiography* flows throughout in Stein's smooth handwriting, seemingly without a break, once she found Toklas's voice. But it took time to find that voice, and the early pages of the *Autobiography* in the first *cahier* stridently refused to give up the riddling Stein style. There are more than the usual interpolations by Toklas in the margins—as Stein's typist, Toklas usually changed little, but here she couldn't refrain from the occasional comment, a "*NO*" or "*Not again.*"[36] It's possible that the *cahiers* were essentially a fair copy—Stein often worked first in smaller notebooks or *carnets*, most of which, for this period, have been lost. Toklas could easily, of course, have dictated passages of the autobiography to Stein, to help her get the voice. Yet having lived together, and having been never apart—not even for the shortest spell, over twenty-five years—Stein would in any case have been extremely well placed to recreate Toklas's talk. And their intimacy had always had a literary element—as Toklas helped Stein, for years, prepare her manuscripts.

Usually, Stein wrote Toklas private notes in her *cahiers*, often in nonsense or rhyme, for her to pick up when she typed them. They gave each other nicknames in this private semi-nonsense world: "Mr. & Mrs. Reciprocal," "Baby," "wifey," "Mr. and Mrs. Cuddle-Wuddle," or "Mr. & Mrs. C.-W."[37] The notes were sometimes sexual doggerel. "Baby's type writing," wrote Stein to Toklas in one skit which Ulla Dydo quotes, "!! No not that / IT no not that / It yes that's it / ByBy no BaBY no / Ba!Y no Baby no / Baby yes."[38] Now in the *Autobiography*, Stein wrote a whole book which was also a kind of love letter.

*

Of course it is impossible to write (not ghostwrite) someone else's auto-biography. By imitating her partner's voice over the course of a whole book, Stein was forced to see everything from her lover's point of view, including herself. This scheme tied a knot in the usual line between subject and object in biography and autobiography. Playfully, the *Autobiography* shortcircuits all usual biographical categories. In her typically acute, faux-naïf manner, Stein herself compared it not with conventional biographies or autobiographies, but with the roots of the novel in fake autobiography. "I am going to write it as simply as Defoe did the autobiography of Robinson Crusoe,"[39] she wrote at the end; and she did the same as Defoe in originally suppressing her own name from the volume.[40] Yet the *Autobiography*, despite ostensibly being by, and about, Toklas, was also so much about Gertrude Stein, that it was, simultaneously, a biography of Stein, written by a scribe who knew her intimately.

The *Autobiography* can also be seen as a group biography of writers and artists working in Paris during the early decades of the twentieth century. Beginning in 1907, the year Toklas met Stein, it tells not only of Picasso and Matisse, but of Fauvism, Cubism, and other pre-war artistic "isms"; the First World War; and 1920s Paris in the period of Modernism and the little magazines. Like many reminiscences, the *Autobiography* is, in effect, an entire book of literary portraits. Here are Georges Braque, Jean Cocteau, T. S. Eliot, F. Scott Fitzgerald, Ford Madox Ford, Ernest Hemingway, Ezra Pound, Erik Satie, Edith Sitwell, and Tristan Tzara—among many others in these bustling pages. Stein engineered the opening chapters of the narrative to begin, after a very concise account of Toklas's life before she came to Paris, with a description of a 1907 dinner party at the rue de Fleurus, where she met several of the painters mentioned, swiftly followed by an account of the vernissage of the *Salon des Indépendants*, where she saw these artists again, and their paintings. Hence from its beginnings the focus of the *Autobiography* is firmly on its gallery of personalities, and indeed the book is designed as a kind of verbal museum, in which these personalities, one by one, are portrayed (and curated) by Stein, who deliberately blurs—one of her favorite maneuvers in the *Autobiography*—descriptions of their art and their lives.

Before the war, most of the figures in the *Autobiography* were visual artists; in the 1920s, writers predominate. The war, which as the *Autobiography* relates, Stein and Toklas spent partly on Majorca, and partly driving around France delivering supplies for the American Fund for French Wounded—broke the Parisian artistic worlds apart. But there were figures, like Stein, who straddled both generations. Of the writers, Ford Madox Ford was one such guiding presence. In the *Autobiography*, Toklas tells how the writers met at a party before the war, when "Violet Hunt and Gertrude Stein were next to each other at the tea table and talked a great deal together. I was next to Ford Madox Hueffer and I liked him very much."[41] Ford is glimpsed again a few pages later, laying a "heavy hand"[42] on Hemingway's shoulder and asking Stein for permission to dedicate a book—which must have been *A Mirror to France*—to her. Almost in return, the ending of the *Autobiography* mentions Ford conspicuously in its final paragraphs, perhaps as a gesture of gratitude, since Ford had also published excerpts of *The Making of Americans* in the *transatlantic review*: "When Ford Madox Ford was editing the Transatlantic Review he once said to Gertrude Stein, I am a pretty good writer and a pretty good editor and a pretty good business man but I find it very difficult to be all three at once."[43]

Privately, in a letter to Van Vechten, Stein wrote that Ford was part of "more or less the old guard."[44] But she respected this old guard, seeing them as a counterpoint to the young upstarts in 1920s Paris. Henry James makes his entrance on the *Autobiography*'s first page, when Alice, at nineteen, writes to him suggesting she turn *The Awkward Age* (1899) into a play. Stein had never met James, despite a near-miss in July 1914, when she arranged a visit to Lamb House through Alvin Langdon Coburn, only to have James cancel with a telegram on the day itself.[45] But she clearly wanted him in the book at the start. Wells, meanwhile, is mentioned respectfully in the *Autobiography*, having written to Stein about *Three Lives*. Those writers younger than Stein, however, were drawn more facetiously. "Wyndham Lewis," Stein declares:

> tall and thin, looked rather like a young frenchman on the rise, perhaps because his feet were very french, at least his shoes. He used to come and sit and meas-ure pictures. I can not say that he actually measured with a measuring-rod but he gave all the effect of being in the act of taking very careful measurement of the canvas, the lines within the canvas and everything that might be of use. Gertrude Stein rather liked him. She particularly liked him one day when he came and told all about his quarrel with Roger Fry. Roger Fry had come in not many days before and had already told all about it. They told exactly the same story only it was different, very different.[46]

Lewis appears as a foreigner to Stein, as he also did around this time to Ford and others. Stein implies that Lewis's Vorticism borrowed from Cubism, or less charitably, that Lewis as a painter had no originality. But Stein softens the blow with her statement that she "rather liked" Lewis, and in her account of Lewis's notorious split with the Bloomsbury-affiliated Roger Fry and his Omega Workshops in 1913—when Fry, according to Lewis, cheated Lewis out of a commission—Stein cleverly sits on the fence.

The *Autobiography* is a long parade of such crisp, detachable sketches. People appear and disappear, are dismissed or appraised in a few lines, almost as if they were paintings. Sometimes the character sketches in the *Autobiography* use techniques Stein had mastered in her earlier portraits. Of Picasso, for instance, Stein writes: "Of course he often says yes when he has no intention of doing what he says yes to, he can't say no, no is not in his vocabulary and you have to know whether his yes means yes or means no."[47] At other points, Stein allows herself more extensive use of anecdote and narration.

Before it became the *Autobiography of Alice B. Toklas*, there were other titles, as Stein tells us: "My Life With The Great, Wives of Geniuses I Have Sat With, My Twenty-Five Years With Gertrude Stein."[48] Early on, "Toklas" also says "before I decided to write this book my twenty-five years with Gertrude Stein, I had often said that I would write, The wives of geniuses I have sat with."[49] She continues:

> I have sat with so many. I have sat with wives who were not wives, of geniuses who were real geniuses. I have sat with real wives of geniuses who were not real geniuses. I have sat with wives of geniuses, of near geniuses, of would be geniuses, in short I have sat very often and very long with many wives and wives of many geniuses.[50]

As well as being a form of translation, an experiment in "other people's words" and their texture, Stein saw the idea of using Toklas's voice as being like the way painters depicted their wives in portraits. She had always been influenced by such paintings. *Three Lives* was written not only during the Picasso sittings, but under Cézanne's *Portrait of Madame Cézanne*, which hung over the writing table in the rue de Fleurus. The *Autobiography* was a literary analogue to these works, reversing the premises of portraying a wife in painting. Where the wives sat mutely, while the "geniuses" caught their beauty on canvas, and at parties had to sit with other wives, the literary portrait of a wife allowed her to speak out. Stein's plan also alluded to the way that writers' wives or partners were so often omitted from the public record of their autobiographies—and found a way to get around, indeed reverse, this. In the *Autobiography*, Toklas, via Stein, gives the long roll-call of wives

she has met: the joke extending as each "genius" often had more than one—
"How they unroll, an endless vista through the years [. . .] Fernande and [. . .]
Madame Matisse and Marcelle Braque and Josette Gris and Eve Picasso and
Bridget Gibb and Marjory Gibb and Hadley and Pauline Hemingway
and Mrs. Sherwood Anderson and Mrs. Bravig Imbs and the Mrs. Ford
Maddox Ford."[51]

The conceit of being just another of these wives—really, "Mrs. Gertrude
Stein"—allowed Toklas, or Stein, to sidestep many practical problems faced
by autobiographers. It allowed Stein to hide behind Toklas, and meant that
the contingency of memoir-writing—the eternal problem of tact when
writing about people whom one knew and were still living—was slightly
dissolved. Stein could be honestly critical, free with her tongue, in a gossipy,
entertaining, slightly malicious way. In the case of her brother, Leo, this enabled
a conspicuous omission, almost verging on semi-deletion, from the story of
her life, which lay in their falling out in 1913, and the fact that they had not
seen each other since. And it allowed Stein to make the absolute centrality
of Toklas to her own life extremely visible, albeit under complex cover,
hiding in plain sight. Writing of herself in the third person, Stein avoided
self-exposure. It was a strange, inspired tactic, which allowed her to write of
herself as a novelist would of a fictional character. She formed a superficial,
entirely external self-portrait, without that unnerving "fluidity" of first-
person writing that Henry James spoke of, and that Stein herself noted in
novels by friends.[52]

The *Autobiography*'s virtuoso use of point of view was a natural development of Stein's techniques in her portraits. Characters are brought in from
strange angles, as Toklas overhears and reports fragments of Stein's conversation about them to someone else: an effect that is lifelike enough to seem
unforced and natural. We hear, via Toklas, not only what Stein thinks of
other people but what other people think of other people too.

Sometimes the indirect, refracted point of view is used to cast new light
on Stein. A meeting with Matisse is reported almost as eavesdropping by
Toklas, as she approaches Matisse and Stein at a party, and hears only snatches
of their talk. "As I came up I heard her say, Oh yes but it would be more
difficult now." "We were talking," Stein tells Toklas, "of a lunch party we had
in here last year," when Stein sat all of the painters opposite one of their
own pictures. Only Matisse noticed. "And now he says it is a proof that I am
very wicked, Matisse laughed and said, yes I know Mademoiselle Gertrude,
the world is a theatre for you."[53] Curiously, as here, the self-portrait Gertrude

gives herself in the third person is not particularly benign. She calls herself a "genius"—tackling the intrinsic egotism of the genre of autobiography audaciously. But she's not afraid to make herself unattractive, referring to her "explosive temper,"[54] or her "reprehensible habit of swearing."[55]

The account of Stein's own early years in the *Autobiography* is brief, enabled partly by the chronology of the narrative's first half. The early chapters step back in time slowly, from "My Arrival in Paris," to "Gertrude Stein in Paris, 1903–1907," to "Gertrude Stein Before She Came To Paris," before moving forwards more sequentially. Only after several chapters, then, are we told where and when Stein was born, how she spent time in Vienna and Paris until she was five, how she grew up in San Francisco and later studied psychology. There is sadness in this account of early years, alluded to but buried in matter-of-fact sentences, as Stein writes of a "lonesome" period in California and "an agony of adolescence."[56] "After the death of first her mother and then her father she and her sister and one brother left California for the East,"[57] Stein writes of her move to Baltimore before university. She soon moves on, enabled once again by this all being Toklas's, not her own, story. Indeed, Stein manages Toklas's voice so well, devoting so many pages to portraying people she knew, that she sometimes merely comes across as a walk-on part, an extra, in the story of her own life.

*

While many autobiographies depict or search for turning-points in the writer's life, the biggest turning-point in Gertrude Stein's later life was the *Autobiography* itself. More than she had dared to hope, the book was an immediate popular success. Yet she felt that the person depicted as herself in the book was not really her; and the knock-on effect of becoming so well-known for something so untrue to what she had always stood for was disturbing. At some stage, too, either in 1932 or 1933, Stein fell out with Toklas, over Stein's first unpublished novel *Q.E.D.*, whose discovery that summer of 1932 is briefly mentioned in the *Autobiography*.[58] *Q.E.D.*'s auto-biographical account of Stein's early love in 1902 for May Bookstaver threw Toklas into a rage of jealousy, when she learned of it now for the first time. Ulla Dydo writes that this was probably after the *Autobiography* was done, in December 1932, although it was thought for some time to have prompted the *Autobiography*.[59] Dydo tells how Toklas's jealousy was such that she made Stein go back through the *Stanzas in Meditation*, crossing out every single word

"May" in the verses—as these might refer to May Bookstaver—substituting "May" with "can." It is still not entirely clear how long Toklas's jealousy lasted. In a chain of biographical Chinese whispers not unlike the complicated refractions of the *Autobiography*, it appears that Toklas herself told Leon Katz that it went on until March 1935, until as Dydo reports via Katz and Toklas, "Stein told Toklas she would leave her unless she stopped goading and bickering."[60]

The *Autobiography* brought money and fame, but it is hard to escape the sense that it was tainted. Before it was even serialized in the *Atlantic Monthly*, starting in May 1933, it caused divisions in Stein's personal relationships. Later in the 1930s, when she had got over most of these ruptures, Stein eventually wrote about the aftermath of the book's success in a follow-up memoir, *Everybody's Autobiography* (1937) which tells what happened to her from 1933 to 1937, and whose essential theme is the unnerving, shattering impact the *Autobiography* had on her life.

The opening chapters of *Everybody's Autobiography* recount the end of many long friendships. Stein writes early on how she and Toklas returned to Paris at the end of 1932; and how the first thing she did was to telephone Picasso. In a scene reflecting back to her sittings for the *Portrait of Gertrude Stein*, but emphasizing the riskier side-effects of literary portraiture, Stein describes how she read aloud from the *Autobiography*, to Picasso and his new wife Olga Khokhlova—rather like when Fernande Olivier read aloud from La Fontaine, while Picasso painted Stein's portrait. Where Picasso's visual portrait of her sealed their friendship, her new portrait of him temporarily served to break it. In her telling of this mirror scene to the 1905–6 portrait sittings, Stein blurs past and present, the current situation and the written world of *Toklas*.

> I began reading it to him, he and I were on the couch together and his wife was sitting on a chair and was talking to Alice Toklas and then they all listened as I began [...] So I began at the beginning with the description of the room as it was and the description of our servant Helen. You made one mistake said Pablo you left out something there were three swords that hung on that wall one underneath the other and he said it was very exciting. Then I went on and Fernande came in. I was reading he was listening and his eyes were wide open and then suddenly his wife Olga Picasso got up and said she would not listen she would go away she said. What's the matter, we said, I do not know that woman she said and left. Pablo said go on reading, I said no you must go after your wife, he said oh I said oh, and he left and until this year and that was two years in between we did not see each other again.[61]

There were to be more broken friendships, especially among the painters depicted in the book; and more criticisms like Picasso's "you made one mistake." Matisse, Braque, and Marie Laurencin were all unamused by Stein's licentious portrayals of them, and, as *Everybody's Autobiography* tells, "they did not like it and they did not get used to it [...] Matisse I never saw again but Braque yes twice and Marie Laurencin once."[62] In 1934–5, several of the artists appeared in a special pamphlet of *transition*, "Testimony Against Gertrude Stein," devoted to correcting the errors they perceived in the *Autobiography*. The pamphlet is a prize exhibit of autobiography's tricky negotiations with truth and fact—and the dangers of depicting subjects who can answer back, as Braque, Matisse, Eugene and Maria Jolas, André Salmon, and Tristan Tzara now all did, in turn, attacking Stein and her version of their past. What's most apparent from the pamphlet is not that Stein had wildly misfired with the facts, however, but the bruised emotional response of people who felt robbed, even maimed, by being portrayed irresponsibly, without their consent. The pamphlet simmers with rage for Stein's "superficial" account, and its popularity. Stein had misunderstood everything, and debased it too, these writers and artists concurred. Only Matisse grudgingly saw the book's artfulness.

Leo also felt his semi-erasure from his sister's story keenly. "God what a liar she is!" he wrote to Mabel Weeks. "Some of her chronology is too wonderful [...] Practically everything that she says of our activities before 1911 is false both in fact and implication, but one of her radical complexes [...] made it necessary practically to eliminate me."[63] "It's the first time I ever read an autobiography of which I knew the authentic facts, and to me it seems sheerly incredible."[64]

As she wrote of the *transition* pamphlet and her fallings-out in the wake of the *Autobiography* in *Everybody's Autobiography*, Stein affected blitheness towards all these accusations. She concentrated on the material success the *Autobiography* brought her: how she bought a new Hermes coat, a new eight-cylinder Ford, and studded collars for her poodle, Basket, with the money. She also installed a telephone in Paris to speak to Bradley every morning, and one in Bilignin—for the next few years, she could be called in summertime on Belley 168.[65]

The summer of 1933, however, after Stein and Toklas had returned to Bilignin, is recounted in a more eerie, off-key way in *Everybody's Autobiography*. Macabre events started happening in Belley. The wife of the manager of the Hotel Pernollet fell to her death from the hotel balcony onto the courtyard.

The death was put down by some to sleepwalking. Not long afterwards, while Janet Scudder and her friend were staying with Stein and Toklas at Bilignin, there was an incident with the servants, who cut off the telephone and sabotaged Gertrude and Janet's cars one morning. Completing the trio of local disturbances was the death of an Englishwoman who lived nearby with Madame Caesar, another friend of Stein and Toklas's, who had come to lunch at Bilignin. She was found dead in a ravine with two bullets in her head, and the Basque cap she often wore "put carefully down on a rock beside her."[66] Suicide was suspected, although the two bullets were a mystery. The case remained unsolved. All these events disquieted Stein, fusing in her psyche with the *Autobiography*, serialized that summer and beginning to have its success. There was the implication that her old self was being killed by the popularity of her simulacrum, and that the replacement of this self was likewise irreversible, self-inflicted.

Stein also became interested in detective stories around this time. Autobiography was, she implied, like a detective story. Both genres turned around the pursuit of a self. Often a self or selves had to be killed, if this pursuit was to take place effectively. Autobiography disinters a succession of dead selves—cast-off shells, outgrown personas, buried fragments of personality which have become discarded or disused—and puts something else in their place. Likewise, the art of biography resembles the crime novel, above all in its preference that the hero be a corpse. The dead woman on the concrete outside the Hotel Pernollet, and the corpse of the Englishwoman down in the ravine, symbolized to Stein what had happened to herself, because of the *Autobiography*. And like the Englishwoman's death, perhaps what had happened was closer to suicide, than to murder.

The genres fuse not only around their pact with death, but also in terms of procedure. Biography and autobiography, as Stein knew, are based on detection, and multiple divergent tellings of the same event—just as in crime novels—from different points of view. They give endless angles on the same story. This repetition, Stein thought, was a key part of these genres. Stein connected the way crime novels retold the same story with the idea of "insistence" or repetition in her portraits. "Anybody can be interested in the story of a crime because no matter how often the witnesses tell the same story the insistence is different," Stein wrote in her *Lectures in America* (1935). For all this repeating, there is no such thing as total repetition, Stein thought; no matter how similar, the story is always slightly different each time. "That is what makes life that the insistence is different, no matter how often you tell the same story if there is anything alive in the telling the emphasis is different."[67]

Stein's interest in autobiography and detective stories in the 1930s also grew from her increasing feeling that novels were no longer feasible. Publicity had become so adept at the creation of fictional characters for mass consumption, it endangered and outdid the novel. "Meredith was the last to produce characters who people felt were alive," Stein later said in an interview. "In the characters of Henry James this is really very little true, the characters do not live very much [...] the novel as a *form* has not been successful in the Twentieth Century. That is why biographies have been more successful than novels. This is due in part to this enormous publicity business."[68] In *Everybody's Autobiography*, alongside her account of the succession of corpses around Belley that summer of 1933, she put the same point differently. "Novels now cannot be written," she asserted, "[...] there is so much publicity so many characters are being created every minute of every day that nobody is really interested in personality enough to dream about personalities."[69] "The only novels possible these days are detective stories," she wrote, "where the only person of any importance is dead."[70] The unconscious subtext of all these reflections on publicity, biography, murder, and character, was, as always, rooted in her own direct experience: rising from the feeling that the Gertrude Stein in the *Autobiography* lived at the expense of what she hoped was her true self.

Certainly, the success of the *Autobiography* had done something fatal to the writer in herself. Throughout that unbalanced summer, she was unable to write anything. "Slowly something changed inside me,"[71] she wrote in *Everybody's Autobiography*. "That summer that first summer after The Autobiography was not a natural summer."[72] "It was a strange year that year and it is a strange year this year. The blue of the sky looks rather black to the eye."[73] The off-key early part of *Everybody's Autobiography* reaches a peak of agitated, superstitious disquiet in nervy reiterations and repetitions about Stein's writer's block.

> All this time I did no writing. I had written and was writing nothing. Nothing inside me needed to be written [...] there was no word inside me. And I was not writing. I began to worry about identity. I had always been I because I had words that had to be written inside me [...] But was I I when I had no written word inside me. It was very bothersome.[74]

Stein did, however, attempt a detective story, based on the mysterious events of that summer, called *Blood on the Dining-Room Floor*. And she made plans for the second memoir which would become *Everybody's Autobiography*, although this only at first resulted in the sketch "And Now," written from November 1933 to early 1934. Stein tried several different titles on the cover of its manuscript: "A Confession," "And Now," "Beginning of another biography," "A True Story."[75] The overwhelming note of this fragment was thwarted, and melancholy, as Stein wrote how this memoir was to differ from the first.

> The other book was gay, this one will not be so gay [...] It is going to be rather sad. What happened from the day I wrote the autobiography to to-day and what do I think about it all, about what happened every day [...] What happened to me was this. When the success began and it was a success I got lost completely lost [...] I lost my personality [...] So many people knowing me I was I no longer and for the first time since I had begun to write I could not write and what was worse I could not worry about not writing and what was also worse I began to think about how my writing would sound to others.[76]

Perhaps Toklas's jealous rage from 1933–5 over the Bookstaver affair lay behind this desolate tone, which seems to reach to the heart of Stein's life, going beyond what the words themselves say, suggesting something deeply and painfully wrong. Toklas's anger certainly made more autobiography very difficult. In the notes for "And Now," there was another instance of a furious crossing-out, as Stein had written, "Some time describe my New York experiences with May Mary"[77] and a line was scrawled across it. The other reason for Stein's sadness was the dawning realization in the wake of her success, that her dream of the *Autobiography* leading people to her other, more experimental work, was indeed only a dream. She had finally found her readership not in her own voice, but by imitating Toklas. Now, she couldn't get her own voice back; or if she could, perhaps no one wanted to hear it. To help break her writer's block, she entertained the idea of collaboration again. What became *Four in America* had its roots in a biography of General Grant she had wanted to write with Sherwood Anderson. She began this alone in October 1933, continuing on her return to Paris that November, writing it all that winter in the city.

One of the four long portraits in *Four in America* is of Henry James, imagining what he would have been like had he not been a writer, but a general—following the conceit of the book's "what if" experiment in biography, which takes four figures and reimagines their roles. General Grant becomes a religious leader; James a general; Wilbur Wright a painter; George Washington a novelist. The portrait of James takes a long time to discuss him at all, but when it does emerge, it is baffling, insinuating, humorous, mischievous, and cryptic. "Would he lose a battle a battle that was begun. Perhaps yes,"[78] Stein writes, as she circles around to the subject. "It is of great importance that Henry James never was married,"[79] she continues, beginning the main theme of the portrait, full of wry hints about James's sexuality, and a subliminal sense that he never really lived, and never really loved.

> I wish every one knew exactly how to feel, about Henry James [...] Henry James had well you might say he had no time [...] it might be that he was uneasy [...] They might be caught alone. Who might be caught alone [...] Henry James was very ready to have it happen for him [...] He had no fortune and misfortune [...] no distress and no relief from any pang. Any pang. Oh yes any pang.[80]

Once *Four in America* was finished, Stein spent the summer of 1934 preparing for the publicity tour scheduled to begin that autumn in America, the first time she had returned for thirty years. As she told in *Everybody's Autobiography*, she fell out with Bradley over plans for it, yet eventually decided to do it, perhaps swayed by another friendly voice. "Ford Madox Ford for many years had been saying that I should go over. Come with me he would say, they feel hurt that you do not come, and you would not like to hurt their feelings, come with me come this January he used to say persuasively."[81]

Stein and Toklas sailed on October 17, 1934, arriving in New York—where, as *Everybody's Autobiography* tells, crowds of reporters were waiting to quiz Stein about herself—on October 24. They had dinner with Carl Van Vechten that evening. During the week-long voyage, as a portent of her coming fame, Stein had spoken with a throat specialist from Newark on board who had a copy of the *Autobiography*, and asked her to autograph it for him. In New York, it seemed as though everybody recognized her.

> We saw a fruit store and we went in. How do you do Miss Stein said the man, how do you do I said, and how do you like it, he said, very much I said [...] He was so natural about knowing my name that it was not surprising and yet we had not expected anything like that to happen [...] and then we went out again on an avenue [...] and then we saw an electric sign moving around a building and it said Gertrude Stein has come and that was upsetting.[82]

Throughout the American trip recounted in detail in *Everybody's Autobiography*, Stein moves disconcertingly between unease, horror, intrigue, and enjoyment of her celebrity, sometimes almost standing outside herself and looking at it, as a phenomenon, before feeling its effects more sharply and directly. The tour was a whirlwind for her and Toklas, accustomed to the rural quiet of Bilignin, but it came off resoundingly well. In *Everybody's Autobiography*, whose second half records impressions of the tour, Stein gives a blow-by-blow travelog of the hotels they stayed at, the cities they visited, the trains and flights they took as they criss-crossed the continent, what they ate, who they met. From the breathless tone, it is clear that the tour was over-whelmingly exciting for Stein, and that the fear and confusion she felt at her celebrity eventually gave way to pleasure.

She found America fascinating. The travelog in *Everybody's Autobiography* opens out into a portrait of the continent in the mid-1930s, seen with native, but slightly alien eyes, as Stein and Toklas darted around it. Stein tells of her experiences flying for the first time, and compares the view of the earth down below to Picasso and Braque's innovation of Cubism. She gets her first sight of advertising: "There on the roads I read Buy your flour meal and meat in Georgia. And I knew that was interesting. Was it prose or was it poetry I knew that it was interesting."[83] In Chicago, she stayed in Thornton Wilder's apartment, and asked to accompany the police in a homicidal squad car, where she witnessed no crimes, to her dismay, but did see a nocturnal walking dance marathon, which she compared to Surrealism. Throughout the entire American trip, her eye roved quizzically high and low. With Toklas always by her side, she seemed to go everywhere, and to meet everyone. By the time Stein and Toklas left America, in May 1935, they were reluctant to go.

Stein finally began writing *Everybody's Autobiography* in 1936, working on it all summer in Bilignin, and back in Paris. Unlike when writing the first *Autobiography*, Stein kept friends posted with her progress, relishing it when she could tell them in letters where she was in the narrative, and when they appeared in it. Towards the end, Stein even announced when she was going to finish it, in the text itself: with the performance of her play "The Wedding Bouquet" at Sadler's Wells in April 1937. She played with the tenses of the book as this deadline rushed up on her, as the account of the recent past in America now began crossing over into the present, until she reached the final line, "any way I like what I have and now it is to-day."[84]

Everybody's Autobiography is not so much a celebrity autobiography—although it is that—as an autobiography about celebrity. If the *Autobiography* took Toklas's voice, the idea behind this follow-up was that it would take everybody's voice. Becoming famous, Stein found, if only after the American trip, was oddly democratic. "Everybody speaking to you everybody knowing you, everybody in a hotel or restaurant noticing you everybody asking you to write your name for them [...]"[85] She put all these conversations into the book, in a textual mosaic of reported speech, whose guiding idea and correspondingly transparent style worked together to portray the new American world where privacy was a thing of the past: the new America, where "they want to make everything something anybody can see by looking."[86] It was everybody's autobiography, too, in the way she saw it as continuing the project of *The Making of Americans*, moving beyond the particularity of biography and life-writing, telling the story of everyone and everything.

Stein also, in *Everybody's Autobiography*, appeared to atone, a little, for the portrayal of Leo in the *Autobiography*. A further strange encounter of the 1933 summer was the sudden arrival in Bilignin of the American writer on anthropology and magic, William Seabrook. In *Everybody's Autobiography*, Stein told how Seabrook called her and came over for dinner. The conversations she had with him—like her, he had writer's block at that time—provide the excuse in the text for a long retrospective account of Gertrude's childhood relations with Leo. It is implied that talking to Seabrook about his problems unlocked, as in a psychoanalytic session, Gertrude's own problems over Leo.

The story Gertrude tells Seabrook begins in utopian togetherness—"we always had been together, when we were very little children we went many miles on dusty roads in California together"[87]—leading to a long drift apart, caused mainly by Leo's disparagement of Gertrude's writing, until "little by little we never met again."[88] It is a sad story, told with more self-exposure than anything in the first autobiography. Later on in *Everybody's Autobiography*, Gertrude also reflected on the others in her family with an unprecedented intimacy, in another flashback folded into the main narrative. During the American tour, in San Francisco, she tells how she returned to the house she grew up in, revisited her school, and found the experience depressing. Something has changed, and it is not the sense of place, so much as of herself. She feels briefly despondent—and then she moves on.

In a style she worked hard at, despite its apparent simplicity, fusing elements of the portraits with a steadier sense of narrative, this second memoir was also an essay about autobiography, or a meta-autobiography,[89] as much as an account of Stein's post-*Autobiography* experience, constantly moving forwards to the time of the writing, endlessly rising into abstract discussions of the genre in which it took part. Stein, as ever, was wary of memory, alert to the shifting recreations of self and identity, and she fixed all this down in her faux-naïf rolling repetitions. "You are never yourself to yourself," she writes:

> except as you remember yourself and then of course you do not believe yourself. That is really the trouble with an autobiography you do not of course you do not really believe yourself why should you, you know so well so very well that it is not yourself, it could not be yourself because you cannot remember right and if you do remember right it does not sound right and of course it does not sound right because it is not right. You are of course never yourself.[90]

In *Everybody's Autobiography*, so largely about Stein's betrayal of herself in the *Autobiography*, it was crucial not to betray herself again. And she didn't. The second autobiography began to close the gap between her split modes of the early 30s, and so enacted a stylistic reformation which was in itself part of Stein's recovery. It took her closer to the present, where she always felt more comfortable, away from the reconstructive traps of memory, the myths of past identities. And as she continued it, she moved from slight suspicion of the facility of autobiography—"autobiography is easy for any one"[91]—to a greater realization of how the form allowed her to write on all her real interests at once. Perhaps only in autobiography could one move, as she did here, from reflections on identity, murder, publicity, and genre, to loosely associated thoughts on serial production, modern America, newspapers, radios, reporters, and food, and continue to provide a narrative and a critique of previous and ongoing books. By the end, the authentic unease of the Belley killings with which *Everybody's Autobiography* began was cleared away conclusively with the triumph of the play.

*

There were many flickers in the background of *Everybody's Autobiography* of the darkening atmosphere of the 1930s, with several mentions of the Spanish Civil War, the Great Depression, and the political uncertainty in Europe. Returning to France from their American tour, Stein and Toklas came back to a country soon to be at war again. Within a few years, most Americans would cross the Atlantic the other way. Stein and Toklas wilfully underplayed the change in the atmosphere. The final chapter of Stein's life, however—also chronicled in a very short memoir and another major autobiography—was to be dominated by war.[92]

In Bilignin, after finishing *Everybody's Autobiography*, Stein began a novel, *Ida*, in June 1937. Later that year, she also began her short book *Picasso*. She never defined it generically, but it was something between another portrait of the painter and a brief biography. As biography, it was pure in outline—like Picasso's sketches—telling, in a broadly chronological way, only the story of the Spaniard's artistic development. Unlike the high gossip of the *Autobiography*, *Picasso* draws clear lines between the work and the life. Stein builds up the portrait with abstract, yet firm observations, which strike to the root of Picasso's character, and she avoids particular and external biographical details. At the same time, Stein used the book to continue setting her career on parallel lines to Picasso's, retelling the story of his portrait of her, insisting on how she had been the only one to understand his early work; and, at the end, in the English edition, juxtaposing two photographs by Cecil Beaton: one of Picasso, and one of herself.

While the Picasso book was being finished, Stein and Toklas were forced to leave the rue de Fleurus, and moved into an apartment at 5 rue Christine in January 1938. The following year, Stein began another memoir, *Paris France*. This started as a charmingly naïve story of Stein's relations with France. A strangely shuffled pack of memories and stray thoughts, *Paris France* turned on a series of reflections on the nineteenth and twentieth centuries, and different nationalities, before it became an eccentric account of the onset of conflict, when France declared war on Germany in September.

Stein and Toklas were in Bilignin when they heard the news of war, and made a rushed trip back to the rue Christine to pick things up—including Cézanne's *Portrait of Madame Cézanne* and Picasso's *Portrait of Gertrude Stein*—before returning to Bilignin to spend the winter in the country: the first Stein had ever spent. In *Paris France*, one can trace how the war crept up on Stein. Its encroachment on the memoir was so inappropriate to the reflections on French ways and customs, that the book recreates the gradual immersion in disaster, as it happened, day by day.

Paris France is sweetly childlike initially, telling of French cats and chickens, the French things in the San Francisco of Stein's youth, French food and French knives and forks, French books, French paintings, and how Paris became the artistic capital of the early twentieth century. Then, without warning, its quaint scheme is overturned, as Stein writes, "all this may be only a fire drill, by all this I mean war and thought of war"[93] [...] "Ah yes the village is sad, the men are all gone"[94] [...] "the war is going on this war and we were all waiting."[95] As Stein and Toklas settled down in Bilignin, a newly rustic note enters the writing. No longer able, throughout the war, to spend winters in Paris, Stein and Toklas had to learn the ways of the French countryside all year round. In *Paris France*, Stein tries out a kind of domestic reportage, telling of her conversations around the countryside of Belley, what the men and women in the village told her every day. She continually returns to the original theme of the book, but "now that it is 1939 and war-time,"[96] the war dominates.

Stein inserted a short children's story into the middle of *Paris France*, originally intended to be quite separate. This was also garnered, as so much of her work now was, from conversations. She had hired a new servant girl, Hélène Bouton; in the children's story "Helen Button" which enters *Paris France*, Stein puts down the stories the real Hélène told her.[97] The non-fictional memoir suddenly incorporates a fictional short story; the sing-song tone begins to tell of atrocity. A dog from behind enemy lines turns into a man in front of Helen's eyes. Helen Button's dog is soon run over. Then Helen Button sees a horse.

> It was pulling a wagon and on the wagon was an animal, nobody had ever seen any animal like it before, it was enormous and it was dead [...] The enormous animal did not have a tail and it did not have any ears. It was an enormous animal and it was war-time [...] Nobody knew where the wagon and the horse went, nobody ever does in war-time.[98]

By January 1940, Stein and Toklas were still thinking of leaving France for another lecture tour in America. Stein also dreamed of making a film of the *Autobiography* in Hollywood. But they did nothing. Day after day in the Bilignin winter, Stein wrote Van Vechten, "we sit before the fire and wonder what we will do, but just at present we continue to sit before the fire [...] and so the time passes, the way it always does in wartime."[99] Stein carried on working, and writing, as ever, soon beginning a new novel, *Mrs. Reynolds*. The war narrative curled within *Paris France* continued in a short piece, "The Winner Loses," published in *The Atlantic Monthly* in November 1940. It carried on the note of domestic war reportage in *Paris France*, telling of life in Bilignin since war was declared, while also functioning as propaganda for the Vichy regime—which Stein supported during these early years of war.

Its tone was also similar to the letters to Wilder and Van Vechten that Stein continued to send to America throughout 1940. Stein writes of the privations and restrictions of the war, in a clear-minded tone without self-pity or melodrama, focusing on how it affected her. The letters tell of writing, and gathering wood, or the daily walks Stein took with her dog while getting food. To Wilder, even in September 1940, Stein pretended to be unperturbed by the war, and still thought of going over to America soon. "We are laying in wood for the winter, it is a fascinating life this, so completely different from anything we xpected [*sic*] to live, and every day is stranger than the day before [...] we walk to Belley all the time, and everybody turns up on foot on bicycles [...] it does not turn out to be at all a solitary life."[100] By December 1940, Stein still doesn't sound anxious. "We have settled down for the winter, I like a country winter, Basket and I have gotten so we can walk 10 or 12 kilometres and not be tired [...] we see a good many people."[101] In September, 1941, Stein wrote Van Vechten, "I suppose I should really have kept a diary, such wonderful conversations that I have every day, and such nice xpressions [...]"[102]

In November 1942, the Vichy regime lost independence, and all of France was occupied by the Germans. Escape to America was now out of the question. So was any more correspondence: the letters to Van Vechten and Wilder stop for the next two years. In February 1943, Stein and Toklas had to move out of their house in Bilgnin to a château in the nearby mountain village and railway junction of Culoz. Around the time of the move, Stein now began her final autobiography, with several early titles, as ever, on its manuscript cover: "Gertrude Stein War Autobiography," "Foreign, Domestic and Civil Wars," "My Emotional Autobiography."[103] This became *Wars I Have Seen*.

*

As an autobiographer, Stein always used a filter or frame for her life. In the *Autobiography*, she used Alice as a vantage point; in *Everybody's Autobiography*, the experience of fame. In *Wars I Have Seen*, she now used war. All these framing devices play with the rules of autobiography. But they were true to Stein's mistrust of the genre's claims to totality, its inevitably selective reordering of facts. Even while the difference between autobiography and memoir lies in how autobiography tells all of a life, compared to the memoir's partial slice, autobiography's completeness is still a myth. All autobiography is literally endless—at both ends of its story. Although it sometimes tells of the very end of life, it does so less than biography; and it can't tell the very beginning, certainly not first-hand. Autobiography, if it is to be made out of memories, lacks a definitive opening. The story of memory is a thing of shards and fragments, beginning statically, with isolated, photographic scenes, before it becomes sequential.

In *Wars I Have Seen*, Stein was intrigued by all this. She was concerned, at the opening, with the authenticity of her earliest memories, distinguishing between real memories of events, and memories made for her through the retellings of family members: memories created by narrative. "I do not know whether to put in the things I do not remember as well as the things I do remember," Stein wrote. "To begin with I was born, that I do not remember but I was told about it quite often [...] the next thing I heard about myself was that I was eight months old."[104] In Vienna, parts of her real memory began, assisted by "some things I could be helped to remember by hearing them told again and again."[105] In looking back at her youth, and her time in California from six years old onwards, Stein was more interested in the patterning of her memories and their unconscious self-selection, than in the story itself. In line with the frame of *Wars*, she also compared her growth with that of the nineteenth and twentieth century's conflicts.

The telling of her life as a mirror to war proved unsustainable, however, and Stein soon caught up with the present of 1943 in Culoz, turning *Wars* into an account of living in occupied France: almost a secret diary. She had never kept a diary or journal before.[106] Scattered throughout with precise dates—although written in one unbroken stream of prose, rather than with the breaks of a journal—the new book began to log what Stein did every day from 1943 until the end of the war. It was to be half-secret, half-public, since Stein wrote it with an eye for future publication in America.

As the distance between the time of the writing and the events being recorded closed up, it was as if, as an autobiographer, despite the war, Stein had been set free. The text crackles with discovery and momentum. Always aware of how autobiography balances two times simultaneously—and especially how it privileges an often half-imaginary past over the more immediate act of writing—Stein was scrupulous about avoiding memory's illusions. It was a mark of her honesty as a writer, her demand for exactitude, even when she appeared most obscure and hard to understand. "It is better not to remember because there is no such thing no such thing as remember,"[107] she wrote in *The Geographical History of America* (1936). And she meant this sincerely. She had struggled throughout her writing life with memory, wanting to set things down only as she saw them in the continuous present. She had betrayed these scruples in the *Autobiography*, and had a serious breakdown in her life, perhaps as a result. In the diary form of *Wars*, she finally found a form where the continuous present was entirely natural and unforced.

In the war itself, she also found a subject which destroyed the past: making everyday living and survival the main focus.

Wars I Have Seen carried on the general movement of Stein's autobiographies: away from talking about herself, to talking about everyone. But it was even more democratic. It was another book based on talk and conversation, growing out of Stein's informal chats with the people she encountered on her rounds in rural wartime France. Each day, she walked out, often to gather food. The daily walk—often resulting in a daily talk with someone met by chance out on the road—became the daily material of the diary. Stein also recorded what she heard on the radio, the other central influence on the book. She told Toklas not to type up the manuscript at first, so that if found by the Germans, it could only be deciphered with difficulty. What Stein built up in these pages again created a homely war reportage which ran counter to much writing about conflict. She knew she was writing history—the diary-like dates in *Wars I Have Seen* are self-consciously aware of their importance for posterity—but she wanted to record the ordinary life history leaves out.

Wars plunges straight into the middle of conflict, like a diary whose early volumes have been lost, beginning during Stein's fourth winter in the country, at the turn of 1942–3. By this time, the war has already gone on so long, no other life was imaginable. Once under way in the continuous present, the beginnings of war in the book felt a long way away. So did an ending. *Wars* was a book which continually seemed to be ending, to be about to be ending, to be about the war ending, to be ending right from the start. Even in the early pages, Stein writes how the end of the war is not far off.

These days of waiting for the end were last days in another way—almost, the days of apocalypse. Only Wells ever imagined anything like this, Stein writes. Or Shakespeare, whose histories Stein pointedly says she is reading during the war. In *Wars*, Stein writes of what she calls the "mediaeval" atmosphere, as everyone is forced to go out looking for food. People travel by bicycle, or with push-carts and boxes to gather wood for winter fires, on foot. We seem epochs away from the Paris of the *Autobiography of Alice B. Toklas*, the America of *Everybody's Autobiography*. In the rustic, conspiratorial atmosphere of *Wars*, people are paranoid and superstitious—not only speculating on the end of the war daily, but reverting to portents and signs. Stein chronicles how the resistance fighters or "maquis" hide up in the mountains; how suspected collaborators are sent tiny matchboxes with threats inside, or little wooden coffins containing a letter and a rope to suggest they hang themselves. She meets old women, families, refugees. They all tell her stories which go into the book, which revels in the thick, expanding network of rumors, of truths and counter-truths, speculations and predictions, the barter of gossip and information between people in the village. *Wars* offers an unexpected culmination of her portrait-writing, as she sketched, page by page, these people she encountered on the road. She no longer tried to define them as types, but in a prose of directness and simplicity, acted as a conduit for their stories, which nearly all inevitably proved to be stories of war.

She was careful throughout *Wars* not to give certain kinds of information. Above all, she avoided mention of her Jewishness. And she avoided direct mention of the Holocaust, although allusions to concentration camps and disappearances are everywhere in the text. Her treatment of these disappearances was evasive, yet omnipresent, quite possibly through her own sense of fear, in this book of conversations where it is always "To-day" or "yesterday." "Anybody can be taken away," Stein writes, "taken up in the street, taken at any time and carried away to work in a far away country and perhaps never to come home again at any age and in any place."[108] "And now and here in 1943, it is just like that, you take a train, you disappear, you move away your house is gone, your children too, your crops are taken away, there is nothing to say [...] anything can come and anything can go and they can say yes and no, and they can say, go [...]"[109]

In *Paris France*, Stein noted how war created a "concentration of isolation";[110] by 1944, this fifth winter of war, this isolation became even more intense when the telephone was suppressed. In early 1944, in the text, as at the time, the interminable waiting becomes unbearable. Stein sees trains mysteriously marked at the station; more people in the villages are taken away. Germans arrive at the house; Stein and Toklas have to put them up until they go. The endless present tense of *Wars* becomes intensely claustrophobic, only rarely punctured by a sudden flash of reminiscence, almost like a ray of light—as when Stein hears of Lake Trasimena on the radio, and remembers back to blissful pre-war long-gone days with Leo:

> When my brother and I were still at college we spent one summer some weeks in Perugia at a pension and there were lots of us there and one day some of us went off to see Lake Trasimena because there was supposed to be a whole army at the bottom well an army of ancient days naturally with gold chariots, and we thought we would like a swim in the lake, and the young men took the boatmen with them at one end of a little island in the middle of the

lake and we girls went to the other end to swim, and we swam without clothes in the sunset in Lake Trasimena.[111]

Back in the darkness of the interminable present, through the web of rumor and counter-rumor, and through the radio, the news of the American landings reaches the villages. But it's only as Stein grows confident of the coming ending of the war that she announces she will end the book when the war ends, rather like the pre-announced marking of an ending in *Everybody's Autobiography*. Then, suddenly, "now at half-past twelve to-day on the radio a voice said attention attention attention and the Frenchman's voice cracked with excitement and he said Paris is free."[112] *Wars* has, by this point, sustained the agonizing continuous present for so long, that this end of the war and the end of the text is euphoric. In a short coda, Stein relates her return with Toklas to Paris, where they found that their treasured paintings at the rue Christine, after all these years, were still intact.

*

As Janet Malcolm writes in *Two Lives*, and Barbara Will writes in *Unlikely Collaboration*, given Stein's Jewishness, her relationship with Toklas, and her celebrity, it is still mysterious how she survived the war, living in occupied France. Her survival was due to her friend Bernard Faÿ, who, despite his own anti-Semitism, used his high position in the Vichy regime to personally secure, from Pétain, the American ladies' protection.[113] Stein met Faÿ in 1926, and noted their first meetings in the *Autobiography*—which Faÿ, a professor specializing in Franco-American relations, translated into French. Faÿ had helped to organize Stein and Toklas's triumphant American tour. During the early years of war, he became director of the Bibliothèque Nationale, replacing a Jew, and assisted the Nazis in persecuting Freemasons. It was Faÿ who suggested that Stein work on a translation of Pétain's speeches in the early years of conflict: speeches in which there was strong anti-Semitic content, and a call for France to side with the Nazi occupiers. How, as a Jew herself, Stein could have devoted herself to this work remains puzzling. Stein worked on these translations from 1941 until early 1943 in Bilignin, even though they remained unfinished, and are not mentioned in *Wars*. Writing to the *sous-préfet* of Belley in 1941, Stein clearly referred to herself as "an American writer working for French propaganda in America"[114]— and mentions the success of *Paris France*—while also arguing for privileges as a vocal supporter of the Vichy regime. It is possible that the speeches were undertaken by Stein to try and broker her own protection; yet she had also shared many of Faÿ's increasingly right-wing political views in the 1930s.

Faÿ's protection of Stein and Toklas began to fall away from late 1942 onwards, however, as he lost his influence: the last time Stein saw Faÿ was in Culoz in autumn 1943.[115] During the period chronicled in detail in *Wars* Stein and Toklas were in a highly precarious, exposed position. Early in *Wars*, Stein tells how her lawyer told her that she and Toklas could now be deported to a concentration camp. But Stein was resolute: "here we are and here we stay."[116] Part of the energy of *Wars* comes through its genuine sense of fear and entirely justified paranoia. "You keep on thinking how quickly anybody can get killed,"[117] Stein writes early on. "Everybody knowing that everything is coming to an end every neighbour is denouncing every neighbour."[118] Even having accepted Faÿ's help would have been dangerous from 1943 onwards—in Culoz, to be accused of collaboration during the war would have been extremely risky, as Stein also suggests in *Wars*: "now in June 1943 something very strange is happening, every day the feeling is strengthening that one or another has been or will be a traitor to something."[119]

After the war, Faÿ was imprisoned as a collaborator. We still do not know exactly what Stein knew or thought of Faÿ's real activities. In a letter to Francis Rose after the war, Stein declared that Faÿ "certainly did certain things he should not have done, but that he ever denounced anybody, no, that I do not believe, in fact I know he did not."[120] But Stein was wrong: Faÿ did denounce people. Stein probably knew that she had compromised herself by accepting Faÿ's help, and in *Wars* itself there is a shift in the text's affiliations, with early sections proving broadly pro-Pétain, and later sections celebrating the Resistance. To some degree Stein's survival was tainted, and she knew this. There is anxiety in *Wars*, most noticeably near the start when Stein writes how she decided to stay in France; but an impersonal steadfastness, a quiet courage and resilience also emerges, even as she grew more and more politically out of her depth as the war went on. For all the evident danger, nowhere is there the sense of utter confusion and loss Stein felt years before in the 1930s, in the months when she fell out with Alice. Toklas is there throughout *Wars*, often silently included in an unexplained "we," whose very complacency suggests that all was well between them, now. As long as they were together—and as long as Stein was writing—nothing on earth could shake her.

Stein survived the war against all odds, hardly seeming to age. But the end of her own story, however, was nearer than she thought. In 1946, she suffered increasingly strong stomach pains, and was diagnosed with cancer. She had lost weight in the war, and put this down to the lack of food. She died on July 27 that year, after an operation. It was a swift end, whose suddenness feels more unexpected after reading *Wars*, which hardly mentions illness, and whose writing is so engaged with survival that it is easy to forget that Stein turned seventy in 1944.

Only in her manuscript *carnets* did she strike at the heart of her life: her love for Toklas. She kept this under cover, more or less, in all her autobiographies. The *Autobiography* made an open secret of it, a declaration as it were of their affiliation, but it could not of course have outlined their passion for each other. It did emphasize, however, the fact that Stein and Toklas were unable to extricate themselves from each other's identity: a fact borne out painfully by Toklas's life after Stein. On July 31, 1946, Alice, alone in the rue Christine, wrote Van Vechten, taking up the correspondence which had been interrupted by the last years of war, with a sense of devastation, depletion, and shock. "The emptiness is so very—very great," Toklas wrote. "Now she is in the vault of the American cathedral on the Quai d'Orsay—and I'm here alone. And nothing more—only what was [...] everything is empty and blurred [...] and I am to stay on here and the Picasso portrait goes to the Metropolitan Museum."[121] Losing the Picasso portrait was like losing part of Stein. Van Vechten wrote back a few days later, with an equally devastated, shocked postscript. "We are lonely too [...] It never occurred to me that Baby could die!"[122]

Wyndham Lewis and Gladys Anne Hoskins on the *Empress of Britain*, September
1939.
Source: Wyndham Lewis collection, #4612. Division of Rare and Manuscript Collections, Cornell
University Library.

7

My life being so difficult a one to live

Wyndham Lewis

I am sitting for myself at present—in fact it is a permanent job...[1]

Wyndham Lewis

After almost a decade spent on the Continent since leaving the Slade School of Drawing, Painting, and Sculpture in 1901, Wyndham Lewis returned to England with a new sense of purpose and urgency concerning his life as a painter and writer. Back in London in 1909, his long, unproductive European period, spent mainly in Paris, with periods in Brittany, Holland, Munich, and Madrid, was essentially over. Lewis, at twenty-seven, had just had his first success in art or literature: the appearance of his short stories of Breton life in the *English Review*. Ford Madox Hueffer had published "The Pole" by "P. Wyndham Lewis"—still in the process of shedding his first name, Percy—in the May 1909 issue, which also carried Conrad's reminiscences. "Some Innkeepers and Bestre" and "Les Saltimbanques" followed later that year. Despite this literary encouragement, Lewis, who oscillated between painting and writing all his life, decided soon afterwards to apply himself, with renewed dedication, to art.

Around 1911, Lewis drew three self-portraits as if taking possession of his talent: a trio of angular visions of himself, in which traces of his youthful wistfulness are overcome by resolution. All three drawings showed an affinity with Picasso's work influenced by African art. In Paris, Lewis had not met Picasso; but he probably heard about him through the bohemian elder painter Augustus John, who visited Picasso's studio and was a mentor to

Lewis in France. In his three self-portraits, Lewis invented his own idea of Cubism, and of himself, as he divided his own face into geometric shapes, breaking up and abstracting his features: tight and brooding, mask-like and vacated; alien, cold, and inhuman. Lewis had been depicted by John several years earlier, in an etching of 1903, and an oil painting of 1905; his expression in both portraits, beneath his luxuriantly dark hair, allowing flickers of his naivety and dreaminess to hover, as if hopefully, around his hard, exclusive, self-focused determination. But in the 1911 self-portraits he is all angles and edges.

Self-portraiture would become a recurring aspect of Lewis's work as an artist, and he produced numerous drawings and paintings of himself, in contradictory guises. Having been classically schooled at the Slade in the Life Room, Lewis used his self-portraits to experiment with identities, to cast himself in roles. "Why try and give the impression of a consistent and indivisible personality?,"[2] he wrote in 1915. He made reinvention sound like an artistic, even moral, obligation. "You must catch the clearness and logic in the midst of contradictions: not settle down and snooze on an acquired, easily possessed and mastered, satisfying shape."[3] In his "Code of a Herdsman," Lewis aired the same theme: "Contradict yourself. In order to live, you must remain broken up."[4] "Leave your front door one day as B.: the next march down the street as E." "A variety of clothes, hats especially, are of help in this wider dramatisation of yourself."[5]

The essence of self-portraiture, for Lewis, was multiplicity. The secret of the self was an illusion, a painting; and it was also through painting that one could remake oneself. In Lewis's first published novel *Tarr* (1918) the young English painter Frederick Tarr imagines the self as "a Chinese puzzle of boxes within boxes, or of insects' discarded envelopes."[6] For Bertha, his lover, at the center of these boxes was "an astral baby"; for himself, though, there was no "live core, but a painting like the rest. —His kernel was a painting, in fact: that was as it should be!"[7] Yet for all his multiplicity, Lewis was always reserved and secretive. Perhaps part of the attraction of showing many faces was that one could, fundamentally, protect oneself.

Lewis produced his most conflicting self-images in the years just after the First World War. For the Group X show at the Mansard Gallery in London in March 1920, he contributed at least four self-portraits, one an oil painting—and nothing else. His pen-and-ink self-portraits of that year, with their black shading looking like woodcuts, saw him improvising with accoutrements and props: pipe, hat, coat, and tie.[8] His face is generally softer and more oval than in the earlier self-portraits. The shading makes a mask of his expression, mournful and slightly anonymous, a face that could disappear in the crowd. A lost painting from this period, *Self-Portrait with Chair and Table*, turns Lewis into a smooth, black, externalized, almost sculptural figure, as if he were painting his shell.[9]

For his one-man show *Tyros and Portraits* at the Leicester Galleries in London in 1921, Lewis exhibited two contrasting self-portraits in oil. In *Portrait of the Artist as the Painter Raphael*, he depicted himself in the act of painting, with the canvas tilting towards him on the left-hand side of the frame, wearing a brown hat and jacket, his eyes direct but strangely flat. He appears calm, studious, and confident, accomplished in his art but also, the title suggests, keen to realign himself with tradition. In *Mr Wyndham Lewis as a Tyro* the background is violent yellow, the hat sharp and black, and the sneering, cartoon-like face hardly recognizable: sour green, eyebrow raised to a point, mouth set in a fixed, toothy grin.[10] Traumatized and empty, the implicit reference of this satirical and harsh self-portrait is to the psychological damage of the war. In 1921, Lewis launched a journal called *The Tyro*, and he made other drawings and paintings of Tyros: manipulated puppets of post-war society, mechanical and childlike, "worked with deft fingers, with a screaming voice underneath."[11]

Throughout the 1920s and 30s, Lewis continued to make drawings of himself in pencil, pen-and-ink on paper, often as an author portrait to accompany his writings, to which he turned with vigor, neglecting art for several years, from around 1923. In two self-portraits from 1927,[12] and his *Self-Portrait with Hat* from 1930,[13] Lewis looks more earnest and bookish. He now sometimes wears spectacles, as in the sober self-image from his 1932 exhibition *Thirty Personalities and a Self Portrait*.[14] In his 1931 *Self Caricature*,[15] later inscribed as *Self-Portrait*, the spectacles are an aspect of his cold, impersonal persona, recalling the sharp, hard lines of his self-drawings from twenty years earlier.

By this time Lewis was "The Enemy." Antagonistic, like a theatrical villain, "The Enemy" was an exaggerated, parodic alias. He enters and exits Lewis's poem *One-Way Song* (1933) "cloaked, masked and booted," spitting green flames, "an 'outcast' and a man 'maudit'."[16] A solitary, shadowy artistic force against contemporary society, unafraid to speak his mind, "The Enemy" was active from 1927, when Lewis launched his journal of that name. Yet after playing at casting himself in the role of villain, Lewis struggled to shake the mask off. In his last recorded self-portrait, a pencil drawing in 1938 for the *London Mercury*, he moved beyond this self-dramatization, yet his depiction still has a slight air of insouciance, with his Peterson pipe, spectacles, and sombrero.[17] In all his self-portraits, Lewis moved between the temptation to portray and construct a tough, aggressive exterior, and another impulse which conveyed his sensitivity. The problem was that the hostile persona was so much more memorable.

Lewis also made portraits of others throughout his life. Even as the self-styled pioneer of Vorticism before the First World War, he often used models to create his abstract paintings, or reverted to naturalism. In 1911, he drew his lover Olive Johnson, the year she had her first child with him, in *Mamie* and *Girl Asleep*.[18] Around the same time he drew another lover, Kate Lechmere, grimacing like the later Tyros, in *Smiling Woman Ascending a Stair* and *The Laughing Woman*. Of the latter's distortions, Lewis declared that "although the forms of the figure and head perhaps look rather unlikely [...] It was done from life."[19] The title of the Vorticist *Portrait of an Englishwoman* (1913), meanwhile, is nothing less than a challenge, or affront, daring the viewer to reconcile its stack of rectangles and diagonals with a flesh-and-blood sitter.

In the years after the war, Lewis threw himself into portraiture. Moving away from Vorticism, he came much closer to representation, though retaining abstract elements, "burying Euclid deep in the living flesh,"[20] as he put it. Wishing to improve his technique, he concentrated on the human figure, working on nudes as well as drawings and paintings of friends, acquaintances, and lovers. His new muse, Iris Barry, was depicted contrastingly, sitting while pregnant with another of his children in *Woman Knitting* (1920); and mutated into an inhuman brooding mass in the oil *Praxitella* (1920–1). Yet in his portraits Lewis was concerned not so much with multiplicity, as with capturing the presence of his subjects, through an intense—and often uncomfortable, for the sitters—focus on appearances. Through portraiture, externality became his artistic philosophy. "Dogmatically, I am for the Great Without, for the method of *external* approach—for the wisdom of the eye,"[21] Lewis wrote in *Men Without Art* (1934). "It is the *shell* of the animal that the plastically-minded artist will prefer."[22] To William Rothenstein, Lewis declared, "I go primarily for the pattern of the structure of the head and insinuate, rather than stress, the 'psyche'."[23]

This external method could be transcendent in its power, Lewis thought, making some portraits, in their extreme likeness, exist outside time. "The reality that is reflected in some portraits," Lewis wrote, referring to Renaissance portraits in particular, "is so fresh and delicate [...] that it is, while you gaze at these reflections, like living yourself, in a peculiar immortality."[24] Portraits took on a life of their own when achieved at this level of mastery. Of a portrait of Violet Schiff, Lewis said he wanted to create "something that will in a sense be *her*."[25] With such ideals, sitting for Lewis was arduous. Even his wife Gladys, a favorite model who married him in 1930 and sat for scores of images, found his scrutiny severe. Some sitters recalled the stream of negative talk issuing from Lewis as he worked; others evoked the silence as he portrayed them. Edith Sitwell, who said she sat for Lewis "every day excepting Sundays, for ten months" from late 1921, wrote that "when one sat to him [...] mice emerged from their holes, and lolled against the furniture."[26] The detail is leveled disparagingly at Lewis, who satirized Sitwell in *The Apes of God* (1930), but it also suggests the devoted absorption of his method of working on portraits.

Sometimes sitters would fall asleep, as happened when Ezra Pound—depicted by Lewis many times in his career after they first met through Ford—sat for one of his portraits. The shrewder T. S. Eliot, also depicted many times by Lewis, was less at his ease. He described Lewis at work on one portrait of himself, "wearing a look of slightly quizzical inscrutability" while he painted, making one "feel that it would be undesirable, though not actually dangerous, to fall asleep in one's chair."[27]

The danger of displeasing the sitter was an intrinsic element of portraiture for Lewis. "Sitters," Lewis wrote in his autobiography *Blasting and Bombardiering* (1937), "are apt to be very nice right up to the final sitting,"[28] when they were disappointed on viewing the finished product. Lewis always associated portraits with money. Whenever he was hard up, he returned to portraits for support. But the terrain was treacherous. A good portrait of a sitter was not always one that made the sitter look good. Sitters whose vanity was wounded were apt to leave without the portrait, and without paying for it. For this reason, many of Lewis's portraits were drawings rather than oil paintings. He could invest his time more cautiously with "portrait-heads in pencil or aquarelle," which "only occupied two or three afternoons,"[29] he wrote in *Blasting*, rather than oils which took far longer. Extracting payment from sitters became one of Lewis's many miseries. Squabbling over a portrait drawing of O. R. Drey, Lewis wrote to his sitter:

> You say, let the original arrangement stand: but where's the *cheque*, old boy? [...] instead of *saying* let the arrangement stand, *do* something; sit down at your desk, draw out your cheque-book, write me a nice polite little note saying you are

sorry there has been any trouble, close your eyes, hold your breath, and write *six*—and there you will be straight with me.[30]

Wrangles with offended sitters bedevilled Lewis's life as a painter. Related problems also surrounded his writing. Lewis was more fiercely satirical as a writer than in his art, and his books often included, recognizably, friends, acquaintances, and other real-life figures. As a writer, Lewis remained faithful to external appearances, however unflattering. Satire, Lewis felt, was truth-telling, a mode between comedy and tragedy: "a *grinning* tragedy."[31]

Pledged as a writer to the external, Lewis scorned the internalized techniques of Virginia Woolf, Gertrude Stein, and Lewis's friend James Joyce. (Lewis never let friendship get in the way of satire or critique.) Stein came under heavy fire, parodied as Satterthwaite in *The Childermass* (1928) and in *Time and Western Man* (1927), which ridicules Stein and the "stuttering," childlike inflections of her "prose song": "a cold suet-roll of fabulously reptilian length. Cut it at any point, it is the same thing; the same heavy, sticky, opaque mass all through, and all along [...] It is mournful and monstrous, composed of dead and inanimate material."[32] Lewis thought such verbal representations of the inner life lacked any firm definition. Joyce's *Ulysses*, Lewis wrote, "imposes a softness, flabbiness, and vagueness everywhere in its bergsonian fluidity."[33] Yet Henry James, never an acquaintance, receives a milder treatment. James "had an excellent eye in his head," Lewis wrote in *Men Without Art*.[34] But James went wrong, Lewis thought, in that "his activities were all turned *inwards* rather than *outwards*."[35]

Vagueness was seldom a feature of Lewis's own novels, often drawn daringly sharply and closely from life, sometimes causing reprisals. Some of those satirized in *The Apes of God* set up counter-attacks on Lewis, including the painter Richard Wyndham, who took out a personal advertisement offering two of Lewis's paintings at bargain prices in *The Times*. Lewis denied that there was any character based on Wyndham; and he produced a flyer, headed "A STOP PRESS EXPLOSION": "ENRAGED Ape of God, believing that he had caught sight of his own features in the crowded mirror of *The Apes of God*, sends up a cry of AGONY!"[36]

Like H. G. Wells—who wrote to Lewis about *The Childermass*, with Lewis replying in turn, complimenting the older writer on *The World of William Clissold* and his articles about war[37]—Lewis made repeated disavowals about the "originals" of his characters. Around the time of *The Apes of God*, he had lunch with Wells and they discussed this very topic. As Lewis recalled in his second autobiography, *Rude Assignment* (1950), Wells found it hard to believe that people could be wounded by such portrayals: "he had some interesting things to say on the subject of the rage that people may *affect to feel*, and their motives."[38] Yet contemporaries were wounded by Lewis's unforgiving take-downs. Virginia Woolf wrote in her diary, in October 1934, about *Men Without Art*: "I know by reason and instinct that this is an attack; that I am publicly demolished."[39] Being at the receiving end of Lewis's barbs was more painful than Wells would acknowledge. But his satire, Lewis thought, was "not portraiture"—"a new world is created out of the shoddy material of everyday, and nothing does, or could, go over into that as it appeared in nature."[40] To publishers, Lewis offered many explanations of this point. In 1926, to Chatto & Windus, Lewis made this self-defense:

> As to your believing that you detect a likeness in some of my personages to people in real life, in that you are mistaken. I have here and there used things, it is true that might suggest some connection. But the cases you choose are not ones I could, I am afraid, remove from my picture. If the bodies I describe fit the morning suits of real people and they [...] lay claim to them, however much the clothes fitted I should not countenance the wearing of such mis-fits by any of my characters, to all of whom I supply suits to measure from *my own* store.[41]

Libel actions from people who saw themselves in his pages became a pressing snag for Lewis in the 1930s, in the years just before he wrote his autobiography in 1937. *Doom of Youth* in 1932 brought two libel actions, as Chatto had foreseen. Switching publishers with *Snooty Baronet* the same year, there was further trouble, with Cassell warning Lewis that his next books must "pass the Library censors."[42] *Filibusters in Barbary*, also in 1932, brought another libel claim; *The Roaring Queen*, submitted by Cape to a solicitor, was withdrawn. Faced with this barrage of writs, Lewis was paranoid, believing there was a conspiracy against him.

These legal vendettas added strain to Lewis's financial woes at this time. Since 1926, he had sustained an outpouring of writing, often publishing several books each year. But he had little money. Medical bills deepened his debts when he became seriously ill in 1932 from grisly complications resulting from the gonorrhea he had when he was younger. Lewis had four major operations in the 1930s, nearly dying during one of them, becoming a long-suffering denizen of what he called, in a letter to Eliot, "hospital land."[43] The experience of illness and dependency fed into paintings such as *The Convalescent* (1933), broaching a new warmth and humanism. Lewis also produced otherworldly and metaphysical imaginary scenes, likewise haunted by hospital, around this time. His novel *The Revenge for Love* (1937) also revealed an interest in creating rounded, emotionally alive, characters, blessed with an interior, rather than purely exterior, life. It was a complete departure in this way from the hard impersonality of his earlier literary work.

At the same time, Lewis had been moving into dangerous territory with his political writing: especially since his articles on Hitler and National Socialism, published as a book in 1931. Lewis's polemical volumes in the 1930s took contradictory positions on Communism and Fascism. They were all, above all, against another war, but they did at times show sympathy for Fascism. In several tracts, including *Left Wings Over Europe* (1936) and *Count Your Dead—They Are Alive!* (1937), Lewis's suspicion of left-wing intellectuals and desire for appeasement made him, in W. H. Auden's phrase, a "lonely old volcano of the Right."[44]

What Lewis called his "anti-war" political books were often shifting and ambiguous. By 1938 he reversed his opinions, especially on Hitler and Germany, and after the war, in *Rude Assignment*, he called most of these political books "futile performances—ill-judged, redundant, harmful of course to me personally, and of no value to anybody else."[45] Fear of the insecurity of another war lay behind their frenzied postures. But no amount of retraction could undo the damage they did to his reputation, as Lewis himself slowly came to realize.

*

Lewis was fifty-four when he published *Blasting and Bombardiering* in October 1937. Despite his recent illnesses, *Count Your Dead* had appeared in April, and *The Revenge for Love* in May. Much of the autobiography was written that spring and summer, being finished in the autumn,[46] although Lewis had the idea of writing it earlier, probably in the autumn of 1936,[47] in the hope of gaining a larger audience, and paying off some of his medical debts. Lewis always distinguished between his "formal" books—his novels—and his "informal" non-fiction, written much faster, "just as one talks, and nearly as fast as talking."[48] A page of *The Revenge for Love*, Lewis wrote in a letter of 1937, "takes me as long to write as twenty pages of *Blasting and Bombardiering*."[49] The autobiography was written at great speed; its tone was also deliberately colloquial.

That year, Lewis was moving house, as he constantly was during the 1920s and 30s, sometimes secretively. His flats since the war had frequently been around Paddington and Bayswater, and he had an unusual habit of renting several different, often tiny, separate spaces for living and work, then shifting between them. In 1937, before his fourth and final major operation, he and Gladys relocated, and that summer he cleared out of 121 Gloucester Terrace,[50] where he had had a workroom since 1934.[51] From July, his London base was nearby at 10 Sussex Gardens before the Lewises arrived in October at 29A Kensington Gardens Studios, Notting Hill Gate, a large third-floor studio with a skylight and kitchen, the living quarters—a living-room, bedroom, and another kitchen—on the floor below.[52]

In several unrealized projects, Lewis had come close to depicting his own life before, as well as in his autobiographical fiction. In 1922, he had planned a novel entitled *The Life of a Tyro*, never written.[53] Then there was a character called "Cantelman," who surfaced in some stories published during the First World War,[54] drawing from Lewis's experiences. In 1930, Pound wrote to Lewis about Cantelman,[55] and Lewis mentioned some "rough war-stories and sketches" used for a "war-book which I started two years ago, have not gone on with, but hope to soon,"[56] possibly referring to the unfinished "Cantelman-Crowd Master" manuscript,[57] parts of which he used in *Blasting*.[58] Perhaps Pound also recalled a letter he received from Lewis in 1916, where Lewis, about to fight in France, announced: "I am writing a book called 'The Bombardier': only in my head, of course [...]"[59]

Blasting and Bombardiering would be another war book itself, indeed another anti-war book, its depiction of the First World War freshly topical in the late 1930s with another conflict looming. Early on, Lewis highlighted the time of the writing, "with a little sketch of how things are shaping—in 1937,"[60] "because it is after all myself in 1937 who is writing about myself as 'blaster' and as bombardier."[61] Lewis promised that there would be no politics in the autobiography, "a private history"[62] free of propaganda. He was clear, too, about what period the autobiography would cover, making ambitious claims about the omission of his life until his thirties:

> This book is about myself. It's the first autobiography to take only a section of a life and leave the rest. Ten years about is the time covered. This is better than starting with the bib and the bottle. How many novels are tolerable that begin with the hero in his cradle? And a good biography is of course a sort of novel [...] This book is about what happened to me in the Great War, and then afterwards in the equally great Peace [...] the war, with a bit of pre-war and post-war sticking to it, fore and aft.[63]

Lewis promised that the autobiography would not venture past 1926, because it was still too near to be seen with clarity. "One only writes 'biographies' about things that are past and over. The present period is by no means over. One couldn't sit down and write a biography about *that*."[64] *Blasting* moves from Lewis's momentary celebrity in the first six months of 1914, to the First World War in London and France, before depicting the early 1920s—its structure "Art-War-Art, in three panels."[65] It is hardly "the first autobiography to take a section of a life and leave the rest," yet its total omission of childhood is radical. Any areas of Lewis's life not concerning his status as a writer and artist, or the war, are left completely out of sight. Lewis pictured the structure of the book in strikingly visual terms—and perhaps his life-long practice of self-portraiture and portraiture made autobiography easier for him—as being "about a little group of people crossing a bridge [...] the bridge, you see, is *the war*."[66]

Alongside himself, Lewis wanted to portray a number of friends in the autobiography. "As well as being about myself, this book is about a number of people in all walks of life,"[67] he wrote. In fact, *Blasting* was initially envisaged as a kind of group biography called "The Men of 1914," before Lewis shifted the focus onto himself during the writing.[68] The people finally included were mainly writers and artists. Many figures also appeared in the reproductions of Lewis's portrait drawings in *Blasting*, including Rebecca West and "The Men of 1914" themselves: Joyce, Pound, and Eliot, all of whom Lewis drew in multiple portraits with sharp, incisive strokes, and whom he characterizes as a group both heroically and nostalgically as "*the first men of a Future that has not materialized*," belonging to "a 'great age' that has not 'come off'."[69]

Lewis noted that he was bound by the "vexatious" laws of libel: "there are limits to the truthfulness in which I may indulge."[70] In a rejected early preface, "A Preliminary Aside to the Reader; Regarding Gossip, and its Pitfalls," Lewis voiced his qualms about biography, as he declared: "I am about to gossip. I am going to be exceedingly 'personal' about certain persons." He blamed the reader: "it is because of *you* that I descend to these picturesque details."[71] As an autobiographer, he was conscious of the irony of depicting impersonal writers such as Eliot—who asserted that "the progress of an artist is a continual self-sacrifice, a continual extinction of personality"[72]—through their lives rather than their work. Part of his motivation, Lewis claimed in *Blasting*, was to give a more truthful account than he thought these people would receive from future biographers. "I must rescue a few people I respect [...] from the obloquy and misrepresentation which must be their unenviable lot."[73] *Blasting* also makes a side-swipe at the "New Biography" practiced by the "Bloomsberries":

> With what assurance people compose accounts of the demeanour and most private thoughts of the departed great! What novelists *a bon marché* those biographists become! Every "great man" to-day knows that he is living potentially a life of fiction. Sooner or later he will find himself the centre of a romance [...] Now for a decade or two those of the Strachey kidney have made a corner in the eminent dead [...] But I, for a change, will stake out a modest claim in the *living*.[74]

In *Blasting*, Lewis organized his life-story with the firm lines of his drawings and novels. Autobiography, he argued, allowed him to assert control. "Don't you often feel about some phase of your existence that it requires going over with a fine comb and putting in order?"[75] In this spirit, he offered views of himself, in different phases and poses. As an autobiographer, Lewis wanted no flapping loose ends; above all, he wanted his life to be neat, as though self-portraiture were akin to a visit to the hairdresser—blessed in a whole page of *Blast*, as Lewis also reminds us in *Blasting*.[76]

The first "panel" of *Blasting* recounts Lewis's breakthrough in 1914, as the leader of the Rebel Art Centre, figurehead of Vorticism and editor of *Blast*. Writing from the pre-war-shadowed present of 1937, Lewis recreated the pre-war-shadowed months of 1914 as a period when art was full of military maneuvers, playing at war, as Marinetti and the Futurists clashed with the Vorticists. In one slapstick sequence which, in its exaggeration and caricature recalls Ford's memoirs of the Pre-Raphaelites in *Ancient Lights*, Lewis intervenes in a dispute between Henri Gaudier and David Bomberg, after Gaudier "threatened at Ford's to sock Bomberg on the jaw"[77]—before Lewis admits that he once seized T. E. Hulme by the throat. "He transfixed me upon the railings of Soho Square,"[78] Lewis writes. All the "*putsches*" of these rival groups are portrayed as essentially comic, as is Vorticism, which "was replete with humour, of course."[79]

So was *Blast*, the "Review of the Great English Vortex," whose first issue appeared on July 1, 1914,[80] and which Lewis gives such prominence in his autobiography. In pages of typographically eccentric headlines between putrid covers variously described as puce, pink, and purple, and whimsical cursings and blessings, *Blast* challenged an entire generation of writers and artists, in a string of manifestos, poems, plays, "vortices and notes," and other oddments, with literary contributors including Pound, Lewis, Ford, and Rebecca West; and illustrations from numerous Vorticists. Despite the inclusion of Ford, Impressionism was one of many targets of the Vorticists: "Our Vortex rushes out like an angry dog at your Impressionistic fuss."[81] But the contributors were certainly far from aligned in their aims. Rebecca West, for example, wondered privately, "Am I a Vorticist? I'm sure it can't be good for Anthony if I am."[82] In *Blasting*, Lewis reproduced—without the typographical quirks of the original or "the scale of the 12 in. high *Blast* page"[83]—some of the *Blast* manifestos, which as he explains, reveled in contradiction:

BLAST HUMOUR—
Quack ENGLISH drug for stupidity and sleepiness.
Arch enemy of REAL [...][84]

Then only a few pages later:

BLESS ENGLISH HUMOUR [...]
The wild MOUNTAIN RAILWAY from IDEA
to IDEA, in the ancient Fair of LIFE.[85]

As Lewis tells it, a shower of invitations reached him as a result of "that comic earthquake, *Blast*,"[86] helping him make his entrée into "society." He was a "lion," enjoying an unprecedented—and he implies, largely unearned—celebrity. At Lady Ottoline Morrell's house, Lewis even met the Prime Minister. On the weekend before the outbreak of war in July, Lewis went up to Berwickshire, to the country-house party hosted by Mary Borden Turner where Ford and Violet Hunt were also present. Lewis had no idea, he writes, of the war on the horizon, and depicts himself as a political naïf. At the party, he belatedly became aware, noting the other guests' concentration on the newspapers, that something momentous was occurring. In a pivotal scene from *Blasting*, at breakfast, Mary Turner and Ford discussed whether England would go to war.

Ford thrust his mouth out, fish-fashion, as if about to gasp for breath. He goggled his eyes and waggled one eyelid about. He just moved his lips a little and we heard him say, in a breathless sotto voce—
"England will."
"England will! But Ford," said Mrs. Turner, "England has a Liberal Government. A Liberal Government cannot declare war."
"Of course it can't," I said, frowning at Ford. "Liberal governments can't go to war. That would not be liberal. That would be conservative."

Ford sneered very faintly and inoffensively [...] "I don't agree," Ford answered, in his faintest voice, with consummate indifference, "because it has always been the Liberals who have gone to war."[87]

This ending of the first "panel" of *Blasting* was a political awakening for Lewis, still only in his early thirties. Lewis also wrote about this moment in his earlier, fictional "Cantelman-Crowd Master" manuscript, where the portrait of Ford (fictionalized as "Leo Makepiece Leo") is more unpleasantly explicit about the older man's habit of associating himself with other great writers, and about Ford's physical appearance and size. Although Ford in *Blasting* is hardly portrayed kindly in external terms—with his thrust-out mouth, goggling eyes, and breathlessness—he is given a certain grudging admiration and respect for his knowledge of the ways of the world, compared to the more innocent Lewis.

In the second "panel" of *Blasting*, the "Cantelman" manuscript reemerges more strongly—as Lewis hands over entirely to "Cantleman" [*sic*] for several chapters. He tells us that Cantleman is a mask for himself,[88] and notes that he has used parts of *Blast 2: War Number* from 1915, written "*on the spot.*"[89] And this is where "Cantleman" material first surfaced.[90] Reassembling texts written over twenty years before, Lewis acts as an impresario of his earlier fictional selves, also saying he has toned down the original, included as its closeness to the events gives it authenticity. He worried that the *Blast 2* material might be too "highbrow" for the autobiography.[91] The switch into the third-person, into fiction, and into a different tone, is novel and jarring. But the dislocation also reflects the momentous confusion as England prepared for war.

Cantleman leaves the house-party abruptly, departing on the night train. He sees scenes of mobilization everywhere as the train lurches south through the small hours. Conversations are woven into a tapestry of reportage and stream-of-consciousness, as Cantleman gives word portraits of people on the train, reaching King's Cross in the morning. Cantleman joins the thronging war-crowds in London, wandering through them like a flâneur to Trafalgar Square, conducting "crowd-experiments."[92] He dissolves into the moods of the crowd, and makes notes on them. "The war was like a great new fashion,"[93] he observes.

*

Lewis, having only just established himself as an artist and writer, was completely unprepared for the war. As he stresses in *Blasting*, it took him by surprise. His first reaction to the tumult was, he writes in the autobiography, to try and continue as usual. For a while he lived at 4 Percy Street, off the Tottenham Court Road, recovering from an "infection"[94]—the gonorrhea which proved debilitating years later—mentioned in the autobiography in fairly cryptic terms. Knowing he would sign up once he was fit, Lewis worked on *Tarr*, and continued with art. In November 1914, he completed a Vorticist panel at South Lodge for Ford and Violet Hunt, and the following year designed the cover for Ford's poem *Antwerp*. In March 1915 he appeared in the Second London Group Show, and in June held the first, only, Vorticist Exhibition. Also that summer, after Gaudier died in France on June 5, and probably before Ford enlisted in July 1915, Lewis recorded another conversation in *Blasting* with Ford, again granted a gift for prophecy, contrasted with Lewis's naivety.

> I was talking to Ford Madox Hueffer about Gaudier's death [. . .] It was absurd, Ford agreed. But there it was, he seemed to think. He seemed to think *fate* was absurd [. . .]
>   "When this War's over," he said, "nobody is going to worry, six months afterwards, what you did or didn't do in the course of it. One month after it's ended, it will be forgotten. Everybody will want to forget it—it will be bad form to mention it. Within a year disbanded 'heroes' will be selling matches in the gutter. No one likes the ex-soldier—if you've lost a leg, more fool you!"
>   "Do you think that?" I said [. . .]
>   "Of course," he answered. "It's always been the same. After all wars that's what's happened."
>   This worldly forecast was verified to the letter.[95]

In *Blasting*, Lewis makes clear he wanted to finish *Tarr* before enlisting,[96] intending to leave at least some kind of literary legacy behind him before he went to France. Harriet Weaver accepted *Tarr* for *The Egoist* in January 1916; Lewis volunteered in March. He bequeathed his possessions to his mother, Anne, who was also looking after his two children with Olive Johnson, the second born in 1913.[97] Lewis spent the rest of 1916 in artillery camps on the south coast of England, initially training as a gunner, then as a bombardier. Through Pound in August 1916, he heard about Ford's shell-shock. Pound had met Ford's brother-in-law. "He said a shell had burst near our friend and that he had had a nervous breakdown,"[98] Pound wrote Lewis. Through Violet Hunt, Lewis was also applying for a commission. He left for France in May 1917, and he was soon at the front and under heavy fire.

Lewis's letters describe the vivid turmoil of the war with immediacy and extraordinary bravado. On June 6, 1917, Lewis was writing to his mother, telling her not to worry: "I am now in the firing line [...] I am writing you this note in my dugout, surrounded by a continuous din from all quarters. Guns of all description blaze away day and night."[99] To Pound, the same day: "Whizzing, banging, swishing and thudding completely surround me."[100] Two days later, to Pound again, Lewis said he had been gassed in his sleep, and missed shells—"coming over every few seconds"[101]—by twenty yards, twice.

Lewis also gave a very thorough account of his war in *Blasting*, again steeped in bravado. While Ford avoided the war in his autobiographies, Lewis gave it pride of place. He was especially concerned to demystify war, to strip it of its "romance." He was keen to write against the "subtle anguish"[102] of the accounts of the late 1920s. He wanted to depict the conflict as a "squalid serio-comedy."[103] Yet the detail of the autobiography, for all its gruffness and imperturbability, amasses a certain gravity. And while its grim humor and anti-romanticism mask Lewis's feelings about the war, its centrality in his account of his life shows his awareness nonetheless that, more than anything else he experienced, it had marked him irrevocably. He was not prepared for the war; nor did he ever really get over it. In *Blasting*, keen to demystify war, Lewis tried to make light of his time as a gunner and battery officer, stressing that his experience was not "fighting" like the infantry, and depicting the long periods of inactivity. Lewis says he hardly ever saw the enemy, while dispatching endless shells towards them. But he was also under continual bombardment, sometimes for days and nights on end.

At the end of June 1917, he came down with "trench fever," as he writes in *Blasting*: his neck and face were swollen, along with his tongue. He was taken to a Casualty Clearing Station near Boulogne, then a convalescent hotel in Dieppe. Despite the stiff comedy of the autobiography, in his letters he was dwelling on his possible death, writing to Pound that if anyone had to write a memoir of him, he would like Pound to do it.[104] In mid-August, he returned to his battery near Nieuwpoort in Belgium. In Nieuwpoort, for almost two months, he was in a battery position under intense shelling day and night. An anecdote in *Blasting* from this time is particularly chilling. One afternoon, Lewis went to Headquarters, and on return saw his position had been hit: his sergeant killed, half a dozen men wounded. Lewis's unemotional tone modulates into solemn, stunned resentment. "As this is written, so it happened. But that is obviously not how men's lives should be taken away from them, for nothing at all."[105]

From the end of September, he was in the Salient, in the Third Battle of Ypres, a semi-aquatic, boggy nightmare, portrayed in *Blasting* in both comic and tragic terms—a "*grinning* tragedy," indeed—as "an epic of mud." Going to his observation post before dawn, in an empty dugout just off the road, a shell "exploded two feet from my head,"[106] Lewis writes in *Blasting*. Soon afterwards, he saw two dead Scottish soldiers, one without a head.[107]

In November, Lewis was granted compassionate leave to return to London, as his mother was ill with pneumonia. Lewis extended his leave in London, he notes in *Blasting*, and heard about the Canadian Government's scheme for war artists. Returning to the front at the end of 1917, he had a new role as a "painter-soldier."[108] As a war artist, he was living in a château along with his old friend Augustus John. He was back in London early in 1918, to complete his war paintings. He was physically unharmed, miraculously; but he must have been psychologically scarred by his experience of being shelled for months on end. Lewis makes his role as a war artist sound relatively frivolous, but he excelled in his paintings of the conflict.

Bitterness only seeps into *Blasting* as the conflict nears its end. Lewis pinpoints how the war was an education for him politically. Under bombardment, Lewis had read Stendhal, Proudhon, and Marx. And now, thinking politically about the war, he gags himself and his rising anger, not unlike Ford's ex-army character "Gringoire" in *No Enemy*, who also has to stop himself saying too much.

In the third and final "panel" of *Blasting*, Lewis gives a sketchy account of his post-war period, in London. His father, Charles, who left Lewis's mother in 1893, and whom Lewis had barely seen for twenty years, died in November 1918, before Lewis's mother died in 1920. Lewis himself was a victim of the post-war flu epidemic, with influenza followed by double pneumonia. He recovered, but only after losing nearly all his hair. Lewis's resumé in *Blasting* of what he had achieved by this point in his life is scathing: "I had accomplished nothing."[109] He had to start anew as a writer and artist, at thirty-six, having lost several crucial years in the war.

As Lewis began painting regular portraits in the early 1920s, the pages of *Blasting* offer a series of anecdotes about his sitters, these short verbal sketches forming a natural counterpart to the narrative of Lewis's new life as a portrait painter in his garden studio in Adam and Eve Mews in Kensington. The last "compartment" of the autobiography gives distilled word portraits of first meeting Joyce, Pound, and Eliot—the device of depicting these figures through brief "meetings" also allowing for concision and pithiness. Lewis met Joyce in Paris with Eliot in the summer of 1920, as he relates. His first meeting with Pound was probably in 1910, in the Vienna Café in New Oxford Street, where Lewis also remembered noticing Wells (before they met) several times: Wells "springing about in a suit too tight for him, as he inducted ladies into chairs."[110] With Eliot, Lewis can't exactly place when he first met him—for he "*slid*" into his consciousness—but it was "in the narrow triangle of Ezra's flat" in Kensington.[111]

Blasting ends with a brief account of 1937; and it is in the third and final "panel" that the omissions and evasions of the autobiography—the most glaring being of Lewis's sexual relationships—make themselves most felt. Even at the outset of *Blasting*, Lewis noted that "1918–26 is a period marked 'strictly private'."[112] His many relationships with women are off limits in *Blasting*, and as in Ford's autobiographies, Lewis's lovers are completely omitted, along with their offspring.

Lewis's two children with Olive Johnson are not even glimpsed in these pages, nor are his two children after the war with Iris Barry, born in 1919 and 1920 respectively, or his child with his first serious girlfriend Ida Vendel, born in 1908. These omissions do however reflect one truth. Lewis hardly saw any of these children. Apart from attempting to provide upkeep, he abandoned them just as he had been abandoned by his father, and he abandoned the women who bore them. He seems to have found any conception of family life completely unimaginable; to have regarded emotion with suspicion or scorn. Women who had affairs with Lewis, meanwhile, did appear, innocuously, in his autobiography, including Sybil Hart-Davis, Mary Borden Turner, and Nancy Cunard. His wife, Gladys Anne, or "Froanna," would have no children, and was also invisible in *Blasting*.

And yet Lewis drew and painted nearly all his women repeatedly, obsessively. It was in his images, not his words or deeds, that his feelings for them emerged. Between 1936 and 1938, for example, as Paul Edwards writes, Lewis produced seven paintings of "Froanna," and many more works on paper.[113] She was highly visible in the *Red Portrait* and *Portrait of the Artist's Wife* in Lewis's show at the Leicester Galleries in December 1937, "Infernos." The couple traveled to Warsaw and Berlin together before the opening, with this trip revealing to Lewis his misjudgment of the German situation. Over the next two years, Lewis returned with vigor to portraiture, remaining in Kensington Gardens Studios, and painting portraits of Pound and Eliot—the latter being painted in March 1938, with sittings in the evenings between

8.30 and midnight, and Lewis continuing with the painting alone during the day.[114] The Eliot portrait was rejected by the Royal Academy, sending Lewis back into the public fray in his preferred role as artistic antagonist.

Much as he liked to satirize society and live in secrecy, "underground," Lewis thrived on company, even if only as something against which to rebel. Despite his seeming misanthropy, he found it hard to live in total isolation, and his satire fed on other people, just as his portraiture literally depended on them too. This was something he would realize over the next few years, as he and Gladys left England for America and Canada on the eve of the Second World War, with Lewis planning to escape the "economic inferno"[115] of war-time Britain, where the encroaching atmosphere of war was making it harder than ever to survive as an artist. In America, Lewis thought, portraits would be easier to come by.

*

Lewis and Froanna left Southampton, sailing for Quebec, on September 2, 1939, the day before Britain declared war on Germany, arriving in Canada on September 8. After a week in Toronto they made their way to New York, where they were based for most of the next year, before being forced to return to Toronto in November 1940 when their American visas expired. They spent the next two-and-a-half years in an apartment suite, 11A, in the Tudor Hotel in Toronto, while Lewis attempted—steadily becoming poorer and poorer—to keep them afloat on portrait commissions. A trip Lewis had imagined would last several months eventually lasted six years, as the war continued, and as Lewis and Froanna's finances dwindled, making the return boat fare out of reach.

As during the First World War, Lewis became a prolific letter-writer during this time. His growing desperation can be traced in numerous accounts to correspondents throughout his residence in America and Canada. Where Gertrude Stein a few years earlier toured America in triumph, disconcerted mainly by her celebrity, Lewis faced not just indifference on his arrival, but even, he thought in his more paranoid moments, hostility. He was utterly dependent on portraits to survive, yet to obtain commissions he had to dress expensively, he thought, and give no outward sign that he and Gladys were hard up. After nearly a year in the Tudor Hotel, in October 1941, he summed things up relatively optimistically to Archibald MacLeish: "Although I have succeeded in making a living of sorts here in Canada—mostly by portrait-painting—it is very gruesome work struggling with people about the shapes of their noses and the size of their feet."[116] But by April 1942, still stuck in the Tudor, he was writing to James Johnson Sweeney:

> Already my life here is unbelievably difficult and my wife nearly crazed with worry. All along I have recognised that millions of people everywhere are suffering in the most terrible way—that my misfortune is merely typical of a universal misery. For my wife's sake even more than for my own (for I feel responsible for what is happening to her) I have incessantly exerted myself to find some solution. I am still doing so. There is no stone that has not been turned over. But all I can say is that [...] I can see no prospect of relief. If I did not have a hotel which providentially does not seem to mind about the payment of rent we should be on the streets.[117]

As ever, Lewis was able to extract humor from the desperation, wryly adding: "I refer to this as my 'Tudor Period'."[118] But the situation was obviously dire, exacerbated by exile, worry, and loneliness. New York, Lewis told one correspondent in summer 1942, "was the worst year of my life—years of illness excepted [...] Today however I am screwed down as firmly as it is possible to be [...] What is going to happen to us in the end I do not know."[119] At one point, he and Gladys were so short of funds, as Paul O'Keeffe relates, that Gladys "was unable to leave the apartment because she had no serviceable shoes."[120] She applied for work in a tarpaulin-sewing factory, but her application was rejected, as were Lewis's applications for teaching positions. The begging letters from Lewis continued; at one particularly low moment he even made veiled threats to his ex-lover Iris Barry, now married and working at MoMA in New York, and also trying to find a publisher for Lewis's novel *The Vulgar Streak* (1941). "Remember, I will show up your bad behaviour,"[121] Lewis wrote to Barry ominously. She sent money.

Lewis wrote about his time in America and Canada in two highly autobiographical books, which together suggest how his initial optimism became privation as the war continued. *America, I Presume* (1940) was written swiftly in the first year abroad, narrated by a bluff Anglo-Indian, Archibald Corcoran, who like Lewis has left England on the eve of the Second World War. Corcoran, with his wife Agatha Morgan—a crime novelist whose latest mystery is called *The Clue of the Silver Snuff-Box*, and who, we are later told, has ghostwritten much of the manuscript—is "booked for a coast-to-coast lecture tour"[122] of the United States. Like Lewis and Gladys, "Corkers" and Agatha arrive in Canada at Quebec and visit Toronto, before New York. Lewis uses *America, I Presume* to offer, through

Corcoran's conservative viewpoint, his jaundiced observations as he travels in America. Stephen Spender recalled being shown a copy containing a "key" to the real identities of its characters[123]—and the novel is a transparent *roman à clef*, close to a travel book or even a polemic, as Lewis uses his slap-dash, "political"-pamphlet-style loquacity to flesh out an essentially plotless narrative. For all its aimlessness and digression, and the jarring effect of the prejudiced, unreliable narrator, the mood of *America, I Presume* is generally blithe and upbeat.

But in *Self Condemned* (1954), mainly written after the ordeal was over, Lewis fictionalized, in gruelling detail, the long confinement in the Tudor Hotel, through his portrayal of the two main characters: René Harding, a professor of history who gives up his career and emigrates to Canada, and his wife, Hester. As René tells each member of his family in turn before departure, he has abandoned history as a discipline. His exile to Canada, unlike Lewis's initial vision of America, is envisaged as hopeless: "an empty interlude, an apprenticeship to death," or "a breathing-space, a period of readjustment."[124]

Self Condemned conveys René's self-reproach in microscopic detail, as he and Hester take up residence in Canada in "the Room," in the Hotel Blundell, "twenty-five feet by twelve about," where they remain for "three years and three months."[125] Stuck in a "senseless captivity,"[126] they are "eco-nomic exiles—exiles by accident, frozen in their tracks, as it were, by the magic of total war."[127] The months turn into years. England recedes—"until it was, at times, hardly real."[128] The Room becomes like an extension of René and Hester themselves, and René resents anyone entering it and seeing their unhappiness. The plight of the exiles is too "small" to be truly tragic, as they know their suffering is eclipsed by the war. Yet it inspires pity. Shame and self-recrimination haunt them, as well as pettiness and futility. Time expands as the war goes on:

> That there was no intention of ending this war, until it had become a total catastrophe *for everybody* was now obvious to him. He did not communicate to Hester his views as to the probable length of the war. He just sat before the radio, and listened to the unfolding of new moves promising, as he interpreted it, the most stupendous evils—sat there, night after night, too shocked to speak at times: at others simply stifling the human instinct to communicate.[129]

The bleakness of *Self Condemned* is lightened by the love which, in their confinement, binds Hester and René together, in a tender and unexpectedly affecting way. Lewis depicts this newly dawning affection, rooted in mutual dependence and shared suffering, with the force of an emotion experienced for the first time. The drawings of Gladys that Lewis made during their time in the Tudor Hotel are also integral to *Self Condemned*. Illustrating the role of Hester, they again make Gladys touchingly visible. In *Self Condemned*, as also happened in the Tudor Hotel in February 1943, there is an immense fire in the hotel, and René's situation eventually changes, as he is offered a column in the local newspaper, and a post as a professor in Canada. René knows he cannot return to London, while Hester longs to do so. Towards the close of the novel, Hester commits suicide, leaving René stunned, a "glacial shell."[130] In an alternative discarded ending of *Self Condemned*, René and Hester return together to London and penury.

But things improved professionally for Lewis later in 1943, when he found a teaching position at Assumption College in Windsor, Ontario, entering a less desperate phase in his sojourn in North America. Lewis and Gladys moved to Windsor in June 1943. In 1944 they spent nearly eight months in St Louis, where Lewis hoped for some large portrait commissions, before returning to Windsor. By May the next year, the Lewises were in Ottawa. They sailed from Quebec to England in August 1945, having borrowed the money for their fares.

Lewis was sixty-two when he and Gladys came back to post-war London. As they returned to Kensington Gardens Studios, vacant throughout the war, the landlord immediately tried to claim six years' back-payment of rent. The top floor studio's glass roof had been smashed during the war from bombing, and although new glass had been installed, the contents of the room had been rained on during a considerable interim period.[131] Meanwhile, dry rot apparently originating in the Christian Science Reading Room below the flat was spreading through the building. Rationing was still in force, and London seemed like a giant ruin. "This is the capital of a dying empire," Lewis wrote to Geoffrey Stone, "—not crashing down in flames and smoke but expiring in a peculiar muffled way."[132] Lewis however was clearly glad to be back among his old haunts and acquaintances.

In 1946 he turned his thoughts to writing another autobiography. In July, Lewis signed a contract with Hutchinson for *Story of a Career*, which he submitted in March or April 1947, under the title *Ascent of Parnassus*.[133] The book, after a long delay, was published in 1950 as *Rude Assignment: A Narrative of my Career Up-to-Date*. At the time of writing, it had been almost a decade since *Blasting*, whose selective slice of Lewis's life left plenty of scope for further treatment. Like *Blasting*, Lewis conceived *Rude Assignment* as having three parts. But war played much less of a role. In part one, "Three Fatalities," Lewis outlines the three "handicaps" he faced—namely, being an intellectual, a satirist, and a political pamphleteer. "Part Two is autobiography," he declared, while the last part is "a biography, and in some cases a restatement in different terms, of a number of my books."[134] The only autobiography in *Rude Assignment*, really, is the careful portion sandwiched in the middle.

*

Autobiography is a form of revision in which parts of one's life can be reordered and reshaped, while offering the illusory satisfaction to the autobiographer of setting the final record "straight." Often, for novelists and artists, the urge to undertake this revision is stirred by a desire to explain elements of their work which might otherwise fall prey to, or be ignored by, uncomprehending critics. Autobiography allows writers to offer their own self-criticism, and to respond to assessments of their work. But the possibility of writing multiple autobiographies also attests to the way that any autobiography, while often aiming to have the "last word," is only another version of, and another slant on, the various aspects of any life and its work. Autobiography seduces with the lure of finality and completeness, while always remaining partial, a portrait. In *Rude Assignment*, Lewis was particularly motivated by an urge to counter distorted portraits of himself that might find themselves in circulation, as he wrote in a passage which curiously recalls Oscar Wilde's *The Picture of Dorian Gray* (1891).

> In the course of controversy, in order to discredit an opponent [...] many disobliging fictions gain currency. A picture of a man is in this way handed down which is a very bad likeness, one that corresponds only slightly with the original. After his death, the painting goes on [...] if only the spurious portrait of oneself gets painted in public [...] if it is brought out into the open to be painted there, then all is well [...] And so long as the living man is still there he can annihilate the phantom: whereas when a phantom himself it would be too late.[135]

This is a haunting meditation on biography and reputation, also echoing the ghostly reverberations of Henry James's thoughts about biography and what the artist could do in self-defense. Where James opted for destruction of documents, Lewis puts his faith in setting forth his own account. *Rude Assignment*, he writes, has been composed in order "to spoil the sport of the irresponsible detractor, to improve my chances of some day not being too much lied about, to clear the path immediately ahead—a simple domestic operation, but long overdue."[136] But it is not his conduct as a man that Lewis defends, or even describes in *Rude Assignment*, so much as the controversial positions in his work. As with *Blasting*, Lewis's personal relationships make no appearance. Once again, as an autobiographer, Lewis is extremely controlled, separating the panels of his text very neatly. At times, the tone of the volume feels like Lewis giving his own defense at an imaginary trial, as he outlines how "the nature of my thinking [...] has resulted in my life being so difficult a one to live."[137]

The first part of *Rude Assignment* is essentially an essay, divided into three sections, on the role of the intellectual, satirist, and political writer, as Lewis gives a "catalogue of my personal handicaps."[138] While *Blasting* had been written for a popular audience, Lewis wished to concede less of his usual "highbrow" stance in *Rude Assignment*; and the fissure between the "two publics" was his very subject in the opening section on being an intellectual. Explaining his role as a satirist, meanwhile, Lewis invokes a host of earlier writers, and discusses the cartoons of David Low and "Vicki." Portrait painting in the twentieth century, he writes, has become unable to deal with reality, as people desire an "improved" version of themselves. This kind of self-deception nonetheless—despite Lewis's ability to stare closely at his own frailties and mistakes—also underlies the project of *Rude Assignment*, particularly in Lewis's account of his politics, as he attempted to readjust his own portrait for posterity.

When "more intimate autobiography"[139] appears in part two, Lewis offers, for the first time as an autobiographer, an account of his youth. Casting his mind back half a century, he recounts making his first "books" at eight; transforming his study at school in Rugby into an "artist's studio";[140] spending weeks each year with his mother in Paris, visiting the Louvre; attending the life-class under Professor Tonks at the Slade, before entering "heaven" with a long sojourn in Paris "in its late sunset."[141] In Paris, Lewis rid himself of his English education and "became a European."[142] Looking back, he dwells on his inactivity throughout his years on the Continent, and how he was supported financially by his mother, during "long vague periods of an indolence now charged with some creative purpose."[143] In one unusual passage, he notes his inability to communicate with other people:

> I remained, beyond the usual period, congealed in a kind of cryptic immaturity. In my social relations the contacts remained, for long, primitive. I recognised dimly this obstruction: was conscious of gaucherie, of wooden responses [...] But I am gazing back into what is a very dark cavern indeed. An ungregarious childhood may have counted for something.[144]

Augustus John noticed this too during his time with Lewis in France. "You never have—it seems to me—given the [idea] of friendship a chance,"[145] John wrote to Lewis in 1907. In his early years, by his own account, Lewis's dealings with others were marked by secrecy, privacy, and a certain truculence. Writing here as if about someone else, in the sometimes awkward language of this second autobiography, admitting that he has no explanation, Lewis tentatively connects his "gaucherie" with his childhood. Later in *Rude Assignment* one also senses him wondering about his later self-ostracism after the war, as he reflects on *The Tyro* and *The Enemy*, and the "note of solitary defiance"[146] he often struck.

But he did become more social returning to London in 1909. In *Rude Assignment*, Lewis recounts going to the office of the *English Review* in Holland Park—and portrays himself through Ford's portrait of him: "Hueffer has described [. . .] 'the moujik' who unexpectedly mounted the stairs, [and] silently left a bundle of manuscript."[147] Ford, Lewis writes, led him to Pound, Eliot, Gaudier Brzeska, and others; and what Lewis calls Ford's "somnolent but systematic sociability" expanded further when he married Violet Hunt. At dinner at "Mrs. Hueffer's," Lewis remembered first meeting Rebecca West: "a dark young maenad then, who burst through the dining-room door (for she was late) like a thunderbolt."[148] Lewis's 1932 pencil drawing of West—nervy, graceful, and melancholy—already in *Blasting*, reappears in *Rude Assignment*, where Lewis continues his word portrait of Ford at some length, satirizing Ford's physical appearance and pretensions, but extolling his virtues as an editor.

> Hueffer was a flabby lemon and pink giant, who hung his mouth open as though he were an animal at the Zoo inviting buns—especially when ladies were present. Over the gaping mouth damply depended the ragged ends of a pale lemon moustache. This ex-collaborator with Joseph Conrad was himself [. . .] a typical figure out of a Conrad book—a caterer, or corn-factor, coming on board—blowing like a porpoise with the exertion—at some Eastern port [. . .] He possessed a vivid and theatrical imagination: he jacked himself up, character as he was in a nautical story, from one of the white business gents in the small tropic port into—I am not quite sure it was not into a *Maugham* story [. . .] But [. . .] Hueffer was probably as good an editor as could be found for an English literary review.[149]

In his autobiographies, Lewis grasped how Ford's reminiscences opened the door to verbal flourishes in return. *Rude Assignment*, which offers less of a group portrait than *Blasting*, despite sketches and asides on Augustus John, Eliot, Joyce, and Pound, still made space for Ford. In this portrait, Lewis mocks Ford's manner, while paying him a homage he would have appreciated, describing him as a fictional character in Conrad, someone from the pages of a book. Lewis saw the self-delusion in Ford that irritated Wells; he also saw how, as an editor, Ford offered himself to others, abandoning his "vanity."[150] Ford helped Lewis form his persona: in his literary portrayals of Lewis, Ford described him as a conspirator, an exotic European. And Lewis accepted this Fordian mask in *Rude Assignment*. "I was for some years spiritually a Russian," Lewis writes, "—a character in some Russian novel. As such I made my bow in London—to the deeply astonished Ford Madox Hueffer."[151]

As it moves past the *English Review*, *Rude Assignment* leads towards the same period as *Blasting*, saying more about Lewis's involvement with Roger Fry and the Omega Workshops in 1913, while being uncharacteristically diplomatic about their falling-out.[152] Lewis also writes of his work decorating the short-lived "Cave of the Golden Calf" nightclub on Heddon Street, off Regent Street, for Madame Strindberg, and the high ideals—worth fighting for—of the immediate pre-war period:

> It was, after all, a new civilisation that I—and a few other people—was making the blueprints for: these things never being more than that. A rough design for a way of seeing for men who as yet were not there [...] I, like all the other people in Europe so engaged, felt it to be an important task. It was more than just picture-making: one was manufacturing fresh eyes for people, and fresh souls to go with the eyes. That was the feeling.[153]

This feeling altered after the war. In the short account of the conflict in *Rude Assignment*, Lewis remarks how the war made him move away in art from abstraction, towards figuration. Writing *Tarr* also dragged him away from abstraction, as novels were necessarily less abstract than art. After the war, "the geometrics which had interested me so exclusively before, I now felt were bleak and empty. They wanted *filling*."[154]

The central reminiscential section of *Rude Assignment* comes, as *Blasting* also did, to an invisible block in the mid-1920s, offering a different reason for it. In the first autobiography, Lewis wrote that the period after this was still too near to be seen clearly; in *Rude Assignment*, he writes that after 1925, writing took up nearly all his existence.[155] Lewis tells us that he had been intending to go up to the Second World War in this second autobiography. But after the mid-1920s, "my personal life has no further relevance. Thenceforth my history is strictly that of my books."[156] In this way, Lewis justifies the final section of *Rude Assignment*, which offers a life through these books, and a reassessment of his *oeuvre*.

In concept, this final part offered Lewis a chance to compose a very fitting text for an impersonal writer and artist such as himself: a purely "intellectual autobiography" in which only the work is reassessed rather than the life. Autobiography and biography are well-suited to depicting the genesis and evolution of works of literature and art, also fitting them together into the larger pattern of an *oeuvre*. This is precisely what Lewis aims to give in this last section, "The Books—a Pattern of Thinking," taking us up to the time of writing.

An ambitious attempt at self-criticism and realignment, the final part of *Rude Assignment* founders partly because of Lewis's very productivity. A long, involved discussion of *The Art of Being Ruled* (1926) sets a level of detail Lewis does not sustain; and where he is expansive on some areas of his *oeuvre* he is cursory about others. The main thread of his interest in his "pattern of thinking" is, he asserts, in focusing on his most controversial books. While Lewis does make important retractions and revisions, above all of his "anti-war" books of the 1930s which he here almost completely disowns, the focus on controversy skews the account, dwelling on some of his least accomplished books, and ignoring his work as an artist. Reproductions of Lewis's art towards the end of *Rude Assignment*—including a delicate pencil sketch of the artist's wife from 1936—only remind us how much is being missed.

Even Lewis himself fairly early on, as he arrives at certain monuments of his career to defend them in *Rude Assignment*, seems to be tiring of his self-appointed task. The autobiographer, looking back at his earlier ideas, alternates between pride, wariness, apology, and bafflement. "Arriving as I do now at *Time and Western Man*," Lewis writes, "I feel that I am standing before a substantial fortress, once full of vigorous defenders, but now silent, probably a place where bats hang upside down and jackals find a musty bedchamber. To be frank, I have no desire to re-enter it."[157] As he reapproaches his political works of the 1930s, the work of salvage becomes a great deal harder, as Lewis acknowledges, writing of his poverty and sickness, seemingly as the only way he can find to explain or excuse the manifold wrong-turns and rash judgments he now finds in some of these volumes. The autobiography ends with an "Envoi," reminiscent of the ending of Wells's *Experiment in Autobiography* in its over-tidiness, as Lewis recomposes his ruffled ego.

> I have gone back to the past in order to defend ideas of twenty years ago with a changed outlook. This, however, turned out to be less troublesome than

might have been expected. Certainly in many particulars I judge the issues in question differently today. In other cases I discovered there was remarkably little change [...] It is character and motives rather than anything else which one has to protect and put out of reach of smearers. No one cares about the intellect—I don't have to worry about *that*, but what the domestic requires in applying for a job—a good character.[158]

*

While Lewis was writing *Rude Assignment* in Kensington Gardens Studios in 1946, and was approaching its initially scheduled deadline of November, he had a bout of flu which kept him inside for several days. Emerging from his illness, he went to buy a newspaper, and was hit by a motorcycle. He continued with the autobiography in a state of semi-immobility, in a "recumbent position"[159] as his leg healed throughout the winter.

For quite some time, Lewis had been aware of a far more serious problem with his health. In Toronto in 1941, he saw an eye specialist who warned him, as he told one correspondent at the time, that "one of my eyes [...] was practically extinct. My other eye would be the same in six months' time—if I had what he thought I had: namely glaucoma."[160] Having formed his artistic philosophy around the eye, and relying for his livelihood in Canada on his ability to paint portraits, Lewis was terrified of losing his sight. He wrote elsewhere in his letters that he first noticed something wrong with his left eye "about two years before the war,"[161] and had been "practically blind"[162] in that eye for years.

While working on another portrait painting of Eliot, in March and April 1949, Lewis noticed he had to come right up to the sitter to see. He began a portrait of Stella Newton a few months later, and needed "to draw still closer and even then I could not quite see."[163] In December 1949 he had his eyes examined again. His teeth, initially thought to be the source of the problem, were removed early in 1950. The large tumor pressing on his optic nerves, the actual cause of the loss of vision, was diagnosed shortly afterwards. Throughout 1950, Lewis's sight rapidly deteriorated, as he wrote in an article, "The Sea-Mists of the Winter," announcing his necessary resignation as art critic of *The Listener*, in May 1951:

I found that I could no longer read the names of streets, see the numbers on houses, or see what stations I was passing through on the railway. About that time everything but banner headlines was invisible: then I found I could no longer read the letters inside the finger-holes of a telephone-dial. At present, if I wish to dial a number, I count the holes with my fingertips until I reach the opening where I know the letter I have to locate is situated [...] When visited by friends [...] I see them after a fashion, but fragmentarily, obliquely, and spasmodically. I can see no one immediately in front of me [...] But an awareness of the bodily presence is always there, and as one turns one's head hither and thither, glimpses constantly recur.[164]

Lewis was advised to have the tumor removed, but he preferred to live with the encroaching darkness, well aware that "the failure of sight which is already so advanced, will of course become worse from week to week."[165] He had had the tumor for years already, possibly since the 1930s. What he called his "unseemly autobiographical outburst"[166] in *The Listener* was strangely calm and humorous, announcing his intentions to continue as a writer, with a Dictaphone, even while abandoning art criticism, "for I can no longer see a picture."[167]

The lifelong dilemma over whether to pursue writing or painting was one thing, at least, resolved by blindness. In the 1950s, he continued to work, evolving a method of writing blind not with a Dictaphone but using sheets of paper with wire stretched across them to guide his script, often managing about six lines per page, before the pages were sorted, typed up, and read back to him. Among other books, he wrote *Self Condemned* in this way, *Monstre Gai* (1955), *Malign Fiesta* (1955), and *The Red Priest* (1956). In 1956, the blind painter was honored by an exhibition at the Tate, *Wyndham Lewis and Vorticism*. After the private view, Lewis was helped into a taxi with Gladys. As John Rothenstein recalled, "there were tears in his eyes":[168] a surprise to anyone who knows how well Lewis held his feelings at bay.

In 1957, the year he died, he had completed the typescript of another novel, *Twentieth Century Palette*. The hero of this unpublished text, as Paul O'Keeffe writes, is a painter, Evelyn Parke, born twenty years later than Lewis and spared the First World War, although he loses an arm in the Second.[169] Lewis wrote to Hugh Kenner about this novel that it was "not about a man who did anything very much, except sleep with his models, and squeeze pigment out of fat tubes. I like his smell, but would not marry him to my favourite girl."[170] Evelyn has things Lewis never did: a father who brought him up (on his own), a prosperous background, and success from the start. "He was ideally placed as an artist," Lewis writes, and "encountered none of the difficulties that handicapped many of those around him."[171] Thus Lewis, blind, at seventy-four, at the end of what he portrayed in *Rude Assignment* as a long life full of handicaps, sought a sustaining vision.

Epilogue

In April 1939, after having been warned by her sister, the painter Vanessa Bell, that if she waited any longer she would "soon be too old,"[1] Virginia Woolf began her notes towards an autobiography, which she called "Sketch of the Past." She was fifty-seven, and she had been writing a biography of Roger Fry for just over a year. "As it happens that I am sick of writing Roger's life, perhaps I will spend two or three mornings making a sketch,"[2] Woolf noted at the outset of this attempt at autobiography, to be written in the gaps, as it were, of her other work: initially, from April to July 1939. After *Roger Fry: A Biography* appeared in 1940, and an almost year-long break from the autobiography, Woolf took up the "free page"[3] of the "Sketch" again from June to November 1940, in the spare time around writing her last novel, "Pointz Hall," which she worked on in the mornings and which became *Between the Acts* (1941).

Woolf had written very different fragments of her life before, in the four chapters of family "Reminiscences" written in her mid-twenties and addressed to Vanessa's first child, Julian Bell, begun before he was born; and in the three wry and convivial pieces she had written to read aloud at the Bloomsbury "Memoir Club" in the 1920s and 30s.[4] She had also been writing a diary for many years, especially from 1917 onwards. She had long intended to use the diaries as a source for writing her autobiography. "Oh yes, I shall write my memoirs out of them, one of these days,"[5] she noted of her diaries (in the diaries themselves) in 1927. In 1938, again in the diaries, she mused on what her intention was in writing "these continual diaries": "Not publication. Revision? A memoir of my own life? Perhaps. Only other things crop up."[6] In June 1939, having begun her "Sketch of the Past," Woolf writes in the diary that "perhaps if I go on with my memoirs [...] I shall make use of it."[7] She very nearly lost the twenty-four volumes of the diaries when the Woolfs' London flat at 37 Mecklenburgh Square, where they had only just moved all their things from their previous London house, 52 Tavistock Square, in 1939, was bombed in October 1940. Coming to London from Monk's House in Rodmell, East Sussex, where she and her husband Leonard had been largely based since the onset of the Second World War, Woolf salvaged the diary volumes from the mess of "litter, glass, black soft dust, plaster powder": "a great mass for my memoirs."[8]

But Woolf never wrote these memoirs in full as she had intended to, and the diaries were not really put to use in her "Sketch": a provisional, improvisatory, "distracted and disconnected"[9] account of her formative memories and years, leading up to, and only just moving beyond, the turn of the twentieth century. So provisional, in fact, does the "Sketch" appear, that at one point Woolf even tells us how she has retrieved it from her waste-paper basket, after deciding to take the autobiography up again in June 1940: "I had been tidying up; and had cast all my life of Roger into that large basket, and with it, these sheets too."[10] She had been looking for the "Sketch" to refresh herself from the "antlike meticulous labour" of correcting the proofs of her now-finished biography of Fry. "Shall I ever finish these notes," Woolf asks herself, "—let alone make a book from them?"[11] The war was pressing in. "Every night the Germans fly over England; it comes closer to this house daily."[12]

In her "Sketch," Woolf did not use the content of her diaries, but she did use all her experience of writing in the form of the diary, to attempt a tentative, experimental, and ongoing account of her life, which announces its own innovations as they occur to her. Not least among these innovations in 1939 is Woolf's use of the present time of writing as a "platform," making her memoir oscillate between diary and autobiography. Woolf had always been suspicious of the fixed, immobile stances of many biographies and autobiographies, in her many scattered remarks on life-writing in her essays and elsewhere, as her biographer Hermione Lee notes.[13] A good biography "is the record of the things that change," Woolf wrote, "rather than of the things that happen."[14] Reviewing a biography of Christina Rossetti, Woolf was wary of, but also beguiled by, how it seemed closed off from the outside world: "Here is the past and all its inhabitants miraculously sealed as in a magic tank," she wrote, with the "little figures [...] rather under life size."[15] In her "Sketch," Woolf avoided the lure of finality and completeness, aiming instead to create a truthful impression of how the present always casts a shadow over portraits of the past.

Throughout her "Sketch," Woolf kept on returning to "the little platform of present time on which I stand,"[16] from which she now looked back. The constant reversion to the present tense does not give the "Sketch" extra clarity: sometimes, quite the opposite, as it highlights fractures in its composition and the muddle of the actual. The autobiography, written in the breaks from the Fry biography, even gives a snapshot of the chaos of the writer's desk. "I look up at my skylight," Woolf writes, "—over the litter of *Athenaeum* articles, Fry letters—all strewn with the sand that comes from the house that is being pulled down next door—I look up and see, as if reflecting it, a sky the colour of dirty water. And the inner landscape is much of a piece."[17] Woolf follows this by recording that the painter Mark Gertler had dined with her the night before, and had declaimed on the "inferiority of what he called 'literature'; compared with the integrity of painting. 'For it always deals with Mr and Mrs Brown,'—he said—with the personal, the trivial, that is; a criticism which has its sting and its chill, like the May sky."[18]

In setting out her early memories in the "Sketch," Woolf herself initially aimed for a painterly purity, as she describes, in almost hallucinatory detail, scenes which have remained in her mind over the long gap of years. Trying to find some order among "the enormous number of things I can remember"[19] and "the number of different ways in which memoirs can be written,"[20] she sets down her first memory, of sitting on her mother's lap and of her mother's dress, "of red and purple flowers on a black ground."[21] This leads to another memory, "which also seems to be my first memory, and in fact it is the most important of all my memories": [22]

> If life has a base that it stands upon, if it is a bowl that one fills and fills and fills—then my bowl without a doubt stands upon this memory. It is of lying half asleep, half awake, in bed in the nursery at St Ives. It is of hearing the waves breaking, one, two, one, two, and sending a splash of water over the beach; and then breaking, one, two, one, two, behind a yellow blind [. . .] If I were a painter I should paint these impressions in pale yellow, silver, and green. There was the pale yellow blind; the green sea; and the silver of the passion flowers.[23]

The preeminence Woolf gives this shimmering memory, although it is an image of flux, is slightly at odds with the provisionality elsewhere so important to her "Sketch"—perhaps suggesting that above all, in the present of 1939, she *wants* this to be her most important memory, with its light and water contrasting with another very early, disturbing memory just a few pages later, of her half-brother Gerald Duckworth exploring her "private parts," against her will, "once when I was very small."[24] "I remember resenting, disliking it—what is the word for so dumb and mixed a feeling? It must have been strong, since I still recall it."[25]

Woolf is the first to question her own memories and how she has reordered them in setting them down on the page. She notes how some memories can be "more real than the present moment,"[26] and how she can "reach a state where I seem to be watching things happen as if I were there."[27] Yet she knows that "as an account of my life they are misleading, because the things one does not remember are as important; perhaps they are more important."[28] Woolf writes of how large parts of her life are defined by what she calls "non-being"[29]—the humdrum, unremarkable, daily stuff of life, "a kind of nondescript cotton-wool"[30] which surrounds everything, including the "moments of being"[31] which stand out by contrast in retrospect, and which Woolf enshrines in her "Sketch." The fluidity of her sense of the past and how well she remembers it is also noted by Woolf. "The past only comes back when the present runs so smoothly that it is like the sliding surface of a deep river," she writes. "Then one sees through the surface to the depths."[32] She finds that the past, glimpsed in this way, gives greater meaning to the present, which sometimes "presses so close that you can feel nothing else."[33] Perhaps she was complaining of the war-time present of 1940, "marooned" in Rodmell "by the bombs in London,"[34] as she wrote in her diary.

The "Sketch" was left unfinished, with its last dated entry in November 1940. On March 28, 1941, Woolf left an undated letter for Leonard on the table in the sitting-room, alongside one for Vanessa, before walking out towards the River Ouse, where she left her stick on the bank, put a heavy stone in her coat pocket, and drowned herself. She had been worried about becoming ill again, and she knew that she might become a burden for Leonard and Vanessa. In her letter to Leonard, she made it very clear that her decision was hers alone and not any fault of his: "Nothing anyone says can persuade me [...] No one could have been so good as you have been. From the very first day till now. Everyone knows that."[35] Turning the page she wrote, finally, "Will you destroy all my papers."[36] Of course Leonard, in the end, did no such thing.

*

Woolf's reflections on life-writing in her "Sketch of the Past" mirror the discoveries of the other writers in *Portraits from Life*, revealing the importance of the time of the writing of autobiography, the unreliability of memory, the search for the shape of a life, and the ways that life-writing is always concerned with other people. The ethics of depicting these others unsettled Woolf, as they haunted all the other writers in this book. In her biography of Roger Fry, she wished to "tell all," yet she also felt a deep respect for privacy. As the daughter of Leslie Stephen, editor of the *Dictionary of National Biography*, Woolf instinctively resisted the proprieties of Victorian biography—as Lytton Strachey, whose biography she had also considered writing when she was beginning *Roger Fry*, had done in *Eminent Victorians* (1918). But even in the late 1930s, Woolf found that pressure from Fry's family made full disclosure of Fry's life impossible. Writing about real people, using their real names, was, Woolf discovered, very difficult.

When each of the novelists in the portraits in this book wrote about themselves and others in their memoirs or autobiographies, they often risked more than in their explicitly fictional texts. While their autobiographies were in many ways another kind of ultimate fiction, they all felt the difference between writing an autobiography and writing novels. Sometimes this difference can seem wafer-thin; yet the difference is there nonetheless. As H. G. Wells wrote in *Boon*, distancing himself from his pseudonym who so violently savaged an ageing Henry James: "Bliss is Bliss and Wells is Wells. And Bliss can write all sorts of things that Wells could not do."[37]

Nowhere are the different risks in autobiographies more apparent than in their portrayal and potential exposure of others. Even in the most seemingly uninhibited account of a life, there are individuals about whom the autobiographer will feel protective, and who are often, because of this, invisible in the autobiography. This protective social side of a genre often seen as introspective, egotistical, and confessional, is perhaps a feature of autobiography most apparent to novelists, used as they are to the relative freedom of masks and personae. The shielding hand of the writer or artist, as in Parmigianino's *Self-Portrait*, is often not self-defensive so much as wary of causing others unnecessary pain.

In the twentieth century, one can trace a steady increase in candor in autobiography—especially in terms of sexual relationships. During the period of *Portraits from Life*, in the first half of the twentieth century, the relationship between candor and privacy was in a radically transitional phase. Some writers felt the impulse to reveal everything, but could only get halfway towards this aim. Others remained wary and essentially private about many things. While Wells and Edith Wharton wrote unpublished, more candid accounts of their sexual relationships that they knew would eventually join their public autobiographies, the other figures in these portraits offer masterpieces of tact, evasion, and discretion. "I never comment on anybody,"[38] Ford wrote to his mother in 1919; and in this light the imaginative gloss and omissions of his reminiscences can also be seen as a form of protection of those intimate with him.

In many of the cases here, autobiography was first conceived almost as a creative holiday: sometimes embarked upon due to the breakdown of imagination, sometimes begun cynically to provide financial relief with minimal effort, sometimes begun as a form of wider life-therapy. Woolf began her "Sketch," as she tells us, "in fits and starts by way of a holiday from Roger."[39] This also happened to be soon after she met Freud in Hampstead for the first time in 1939—and while, unusually, Woolf began her project as a break not from fiction but from biography, she is not alone in her vision of autobiography as being potentially reinvigorating. But the frequently longed-for therapeutic side of autobiography seldom operates as simplistically as is often hoped; and once begun, the task of autobiography often becomes much more uncomfortable, implicatory, and engrossing than envisaged.

Each of the seven writers in *Portraits from Life*, once they had started, wrote their own lives—in part or in full—more than once; and they often planned to write more autobiography than they eventually did, even when they wrote their lives very fully. Each self-portrait often stimulates another attempt, as the writer becomes simultaneously more practiced as an autobiographer, while also more conscious of the insufficiencies of any one version of a life.

Multiple versions also occur because memory is constantly rewriting the script. If, in fiction, imagination is actively courted and fused with memory, the project of autobiography is often to attempt to transcribe memories which have *not* been tinted by the imagination in this way. And of course this is impossible. Each time a memory is recalled, it is to some extent rewritten in the mind, even before it is rewritten on the page. Autobiography often stimulates a very conscious act of memory that is the opposite of the unconscious, involuntary memory identified by Proust. One of the proofs of autobiography and reminiscence is that memory *can* be stimulated in an active way, aided and abetted by props, spurs, and documentary materials such as photographs, diaries, and old letters, just as much as memory also works autonomously by association or by accident, triggered off by places, smells, or tastes, as with Proust's *madeleine*. But the fickle nature of memory also begs many questions, which are highlighted when memories are written down in autobiographies. Writing of her mother, Woolf notes, "how difficult it is to single her out as she really was; to imagine what she was thinking, to put a single sentence into her mouth! I dream; I make up pictures of a summer's afternoon."[40]

*

Taken together, the portraits in this book, in the very widest sense, ultimately throw the most searching light not on the inevitable intertwinings of fact and fiction, the unreliabilities of memory and imagination, or the endless dance between past and present, so much as revealing, sadly and starkly, the nature of the human life cycle. While every autobiography is unique, as with any single life, this group portrait also highlights the opposite: how each of these writers' stories, on a much larger level, is the same story. In this reading, quite unlike in the realm of fiction where the writer can fix every-thing exactly as he or she wishes, and assumes the hubristic role of creator, autobiography always becomes the quest to understand the quirks of fate, and the randomness of destiny.

Woolf, in her "Sketch," notes how her instinct for writing, she thinks, is an attempt to make sense of, to find order in, perhaps to control, the moments of shock when the outside world often violently breaks into her life, giving a flashing illumination of a "pattern." "I would reason that if life were thus made to rear and kick, it was a thing to be ridden,"[41] Woolf writes:

> I feel that I have had a blow [...] it is a token of some real thing behind appearances; and I make it real by putting it into words. It is only by putting it into words that I make it whole; this wholeness means that it has lost its power to hurt me; it gives me, perhaps because by doing so I take away the pain, a great delight to put the severed parts together. Perhaps this is the strongest pleasure known to me.[42]

Part of the impulse to write fiction comes from the sense of power it grants its author, giving coherence, even mastery, to experience. For writers of autobiography, the search for a pattern amidst the sometimes overwhelming fullness of life is also inevitable. But it can be harder to grasp finally, with the same tight grip as in fiction. H. G. Wells, at the close of his third auto-biography, the posthumous *H. G. Wells in Love*, after years of obsessive life-writing, came to the realization that destiny, or fate, is the subtext of all autobiography. In the "Note on Fate and Individuality" written in 1935 and put at the end of *H. G. Wells in Love* by Gip Wells in his role as editor of his father's autobiography, H. G. wrote:

> It is impossible, I find, to write autobiography with as much sincerity as I have sought, telling of limitations, frustrations, intrinsic failure and accepted defeats, without the picture beginning to take on more and more the quality of a fated destiny, without feeling more and more plainly how close one's experiences have come to those of a creature of innate impulses, caught by circumstances and making an ineffectual buzzing about it like a fly on a fly-paper.[43]

Wells wrote that he rejected this view of predestination with every bone in his body, vehemently asserting free will—"some flies (a little sticky perhaps and hampered) do somehow get away from the fly-paper of circumstance."[44] But the image bothered him. As Gip notes, this ending of the "Postscript" to *H. G. Wells in Love* "survived all of the subsequent revisions virtually unchanged and was still present as the peroration in the final typescript. But my father had drawn a pencil line through it, both in the contents table and in the text of that last typescript, so he may have wished to exclude it for some reason."[45] Wells eventually gifted these views on fate to a fictional character instead, as Gip writes: "Meanwhile, almost the whole of this 'Note' was put into the mouth of the mythical Steele in *The Anatomy of Frustration*."[46]

Perhaps something like this thought occurs to all writers of autobiography—that what we thought was entirely our own narrative, our own decisions, words, reactions, and thoughts, has actually been penned, at least in part, by someone (or something) else. The tension in this realization often keeps autobiographers trying continually to make sense of the life-stories they have both chosen and been given: until, finally, they run out of time.

Notes

INTRODUCTION

1. Nathaniel Hawthorne, *American Notebooks*. Quoted in Richard Brilliant, *Portraiture* (London: Reaktion, 1991), 178.
2. Giorgio Vasari, *Lives of the Painters*, Volume V, 221–2, trans. G. du C. de Vere (New York: Abrams, 1979), 1139–40.
3. Giorgio Vasari, *Lives of the Painters*, 1139–40.
4. Giorgio Vasari, *Lives of the Painters*, 1139–40.
5. John Ashbery, "Self-Portrait in a Convex Mirror," in *The New York Poets: An Anthology*, ed. Mark Ford (Manchester: Carcanet, 2004), 81.
6. John Ashbery, "Self-Portrait in a Convex Mirror," 81.
7. Leon Edel, *The Age of the Archive* (Center for Advanced Studies, Wesleyan University, 1966), 21.
8. Autobiography is of course notoriously hard to define. The French critic Philippe Lejeune, in his essay "The Autobiographical Contract," reflects that autobiography "is as much a way of reading as a kind of writing." See "The Autobiographical Contract," in Tzvetan Todorov, ed., *French Literary Theory Today* (Cambridge: Cambridge University Press, 1982), 220. But Lejeune has also offered the most tenacious definition of an autobiography: "a retrospective prose narrative produced by a real person concerning his own existence, focusing on his individual life, in particular on the development of his personality." See "The Autobiographical Contract," 193.
9. Edmund Gosse, *Father and Son: A Study of Two Temperaments*, ed. Michael Newton (Oxford: Oxford University Press, 2004), 3.
10. Virginia Woolf, "The New Biography," in Leonard Woolf, ed., *Collected Essays IV* (London: Hogarth Press, 1967), 229.
11. Virginia Woolf, "The New Biography," 229.
12. Virginia Woolf, "The New Biography," 231.
13. Virginia Woolf, "The New Biography," 231.
14. Virginia Woolf, "Sketch of the Past," in *Moments of Being*, ed. Jeanne Schulkind (London: Pimlico, 2002), 92.
15. "Sketch of the Past," *Moments of Being*, 92.
16. Virginia Woolf, "The Art of Biography," in *The Death of the Moth and Other Essays* (London: Hogarth, 1942), 124.

17. Edmund Gosse, "The Custom of Biography," *Anglo-Saxon Review*, VIII (March 1901), 195.
18. "Sketch of the Past," *Moments of Being*, 87.
19. As Paul John Eakin wrote in 1988, "writing an autobiography is usually not itself presented as a major event in the life of the biographical subject... There are, in fact, very few examples one can point to in the practice of biography that direct attention to the biographical significance of the writing of an *autobiography* in the life of its subject." See Paul John Eakin, "Henry James's 'Obscure Hurt': Can Autobiography Serve Biography?," *New Literary History*, 19:3 (Spring, 1988), 676, 680.
20. Hermione Lee, *Body Parts: Essays on Life-Writing* (London: Chatto & Windus, 2005), 6.
21. Susan Sontag, *Reborn: Early Diaries 1947–1963* (London: Hamish Hamilton, 2009), 166.
22. Marcel Proust, *A la recherche du temps perdu*, trans. C. K. Scott Moncrieff and Terence Kilmartin, revised by D. J. Enright (London: Chatto & Windus/Vintage, 1992), Volume VI, 253.
23. Leon Edel, *The Age of the Archive*, 21.

CHAPTER I

1. Joseph Conrad to Sidney Colvin, December 28, 1908, *The Collected Letters of Joseph Conrad*, ed. Frederick R. Karl and Laurence Davies, Volume 4 (Cambridge: Cambridge University Press, 1990), 175.
2. Joseph Conrad to J. M. Barrie, December 31, 1903, *Collected Letters*, Volume 3, 104.
3. Joseph Conrad to John Galsworthy, January 7 or 14, 1904, *Collected Letters*, Volume 3, 109.
4. Joseph Conrad to George Gissing, December 1, 1903, *Collected Letters*, Volume 9, 95.
5. Joseph Conrad to Catherine Hueffer, December 26, 1903, *Collected Letters*, Volume 9, 95.
6. From an entry in Olive Garnett's diary, quoted in Leon Edel, *Henry James: A Life* (London: Collins, 1987), 525.
7. Zdzisław Najder, *Joseph Conrad: A Chronicle* (Cambridge: Cambridge University Press, 1983), 239.
8. Henry James to H. G. Wells, October 7, 1902. Quoted in Nicholas Delbanco, *Group Portrait* (London: Faber, 1982), 146–7.
9. For more on the mooted James–Wells collaboration, see Nicholas Delbanco, *Group Portrait*, 145–51.
10. Jessie Conrad, *Joseph Conrad and His Circle* (London: Jarrolds, 1935), 157.
11. Both these accusations appear in chapter nine of Jessie Conrad's *Joseph Conrad and His Circle* (London: Jarrolds, 1935), among other denunciations of Ford.
12. Ford Madox Ford, *Joseph Conrad: A Personal Remembrance* (London: Duckworth, 1924), 11.

13. Joseph Conrad to H. G. Wells, February 7, 1904, *Collected Letters*, Volume 3, 112.

14. Joseph Conrad to H. G. Wells, February 7, 1904, *Collected Letters*, Volume 3, 112.

15. Joseph Conrad to Sidney Colvin, March 4, 1904, *Collected Letters*, Volume 3, 119.

16. Joseph Conrad to James B. Pinker, March 4[14?], 1904, *Collected Letters*, Volume 3, 121. "No 6 of the Mor of the Sea finished last night."

17. Joseph Conrad to Pinker, March 7, 1904, *Collected Letters*, Volume 3, 120–1.

18. Joseph Conrad to Ford, May 29, 1904, *Collected Letters*, Volume 3, 142.

19. John Conrad, *Joseph Conrad: Times Remembered* (Cambridge: Cambridge University Press, 1981), 62.

20. Joseph Conrad to Pinker, February 1904, *Collected Letters*, Volume 3, 114.

21. Joseph Conrad to Pinker, April 18, 1904, *Collected Letters*, Volume 3, 133.

22. Quoted in Najder, *Joseph Conrad: A Chronicle*, 324.

23. H. G. Wells to Joseph Conrad, 1906, *The Correspondence of H. G. Wells*, ed. David C. Smith (London: Pickering & Chatto, 4 vols., 1998), Volume 2, 103.

24. Joseph Conrad, "Author's Note" to *The Mirror of the Sea* in *A Personal Record* and *The Mirror of the Sea*, ed. Mara Kalnins (London: Penguin, 1998), 134.

25. *The Mirror of the Sea*, 176.

26. *The Mirror of the Sea*, 176.

27. *The Mirror of the Sea*, 177.

28. Jessie Conrad, *Joseph Conrad as I Knew Him* (London: Heinemann, 1926), 18.

29. *The Mirror of the Sea*, 190–1.

30. As Najder notes, in *A Chronicle*, 49, Hans Van Marle, after detailed research in Marseilles, ascertained "that in the period in question not one out of thirty-five hundred ships that docked at Marseilles bore the name *Tremolino* or was commanded by Dominic Cervoni."

31. See Frederick Karl, *The Three Lives* (London: Faber, 1979), 171 for more on fact and fiction in *The Mirror of the Sea*.

32. See Frederick Karl, *The Three Lives*, 142; Najder also notes Norman Sherry's discovery of the real-life son of César Cervoni, in *Joseph Conrad: A Chronicle*, 49.

33. Joseph Conrad to Pinker, February 4, 1917, *Collected Letters*, Volume 6, 25.

34. Conrad also briefed his friend Sidney Colvin, who was reviewing the book for *The Observer*, to emphasize its autobiographical elements in his review.

35. Jessie Conrad, *Joseph Conrad as I Knew Him*, 16.

36. Letter to A. T. Saunders, quoted in Norman Sherry, *Conrad's Eastern World* (Cambridge: Cambridge University Press, 1966), 13.

37. Joseph Conrad to the Baroness Janina de Brunnow, October 2, 1897. Quoted in Frederick Karl, *The Three Lives*, 404.

38. Jessie Conrad, *Joseph Conrad and his Circle*, 119.

39. *A Personal Record*, 10.

40. See Najder, *Joseph Conrad: A Chronicle*, 341, for more on this theory.

41. *A Personal Record*, 101.

42. Joseph Conrad to Edward Garnett, August 28, 1908, *Collected Letters*, Volume 4, 112.

43. Joseph Conrad to Pinker, September 18, 1908, *Collected Letters*, Volume 4, 125.

44. Ford Madox Ford, *Return to Yesterday* (London: Gollancz, 1931), 195.

45. Ford Madox Ford, *Return to Yesterday*, 197.

46. Joseph Conrad to Pinker, September 18, 1908, *Collected Letters*, Volume 4, 125.

47. Joseph Conrad to Pinker, October 7, 1908, *Collected Letters*, Volume 4, 138−9.

48. Joseph Conrad to Harpers, October 31, 1909, *Collected Letters*, Volume 4, 284.

49. Najder, *Joseph Conrad: A Chronicle*, 373.

50. Joseph Conrad to H. G. Wells, September 25, 1908, *Collected Letters*, Volume 4, 129.

51. Joseph Conrad to Ford, September 29, or October 6, 1908, *Collected Letters*, Volume 4, 131.

52. Joseph Conrad to Pinker, October 7, 1908, *Collected Letters*, Volume 4, 138−9.

53. Joseph Conrad to Pinker, December 9, 1908, *Collected Letters*, Volume 4, 159.

54. Joseph Conrad to E. V. Lucas, June 3, 1909, *Collected Letters*, Volume 4, 247.

55. "The First Thing I Remember," in *Congo Diary and Other Uncollected Pieces*, ed. Zdisław Najder (New York, 1978), 98−9.

56. "The First Thing I Remember," 98−9.

57. "The First Thing I Remember," 98−9.

58. "The First Thing I Remember," 98−9.

59. Zdzisław Najder was the first to reveal this influence of Bobrowski's *Memoirs* on the reminiscences.

60. Joseph Conrad to Wells, November 3, 1908, *Collected Letters*, Volume 4, 149.

61. Ford Madox Ford, *Joseph Conrad: A Personal Remembrance*, 180.

62. Joseph Conrad, "Stephen Crane: a Preface to Thomas Beer's 'Stephen Crane'," *Last Essays* (London: Dent, 1926), 93.

63. Joseph Conrad, "Stephen Crane: a Preface to Thomas Beer's 'Stephen Crane'," 93.

64. Joseph Conrad, "Henry James: An Appreciation," *Notes on Life and Letters* (London: Dent, 1921), 17.

65. Joseph Conrad, "A Familiar Preface" to *A Personal Record*, 17.

66. *A Personal Record*, 19.

67. Much later, in 1918, Gosse and Conrad corresponded, with Gosse sending Conrad a copy of *Father and Son*, and asking Conrad to send him *A Personal Record*. See *Collected Letters*, Volume 6, 209.

68. *A Personal Record*, 19.

69. *A Personal Record*, 19.

70. *A Personal Record*, 32.

71. *A Personal Record*, 24.

72. *A Personal Record*, 24.

73. *A Personal Record*, 24.

74. *A Personal Record*, 27.

75. *A Personal Record*, 28.

76. *A Personal Record*, 28.

77. *A Personal Record*, 28.

78. *A Personal Record*, 32.

79. *A Personal Record*, 32.

80. *A Personal Record*, 34.

81. *A Personal Record*, 69.

82. *A Personal Record*, 68.

83. *A Personal Record*, 74.

84. *A Personal Record*, 89.

85. *A Personal Record*, 92.

86. *A Personal Record*, 95.

87. *A Personal Record*, 96.

88. *A Personal Record*, 96.

89. *A Personal Record*, 127.

90. Henry James to Violet Hunt, November 2, 1909, in *Henry James Letters*, ed. Leon Edel (Cambridge, MA: Harvard University Press, 4 vols., 1974–84), Volume 4, 533. Hunt also publishes this letter in her memoir *The Flurried Years* (London: Hurst & Blackett, 1926), 88.

91. Quoted in Najder, *Joseph Conrad: A Chronicle*, 349–50.

92. Joseph Conrad to Ford Madox Ford, April 28, or May 5, 1909, *Collected Letters*, Volume 4, 223.

93. Joseph Conrad to Ford Madox Ford, May 20, 1909, *Collected Letters*, Volume 4, 236–7.

94. Joseph Conrad to Ford Madox Ford, July 31, 1909, *Collected Letters*, Volume 4, 263.

95. Joseph Conrad to Ford Madox Ford, July 31, 1909, *Collected Letters*, Volume 4, 263.

96. Joseph Conrad to Ford Madox Ford, July 31, 1909, *Collected Letters*, Volume 4, 263.

97. Joseph Conrad to Ford Madox Ford, July 31, 1909, *Collected Letters*, Volume 4, 263.

98. Joseph Conrad to Austin Harrison, February 15, 1912, *Collected Letters*, Volume 5, 20.

99. Walter Benjamin, "A Berlin Chronicle," in *One-Way Street* (London: Verso, 1997 ed.), 295.

100. Joseph Conrad, "Poland Revisited," in *Notes on Life and Letters* (London: Dent, 1921), 149.

101. "Poland Revisited," 150.

102. "Poland Revisited," 164.

103. "Poland Revisited," 168.

104. "Poland Revisited," 168.

105. "Poland Revisited," 169.

106. Conrad had been asked in 1904 for any early material he had, to be printed in a newspaper. He wrote to Ford: "If you have something written that you do *not* care for *in the least* send it on. I'll put in a few of my jargon phrases and send it on. As I remarked: nothing matters—and we are intimate enough to say anything to each other. You may as well have their modest cheque. If the thing shocks you, tear the sweet note up." *Collected Letters*, Volume 3, 152.

107. Joseph Conrad to James Pinker, August 4, 1909, *Collected Letters*, Volume 4, 254–5.

108. Joseph Conrad to David Meldrum, December 31, 1909, *Collected Letters*, Volume 4, 312.

109. Ford Madox Ford to Joseph Conrad, November 15, 1923, in Ludwig, *Letters*, 157.

110. Frederick Karl, *The Three Lives*, 897.

111. Joseph Conrad to Ford Madox Ford, quoted in Najder, *A Chronicle*, 483.
112. Jessie Conrad, *Joseph Conrad as I Knew Him*, 159.

CHAPTER 2

1. Henry James, *William Wetmore Story and His Friends; From Letters, Diaries, and Recollections*, Volume 2 (Edinburgh: William Blackwood and Sons, 1903), 198.
2. Henry James to Edith Wharton, March 16, 1912, *Henry James Letters IV*, ed. Leon Edel (Cambridge, MA: Belknap Press, 1984), 605.
3. Leon Edel, *Henry James: The Master 1901–1916* (Philadelphia: Lippincott, 1972), 460.
4. Leon Edel, *The Master 1901–1916*, 488.
5. See, for example, Henry James, *The Art of the Novel: Critical Prefaces*, ed. R. P. Blackmur (New York: Scribner, 1935), 148. There are many other instances.
6. See, for example, Henry James, *Autobiography*, ed. Frederick W. Dupee (London: W. H. Allen, 1956), 84.
7. For a much more recent volume collecting *A Small Boy and Others*, *Notes of a Son and Brother*, and *The Middle Years*, alongside other, shorter autobiographical pieces, see Philip Horne, ed., Henry James, *Autobiographies* (New York: The Library of America, 2016).
8. A recurring phrase in the New York prefaces, see, e.g. *The Art of the Novel*, 236.
9. *The Art of the Novel*, 47.
10. Henry James, *Partial Portraits*, with intro. by Leon Edel (Ann Arbor: University of Michigan Press, 1970), essay on George du Maurier, 327.
11. *The Art of the Novel*, 320–1.
12. Henry James, *The Complete Notebooks of Henry James*, ed. Leon Edel and Lyall H. Powers (New York: Oxford University Press, 1987), 54; the observation was Hippolyte Taine's, over lunch with James, although James thought it sufficiently noteworthy to jot it down.
13. Henry James to H. G. Wells, 1913, quoted in Nicholas Delbanco, *Group Portrait* (London: Faber, 1982), 161.
14. For more on James's autobiographical writings in his later years across several genres, see Oliver Herford, *Henry James's Style of Retrospect: Late Personal Writings 1890–1915* (Oxford: Oxford University Press, 2016).
15. *The Complete Notebooks of Henry James*, 214.
16. *Partial Portraits*, essay on Robert Louis Stevenson, 138.
17. See Henry James to Harry James, November 15–18, 1913, *The Letters of Henry James*, ed. Percy Lubbock (London: Macmillan, 1920), Volume II, 357. "From the moment of those of my weeks in Cambridge of 1911 during which I began, by a sudden turn of talk with your Mother, to dally with the idea of a 'Family Book', this idea took on for me a particular light, the light which hasn't varied, through all sorts of discomfitures and difficulties—and disillusionments, and in which in fact I have put the thing through. That turn of talk was the germ, it dropped the seed."

18. From preface to Somerset Maugham, ed., *The Greatest Stories of All Time* (1939). Quoted in *Henry James Letters IV*, ed. Leon Edel, 364.

19. Henry James to Harry James, January 13, 1913, *The Letters of Henry James*, ed. Percy Lubbock, Volume II, 302.

20. Harry James to William James, March 9, 1910, quoted in Leon Edel, *The Master 1901–1916*, 440.

21. *The Complete Notebooks of Henry James*, 314.

22. Henry James to Edith Wharton, June 10, 1910, quoted in Leon Edel, *The Master 1901–1916*, 443.

23. *The Complete Notebooks of Henry James*, 214.

24. *The Complete Notebooks of Henry James*, 237.

25. *The Complete Notebooks of Henry James*, 331.

26. Henry James to Theodora Bosanquet, October 27, 1911, ed. Edel, *Henry James Letters IV*, 589.

27. Henry James to Edith Wharton, November 19, 1911, ed. Edel, *Henry James Letters IV*, 590–2.

28. Henry James to Theodora Bosanquet, November 2, 1911, ed. Edel, *Henry James Letters IV*, 590.

29. *The Complete Notebooks of Henry James*, 80.

30. Theodora Bosanquet, "Henry James at Work" (London: Hogarth Essays, 1924), 11.

31. Theodora Bosanquet, "Henry James at Work," 11.

32. Henry James, *Autobiography*, 460.

33. Theodora Bosanquet, "Henry James at Work," 10.

34. *The Art of the Novel*, 185.

35. *The Art of the Novel*, 59.

36. *Autobiography*, 494.

37. Leon Edel, *The Master 1901–1916*, 19.

38. Leon Edel, *The Master 1901–1916*, 19.

39. Henry James, "The Beast in the Jungle," in *The Novels and Tales of Henry James* ["New York Edition"] 24 vols. New York: Scribner's (London: Macmillan, 1908–9), Volume 17, 64.

40. *Autobiography*, 496.

41. *Autobiography*, 38.

42. *Autobiography*, 95.

43. *Autobiography*, 123.

44. *Autobiography*, 157.

45. *Autobiography*, 161.

46. *The Art of the Novel*, 164.

47. *Autobiography*, 32.

48. Henry James to Harry James, quoted in Adeline R. Tintner, "Autobiography as Fiction: 'The Usurping Consciousness' as Hero of James's Memoirs," *Twentieth Century Literature*, 23:2 (1977), 242.

49. Henry James to Harry James, November 26, 1911, in Philip Horne, ed., *Henry James: A Life in Letters* (London: Allen Lane, 1999), 503.

50. *Autobiography*, 118.

51. *Autobiography*, 42.

52. F. W. Dupee, introduction to Henry James, *Autobiography*, xiv.

53. *William Wetmore Story and his Friends*, Volume 2, 14.

54. Henry James to Harry James, July 16, 1912, ed. Lubbock, *The Letters of Henry James*, II, 248.

55. *The Complete Notebooks of Henry James*, 335.

56. *The Complete Notebooks of Henry James*, 357.

57. Henry James to Mrs. William James, November 13, 1911, in Philip Horne, ed., *Henry James: A Life in Letters*, 503–4.

58. *The Complete Notebooks of Henry James*, 368.

59. Henry James to Harry James, November 25, 1912, ed. Edel, *Henry James Letters* IV, 798.

60. *Autobiography*, 272.

61. *Autobiography*, 492.

62. *Autobiography*, 414–15.

63. *Autobiography*, 283.

64. *Autobiography*, 530–1.

65. *Autobiography*, 511.

66. Henry James to Harry James, ed. Edel, *Henry James Letters* IV, 803.

67. Henry James to Harry James, ed. Edel, *Henry James Letters* IV, 803–4.

68. See Tamara Follini, "Pandora's Box: The Family Correspondence in *Notes of a Son and Brother*," *Cambridge Quarterly*, 25 (1996), 26–40 for more on James's alterations to the family letters.

69. Henry James to Harry James, November 15–18, 1913, ed. Lubbock, *The Letters of Henry James* II, 358–9.

70. Lyndall Gordon, *A Private Life of Henry James: Two Women and His Art* (London: Chatto & Windus, 1998), 352.

71. Henry James to Harry James, November 15–18, 1913, ed. Edel, *Henry James Letters* IV, 803: "I daresay I did instinctively regard it at last as all *my* truth, to do what I would with." The letter from Henry James to Henrietta Temple, May 5, 1914, uses the same phrase about Minny's letters, "[…] sending them to *me* (to do what I would with)." Quoted in Gordon, *A Private Life of Henry James*, 356.

72. Leon Edel, *The Master 1901–1916*, 366. The scene appears in H. G. Wells, *Experiment in Autobiography*, Volume II (London: Faber, 1984), 538.

73. *The Art of the Novel*, 164.

74. *The Complete Notebooks of Henry James*, 66.

75. Henry James, "She and He: Recent Documents," in *Literary Criticism: French Writers, Other European Writers, The Prefaces to the New York Edition*, ed. Leon Edel and Mark Wilson (New York: The Library of America, 1984), 740.

76. "She and He: Recent Documents," 740.

77. "She and He: Recent Documents," 742–3.

78. *Autobiography*, 111.

79. Quoted in Leon Edel, *The Master 1901–1916*, 537.

80. Henry James, "Gustave Flaubert," in *Literary Criticism: French Writers, Other European Writers, The Prefaces to the New York Edition*, ed. Leon Edel and Mark Wilson, 297.

81. See Henry James to Charles Scribner's Sons, February 16, 1915, in Edel, *Henry James Letters* IV, 736. "My Tillapenny shall certainly be Tullafinny on the next opportunity – though I am sorry it should have to, being as it is, I think, slightly the less ugly form of the two [...] I thank your correspondent particularly for setting right my error in using U.S.C.T. when I should have named the 55th Massachusetts; an error for which I blush, feeling it now, as Prof. Wilder says, a bad one. We must absolutely attend to it. I can only plead in attenuation that my remoteness from sources of reference and refreshments of memory laid frequent traps, no doubt, for my poor old imagination." As Oliver Herford points out, James did at least intend for the facts, references, and allusions in *A Small Boy and Others* and *Notes of a Son and Brother* to be correct. In an earlier letter, to Thomas Sargent Perry on September 17, 1913, he wrote: "these and their like are all ghostly little facts—but [...] as I go over the heterogeneous pages I want to *verify* [...] it should be right, as all should be." See Oliver Herford, *Henry James's Style of Retrospect* (Oxford: Oxford University Press, 2016), 77.

82. Anonymous review of Proust's *Du Côté de Chez Swann*, *TLS*, December 4, 1913, by A. B. Walkley.

83. Henry James to Harry James, April 7, 1914. Quoted in Carol Holly, "Absolutely Acclaimed: The Cure for Depression in James's Final Phase," *The Henry James Review* 8:2 (1987), 133.

84. H. G. Wells, *Experiment in Autobiography*, Volume II, 611.

CHAPTER 3

1. Ford Madox Ford to H. G. Wells, November 20, 1908, quoted in Max Saunders, *Ford Madox Ford: A Dual Life*, Volume II (Oxford: Oxford University Press, 1996), 438.

2. Ford Madox Ford, *Joseph Conrad* (London: Duckworth, 1924), 25.

3. Max Saunders, *Ford Madox Ford: A Dual Life*, Volume II, 467.

4. Fernando Pessoa, *Selected Prose*, ed. trans. Richard Zenith (New York: Grove, 1998), 40. "Fernando Pessoa himself would be a pagan, were he not a ball of string inwardly wound around itself."

5. Violet Hunt, *The Flurried Years* (London: Hurst & Blackett, 1926), 213. See Max Saunders, *Ford Madox Ford: A Dual Life*, Volume I, 368.

6. Ford Madox Ford, *Mightier Than the Sword* (London: Allen & Unwin, 1938), 36.

7. Leon Edel, *Henry James: A Life* (London: Collins, 1987), 655.

8. Ford Madox Hueffer, *Henry James: A Critical Study* (London: Secker, 1914), 82–90.

9. Arthur Mizener, *The Saddest Story: A Biography of Ford Madox Ford* (London: The Bodley Head, 1971), xxi.

10. David Dow Harvey, *Ford Madox Ford: 1873–1939: A Bibliography of Works and Criticism* (Princeton: Princeton University Press, 1962), 147.

11. Quoted in David Dow Harvey, *Ford Madox Ford: 1873–1939: A Bibliography of Works and Criticism*, 157.

12. Max Saunders, *Ford Madox Ford: A Dual Life*, Volume I, 227–8.

13. Ford Madox Ford, *Return to Yesterday* (London: Victor Gollancz, 1931), 359.

14. Ford, "Literary Portraits—V.; Miss Violet Hunt and 'The Desirable Alien',," *Outlook*, 32 (October 11, 1913), 497–8. Quoted in Saunders, *Ford Madox Ford: A Dual Life*, Volume I, 238–9.

15. Violet Hunt, *The Flurried Years*, 21.

16. Violet Hunt, *The Flurried Years*, 93.

17. According to Harvey's bibliography, 33, chapters I, II, III, and V appeared in *Harper's* in February, April, October 1910; March 1911 with slight changes; chapters XI, IV in *Fortnightly* in October 1910 and March 1911.

18. Max Saunders, *Ford Madox Ford: A Dual Life*, Volume I, 314.

19. See Saunders, *Ford Madox Ford: A Dual Life*, Volume I, 350–1.

20. Violet Hunt, *The Flurried Years*, 187.

21. See Saunders, *Ford Madox Ford: A Dual Life*, Volume I, 305–45.

22. Ford Madox Hueffer, *Ancient Lights and Certain New Reflections* (London: Chapman and Hall, 1911), xiv–xv.

23. *Ancient Lights*, vii.

24. *Ancient Lights*, viii.

25. *Ancient Lights*, viii.

26. *Ancient Lights*, viii–ix.

27. *Ancient Lights*, ix.

28. *Ancient Lights*, ix.

29. *Ancient Lights*, x.

30. *Ancient Lights*, vii–viii.

31. *Ancient Lights*, x.

32. *Ancient Lights*, xii.

33. *Ancient Lights*, 2.

34. *Ancient Lights*, 253.

35. *Ancient Lights*, facing 5.

36. *Ancient Lights*, 226.

37. *Ancient Lights*, 229.

38. *Ancient Lights*, 5.

39. *Ancient Lights*, 14.

40. *Ancient Lights*, 22.

41. Ford to James B. Pinker, January 1911, *Letters of Ford Madox Ford*, ed. Richard M. Ludwig (Princeton: Princeton University Press, 1965), 46–7.

42. *Ancient Lights*, 295.

43. *Ancient Lights*, 296.

44. Ford Madox Brown, *The Diary of Ford Madox Brown*, ed. Virginia Surtees (New Haven: Yale University Press, 1981), 80.

45. Ford, "Literary Portraits XLIII: Mr Wyndham Lewis and Blast," quoted in Sondra Stang, ed., *The Ford Madox Ford Reader* (Manchester: Carcanet, 1986), 175.

46. Ford, "Literary Portraits XLIII: Mr Wyndham Lewis and Blast," 173–4.

47. Ford, "Literary Portraits XLVIII. M. Charles-Louis Philippe and 'Le Père Perdrix'," *Outlook*, 34 (August 8, 1914), 174–5. Quoted in Ford Madox Ford, *War Prose*, ed. Max Saunders (Manchester: Carcanet, 1999), 207.

48. Ford, "Dedicatory Letter to Stella Ford," *The Good Soldier* (London: Penguin, 2002), 4.

49. Ford Madox Hueffer, "Footsloggers," in *On Heaven and Poems Written in Active Service* (London: John Lane, 1918), 72.

50. Ford Madox Ford, *It Was the Nightingale* (London: Heinemann, 1934), 175.

51. *It Was the Nightingale*, 175.

52. Ford to F. S. Flint, Red Ford Cottage, June 23, 1920, *Letters of Ford Madox Ford*, ed. Richard Ludwig, 105.

53. Ford to Alec Waugh, July 26, 1920, *Letters of Ford Madox Ford*, ed. Richard Ludwig, 116.

54. Ford Madox Hueffer, *Thus to Revisit* (London: Chapman and Hall, 1921), 20.

55. *Thus to Revisit*, 22.

56. *Thus to Revisit*, 39.

57. *Thus to Revisit*, 113.

58. *Thus to Revisit*, 113.

59. *Thus to Revisit*, 121.

60. *Thus to Revisit*, 48.

61. *Thus to Revisit*, 193.

62. *Thus to Revisit*, 186–7.

63. *It Was the Nightingale*, 137–8.

64. Ford to Victor Gollancz, March 1, 1932, *Letters of Ford Madox Ford*, ed. Richard Ludwig, 204.

65. Ford to James B. Pinker, January 22, 1920, quoted in Max Saunders, *Ford Madox Ford: A Dual Life*, Volume II, 80.

66. Ford Madox Ford, *No Enemy* (New York: Macaulay, 1929), 100.

67. *No Enemy*, 164–5.

68. *No Enemy*, 190.

69. See Max Saunders, *Ford Madox Ford: A Dual Life*, Volume II, 158.

70. *It Was the Nightingale*, 285.

71. For more on the *transatlantic review*, see Bernard J. Poli, *Ford Madox Ford and the Transatlantic Review* (New York: Syracuse University Press, 1967).

72. Ford to H. G. Wells, October 14, 1923, in Richard Ludwig, *Letters of Ford Madox Ford*, 154.

73. Ford to Joseph Conrad [n.d., but between October 7 and 13, 1923], Yale. Quoted in Max Saunders, *Ford Madox Ford: A Dual Life*, Volume II, 139.

74. Ford Madox Ford, *Joseph Conrad: A Personal Remembrance* (London: Duckworth, 1924), 23.

75. *Joseph Conrad*, 5–6.
76. See *Joseph Conrad*, 73.
77. See, for example, Ford on Conrad's identification with figures whose memoirs or biographies he read, and the importance he attached to, say, having Christina Rossetti's desk in the Pent, *Joseph Conrad*, 89.
78. *Joseph Conrad*, 81.
79. *Joseph Conrad*, 81.
80. *Joseph Conrad*, 82.
81. *Joseph Conrad*, 82.
82. *Joseph Conrad*, 123.
83. H. G. Wells, "Letter to the editor," *English Review*, XXXI (August 1920), 178–9. See Harvey, *Ford Madox Ford: 1873–1939*, 335–6.
84. *Joseph Conrad*, 49.
85. Ford Madox Hueffer, "Footsloggers," in *On Heaven*, 68.
86. *Return to Yesterday*, vii.
87. *Return to Yesterday*, vii.
88. *Return to Yesterday*, vii.
89. *Return to Yesterday*, vii.
90. *Return to Yesterday*, 3.
91. *Return to Yesterday*, 8.
92. Harvey notes, in his bibliography of Ford, 75, that "there are, besides many echoes from earlier works, particularly *Ancient Lights* and *Thus to Revisit* [...] two chapters reprinted, with very little change from earlier published periodical articles [...] Ford makes no explicit acknowledgement of these earlier publications. In addition the sketches of Meary Walker and Meary Spratt in Chapter I, Part Three, first appeared in *Women & Men*."
93. Ford to Hugh Walpole, March 30, 1930, *Letters of Ford Madox Ford*, ed. Richard Ludwig, 193.
94. *Return to Yesterday*, ix.
95. *Return to Yesterday*, 213.
96. *Return to Yesterday*, 22.
97. *Return to Yesterday*, 213–14.
98. *Return to Yesterday*, 13.
99. *Return to Yesterday*, 24.
100. *Return to Yesterday*, 52.
101. *Return to Yesterday*, 109.
102. *Return to Yesterday*, 202.
103. *Return to Yesterday*, 109.
104. *Return to Yesterday*, 418.
105. *Return to Yesterday*, 418.
106. *Return to Yesterday*, 435–6.
107. *Return to Yesterday*, 435–6.
108. According to Harvey's bibliography, 78.
109. *Return to Yesterday*, 139.

110. *It Was the Nightingale*, vi.
111. *It Was the Nightingale*, vi.
112. *It Was the Nightingale*, vi.
113. *It Was the Nightingale*, x.
114. *It Was the Nightingale*, 3.
115. *It Was the Nightingale*, 15.
116. *It Was the Nightingale*, 17.
117. *It Was the Nightingale*, 88.
118. *It Was the Nightingale*, 66–7.
119. *It Was the Nightingale*, 49.
120. *It Was the Nightingale*, 173–4.
121. *It Was the Nightingale*, 161.
122. *It Was the Nightingale*, 161.
123. *It Was the Nightingale*, 161.
124. James Mellow, *Charmed Circle: Gertrude Stein & Company* (London: Phaidon, 1974), 242.
125. *It Was the Nightingale*, 161.
126. Stella Bowen, *Drawn from Life* (London: Virago, 1984), 171.
127. *It Was the Nightingale*, 189.
128. Ford Madox Ford, *Some Do Not…* in Max Saunders, ed., *Some Do Not…(Parade's End 1)* (Manchester: Carcanet, 2010), 3.
129. *It Was the Nightingale*, 192.
130. *It Was the Nightingale*, 139.
131. *It Was the Nightingale*, 158–9.
132. *It Was the Nightingale*, 233–4.
133. Stella Bowen, *Drawn from Life*, 62.
134. Stella Bowen, *Drawn from Life*, 164.
135. As Max Saunders writes, Ford "cultivated the enjoyment of disbelief, the savouring of the sceptical after-taste. He was the great twentieth-century writer about the great nineteenth-century topic: doubt." See Saunders, *Ford Madox Ford: A Dual Life*, Volume II, 192.

CHAPTER 4

1. Edith Wharton to Bernard Berenson, November 23, 1912, on her novel *The Reef*. From *The Letters of Edith Wharton*, ed. R. W. B. Lewis and Nancy Lewis (London: Simon & Schuster, 1988), 284.
2. Edith Wharton, *A Backward Glance* (New York, London: Appleton-Century, 1934), 177.
3. Edith Wharton to Mary Cadwalader Jones, Sainte-Claire, December 26, 1920, *Letters*, ed. Lewis, 436.
4. Edith Wharton to Rutger B. Jewett, February 21, 1923, *Letters*, ed. Lewis, 464–5.
5. Edith Wharton to Rutger B. Jewett, February 21, 1923, *Letters*, ed. Lewis, 464–5.

6. Edith Wharton to Rutger B. Jewett, February 21, 1923, *Letters*, ed. Lewis, 464–5.

7. Edith Wharton to Rutger B. Jewett, February 21, 1923, *Letters*, ed. Lewis, 464–5.

8. Edith Wharton to Rutger B. Jewett, February 21, 1923, *Letters*, ed. Lewis, 464–5.

9. Shari Benstock's *No Gifts From Chance: A Biography of Edith Wharton* (New York: Scribner's, 1994), is consistently good on Wharton's reading of biographies and autobiographies. See, e.g., 162, 181, 253, 263.

10. See Wharton's 1902 review of Herbert W. Paul's *Matthew Arnold*, in *The Uncollected Critical Writings of Edith Wharton*, ed. Frederick Wegener (Princeton: Princeton University Press, 1996), 94–8.

11. See Hermione Lee, *Edith Wharton* (London: Chatto & Windus, 2007), 653.

12. From *Quaderno dello Studente*, quoted in R. W. B. Lewis, *Edith Wharton: A Biography* (New York: Harper & Row), 1975, xii.

13. From *Quaderno dello Studente*, quoted in R. W. B. Lewis, *Edith Wharton*, xii.

14. R. W. B. Lewis, *Edith Wharton*, xii.

15. Hermione Lee, *Edith Wharton*, 638.

16. Cynthia Griffin Wolff, in *A Feast of Words: The Triumph of Edith Wharton* (Oxford: Oxford University Press, 1977), 417, asserts that "Life & I," "almost certainly serving as a first draft of the published autobiography, *A Backward Glance*," was "probably written as early as 1920 or 1922." In the notes of Edith Wharton, *Novellas and Other Writings* (New York: Library of America, 1990), 1136, Wolff writes that "Life & I," "never completed," may pre-date the 1923 Jewett letter.

17. "Life & I," in Edith Wharton, *Novellas and Other Writings*, 1074.

18. "Life & I," 1074.

19. "Life & I," 1072.

20. "Life & I," 1071.

21. "Life & I," 1072.

22. "Life & I," 1072.

23. "Life & I," 1080.

24. "Life & I," 1082.

25. "Life & I," 1093.

26. "Life & I," 1087.

27. "Life & I," 1088.

28. "Life & I," 1087.

29. "Life & I," 1087.

30. R. W. B. Lewis, *Edith Wharton*, xi.

31. Edith Wharton to Bernard Berenson, February 18, 1931, *Letters*, ed. Lewis, 534.

32. Nor, it transpires, did Edel really want to write the Berry biography. According to Lewis, the whole project was a complicated cover for one of Edel's friends, who wanted to see Wharton's letters to Berry. Edel went to St. Brice in June 1931, and agreed to abandon the Berry project. See Lewis, *Edith Wharton*, 501.

33. Edith Wharton to Mary Berenson, June 4, 1932, *Letters*, ed. Lewis, 553.

34. Edith Wharton to Gaillard Lapsley, March 2, 1933, *Letters*, ed. Lewis, 557.
35. Shari Benstock, *No Gifts From Chance*, 433.
36. *A Backward Glance*, vii.
37. *A Backward Glance*, vii.
38. *A Backward Glance*, 1.
39. *A Backward Glance*, 1.
40. *A Backward Glance*, 7.
41. *A Backward Glance*, 37.
42. *A Backward Glance*, 24.
43. *A Backward Glance*, 46.
44. *A Backward Glance*, 82.
45. *A Backward Glance*, 70.
46. For a full account of the 1914 manuscript of "Literature," see Nancy R. Leach, "Edith Wharton's Unpublished Novel," *American Literature*, 25:3 (November 1953), 334–53.
47. *A Backward Glance*, 113.
48. *A Backward Glance*, 169.
49. *A Backward Glance*, 172.
50. *A Backward Glance*, 172.
51. *A Backward Glance*, 175.
52. Edith Wharton to Gaillard Lapsley, early 1916, quoted in Lewis, *Edith Wharton*, 383.
53. *A Backward Glance*, 248.
54. *A Backward Glance*, 178.
55. *A Backward Glance*, 179.
56. *A Backward Glance*, 179.
57. Millicent Bell, *Edith Wharton and Henry James: The Story of Their Friendship* (New York: George Braziller, 1965), 147.
58. *A Backward Glance*, 180.
59. *A Backward Glance*, 323.
60. *A Backward Glance*, 241.
61. *A Backward Glance*, 193–4.
62. *A Backward Glance*, 231.
63. Edith Wharton to Morton Fullerton, March 19, 1910, *Letters*, ed. Lewis, 201–2.
64. *A Backward Glance*, 90.
65. Grace Kellogg, *The Two Lives of Edith Wharton: The Woman and Her Work* (New York: Appleton-Century, 1965), 64.
66. "Life & I," 1075.
67. *A Backward Glance*, 215–16.
68. *A Backward Glance*, 221–2.
69. *A Backward Glance*, 170–1.
70. *A Backward Glance*, 170–1.
71. *A Backward Glance*, 170–1.
72. *A Backward Glance*, 379.

73. See Edith Wharton, *The Writing of Fiction* (New York: Scribner's, 1925), 78. What sets "apart the born novelist from the authors of self-confessions in the novel-form [...] [is] the absence of the objective faculty in the latter. The subjective writer lacks the power of getting far enough away from his story to view it as a whole and relate it to its setting; his minor characters remain the mere satellites of the principal personage (himself), and disappear when not lit up by their central luminary."

74. *A Backward Glance*, 210–11.

75. *A Backward Glance*, 210–11.

76. Henry James, *The Art of the Novel*, 320–1.

77. Henry James to H. G. Wells, 1913, quoted in Nicholas Delbanco, *Group Portrait*, 161.

78. From "The Fullness of Life." Quoted, among other places—nearly every writer on Wharton uses this quotation, since it is so central to understanding how she saw herself—by Lewis, *Edith Wharton*, 65–6.

79. Hermione Lee, *Edith Wharton*, 10.

80. The Life Apart, 670. First published in 1994 in *American Literature* (66:4), December 1994. "Texts and Contexts of Edith Wharton's Love Diary," ed. Kenneth M. Price and Phyllis McBride, 663–88.

81. *A Backward Glance*, 6.

82. Cynthia Griffin Wolff, *A Feast of Words: The Triumph of Edith Wharton*, 147.

83. The Life Apart, 676.

84. The Life Apart, 679.

85. The Life Apart, 680.

86. The Life Apart, 680.

87. The Life Apart, 683.

88. The Life Apart, 683.

89. The Life Apart, 683.

90. "Terminus," quoted in Lewis, *Edith Wharton*, 259–60.

91. "Terminus," 259–60.

92. "Terminus," 259–60.

93. Lewis, *Edith Wharton*, 259.

94. Edith Wharton to Morton Fullerton, August 26, 1908, *Letters*, ed. Lewis, 162.

95. The Life Apart, 673.

96. The Life Apart, 674.

97. Edith Wharton to Morton Fullerton, May 20, 1908, *Letters*, ed. Lewis, 145.

98. Edith Wharton to Morton Fullerton, June 5, 1908, *Letters*, ed. Lewis, 147.

99. In a late letter, Wharton wrote: "I feel about my houses as a crab must about its carapace." Edith Wharton to Mary Cadwalader Jones, April 10, 1934, *Letters*, ed. Lewis, 577.

100. The Life Apart, 671.

101. The Life Apart, 672.

102. Edith Wharton to Morton Fullerton, July 1, 1908, *Letters*, ed. Lewis, 156.

103. Edith Wharton to Sara Norton, November 18, 1908, *Letters*, ed. Lewis, 166.

104. See Edith Wharton, *The Uncollected Critical Writings*, ed. Wegener, 287.

105. Edith Wharton to John L. B. Williams, March 17, 1937, [Yale], quoted in Wegener, 287.

106. "A Little Girl's New York," Wegener, 274.

107. "A Little Girl's New York," Wegener, 277.

108. Edith Wharton to Mrs. Royall Tyler, May 23, 1936, *Letters*, ed. Lewis, 594–5.

109. Edith Wharton to Minnie Jones, January 24, 1932, quoted in Benstock, *No Gifts From Chance,* 431.

110. Edith Wharton to Mary Berenson, October 11, 1936, *Letters*, ed. Lewis, 598.

111. Edith Wharton to Mary Berenson, October 11, 1936, *Letters*, ed. Lewis, 598.

CHAPTER 5

1. Letter from H. G. Wells to "Mrs Tooley," October–November 1908. See David C. Smith, ed., *The Correspondence of H. G. Wells*, Volume II, 1904–1918 (London: Pickering & Chatto, 1998), 228.

2. H. G. Wells to the Editor, *Queen*, July 6, 1900. *The Correspondence of H. G. Wells*, ed. David C. Smith, Volume I, 1880–1903, 359–60.

3. H. G. Wells to Ford Madox Ford, November 14, 1908. Quoted in Max Saunders, *Ford Madox Ford: A Dual Life*, Volume II, 438.

4. H. G. Wells to Frederick Macmillan, c.September 26, 1910. *The Correspondence of H. G. Wells*, ed. David C. Smith, Volume II, 1904–1918, 286.

5. As Geoffrey West writes in *H. G. Wells: A Sketch for a Portrait* (London: Gerald Howe, 1930), 186: "To-day Wells feels that he should have set them [the Webbs] boldly in his novel under their own names."

6. One of many examples: in his *Experiment in Autobiography*, Volume I (London: Faber, 1984), 171, Wells writes: "In a novel of mine called *Love & Mr Lewisham* which is about just such a Grammar School teacher as I was, I have described how he had pinned up on his wall a 'Schema', planned to make the utmost use of his time and opportunities. I made that *Schema*." At the same time, Wells in later life became more and more touchy about other people depicting him in their memoirs or novels. His late correspondence from the 1930s on is strewn with letters from Wells to various publishers threatening libel suits.

7. Henry James to H. G. Wells, March 3, 1911. Quoted in Norman and Jeanne MacKenzie, *The Time Traveller: The Life of H. G. Wells* (London: Weidenfeld & Nicolson, 1973), 271.

8. H. G. Wells, *Boon, The Mind of the Race, The Wild Asses of the Devil and The Last Trump* (London: Unwin, 1915), 98.

9. H. G. Wells, *Boon*, 118.

10. H. G. Wells, *Boon*, 100.

11. As Lovat Dickson writes, "Wells continued publicly to maintain that the true authorship lay with another; the most he would admit was that the book was of 'blended' origin." See *H. G. Wells: His Turbulent Life and Times* (Basingstoke: Macmillan, 1969), 260.

12. H. G. Wells, *Boon*, 123.

13. H. G. Wells, *Boon*, 169.

14. H. G. Wells, *Boon*, 169.

15. H. G. Wells, *Boon*. Quoted in David C. Smith, *H. G. Wells: Desperately Mortal* (New Haven: Yale University Press, 1986), 170.

16. H. G. Wells, *The World of William Clissold*, Volume I (London: Ernest Benn, 1926), i.

17. H. G. Wells, *The World of William Clissold*, Volume I, i.

18. H. G. Wells, *The World of William Clissold*, Volume I, ii–iii.

19. As David C. Smith writes, *William Clissold* can, of course, be seen "as a trial run" for Wells's *Experiment in Autobiography*. Reviewers took little notice of Wells's stipulations, as Smith also reveals. "When the book was reviewed in *Nature*, the reviewer, Henry E. Armstrong, called it Wells's autobiography—'a photograph taken with a wide lens, but not a very deep focus'." See *Desperately Mortal*, 417–18.

20. H. G. Wells, preface to *The New Machiavelli* (London: Penguin, 2005), 3.

21. H. G. Wells, *The New Machiavelli*, 3.

22. H. G. Wells to Edward Clodd, March 30, 1904. *The Correspondence of H. G. Wells*, Volume II, 19.

23. This is also recounted by Wells in a much later letter to Edmund Gosse. *Correspondence of H. G. Wells*, Volume II, 434. Here it is dated as Summer 1915, but there is some confusion since the same letter appears in the *Correspondence*, Volume III, 215, dated as Summer 1926.

24. David C. Smith, in *The Correspondence of H. G. Wells*, Volume II, 14, notes that Wells's proposed preface was printed in *Monthly Review* as "George Gissing: An Impression" (August 1904), 160–72. S. J. James also discusses the Gissing–Wells relationship, and the *Veranilda* preface, in "The Truth about Gissing: Reassessing the Literary Friendship of George Gissing and H. G. Wells," *The Wellsian*, 24 (2001), 2–21.

25. See MacKenzies, *The Time Traveller*, 334.

26. Alan Judd, *Ford Madox Ford* (London: Collins, 1990), 104.

27. Hermione Lee, *Virginia Woolf* (London: Vintage, 1997), 4.

28. "Geoffrey West" was the pseudonym chosen by the young Geoffrey Wells, who was no relation to H. G.

29. Geoffrey West, *H. G. Wells: A Sketch for a Portrait*, iv.

30. Wells's introduction to Geoffrey West, *H. G. Wells*, 13.

31. Wells's introduction to Geoffrey West, *H. G. Wells*, 13.

32. See Wells's own description of his "*Drive*" in a revealing letter to Rebecca West. Quoted in Gordon Ray, *H. G. Wells and Rebecca West* (Basingstoke: Macmillan, 1974), xviii.

33. As recounted in David C. Smith, *H. G. Wells: Desperately Mortal*, 157.

34. H. G. Wells, *The Bulpington of Blup* (London: Hutchinson, 1932), 403.

35. H. G. Wells, *The Bulpington of Blup*, 403.

36. H. G. Wells, *Experiment in Autobiography*, Volume I, 24.

37. *Experiment in Autobiography*, Volume I, 15.

38. *Experiment in Autobiography*, Volume I, 37.

39. *Experiment in Autobiography*, Volume I, 36.

40. *Experiment in Autobiography*, Volume II, 435.

41. *Experiment in Autobiography*, Volume I, 33–4.

42. *H. G. Wells in Love* (London: Faber, 1984), 102.

43. *Experiment in Autobiography*, Volume II, 827.

44. *Experiment in Autobiography*, Volume II, 417–18.

45. *Experiment in Autobiography*, Volume II, 494–5.

46. *Experiment in Autobiography*, Volume I, 28.

47. And yet, as John S. Partington writes, Wells's theory of global governance has been hugely influential. If Wells is not credited as much as he should be for his cosmopolitan ideas, this is perhaps because "he broke with organized campaigns for world government" and "never actually produced a single consolidated book containing his theory of global governance." See *Building Cosmopolis: The Political Thought of H. G. Wells* (Aldershot: Ashgate, 2003), 9.

48. Michael Draper, "Wells, Jung and the Persona," *English Literature in Transition*, 30:4 (1987), 437–49.

49. H. G. Wells to S. S. Kotelianski, January 8, 1933. *The Correspondence of H. G. Wells*, Volume III, 465.

50. Anthony West, in *H. G. Wells: Aspects of a Life* (London: Hutchinson, 1984), 381, writes that the correct name for this house is "Uppark," not "Up Park," which "has been copied from book to book on Wells, following the lead given by him in his autobiography." But I have followed Wells.

51. *Experiment in Autobiography*, Volume II, 737.

52. *Experiment in Autobiography*, Volume I, 76.

53. Anthony West, an acute reader of Wells's autobiography, isn't quite convinced by the broken tibia story, noting that "my father drops his account of the accident and its sequel into the narrative between two curious passages, the first concerned with his mother, and the second with the beginnings of his interest in sex." *Aspects of a Life*, 179.

54. *Experiment in Autobiography*, Volume I, 311.

55. *Experiment in Autobiography*, Volume I, 280.

56. *Experiment in Autobiography*, Volume I, 280.

57. *Experiment in Autobiography*, Volume II, 419.

58. *Experiment in Autobiography*, Volume II, 439.

59. *Experiment in Autobiography*, Volume II, 439.

60. Gene K. Rinkel and Margaret E. Rinkel, *The Picshuas of H. G. Wells: A Burlesque Diary* (Urbana: University of Illinois Press, 2006), 40.

61. *Experiment in Autobiography*, 439.

62. *Experiment in Autobiography*, 444.

63. *Experiment in Autobiography*, 444.

64. *Experiment in Autobiography*, 442–3.

65. Gene K. Rinkel and Margaret E. Rinkel, *The Picshuas of H. G. Wells: A Burlesque Diary*, 101.

66. Janet Malcolm, *Two Lives: Gertrude and Alice* (New Haven and London: Yale University Press, 2007), 205–6.

67. *Experiment in Autobiography*, Volume II, 490.

68. *Experiment in Autobiography*, Volume II, 619.

69. *Experiment in Autobiography*, Volume II, 620.

70. *Experiment in Autobiography*, Volume II, 620.

71. *Experiment in Autobiography*, Volume II, 615.

72. *Experiment in Autobiography*, Volume II, 615–16.

73. *Experiment in Autobiography*, Volume II, 618.

74. *Experiment in Autobiography*, Volume II, 622.

75. *Experiment in Autobiography*, Volume II, 617.

76. *Experiment in Autobiography*, Volume II, 536.

77. *Experiment in Autobiography*, Volume II, 535.

78. *Experiment in Autobiography*, Volume II, 599.

79. *Experiment in Autobiography*, Volume II, 623.

80. *Experiment in Autobiography*, Volume II, 493.

81. *Experiment in Autobiography*, Volume II, 503.

82. The lack of data in the last parts of the *Experiment* has been well-noted by previous critics. David C. Smith, for example, notes that the first fifty years of Wells's life are laid out in considerable detail, while "the last twenty years were treated very lightly, and the second section of the book is a restatement of his political and social philosophy." See *Desperately Mortal*, 418.

83. *Experiment in Autobiography*, Volume II, 799.

84. *Experiment in Autobiography*, Volume II, 798.

85. *Experiment in Autobiography*, Volume II, 822.

86. *Experiment in Autobiography*, Volume II, 824.

87. Lovat Dickson, *H. G. Wells: His Turbulent Life and Times* (Basingstoke: Macmillan, 1969), 3.

88. Anthony West, *H. G. Wells: Aspects of a Life*, 124.

89. See Deborah McDonald and Jeremy Dronfield, *A Very Dangerous Woman: The Lives, Loves and Lies of Russia's Most Seductive Spy* (London: Oneworld, 2015) for a recent account of Moura's love affairs and career as a spy.

90. Andrea Lynn, *Shadow Lovers: The Last Affairs of H. G. Wells* (Oxford: Westview, 2001), 113.

91. *H. G. Wells in Love*, 16.

92. *H. G. Wells in Love*, 17.

93. *H. G. Wells in Love*, 18.

94. Andrea Lynn, *Shadow Lovers: The Last Affairs of H. G. Wells*, 28.

95. See Andrea Lynn, *Shadow Lovers: The Last Affairs of H. G. Wells*, 28, for more on these cuts.

96. Andrea Lynn, *Shadow Lovers: The Last Affairs of H. G. Wells*, 25.

97. *H. G. Wells in Love*, 234.

98. *H. G. Wells in Love*, 234.

99. *H. G. Wells in Love*, 234.
100. Indeed, Martha Gellhorn always refuted, throughout her life, the idea that she had anything more than a close friendship with the much older Wells. See Caroline Moorehead, *Martha Gellhorn: A Life* (London: Vintage, 2004), 114–16.
101. See, for example, John Huntingdon, "H. G. Wells: Problems of an Amorous Utopian," *Literature in Transition*, 30:4 (1987), 411–22.
102. *H. G. Wells in Love*, 31.
103. *H. G. Wells in Love*, 32.
104. *H. G. Wells in Love*, 63.
105. Anthony West plausibly asserts that the scandal that was made of Wells's affair with Amber Reeves (a key omission in the *Experiment*) affected Wells more deeply than nearly anything else in his life. *Aspects of a Life*, 332.
106. *H. G. Wells in Love*, 96.
107. *H. G. Wells in Love*, 96–7.
108. *H. G. Wells in Love*, 235.
109. *H. G. Wells in Love*, 69.
110. *H. G. Wells in Love*, 176.
111. "No consolidated John Smith wakes up. There are endless variants of the theme we recognize and which recognizes itself as John Smith [...] All the John Smiths, from John Smith 1 to John Smith 5,000 or John Smith 5,000,000, have a common core in this belief that John Smith is really one person, because they are not only all aboard the same body, but also built round a similar conception of himself, his *persona* as Jung has it. *But in fact they are a collection of mutually replaceable individual systems held together in a common habitation*. One ascends; another fades before it." See *'42 to '44: A Contemporary Memoir* (London: Secker, 1944), 171.
112. David C. Smith, *H. G. Wells: Desperately Mortal*, 361.
113. *H. G. Wells in Love*, 190.
114. *H. G. Wells in Love*, 192.
115. *H. G. Wells in Love*, 183.
116. *H. G. Wells in Love*, 183.
117. From G. K. Chesterton, *Autobiography*. Quoted in MacKenzies, *The Time Traveller*, 341.
118. *The World of William Clissold*, 575.
119. *The World of William Clissold*, 575.
120. Philippe Lejeune and Victoria A. Lodewick, "How Do Diaries End?," *Biography*, 24:1 (2001), 99–112.
121. *H. G. Wells in Love*, 200.
122. Andrea Lynn, *Shadow Lovers: The Last Affairs of H. G. Wells*, 449.

CHAPTER 6

1. Gertrude Stein, *The Geographical History of America* (Baltimore: Johns Hopkins University Press, 1995), edited with an introduction by William Gass, 105.

2. Much to the dismay of some Picasso scholars. In a catalogue essay in *Matisse Picasso*, by Elizabeth Cowling, Anne Baldessari, John Elderfield, John Golding, Isabelle Monod-Fontaine, and Kirk Varnedoe (London: Tate Publishing, 2002), John Elderfield notes the fact that Stein's account is the only first-hand record, and queries the validity of her claim that there were eighty or ninety sittings— more than was usual for Picasso. See the footnotes to his essay, 348.

3. Gertrude Stein, *The Autobiography of Alice B. Toklas* (London: The Bodley Head, 1933), 50.

4. *The Autobiography of Alice B. Toklas*, 51.

5. *The Autobiography of Alice B. Toklas*, 51.

6. *The Autobiography of Alice B. Toklas*, 54–5.

7. *The Autobiography of Alice B. Toklas*, 57.

8. *The Autobiography of Alice B. Toklas*, 61.

9. *The Autobiography of Alice B. Toklas*, 13.

10. Gertrude Stein, *Picasso*, English edition (London: Batsford, 1938), 8.

11. For more conceptualizations of the "portrait transaction" in different periods, see, for example, the essays by Angela Rosenthal and David Lomas in Joanna Woodall, ed., *Portraiture* (Manchester: Manchester University Press, 1997), 147–88.

12. *Seeing Gertrude Stein*, ed. Wanda M. Corn and Tirza True Latimer (Berkeley: University of California Press, 2011) provides a detailed overview of the many portraits, in many media, for which Stein sat during her life.

13. Brenda Wineapple, in *Sister Brother* (London: Bloomsbury, 1996), 270, writes that Stein "instructed Emily Dawson, Mary Berenson's cousin, to send from London the English translations of the diary and letters of Madame D'Arblay (Fanny Burney), as well as the letters of Lady Mary Wortley Montagu and Hugh Walpole, and the memoirs, if such existed, of William Tecumseh Sherman, Abraham Lincoln, and John Adams."

14. Diana Souhami, *Gertrude and Alice* (London: Weidenfeld & Nicolson, 1991), 80.

15. Wendy Steiner, in *Exact Resemblance to Exact Resemblance* (New Haven: Yale University Press, 1978) has much to say about the relation of Stein's portraiture to older traditions, including Pope.

16. William James, *The Principles of Psychology*, reprint (Dover Publications, 1950), 238–9. Quoted in S. C. Neuman, *Gertrude Stein: Autobiography and the Problem of Narration* (Boston: Northeastern University Press, 1979), 37.

17. Wendy Steiner, *Exact Resemblance to Exact Resemblance*, 23.

18. Gertrude Stein, *The Autobiography of Alice B. Toklas*, 170.

19. Gertrude Stein, *Picasso*, 15.

20. Stella Bowen, *Drawn From Life* (London: Virago, 1941), reprint, 1984, 215.

21. Gertrude Stein, *A Portrait of One: Harry Phelan Gibb*, in *Geography & Plays* (Boston: Four Seas, 1922), 201.

22. Gertrude Stein, "Susie Asado," in *Geography & Plays*, 13.

23. Gertrude Stein, "Sherwood's Sweetness," in *Reflection on the Atomic Bomb*, Volume One of the Previously Uncollected Writings of Gertrude Stein, ed. Robert Bartlett Haas (Los Angeles: Black Sparrow Press, 1975), 61.

24. Wendy Steiner, in *Exact Resemblance to Exact Resemblance*, suggests that there are three phases of portraiture in Stein's work. While useful, especially in marking out the first two phases, Steiner's division into three phases breaks down rather in the third phase, which is more heterogeneous and hard to classify. I think it is fair to mark out a fourth phase of portraiture, as I do here, in the narrative portraits and the autobiographies, even though the general tradition of many Stein critics is to denigrate the autobiographies and see them either in opposition to the more "serious" experimental work, or as a relaxation of it. This chapter looks at the fourth phase of narrative portraiture, in the autobiographies, in detail, and shows that it too had its own phases.

25. Ulla E. Dydo, *Gertrude Stein: The Language That Rises* (Evanston: Northwestern University Press, 2003), 7.

26. Linda Wagner-Martin, in *Favoured Strangers: Gertrude Stein and her Family* (New Brunswick: Rutgers University Press, 1995), 197, gives a sense of just how many memoirs by Stein's friends had recently appeared. "The model Kiki of Montparnasse had written her memoirs," writes Wagner-Martin, "[...] so had Fernande Olivier [...] Memoirs by friends Lincoln Steffens, Frank Harris, Theodore Dreiser, Muriel Draper, Sherwood Anderson, Ford Madox Ford, Janet Scudder, Isadora Duncan, Emma Goldman, Margaret Anderson, Amelia Earhart, Helen Keller, Gertrude Atherton, Mabel Dodge, and Mary Austin also appeared. Gertrude read the good reviews of Robert Graves's *Goodbye to All That*, which he had written in eight weeks during a summer, and of Natalie Barney's *Aventures de l'esprit*."

27. *The Autobiography of Alice B. Toklas*, 268.

28. *The Autobiography of Alice B. Toklas*, 212.

29. *The Autobiography of Alice B. Toklas*, 268.

30. Gertrude Stein, "The Story of a Book," in *How Writing is Written*, Volume Two of the Previously Uncollected Writings of Gertrude Stein, ed. Robert Bartlett Haas (Los Angeles: Black Sparrow Press, 1974), 61.

31. Gertrude Stein to Fania Marinoff, August 9, 1932. Quoted in Edward Burns, *The Letters of Gertrude Stein and Carl Van Vechten*, Volume I (New York: Columbia University Press, 1986), 258.

32. Gertrude Stein, *Stanzas in Meditation*, from Volume Six of the Yale Edition of the Unpublished Writings of Gertrude Stein, ed. Carl Van Vechten (New Haven: Yale University Press, 1956), 77.

33. This is mentioned in Ulla Dydo, *The Language That Rises*, 537. Of all Stein critics, Dydo has written the most about, and seems to have the most interest in, Stein's manuscripts; and her book offers detailed analysis of them.

34. Edward Burns, in an Appendix to Volume II of *The Letters of Gertrude Stein and Carl Van Vechten*, 852, writes: "From various materials in the Yale archives, it is clear that Stein actually began *The Autobiography of Alice B. Toklas* in the early summer. Her reference to those six weeks in the fall is a smooth concealing manoeuvre." Burns also has his doubts about the table Stein says she sat at when she wrote the book. "The table," writes Burns, "(now in a private collection in

Germany) would appear to be too small and unsteady to have been used as a work table." Burns, *Letters of GS and CVV*, Volume I, 263.

35. Gertrude Stein, "A Transatlantic Interview—1946," in *A Primer for the Gradual Understanding of Gertrude Stein*, ed. Robert Bartlett Haas (Los Angeles: Black Sparrow Press, 1973), 19.

36. See Linda Wagner-Martin, *Favoured Strangers: Gertrude Stein and her Family*, 199–200.

37. All these names were discovered through Ulla Dydo's work with the manuscripts; she writes brilliantly on the secret exchanges between Stein and Toklas. See Dydo, *The Language That Rises*, 51.

38. Quoted in Dydo, *The Language That Rises*, 50.

39. *The Autobiography of Alice B. Toklas*, 268.

40. As Wanda M. Corn notes, the first edition's title page said simply *The Autobiography of Alice B. Toklas*, without naming Stein; and the caption for the Man Ray photograph used for the cover also made no mention of Stein, "even though she was at her desk in the picture." *Seeing Gertrude Stein*, 212.

41. *The Autobiography of Alice B. Toklas*, 231.

42. *The Autobiography of Alice B. Toklas*, 235.

43. *The Autobiography of Alice B. Toklas*, 268.

44. Gertrude Stein to Carl Van Vechten, March 17, 1924. Quoted in Edward Burns, ed., *The Letters of Gertrude Stein and Carl Van Vechten 1913–1946*, Volume I, 95.

45. See James Mellow, *Charmed Circle: Gertrude Stein and Company* (London: Phaidon, 1974), 212. The telegram read: "Sorry to say unable to receive here at present any visits from London. Have come down for complete retirement. Henry James."

46. *The Autobiography of Alice B. Toklas*, 134.

47. *The Autobiography of Alice B. Toklas*, 12.

48. *The Autobiography of Alice B. Toklas*, 268.

49. *The Autobiography of Alice B. Toklas*, 15.

50. *The Autobiography of Alice B. Toklas*, 15.

51. *The Autobiography of Alice B. Toklas*, 97.

52. In a letter to Carl Van Vechten, July 21, 1925, Stein wrote: "it is rather strange but for the first time there is you around through and behind it [...] the you has come in differently in a way it seems to have gotten out of your control you I mean and gotten into the book, it intrigues and puzzles me [...] it bothers and kind of pleases me [...]" See Edward Burns, ed., *Letters of Gertrude Stein and Carl Van Vechten*, Volume I, 119. In 1923 Stein wrote to Sherwood Anderson about his novel *Many Marriages*, "there is perhaps a little bit too much tendency to mix yourself and the hero together, it is a little your weakness in your long things." Quoted in Elizabeth Sprigge, *Gertrude Stein: Her Life and Work* (London: Hamish Hamilton, 1957), 133.

53. *The Autobiography of Alice B. Toklas*, 16.

54. *The Autobiography of Alice B. Toklas*, 12.

55. *The Autobiography of Alice B. Toklas*, 98.

56. *The Autobiography of Alice B. Toklas*, 83.

57. *The Autobiography of Alice B. Toklas*, 83.

58. *The Autobiography of Alice B. Toklas*, 92–3.

59. Ulla Dydo relates in *The Language That Rises* that although she herself, in her article "Stanzas in Meditation: The Other Autobiography" in *Gertrude Stein Advanced: An Anthology of Criticism*, ed. Richard Kostelanetz (Jefferson, NC: McFarland, 1990), 112–27, had argued that the tension in the *Stanzas* resulted from Alice's anger and jealousy over *Q.E.D.*, she now thinks that Alice only read *Q.E.D.* and became jealous in December 1932, i.e. after both the *Stanzas* and the *Autobiography* were written. Linda Wagner-Martin attributes the writing of the *Autobiography* to an attempt to appease Alice in her anger—yet if Dydo's later findings are correct, this is unlikely.

60. Ulla Dydo, *The Language That Rises*, 499.

61. Gertrude Stein, *Everybody's Autobiography* (London: Heinemann, 1938), 5–6.

62. *Everybody's Autobiography*, 21.

63. Leo Stein to Mabel Weeks, quoted in John Malcolm Brinnin, *The Third Rose: Gertrude Stein and Her World* (London: Weidenfeld & Nicolson, 1960), 311.

64. Quoted in Diana Souhami, *Gertrude & Alice* (London: Weidenfeld & Nicolson, 1991), 194.

65. Ulla Dydo is the source for "Belley 168," in *The Language That Rises*, 547.

66. *Everybody's Autobiography*, 66.

67. *Lectures in America* (New York: Random House, 1935), 167.

68. Gertrude Stein, "A Transatlantic Interview—1946," in *A Primer for the Gradual Understanding of Gertrude Stein*, ed. Robert Bartlett Haas, 21.

69. *Everybody's Autobiography*, 53.

70. *Everybody's Autobiography*, 82.

71. *Everybody's Autobiography*, 32.

72. *Everybody's Autobiography*, 38.

73. *Everybody's Autobiography*, 50.

74. *Everybody's Autobiography*, 49.

75. See Dydo, *The Language That Rises*, 574.

76. Gertrude Stein, "And Now," quoted in Robert Bartlett Haas, ed., *How Writing is Written*, Volume Two of the Previously Uncollected Writings of Gertrude Stein, 63.

77. Quoted in *The Language That Rises*, 576.

78. *Four in America* (reprint: Books for Libraries Press, 1969), 138.

79. *Four in America*, 143.

80. *Four in America*, 152–8.

81. *Everybody's Autobiography*, 94.

82. *Everybody's Autobiography*, 150.

83. *Everybody's Autobiography*, 220.

84. *Everybody's Autobiography*, 278.

85. *Everybody's Autobiography*, 153.

86. *Everybody's Autobiography*, 168.

87. *Everybody's Autobiography*, 57.

88. *Everybody's Autobiography*, 61.

89. S. C. Neuman, in *Gertrude Stein: Autobiography and the Problem of Narration*, 16, and elsewhere in this monograph, was one of the first critics to have noted how *Everybody's Autobiography* functions as a meta-autobiography.

90. *Everybody's Autobiography*, 53.

91. *Everybody's Autobiography*, xi.

92. As John Whittier-Ferguson writes, Stein spent "the last years of her life living in wartime, musing on the causes and effects and experience of war, and working war into her art and her theories about art." See "The Liberation of Gertrude Stein: War and Writing," *Modernism/modernity*, 8:3 (2001), 406.

93. Gertrude Stein, *Paris France* (Liveright reprint, 1970), 30.

94. *Paris France*, 33.

95. *Paris France*, 37.

96. *Paris France*, 44.

97. See Edward Burns, ed., *Letters of GS and CVV*, Volume II, 652, for more on how Stein's real conversations with Hélène Bouton became the material for the Helen Button story.

98. *Paris France*, 89.

99. Gertrude Stein to Carl Van Vechten, postmark: January 10, 1940, in Burns, ed., *Letters of GS and CVV*, Volume II, 663.

100. Gertrude Stein to Thornton Wilder, postmark: September 15, 1940. In *The Letters of Gertrude Stein and Thornton Wilder*, ed. Edward Burns and Ulla E. Dydo with William Rice (New Haven: Yale University Press, 1996), 270.

101. Gertrude Stein to Thornton Wilder, postmark: December 18, 1940. *Letters of GS and TW*, 276.

102. Gertrude Stein to Carl Van Vechten, postmark: September 9, 1941. *Letters of GS and CVV*, Volume II, 736.

103. Dydo and Burns tell how these titles are on the first notebook. See *Letters of GS and TW*, 417. Another title for the book was *All Wars are Interesting*. This is how the forthcoming book is mentioned in the article "The Liberation of Gertrude Stein" in *Life*, October 2, 1944.

104. *Wars I Have Seen* (London: Batsford, 1945), 1.

105. *Wars I Have Seen*, 1.

106. The nearest she came was the experimental piece "A Diary" in the 1920s: a short text mainly about trying to keep a diary, and deciding against it. "Will there be a diary a daily diary. There will not be a daily diary [...]" See "A Diary" in "Alphabets and Birthdays," Volume Seven of the Yale Edition of the Unpublished Writings of Gertrude Stein, ed. Carl Van Vechten (New Haven: Yale University Press, 1957).

107. Gertrude Stein, *The Geographical History of America*, 64.

108. *Wars I Have Seen*, 54.

109. *Wars I Have Seen*, 16.

110. *Paris France*, 65.

111. *Wars I Have Seen*, 134.

112. *Wars I Have Seen*, 156.

113. The most detailed account to date of Stein's relationship with Faÿ is Barbara Will's *Unlikely Collaboration: Gertrude Stein, Bernard Faÿ and the Vichy Dilemma* (New York: Columbia University Press, 2011). This builds on Malcolm's account, and reveals a good deal about Faÿ's wartime activities; but what Stein really knew of these remains in question.

114. Quoted in Barbara Will, *Unlikely Collaboration: Gertrude Stein, Bernard Faÿ and the Vichy Dilemma*, 135.

115. *Unlikely Collaboration: Gertrude Stein, Bernard Faÿ and the Vichy Dilemma*, 181.

116. *Wars I Have Seen*, 32.

117. *Wars I Have Seen*, 13.

118. *Wars I Have Seen*, 23.

119. *Wars I Have Seen*, 26.

120. Gertrude Stein letter to Francis Rose, n.d., Gertrude Stein collection, Harry Ransom Humanities Research Center, Austin. Quoted in Barbara Will, *Unlikely Collaboration: Gertrude Stein, Bernard Faÿ and the Vichy Dilemma*, 181.

121. Alice Toklas to Carl Van Vechten, July 31, 1946. *Letters of GS and CVV*, Volume II, 834–5.

122. Carl Van Vechten to Alice Toklas, August 4, 1946. *Letters of GS and CVV*, Volume II, 839.

CHAPTER 7

1. Wyndham Lewis to William Rothenstein *c.*1922, as quoted by Rothenstein in *Men and Memories, 1900–22*, Volume 2 (London: Faber, 1932), 378.

2. "Wyndham Lewis Vortex No. 1," in *Blast: War Number* (July 1915), 91.

3. "Wyndham Lewis Vortex No. 1," in *Blast: War Number* (July 1915), 91.

4. "The Code of a Herdsman," 1917, in *The Essential Wyndham Lewis: An Introduction to His Work*, ed. Julian Symons (London: André Deutsch, 1989), 29.

5. "The Code of a Herdsman" (1917), in *The Essential Wyndham Lewis: An Introduction to His Work*, ed. Julian Symons, 26–7.

6. Wyndham Lewis, *Tarr*, ed. Scott W. Klein (Oxford: Oxford University Press, 2010), 46.

7. Wyndham Lewis, *Tarr*, 46.

8. For reproductions of six self-portraits from 1920, see Walter Michel, *Wyndham Lewis: Paintings and Drawings* (London: Thames and Hudson, 1971), plate 53.

9. *Self-Portrait with Chair and Table* is reproduced in Walter Michel, *Wyndham Lewis: Paintings and Drawings*, plate 66.

10. Both the *Portrait of the Artist as the Painter Raphael* and *Mr Wyndham Lewis as a Tyro* have been widely reproduced in monographs on Lewis's art. See for example, *Wyndham Lewis: Portraits*, ed. Paul Edwards with Richard Humphreys (London: National Portrait Gallery, 2008), 24–6.

11. *Wyndham Lewis on Art: Collected Writings, 1913–1956*, ed. Walter Michel and C. J. Fox (London: Thames and Hudson, 1969), 190.

12. See Walter Michel, *Wyndham Lewis: Paintings and Drawings*, plate 99.

13. See *Wyndham Lewis: Portraits*, ed. Paul Edwards with Richard Humphreys, 27 for a color reproduction of this self-portrait.

14. See *Wyndham Lewis: Portraits*, ed. Paul Edwards with Richard Humphreys, 29.

15. See Walter Michel, *Wyndham Lewis: Paintings and Drawings*, plate 99.

16. Wyndham Lewis, *One-Way Song* (London: Faber, 1933), 44, 56.

17. See *Wyndham Lewis: Portraits*, ed. Paul Edwards with Richard Humphreys, 30.

18. Paul O'Keeffe notes that the identification of Olive Johnson for these two drawings is "unmistakable." See O'Keeffe, *Some Sort of Genius: A Life of Wyndham Lewis* (London: Jonathan Cape, 2000), 105.

19. Quoted in Paul Edwards, *Wyndham Lewis: Painter and Writer* (New Haven: Yale University Press, 2000), 58.

20. Wyndham Lewis, "Super-Nature Versus Super-Real," in *Wyndham Lewis the Artist: From "Blast" to Burlington House* (London: Laidlaw and Laidlaw, 1939), 59.

21. Wyndham Lewis, *Men Without Art* (London: Cassell, 1934), 128.

22. Wyndham Lewis, *Men Without Art*, 120.

23. William Rothenstein, *Since Fifty: Men and Memories 1922–1938* (New York, 1940), 73; quoted in W. K. Rose, *The Letters of Wyndham Lewis* (London: Methuen, 1963), 259.

24. Wyndham Lewis, "The Credentials of the Painter," in *Creatures of Habit and Creatures of Change: Essays on Art, Literature and Society 1914–1956*, ed. Paul Edwards (Los Angeles: Black Sparrow Press, 1989), 68–9.

25. Lewis to Sydney Schiff, March 22, 1922, (BL), quoted in Paul O'Keeffe, *Some Sort of Genius*, 237.

26. Edith Sitwell to Lady Snow, January 8, 1951 in Edith Sitwell, *Selected Letters*, ed. John Lehmann and Derek Parker (London: Macmillan, 1970), 231.

27. Quoted in Jeffrey Meyers, *The Enemy: A Biography of Wyndham Lewis* (London: Routledge, 1980), 292. Eliot's statement originally comes from an article, "White Light," in *Time* (May 30, 1949), 60.

28. Wyndham Lewis, *Blasting and Bombardiering* (London: Eyre and Spottiswoode, 1937), 215.

29. Wyndham Lewis, *Blasting and Bombardiering*, 215.

30. Lewis to O. R. Drey, September 4, 1925, in Rose, *The Letters of Wyndham Lewis*, 162.

31. Wyndham Lewis, "Studies in the Art of Laughter," *The London Mercury*, 30:180 (October 1934), 509–15. Quoted in Geoffrey Wagner, *Wyndham Lewis: A Portrait of the Artist as the Enemy* (London: Routledge & Kegan Paul, 1957), 515.

32. Wyndham Lewis, *Time and Western Man*, ed. Paul Edwards (Los Angeles: Black Sparrow Press, 1993), 59.

33. Wyndham Lewis, *Time and Western Man*, ed. Paul Edwards, 101.

34. Wyndham Lewis, *Men Without Art*, 149.

35. Wyndham Lewis, *Men Without Art*, 153.

36. Quoted in O'Keeffe, *Some Sort of Genius*, 294.

37. See W. K. Rose, *The Letters of Wyndham Lewis*, 180.

38. Wyndham Lewis, *Rude Assignment: A Narrative of my Career Up-to-Date* (London: Hutchinson, 1950).

39. Virginia Woolf, October 11, 1934, in *A Writer's Diary*, ed. Leonard Woolf (London: Hogarth Press, 1953), 220–1. Quoted in Meyers, *The Enemy*, 166.

40. Wyndham Lewis, *Rude Assignment*, 199.

41. Wyndham Lewis to C. H. Prentice, April 12, 1926, in W. K. Rose, *The Letters of Wyndham Lewis*, 167.

42. Quoted in Paul O'Keeffe, *Some Sort of Genius*, 320–1.

43. Wyndham Lewis to T. S. Eliot, July 31, 1936. Quoted in O'Keeffe, *Some Sort of Genius*, 361.

44. W. H. Auden and Louis MacNeice, *Letters from Iceland* (London: Faber, 1937), 233.

45. Wyndham Lewis, *Rude Assignment*, 209.

46. Lewis mentions "May 1937" on 94; "June 26, 1937" on 222 and "autumn 1937" on 303 of *Blasting and Bombardiering*, 1937 edition.

47. Thomas R. Smith, Introduction to Wyndham Lewis, "Preliminary Aside to the Reader; Regarding Gossip, and its Pitfalls," *Modernism/modernity*, 4:2, 182.

48. From an interview with Lewis by Louise Morgan, in *Writers at Work* (London: Chatto & Windus, 1931). Quoted in Meyers, *The Enemy*, 200.

49. Lewis to the editor of "Twentieth Century Verse," November 21, 1937, quoted in W. K. Rose, *The Letters of Wyndham Lewis*, 247.

50. See Meyers, *The Enemy*, 231.

51. See Paul O'Keeffe, *Some Sort of Genius*, 346.

52. See Paul O'Keeffe, *Some Sort of Genius*, 369.

53. See Paul O'Keeffe, *Some Sort of Genius*, 237.

54. "Cantelman" fragments appeared in *Blast 2* (1915) and the *Little Review* (1917), for example, in different versions and with "Cantelman" given different names. See Tom Holland's PhD thesis "Ezra Pound, Wyndham Lewis, and the Crowd" (York, 2007).

55. Ezra Pound to Wyndham Lewis, February 13, 1930, in *Pound/Lewis: The Letters of Ezra Pound and Wyndham Lewis*, ed. Timothy Materer (London: Faber, 1985), 169.

56. Wyndham Lewis to Ezra Pound, before June 1930, in *Pound/Lewis*, 171.

57. The manuscript is in Cornell University, Ithaca. Wyndham Lewis, *Cantelman-Crowd Master* mss. and tss. Wyndham Lewis Papers. Cornell University, Ithaca. See "Ezra Pound, Wyndham Lewis, and the Crowd" by Tom Holland (York, 2007) for a reproduction of this text. As Holland notes, the spelling of "Cantelman" by Lewis was different in the manuscript ("Cantelman") and in *Blasting and Bombardiering* ("Cantleman").

58. The short sketches "The King of the Trenches," "Cantleman's Spring-Mate," and "The War Baby" were also published by Lewis's wife in the posthumous 1967 edition of *Blasting and Bombardiering* (London: Calder & Boyars, 1967), these stories being described by her in a brief preface as "part of an unfinished war book."

59. Wyndham Lewis to Ezra Pound, August 20, 1916. In W. K. Rose, *The Letters of Wyndham Lewis*, 83.
60. *Blasting and Bombardiering*, 1937, 19.
61. *Blasting and Bombardiering*, 1937, 16.
62. *Blasting and Bombardiering*, 1937, 19.
63. *Blasting and Bombardiering*, 1937, 1.
64. *Blasting and Bombardiering*, 1937, 2.
65. *Blasting and Bombardiering*, 1937, 67.
66. *Blasting and Bombardiering*, 1937, 2.
67. *Blasting and Bombardiering*, 1937, 2.
68. Thomas R. Smith, Introduction to Wyndham Lewis, "Preliminary Aside to the Reader; Regarding Gossip, and its Pitfalls," 182.
69. *Blasting and Bombardiering*, 1937, 258.
70. *Blasting and Bombardiering*, 1937, 9.
71. Thomas R. Smith, Introduction to Wyndham Lewis, "Preliminary Aside to the Reader; Regarding Gossip, and its Pitfalls," 183.
72. T. S. Eliot, ed. Frank Kermode, *Selected Prose* (London: Faber, 1975), 40.
73. *Blasting and Bombardiering*, 1937, 14.
74. *Blasting and Bombardiering*, 1937, 13.
75. *Blasting and Bombardiering*, 1937, 6.
76. *Blasting and Bombardiering*, 1937, 43, 46.
77. *Blasting and Bombardiering*, 1937, 39.
78. *Blasting and Bombardiering*, 1937, 39.
79. *Blasting and Bombardiering*, 1937, 40.
80. *Blast* is dated June 20, but did not appear until July 1, 1914.
81. *Blast*. No. 1 (June 1914), 149.
82. From *The Selected Letters of Rebecca West*, ed. Bonnie Kime Scott (New Haven: Yale University Press, 2000), 23.
83. *Blasting and Bombardiering*, 1937, 43.
84. *Blasting and Bombardiering*, 1937, 44.
85. *Blasting and Bombardiering*, 1937, 47.
86. *Blasting and Bombardiering*, 1937, 54.
87. *Blasting and Bombardiering*, 1937, 62–3.
88. *Blasting and Bombardiering*, 1937, 69.
89. *Blasting and Bombardiering*, 1937, 89.
90. Although Cantleman himself does not appear in *Blast 2*, as Lewis says, the material is similar.
91. *Blasting and Bombardiering*, 1937, 68.
92. *Blasting and Bombardiering*, 1937, 84.
93. *Blasting and Bombardiering*, 1937, 81.
94. *Blasting and Bombardiering*, 1937, 50.
95. *Blasting and Bombardiering*, 1937, 183.
96. *Blasting and Bombardiering*, 1937, 91.
97. W. K. Rose, *The Letters of Wyndham Lewis*, 78.
98. See W. K. Rose, *The Letters of Wyndham Lewis*, 83–4.

99. Lewis to his mother, France, June 6, 1917, in W. K. Rose, *The Letters of Wyndham Lewis*, 88–9.

100. Lewis to Pound, June 6, 1917, in *Pound/Lewis*, 73.

101. Lewis to Pound, June 8, 1917, in *Pound/Lewis*, 73–4.

102. *Blasting and Bombardiering*, 1937, 8.

103. *Blasting and Bombardiering*, 1937, 205.

104. Lewis to Pound, No. 8 (Michelham) Home for Convalescent British Officers, France, July 26, 1917, *Pound/Lewis*, 90.

105. *Blasting and Bombardiering*, 1937, 154.

106. *Blasting and Bombardiering*, 1937, 163.

107. *Blasting and Bombardiering*, 1937, 164.

108. *Blasting and Bombardiering*, 1937, 189.

109. *Blasting and Bombardiering*, 1937, 212.

110. *Blasting and Bombardiering*, 1937, 282.

111. *Blasting and Bombardiering*, 1937, 283.

112. *Blasting and Bombardiering*, 1937, 5.

113. Paul Edwards, *Wyndham Lewis: Portraits*, 91.

114. See Paul O'Keeffe, *Some Sort of Genius*, 379.

115. From a letter to Naomi Mitchison, quoted in Paul O'Keeffe, *Some Sort of Genius*, 396.

116. Lewis to Archibald MacLeish, Toronto, October 21, 1941, in W. K. Rose, 302.

117. Lewis to James Johnson Sweeney, April 30, 1942 (Cornell), quoted in O'Keeffe, *Some Sort of Genius*, 449.

118. Lewis to James Johnson Sweeney, April 30, 1942, (Cornell), quoted in O'Keeffe, *Some Sort of Genius*, 449.

119. Lewis to Eric Kennington, Toronto, June 26[?], 1942, in W. K. Rose, *The Letters of Wyndham Lewis*, 325.

120. Paul O'Keeffe, *Some Sort of Genius*, 450.

121. Lewis to Iris Barry, July 18, 1942 (Cornell). In Meyers, *The Enemy*, 255.

122. Wyndham Lewis, *America, I Presume* (New York: Howell, Soskin, 1940), 33.

123. Paul O'Keeffe, *Some Sort of Genius*, 404.

124. Wyndham Lewis, *Self Condemned*, 1954. Reprint, ed. Rowland Smith (Los Angeles: Black Sparrow Press, 1983), 162–3.

125. Lewis, *Self Condemned*, 169.

126. Lewis, *Self Condemned*, 177.

127. Lewis, *Self Condemned*, 176.

128. Lewis, *Self Condemned*, 210.

129. Lewis, *Self Condemned*, 245.

130. Lewis, *Self Condemned*, 407.

131. Lewis to D. D. Paige, August 17, 1947 (Cornell). Quoted in Meyers, *The Enemy*, 286.

132. Lewis to Geoffrey Stone, January 15, 1948, in W. K. Rose, *The Letters of Wyndham Lewis*, 427.

133. Paul O'Keeffe, *Some Sort of Genius*, 520.

134. Lewis, *Rude Assignment*, 12.

135. Lewis, *Rude Assignment*, 10–11.
136. Lewis, *Rude Assignment*, 103.
137. Lewis, *Rude Assignment*, 10.
138. Lewis, *Rude Assignment*, 13.
139. Lewis, *Rude Assignment*, 103.
140. Lewis, *Rude Assignment*, 110.
141. Lewis, *Rude Assignment*, 113.
142. Lewis, *Rude Assignment*, 113.
143. Lewis, *Rude Assignment*, 117.
144. Lewis, *Rude Assignment*, 118.
145. Augustus John to Lewis, June 1907, quoted in Michael Holroyd, *Augustus John* (London: Penguin, 1976), 173n–174n.
146. Lewis, *Rude Assignment*, 197.
147. Lewis, *Rude Assignment*, 121.
148. Lewis, *Rude Assignment*, 122.
149. Lewis, *Rude Assignment*, 122.
150. Lewis, *Rude Assignment*, 122.
151. Lewis, *Rude Assignment*, 148.
152. Lewis, *Rude Assignment*, 124.
153. Lewis, *Rude Assignment*, 125.
154. Lewis, *Rude Assignment*, 129.
155. Lewis, *Rude Assignment*, 140.
156. Lewis, *Rude Assignment*, 139.
157. Lewis, *Rude Assignment*, 192.
158. Lewis, *Rude Assignment*, 221–2.
159. Lewis, *Rude Assignment*, 188.
160. Lewis to Frank Morley, October 17, 1941 in W. K. Rose, *The Letters of Wyndham Lewis*, 299–301.
161. Lewis to David Kahma, July 5, 1951, in W. K. Rose, *The Letters of Wyndham Lewis*, 541.
162. Lewis to David Kahma, July 5, 1951, in W. K. Rose, *The Letters of Wyndham Lewis*, 541.
163. Lewis, "The Sea-Mists of the Winter," *The Listener*, 45:1158 (May 10, 1951). Reprinted in *Wyndham Lewis: An Anthology of his Prose*, ed. E. W. F. Tomlin (London: Methuen, 1969), 394.
164. Lewis, "The Sea-Mists of the Winter," in *WL: An Anthology of his Prose*, ed. E. W. F. Tomlin, 395–6.
165. Lewis, "The Sea-Mists of the Winter," in *WL: An Anthology of his Prose*, ed. E. W. F. Tomlin, 396.
166. Lewis, "The Sea-Mists of the Winter," in *WL: An Anthology of his Prose*, ed. E. W. F. Tomlin, 397.
167. Lewis, "The Sea-Mists of the Winter," in *WL: An Anthology of his Prose*, ed. E. W. F. Tomlin, 397.

168. John Rothenstein, "Introduction," in Jane Farrington, *Wyndham Lewis* (London: Lund Humphries in association with the City of Manchester Art Galleries, 1980), 13.

169. Paul O'Keeffe, *Some Sort of Genius*, 615.

170. Wyndham Lewis to Hugh Kenner, *c.*March 1956, in W. K. Rose, *The Letters of Wyndham Lewis*, 564.

171. Paul O'Keeffe, *Some Sort of Genius*, 616.

EPILOGUE

1. Virginia Woolf, "Sketch of the Past," in *Moments of Being*, ed. Jeanne Schulkind (London: Pimlico, 2002), 78.

2. "Sketch of the Past," *Moments of Being*, 78.

3. "Sketch of the Past," *Moments of Being*, 122.

4. These pieces, "22 Hyde Park Gate," "Old Bloomsbury," and "Am I a Snob?" were presented to the Memoir Club in 1920–1, 1921–2, and 1936 respectively. See the Editor's Note to *Moments of Being*, 171–5.

5. Virginia Woolf, February 3, 1927, in *The Diary of Virginia Woolf*, ed. Anne Olivier Bell and Andrew McNeillie, 5 vols. (London: Hogarth Press, 1977–84), Volume III, 125.

6. Virginia Woolf, August 17, 1938, in *The Diary of Virginia Woolf*, ed. Anne Olivier Bell and Andrew McNeillie, 5 vols. (London: Hogarth Press, 1977–84), Volume V, 162.

7. Virginia Woolf, June 29, 1939, in *The Diary of Virginia Woolf*, ed. Anne Olivier Bell and Andrew McNeillie, Volume V, 222.

8. Virginia Woolf, October 20, 1940, in *The Diary of Virginia Woolf*, ed. Anne Olivier Bell and Andrew McNeillie, Volume V, 330–2.

9. "Sketch of the Past," *Moments of Being*, 105.

10. "Sketch of the Past," *Moments of Being*, 109.

11. "Sketch of the Past," *Moments of Being*, 109.

12. "Sketch of the Past," *Moments of Being*, 109.

13. Hermione Lee, *Virginia Woolf* (London: Vintage, 1997), 10–11.

14. Virginia Woolf, "Stopford Brooke," *TLS*, November 29, 1917, in *The Essays of Virginia Woolf*, Volume II, ed. Andrew McNeillie (London: Hogarth Press, 1986), 184.

15. Virginia Woolf, *Collected Essays*, Volume IV, ed. Leonard Woolf (London: Chatto & Windus, 1966–7), 54.

16. "Sketch of the Past," *Moments of Being*, 96.

17. "Sketch of the Past," *Moments of Being*, 96.

18. "Sketch of the Past," *Moments of Being*, 96.

19. "Sketch of the Past," *Moments of Being*, 78.

20. "Sketch of the Past," *Moments of Being*, 78.

21. "Sketch of the Past," *Moments of Being*, 78.

22. "Sketch of the Past," *Moments of Being*, 78–9.
23. "Sketch of the Past," *Moments of Being*, 78–9.
24. "Sketch of the Past," *Moments of Being*, 82.
25. "Sketch of the Past," *Moments of Being*, 82.
26. "Sketch of the Past," *Moments of Being*, 80.
27. "Sketch of the Past," *Moments of Being*, 80.
28. "Sketch of the Past," *Moments of Being*, 83.
29. "Sketch of the Past," *Moments of Being*, 83.
30. "Sketch of the Past," *Moments of Being*, 84.
31. "Sketch of the Past," *Moments of Being*, 83.
32. "Sketch of the Past," *Moments of Being*, 108.
33. "Sketch of the Past," *Moments of Being*, 108.
34. Virginia Woolf, December 19, 1940, in *The Diary of Virginia Woolf*, ed. Anne Olivier Bell and Andrew McNeillie, Volume V, 345.
35. Virginia Woolf to Leonard Woolf, March 28?, 1941, *The Letters of Virginia Woolf*, ed. Nigel Nicolson and Joanne Trautmann, 6 vols. (London: Hogarth Press, 1975–80), Volume VI, 3710, 486–9.
36. Virginia Woolf to Leonard Woolf, March 28?, 1941, *The Letters of Virginia Woolf*, ed. Nigel Nicolson and Joanne Trautmann, Volume VI, 3710, 486–9.
37. H. G. Wells, *Boon*, quoted in David C. Smith, *H. G. Wells: Desperately Mortal*, 170.
38. Ford Madox Ford to Catherine Hueffer, July 3, 1919, Stow Hill Papers, BH Box 1, File 6, House of Lords Record Office London. Quoted in Ros Pesman, "Autobiography, Biography and Ford Madox Ford's Women," in *Women's History Review*, 8:4 (1999), 657.
39. "Sketch of the Past," *Moments of Being*, 87.
40. "Sketch of the Past," *Moments of Being*, 98.
41. "Sketch of the Past," *Moments of Being*, 141.
42. "Sketch of the Past," *Moments of Being*, 85.
43. H. G. Wells, *H. G. Wells in Love*, ed. G. P. Wells (London: Faber, 1984), 236.
44. H. G. Wells, *H. G. Wells in Love*, 236.
45. H. G. Wells, *H. G. Wells in Love*, 236.
46. H. G. Wells, *H. G. Wells in Love*, 236.

Acknowledgments

This book has been many years in the making. I would like to thank everyone at Oxford University Press for all their support and faith in this book from the start, especially Jacqueline Norton, for responding so warmly to the initial idea, and Aimee Wright for her patience and diligence throughout the editorial process. Thanks also to Eleanor Collins and Lowri Ribbons, as well as my copyeditor Christine Ranft, and Elakkia Bharathi at SPI Global. I am deeply grateful to the readers for OUP for their detailed comments and thoughtful advice. Thanks are also due to the Arts and Humanities Board and the Arts and Humanities Research Council for supporting my research at MA and PhD level, and to the Leverhulme Trust for an Early Career Fellowship which enabled me to see this book through to its completion.

Throughout the writing of this book I have been sustained by advice and encouragement from friends, teachers, and colleagues. My first debt is to Max Saunders for supervising my doctorate at King's College London, and for offering numerous suggestions which I hope have found their way into this book in some form. I have also benefited from the comments of many other people who read parts of this project, including Sara Haslam, Philip Horne, Richard Kirkland, Hermione Lee, David Miller (who gave me the title for the Conrad chapter and invaluable information about Lilian Hallowes), Leonée Ormond, Anna Snaith, and Martin Stannard (for whose encouragement during the final stages of the book I am extremely grateful). At the Centre for Life-Writing Research at King's College London, I also owe thanks to Clare Brant and Lara Feigel, and to all the participants of "The Writer's Diary" conference in 2014.

At the University of the West Indies at Cave Hill, I would like to thank Andrew Armstrong, Jane Bryce, Nicola Hunte, and Robert Leyshon. For support and encouragement during the last phases, thanks also to my colleagues at Kingston University, London: especially Chiara Alfano, Matthew Birchwood, Fred Botting, Tina Chanter, Norma Clarke, Martin Dines, Meg Jensen, Jane Jordan, Patricia Phillippy, Anne Rowe, Sara Upstone, and Maurice Walsh.

Many thanks also, for various reasons, to James Burrell, Barbara Ching, Edward Clarke, Laura Colombino, Andy Cooke, Jane Darcy, Brian Dillon, Rozalind Dineen, Laura Douglas, Dominic Elliot, Natalya Elliot, Tom Fleming, Mark Ford, Dan Fox, Oliver Herford, Jennifer Higgie, Ross Hornblower, Maria Kilcoyne, Brian MacArthur, Bridget MacArthur, Brenda Maddox, Catharine Morris, John Mullan,

Katie Law, Toby Lichtig, Angela McRobbie, Nathaniel Mellors, Seamus O'Malley, Pelagia Pais, Huw Price, Rob Riley, James Roberts, David Sexton, Hugo Shuttleworth, Monica Soeting, Anna Vaux, Maureen Waller, and Jonathan Walton.

Special thanks to all my family: to my brother and to my parents, with love, for all their support over the years. Much love to my two children, Nina and James.

For permission to reproduce images and quote from unpublished materials I am grateful to United Agents LLP (for H. G. Wells); the Hill-Stead Museum; the Division of Rare and Manuscript Collections at Cornell University Library; the Watkins/Loomis Agency (for Edith Wharton); Keystone-France/Getty Images; and The Cecil Beaton Archive at Sotheby's. For permission to quote from John Ashbery's "Self-Portrait in a Convex Mirror" I am extremely grateful to Penguin Random House in America and to Carcanet Press in the UK. The title *Portraits from Life* comes from Ford Madox Ford's volume of literary portraits published in America in 1937.

And finally, thanks and love to Tessa, as always.

Select bibliography

Anderson, Linda. *Autobiography*. London: Routledge, 2001.

Ashbery, John. *Self-Portrait in a Convex Mirror*. London: Penguin, 1976.

Atkinson, Juliette. *Victorian Biography Reconsidered: A Study of Nineteenth-Century "Hidden" Lives*. Oxford: Oxford University Press, 2010.

Auchincloss, Louis. *Edith Wharton: A Woman in Her Time*. London: Michael Joseph, 1971.

Auden, W. H. and Louis MacNeice. *Letters from Iceland*. London: Faber, 1937.

Baines, Jocelyn. *Joseph Conrad: A Critical Biography*. London: Weidenfeld & Nicolson, 1960.

Barthes, Roland. *Camera Lucida*. 1981. Reprint. London: Vintage, 1993.

Batchelor, John. *The Edwardian Novelists*. London: Duckworth, 1982.

Batchelor, John. *H. G. Wells*. Cambridge: Cambridge University Press, 1985.

Batchelor, John. *The Life of Joseph Conrad: A Critical Biography*. Oxford: Blackwell, 1994.

Batchelor, John, ed. *The Art of Literary Biography*. Oxford: Oxford University Press, 1995.

Beaujour, Michel. Trans. Yara Milos. *Poetics of the Literary Self-Portrait*. New York: New York University Press, 1992.

Belford, Barbara. *Violet: The Story of the Irrepressible Violet Hunt and Her Circle of Lovers and Friends—Ford Madox Ford, H. G. Wells, Somerset Maugham, and Henry James*. New York: Simon & Schuster, 1990.

Bell, Millicent. *Edith Wharton and Henry James: The Story of their Friendship*. New York: George Braziller, 1965.

Bell, Millicent. "Henry James and the Fiction of Autobiography." *The Southern Review*, 18 (1982), 463–79.

Belloli, Lucy. "The Evolution of Picasso's Portrait of Gertrude Stein." *The Burlington Magazine*, 141:1150 (January 1999), 12–18.

Benjamin, Walter. *One-Way Street*. London: Verso, 1997.

Benjamin, Walter. *Illuminations*. London: Pimlico, 1999.

Benstock, Shari. *No Gifts From Chance: A Biography of Edith Wharton*. London: Hamish Hamilton, 1994.

Berger, John. *Ways of Seeing*. London and Harmondsworth: BBC and Penguin, 1972.

Bergonzi, Bernard. *The Early H. G. Wells*. Manchester: Manchester University Press, 1961.

Bosanquet, Theodora. *Henry James at Work*. London: Hogarth Press, 1927.

Bowen, Stella. *Drawn from Life*. 1941. Reprint. London: Virago, 1984.

Braque, Georges, Eugene Jolas, Maria Jolas, Henri Matisse, André Salmon, and Tristan Tzara. *Testimony against Gertrude Stein*. Transition pamphlet No. 1. Supplement to *transition* 1934–5. The Hague: Servire Press, 1935.

Brebach, Raymond. *Joseph Conrad, Ford Madox Ford and the Making of Romance*. Ann Arbor: UMI Research Press, 1985.

Bridgman, Richard. *Gertrude Stein in Pieces*. New York: Oxford University Press, 1970.

Brilliant, Richard. *Portraiture*. London: Reaktion, 1991.

Brinnin, John Malcolm. *The Third Rose: Gertrude Stein and Her World*. Boston: Little, Brown, 1959.

Brome, Vincent. *H. G. Wells: A Biography*. London: Longmans, Green, 1951.

Bruss, Elizabeth. *Autobiographical Acts: The Changing Situation of a Literary Genre*. Baltimore: Johns Hopkins University Press, 1976.

Buckley, Jerome Hamilton. *The Turning Key: Autobiography and the Subjective Impulse Since 1800*. Cambridge, MA: Harvard University Press, 1984.

Caramello, Charles. *Henry James, Gertrude Stein, and the Biographical Act*. Chapel Hill: University of North Carolina Press, 1996.

Carr, Helen. *The Verse Revolutionaries: Ezra Pound, H. D. and the Imagists*. London: Jonathan Cape, 2009.

Chantler, Ashley and Rob Hawkes, eds. *An Introduction to Ford Madox Ford*. Farnham: Ashgate, 2015.

Coe, Richard N. *When the Grass was Taller: Autobiography and the Experience of Childhood*. New Haven: Yale University Press, 1984.

Cohen, Rachel. *A Chance Meeting: Intertwined Lives of American Writers and Artists, 1854–1967*. London: Jonathan Cape, 2004.

Conrad, Borys. *My Father: Joseph Conrad*. London: Calder & Boyars, 1970.

Conrad, Jessie. *Joseph Conrad as I Knew Him*. London: Heinemann, 1926.

Conrad, Jessie. *Joseph Conrad and His Circle*. London: Jarrolds, 1935.

Conrad, John. *Joseph Conrad: Times Remembered*. Cambridge: Cambridge University Press, 1981.

Conrad, Joseph. *Almayer's Folly*. 1895. Reprint. London: Everyman Library, 1995.

Conrad, Joseph. *Youth: A Narrative*. 1898. Reprint (with *The End of the Tether*, 1902). London: Penguin, 1975.

Conrad, Joseph. *Heart of Darkness*. 1899. Reprint. London: Penguin, 1995.

Conrad, Joseph. *Nostromo: A Tale of the Seaboard*. 1904. Reprint. London: Penguin, 1971.

Conrad, Joseph. *The Secret Agent*. 1907. Reprint. London: Penguin, 2007.

Conrad, Joseph. *Under Western Eyes*. 1911. Reprint. London: Penguin, 2007.

Conrad, Joseph. *The Shadow-Line: A Confession*. 1917. Reprint. London: Penguin, 1986.

Conrad, Joseph. *The Arrow of Gold*. 1919. London: Dent, 1924.

Conrad, Joseph. *Notes on Life and Letters*. 1921. London: Dent, 1924.

Conrad, Joseph. *Last Essays*. London: Dent, 1926.

Conrad, Joseph. *Congo Diary and Other Uncollected Pieces*. Ed. Zdzisław Najder. New York: Doubleday, 1978.

Conrad, Joseph. *The Collected Letters of Joseph Conrad*. 9 vols. Ed. Laurence Davies and Frederick Karl. Cambridge: Cambridge University Press, 1983–2007.

Conrad, Joseph. *The Mirror of the Sea* and *A Personal Record*. Ed. Mara Kalnins. London: Penguin, 1998.

Corbett, David Peters, ed. *Wyndham Lewis and the Art of Modern War*. Cambridge: Cambridge University Press, 1998.

Cork, Richard. *Vorticism and Abstract Art in the First Machine Age*. Volume 1: *Origins and Development*; Volume 2: *Synthesis and Decline*. London: Gordon Fraser, 1976.

Cork, Richard. *Wyndham Lewis: The Twenties*. London: Anthony d'Offay, 1984.

Corn, Wanda M. and Tirza True Latimer, eds. *Seeing Gertrude Stein: Five Stories*. Berkeley: University of California Press, 2011.

Curle, Richard. *Joseph Conrad: A Study*. London: Kegan, Paul, Trench, Trubner, 1914.

Curle, Richard. *The Last Twelve Years of Joseph Conrad*. London: Sampson Low, 1928.

Curle, Richard. *Joseph Conrad and His Characters*. London: Heinemann, 1957.

De Man, Paul. "Autobiography as De-Facement." *Modern Language Notes*, 94:5 (1979), 919–30.

De Vinne, Christine. "Begging the Question of Confession: Joseph Conrad's *A Personal Record*." *Prose Studies*, 25:3 (December 2002), 82–99.

Delaney, Paul. *British Autobiography in the Seventeenth Century*. London: Routledge, 1969.

Delbanco, Nicholas. *Group Portrait*. London: Faber, 1982.

Demory, Pamela. "Ambivalence in Joseph Conrad's *A Personal Record*: The Anti-Autobiographical Autobiography." *Pacific Coast Philology*, 32:1 (1997), 54–65.

Dickson, Lovat. *H. G. Wells: His Turbulent Life and Times*. London: Macmillan, 1969.

Dillon, Brian. *Tormented Hope: Nine Hypochondriac Lives*. London: Penguin Ireland, 2009.

Dillon, Brian. *Objects in This Mirror: Essays*. Berlin: Sternberg Press, 2014.

Draper, Michael. *H. G. Wells*. Basingstoke: Macmillan, 1987.

Draper, Michael. "Wells, Jung and the Persona." *English Literature in Transition*, 30:4 (1987), 437–49.

Dupee, F. W. *Henry James*. London: Methuen, 1951.

Dydo, Ulla E. "*Stanzas in Meditation*: The Other Autobiography." *Chicago Review*, 35 (1985), 4–20.

Dydo, Ulla E. *Gertrude Stein: The Language That Rises 1923–1934*. With William Rice. Evanston: Northwestern University Press, 2003.

Dyer, Geoff. *The Ongoing Moment*. London: Little, Brown, 2005.

Eakin, Paul John. *Fictions in Autobiography: Studies in the Art of Self Invention*. Princeton: Princeton University Press, 1985.

Eakin, Paul John. "Henry James's 'Obscure Hurt': Can Autobiography Serve Biography?," *New Literary History*, 19:3 (Spring 1988), 675–92.

Eakin, Paul John. *How Our Lives Become Stories: Making Selves*. Ithaca and London: Cornell University Press, 1999.

Eakin, Paul John, ed. *The Ethics of Life-Writing*. Ithaca and London: Cornell University Press, 2004.

Edel, Leon. *The Life of Henry James*. 5 vols. Philadelphia: Lippincott, 1953–72.

Edel, Leon. *Literary Biography*. London: Rupert Hart-Davis, 1957.

Edel, Leon. *Henry James and H. G. Wells: A Record of Their Friendship, Their Debate on the Art of Fiction, and Their Quarrel*. Ed. with Gordon N. Ray. Urbana: University of Illinois Press, 1958.

Edel, Leon. "The Age of the Archive." Middletown, CT: Wesleyan University Press, 1966.

Edel, Leon. *Henry James: A Life*. New York: Harper & Row, 1985.

Edel, Leon. *Writing Lives*. New York and London: Norton, 1987.

Edwards, Paul. *Wyndham Lewis: Art and War*. London: The Wyndham Lewis Memorial Trust in association with Lund Humphries, 1992.

Edwards, Paul. *Wyndham Lewis: Painter and Writer*. New Haven: Yale University Press, 2000.

Edwards, Paul, with Richard Humphreys. *Wyndham Lewis: Portraits*. London: National Portrait Gallery, 2008.

Egan, Susanna. *Patterns of Experience in Autobiography*. Chapel Hill: University of North Carolina Press, 1984.

Egan, Susanna. *Mirror Talk: Genres of Crisis in Contemporary Autobiography*. Chapel Hill and London: University of North Carolina Press, 1999.

Eliot, T. S. *Selected Prose*. Ed. Frank Kermode. London: Faber, 1975.

Ellis, David. *Literary Lives*. Edinburgh: Edinburgh University Press, 2000.

Farrington, Jane. *Wyndham Lewis*. London: Lund Humphries in association with the City of Manchester Art Galleries, 1980.

Finney, Brian. *The Inner I: British Literary Autobiography of the Twentieth Century*. London: Faber and Faber, 1985.

Fleishman, Avrom. *Figures of Autobiography: The Language of Self-Writing*. Berkeley: University of California Press, 1983.

Foot, Michael. *H. G.: The History of Mr Wells*. London and New York: Doubleday, 1995.

Ford, Madox Ford. *Ford Madox Brown*. London: Longmans, Green, 1896.

Ford, Madox Ford. *The Cinque Ports*. Edinburgh and London: William Blackwood and Sons, 1900.

Ford, Madox Ford. *The Inheritors*. With Joseph Conrad. London: Heinemann, 1901.

Ford, Madox Ford. *Rossetti*. London: Duckworth, 1902.

Ford, Madox Ford. *Romance*. With Joseph Conrad. London: Smith, Elder, 1903.

Ford, Madox Ford. *Hans Holbein*. London: Duckworth, 1905.

Ford, Madox Ford. *The Soul of London*. London: Alston Rivers, 1905.

Ford, Madox Ford. *The Spirit of the People*. London: Alston Rivers, 1907.

Ford, Madox Ford. *Ancient Lights and Certain New Reflections*. London: Chapman and Hall, 1911.

Ford, Madox Ford. *The Simple Life Limited*. Pseud. "Daniel Chaucer." London: John Lane, 1911.

Ford, Madox Ford. *The New Humpty-Dumpty*. Pseud. "Daniel Chaucer." London: John Lane, 1912.

Ford, Madox Ford. *Henry James*. London: Martin Secker, 1914.

Ford, Madox Ford. *The Good Soldier*. London: John Lane, 1915.

Ford, Madox Ford. *Zeppelin Nights*. With Violet Hunt. London: John Lane, 1915.

Ford, Madox Ford. *Thus to Revisit*. London: Chapman and Hall, 1921.

Ford, Madox Ford. *Women & Men*. Paris: Three Mountains Press, 1923.

Ford, Madox Ford. *Joseph Conrad: A Personal Remembrance*. London: Duckworth, 1924.

Ford, Madox Ford. *Some Do Not…* London: Duckworth, 1924.

Ford, Madox Ford. *No More Parades*. London: Duckworth, 1925.

Ford, Madox Ford. *A Man Could Stand Up—*. London: Duckworth, 1926.

Ford, Madox Ford. *A Mirror to France*. London: Duckworth, 1926.

Ford, Madox Ford. *Last Post*. London: Duckworth, 1928.

Ford, Madox Ford. *No Enemy*. New York: Macaulay, 1929.

Ford, Madox Ford. *Return to Yesterday*. London: Victor Gollancz, 1931.

Ford, Madox Ford. *It Was the Nightingale*. London: William Heinemann, 1934.

Ford, Madox Ford. *Mightier Than the Sword*. London: George Allen & Unwin, 1938. [First published as *Portraits from Life*. Boston: Houghton Mifflin, 1937.]

Ford, Madox Ford. *Letters of Ford Madox Ford*. Ed. Richard M. Ludwig. Princeton: Princeton University Press, 1965.

Ford, Madox Ford. *War Prose*. Ed. Max Saunders. Manchester: Carcanet, 1999.

Gallup, Donald, ed. *The Flowers of Friendship: Letters Written to Gertrude Stein*. New York: Alfred A. Knopf, 1953.

Goldring, Douglas. *South Lodge: Reminiscences of Violet Hunt, Ford Madox Ford and the English Review Circle*. London: Constable, 1943.

Goldring, Douglas. *The Last Pre-Raphaelite: A Record of the Life and Writings of Ford Madox Ford*. London: Macdonald, 1948.

Gordon, Lyndall. *A Private Life of Henry James: Two Women and His Art*. London: Chatto & Windus, 1998.

Gosse, Edmund. "The Custom of Biography." *Anglo-Saxon Review*, VIII (March 1901), 195–208.

Gosse, Edmund. *Father and Son: A Study of Two Temperaments*. Ed. Michael Newton. Oxford: Oxford University Press, 2004.

Green, Robert. *Ford Madox Ford: Prose and Politics*. Cambridge: Cambridge University Press, 1981.

Greene, Graham. *A Sort of Life*. London: Simon & Schuster, 1971.

Hammond, J. R. *Herbert George Wells: An Annotated Bibliography of His Works*. New York: Garland, 1977.

Hammond, J. R. *H. G. Wells and Rebecca West*. New York: Harvester Wheatsheaf, 1991.

Hammond, J. R. *An H. G. Wells Chronology*. Basingstoke: Palgrave Macmillan, 1999.

Hampson, Robert. *Joseph Conrad: Betrayal and Identity*. London: Macmillan, 1992.

Hampson, Robert. *Conrad's Secrets*. Basingstoke: Palgrave Macmillan, 2012.

Handley-Read, Charles. *The Art of Wyndham Lewis*. London: Faber, 1951.

Harvey, David Dow. *Ford Madox Ford: 1873–1939: A Bibliography of Works and Criticism*. Princeton: Princeton University Press, 1962.

Haslam, Sara. *Fragmenting Modernism: Ford Madox Ford, the Novel and the Great War*. Manchester: Manchester University Press, 2002.

Haslam, Sara, ed. *Ford Madox Ford and the City*. International Ford Madox Ford Studies 4. Amsterdam/New York: Rodopi, 2005.

Hawkes, Rob. *Ford Madox Ford and the Misfit Moderns: Edwardian Fiction and the First World War*. Basingstoke: Palgrave Macmillan, 2012.

Herford, Oliver. *Henry James's Style of Retrospect*. Oxford: Oxford University Press, 2016.

Hewitt, Leah D. *Autobiographical Tightropes*. Lincoln: University of Nebraska Press, 1990.

Hobhouse, Janet. *Everybody Who Was Anybody: A Biography of Gertrude Stein*. London: Weidenfeld & Nicolson, 1975.

Holland, Tom. "Ezra Pound, Wyndham Lewis, and the Crowd." PhD Thesis. University of York, 2007.

Holly, Carol. "Henry James's Autobiographical Fragment: 'The Turning Point of My Life'." *Harvard Library Bulletin*, 31 (1983), 40–51.

Holly, Carol. "'Absolutely Acclaimed': The Cure for Depression in James's Final Phase." *Henry James Review*, 8:2 (1987), 126–38.

Holly, Carol. "The Family Politics of the 'Family Book'." *Henry James Review*, 10 (1989), 98–100.

Holly, Carol. *Intensely Family: The Inheritance of Family Shame and the Autobiographies of Henry James*. Madison: University of Wisconsin Press, 1995.

Holroyd, Michael. *Augustus John*. London: Penguin, 1976.

Holroyd, Michael. *Works on Paper: The Craft of Biography and Autobiography*. London: Little, Brown, 2002.

Homberger, Eric and John Charmley, eds. *The Troubled Face of Biography*. London: Macmillan, 1988.

Horne, Philip. *Henry James and Revision: The New York Edition*. Oxford: Oxford University Press, 1990.

Hunt, Violet. *The Desirable Alien: At Home in Germany*. With a preface and two additional chapters by Ford Madox Hueffer. London: Chatto & Windus, 1913.

Hunt, Violet. *The Flurried Years*. London: Hurst & Blackett, 1926.

Huntingdon, John. "H. G. Wells: Problems of an Amorous Utopian." *Literature in Transition*, 30:4 (1987), 411–22.

James, Alice, ed. Anna Robeson Burr. *Alice James: Her Brothers—Her Journal*. New York: Dodd, Mead and Co, 1934.

James, Henry. *Daisy Miller*. 1878. Reprint. London: Penguin Classics, 2007.

James, Henry. *Hawthorne*. New York: Harper & Brothers, 1879.

James, Henry. *The Portrait of a Lady*. 1881. Reprint. Oxford: Oxford University Press, 1995.

James, Henry. *The Bostonians*. 1886. Reprint. New York: Vintage, 1991.

James, Henry. *The Aspern Papers*. 1888. Reprint. London: Everyman, 1994.

James, Henry. *Partial Portraits*. 1888. Reprint, with intro. by Leon Edel. Ann Arbor: University of Michigan Press, 1970.

James, Henry. *What Maisie Knew*. 1897. Reprint. Oxford: Oxford University Press, 1996.

James, Henry. *William Wetmore Story and His Friends: From Letters, Diaries, and Recollections*. 1903. 2 vols. Edinburgh: William Blackwood and Sons, 1903.

James, Henry. *English Hours*. 1905. Reprint. Ed. Alma Louise Lowe. London: Heinemann, 1960.

James, Henry. *The Novels and Tales of Henry James* (New York Edition). 24 vols. New York: Scribner's, 1907–9.

James, Henry. *The Turn of the Screw and Other Short Fiction*. 1908. Reprint, with an introduction by R. W. B. Lewis. New York: Bantam Books, 1981.

James, Henry. *A Small Boy and Others*. London: Macmillan, 1913.

James, Henry. *Notes of a Son and Brother*. London: Macmillan, 1914.

James, Henry. *The Middle Years*. New York: Scribner's, 1917.

James, Henry. *The Letters of Henry James*. Ed. Percy Lubbock. 2 vols. London: Macmillan, 1920.

James, Henry. *The Art of the Novel: Critical Prefaces*. New York: Scribner's, 1934.

James, Henry. *Autobiography*. Ed. Frederick. W. Dupee. London: W. H. Allen, 1956.

James, Henry. *The Complete Tales of Henry James*. Ed. Leon Edel. 12 vols. London: Rupert Hart-Davis, 1962–4.

James, Henry. *Henry James: Letters*. Ed. Leon Edel. 4 vols. Cambridge, MA: Belknap Press, 1974–84.

James, Henry. *Literary Criticism*. Ed. Leon Edel and Mark Wilson. 2 vols. New York and Cambridge: Library of America, 1984.

James, Henry. *The Complete Notebooks of Henry James*. Ed. Leon Edel and Lyall Powers. New York: Oxford University Press, 1987.

James, Henry. *Henry James and Edith Wharton: Letters 1900–1915*. Ed. Lyall H. Powers. London: Weidenfeld & Nicolson, 1990.

James, Henry. *Henry James: A Life in Letters*. Ed. Philip Horne. London: Allen Lane, 1999.

James, Henry. *The Complete Letters of Henry James*. Ed. Pierre A. Walker and Greg Zacharias. Nebraska: University of Nebraska Press, 2007–ongoing.

James, Henry. *Autobiographies*. Ed. Philip Horne. New York: Library of America, 2016.

James, William. *The Principles of Psychology*. Reprint. Cambridge, MA: Harvard University Press, 1981.

Jean-Aubry, G. *Joseph Conrad: Life and Letters*. 2 vols. London: Heinemann, 1927.

Jean-Aubry, G. *The Sea Dreamer: A Definitive Biography of Joseph Conrad*. Trans. Helen Sebba. London: Allen & Unwin, 1957.

Jefferson, Ann. *Biography and the Question of Literature in France*. Oxford: Oxford University Press, 2007.

Jolly, Margaretta, ed. *The Encyclopaedia of Life Writing*. 2 vols. London: Fitzroy Dearborn, 2001.

Jolly, Margaretta. *In Love and Struggle: Letters in Contemporary Feminism*. New York: Columbia University Press, 2008.

Joslin, K. and A. Price, eds. *Wretched Exotic: Essays on Edith Wharton in Europe*. New York: Peter Lang, 1993.

Judd, Alan. *Ford Madox Ford*. London: Collins, 1990.

Kaplan, Fred. *Henry James: The Imagination of Genius: A Biography*. London: Hodder, 1992.

Karl, Frederick. *Joseph Conrad: The Three Lives*. London: Faber, 1979.

Kellogg, Grace. *The Two Lives of Edith Wharton: The Woman and her Work*. New York: Appleton-Century, 1965

Klein, Scott. *The Fictions of James Joyce and Wyndham Lewis: Monsters of Nature and Design*. Cambridge: Cambridge University Press, 1994.

Knowles, Owen. *A Conrad Chronology*. London: Macmillan, 1989.

Leach, Nancy R. "Edith Wharton's Unpublished Novel." *American Literature*, 25:3 (1953), 334–53.

Leader, Zachary, ed. *On Life-Writing*. Oxford: Oxford University Press, 2015.

Lee, Hermione. *Virginia Woolf*. London: Vintage, 1997.

Lee, Hermione. *Body Parts: Essays on Life-Writing*. London: Chatto & Windus, 2005.

Lee, Hermione. *Edith Wharton*. London: Chatto & Windus, 2007.

Lee, Hermione. *Biography: A Very Short Introduction*. Oxford: Oxford University Press, 2009.

Lejeune, Philippe. *Le pacte autobiographique*. Paris: Editions du Seuil, 1975.

Lejeune, Philippe. "Autobiography in the Third Person." *New Literary History*, 9:1 (1977), 27–50.

Lejeune, Philippe. "The Autobiographical Contract." In *French Literary Theory Today*, ed. Tzvetan Todorov. Cambridge: Cambridge University Press, 1982, 192–222.

Lejeune, Philippe. *On Autobiography*. Ed. Paul John Eakin. Minneapolis: University of Minnesota Press, 1988.

Lejeune, Philippe and Victoria A. Lodewick. "How Do Diaries End?" *Biography*, 24:1 (2001), 99–112.

Lewis, R. W. B. *Edith Wharton: A Biography*. New York: Harper & Row, 1975.

Lewis, R. W. B. *The Jameses: A Family Narrative*. New York: Farrar, Straus and Giroux, 1991.

Lewis, Wyndham. *Blast*. Number 1 (June 1914).

Lewis, Wyndham. *Blast: War Number* (July 1915).

Lewis, Wyndham. *The Caliph's Design: Architects! Where is your Vortex?* 1919. Reprint, ed. Paul Edwards. Los Angeles: Black Sparrow Press, 1986.

Lewis, Wyndham. *The Apes of God*. 1930. Reprint. Los Angeles: Black Sparrow Press, 1981.

Lewis, Wyndham. *Thirty Personalities and a Self-Portrait*. London: Desmond Harmsworth, 1932.

Lewis, Wyndham. *One-Way Song*. London: Faber, 1933.

Lewis, Wyndham. *Men Without Art*. London: Cassell, 1934.

Lewis, Wyndham. *Blasting and Bombardiering*. London: Eyre & Spottiswoode, 1937.

Lewis, Wyndham. *The Revenge for Love*. 1937. Reprint, ed. Reed Way Dasenbrock. Los Angeles: Black Sparrow Press, 1991.

Lewis, Wyndham. *Wyndham Lewis the Artist: From "Blast" to Burlington House*. London: Laidlaw and Laidlaw, 1939.

Lewis, Wyndham. *America, I Presume*. New York: Howell, Soskin, 1940.

Lewis, Wyndham. *Rude Assignment: A Narrative of my Career Up-to-Date*. London: Hutchinson, 1950.

Lewis, Wyndham. *Rotting Hill*. 1951. Reprint, ed. Paul Edwards. Los Angeles: Black Sparrow Press, 1986.

Lewis, Wyndham. "The Sea-Mists of the Winter," *The Listener*, 45:1158 (May 10, 1951).

Lewis, Wyndham. *Self Condemned*. 1954. Reprint, ed. Rowland Smith. Los Angeles: Black Sparrow Press, 1983.

Lewis, Wyndham. *The Letters of Wyndham Lewis*. Ed. W. K. Rose. London: Methuen, 1963.

Lewis, Wyndham. *Blasting and Bombardiering*. London: Calder & Boyars, 1967.

Lewis, Wyndham. *Wyndham Lewis: An Anthology of his Prose*. Ed. E. W. F. Tomlin. London: Methuen, 1969.

Lewis, Wyndham. *Wyndham Lewis on Art: Collected Writings, 1913–1956*. Ed. Walter Michel and C. J. Fox. London: Thames & Hudson, 1969.

Lewis, Wyndham. *The Complete Wild Body*. Ed. Bernard Lafourcade. Los Angeles: Black Sparrow Press, 1982.

Lewis, Wyndham. *Pound/Lewis: The Letters of Ezra Pound and Wyndham Lewis*. Ed. Timothy Materer. London: Faber, 1985.

Lewis, Wyndham. *Creatures of Habit and Creatures of Change: Essays on Art, Literature and Society 1914–1956*. Ed. Paul Edwards. Los Angeles: Black Sparrow Press, 1989.

Lewis, Wyndham. *The Essential Wyndham Lewis: An Introduction to His Work*. Ed. Julian Symons. London: André Deutsch, 1989.

Lewis, Wyndham. *Time and Western Man*. Ed. Paul Edwards. Los Angeles: Black Sparrow Press, 1993.

Lewis, Wyndham. *Tarr* (1928 edn). Ed. Scott W. Klein. Oxford: Oxford University Press, 2010.

Lewis, Wyndham. "A Preliminary Aside to the Reader; Regarding Gossip, and its Pitfalls." Ed. Thomas R. Smith. *Modernism/modernity*, 4:2 (1997), 181–7.

Lindberg-Seyerstad, Brita, ed. *A Literary Friendship: Correspondence Between Caroline Gordon and Ford Madox Ford*. Knoxville: University of Tennessee Press, 1999.

Lubbock, Percy. *Portrait of Edith Wharton*. London: Jonathan Cape, 1947.

Lynn, Andrea. *Shadow Lovers: The Last Affairs of H. G. Wells*. Oxford: Westview, 2001.

Mackenzie, Norman and Jeanne. *The Time Traveller: The Life of H. G. Wells*. London, 1973.

Macshane, Frank. *The Life and Work of Ford Madox Ford*. London: Routledge, 1965.

Madox Brown, Ford. *The Diary of Ford Madox Brown*. Ed. Virginia Surtees. New Haven: Yale University Press, 1981.

Mainwaring, Marion. *Mysteries of Paris: The Quest for Morton Fullerton*. London: University Press of New England, 2000.

Malcolm, Janet. *The Silent Woman: Sylvia Plath and Ted Hughes.* 1994. Reprint. London: Granta, 2005.

Malcolm, Janet. *Two Lives: Gertrude and Alice.* New Haven: Yale University Press, 2007.

Malcolm, Janet. *Forty-One False Starts: Essays on Artists and Writers.* London: Granta, 2013.

Man Ray. *Self Portrait.* London: Bloomsbury, 1963.

Marcus, Laura. *Auto/biographical Discourses.* Manchester: Manchester University Press, 1994.

Matthiessen, F. O. *The James Family: Including Selections from the Writings of Henry James Senior, William, Henry, & Alice James.* New York: Knopf, 1948.

Matz, Jesse. *Literary Impressionism and Modernist Aesthetics.* Cambridge: Cambridge University Press, 2001.

McDonald, Deborah and Jeremy Dronfield. *A Very Dangerous Woman: The Lives, Loves and Lies of Russia's Most Seductive Spy.* London: Oneworld, 2015.

McWhirter, David, ed. *Henry James's New York Edition: The Construction of Authorship.* Stanford: Stanford University Press, 1995.

Mellow, James R. *Charmed Circle: Gertrude Stein & Company.* London: Phaidon Press, 1974.

Meyer, Bernard C. *Joseph Conrad: A Psychoanalytic Biography.* Princeton: Princeton University Press, 1967.

Meyers, Jeffrey. *The Enemy: A Biography of Wyndham Lewis.* London: Routledge, 1980.

Meyers, Jeffrey. *Joseph Conrad: A Biography.* London: John Murray, 1991.

Michel, Walter. *Wyndham Lewis: Paintings and Drawings.* London: Thames & Hudson, 1971.

Miller, David. "Amanuensis: A Biographical Sketch of Lilian Hallowes, 'Mr. Conrad's Secretary'." *The Conradian*, 31.2 (2006), 86–103.

Millgate, Michael. *Testamentary Acts: Browning, Tennyson, James, Hardy.* Oxford: Clarendon Press, 1992.

Misch, Georg. *A History of Autobiography in Antiquity.* Trans. E. W. Dickes, 2 vols. London: Routledge & Kegan Paul, 1950.

Mizener, Arthur. *The Saddest Story: A Biography of Ford Madox Ford.* London: The Bodley Head, 1972.

Morf, Gustav. *The Polish Heritage of Joseph Conrad.* London: Sampson, Low, Marston, 1930.

Morgan, Louise. *Writers at Work.* London: Chatto & Windus, 1931.

Moser, Thomas C. *The Life in the Fiction of Ford Madox Ford.* Princeton: Princeton University Press, 1980.

Murray, Brian. *H. G. Wells.* New York: Continuum, 1990.

Nadel, Ira. *Biography: Fiction Fact & Form.* London: Macmillan, 1984.

Nadel, Ira. "Gertrude Stein and Henry James," in *Gertrude Stein and the Making of Literature*, ed. Shirley Neuman and Ira B. Nadel. Boston: Northeastern University Press, 1988, 81–97.

Najder, Zdzisław, ed. *Conrad's Polish Background: Letters to and from Polish Friends.* Trans. Halina Carroll. London: Oxford University Press, 1964.

Najder, Zdzisław, ed. *Conrad Under Familial Eyes*. Cambridge: Cambridge University Press, 1983.

Najder, Zdzisław. *Joseph Conrad: A Chronicle*. Cambridge: Cambridge University Press, 1983.

Najder, Zdzisław. *Joseph Conrad: A Life*. Revised edition of "A Chronicle," with more on the composition of *The Mirror of the Sea* and *A Personal Record*. London: Camden House, 2007.

Neuman, S. C. *Gertrude Stein: Autobiography and the Problem of Narration*. ELS Monograph Series No. 18. Victoria, BC: English Literary Studies, University of Victoria, 1979.

Novick, Sheldon M. *Henry James: The Young Master*. New York: Random House, 1996.

Novick, Sheldon M. *Henry James: The Mature Master*. New York: Random House, 2007.

O'Keeffe, Paul. *Some Sort of Genius: A Life of Wyndham Lewis*. London: Jonathan Cape, 2000.

O'Malley, Seamus. *Making History New: Modernism and Historical Narrative*. New York: Oxford University Press, 2015.

Olney, James. *Metaphors of Self: The Meaning of Autobiography*. Princeton: Princeton University Press, 1972.

Olney, James, ed. *Autobiography: Essays Theoretical and Critical*. Princeton: Princeton University Press, 1980.

Olney, James, ed. *Studies in Autobiography*. Oxford: Oxford University Press, 1988.

Ormond, Leonée. *George du Maurier*. London: Routledge & Kegan Paul, 1969.

Padover, Saul K. *Confessions and Self-Portraits: 4600 Years of Autobiography*. New York: The John Day Company, 1957.

Pascal, Roy. *Design and Truth in Autobiography*. London: Routledge, 1960.

Pesman, Ros. "Autobiography, Biography and Ford Madox Ford's Women." *Women's History Review*, 8:4 (1999), 655–70.

Pessoa, Fernando. *Selected Prose*. Ed. and trans. Richard Zenith. New York: Grove, 1998.

Pessoa, Fernando. *The Book of Disquiet*. Ed. and trans. Richard Zenith. London: Allen Lane, 2001.

Phillips, Adam. *Houdini's Box*. London: Faber & Faber, 2001.

Pilling, John. *Autobiography and Imagination: Studies in Self-Scrutiny*. London: Routledge, 1981.

Poli, Bernard. *Ford Madox Ford and the Transatlantic Review*. Syracuse, NY: Syracuse University Press, 1967.

Posnock, Ross. *The Trial of Curiosity: Henry James, William James, and the Challenge of Modernity*. New York: Oxford University Press, 1991.

Prescott, Lynda. "Autobiography as Evasion: Joseph Conrad's *A Personal Record*." *Journal of Modern Literature*, 28:1 (2004), 177–88.

Price, Alan. *The End of the Age of Innocence: Edith Wharton and the First World War*. New York: St. Martin's Press, 1996.

Proust, Marcel. *In Search of Lost Time*. Trans. C. K. Scott Moncrieff and Terence Kilmartin, revised by D. J. Enright. 6 vols. London: Chatto & Windus/Vintage, 1992.

Ray, Gordon. *H. G. Wells and Rebecca West*. London: Macmillan, 1974.

Richardson, John. *A Life of Picasso*. 3 vols. London: Jonathan Cape, 1991–ongoing.

Rinkel, Gene K. and Margaret E. *The Picshuas of H. G. Wells: A Burlesque Diary*. Urbana: University of Illinois Press, 2006.

Roth, Philip. *The Facts: A Novelist's Autobiography*. London: Jonathan Cape, 1988.

Rothenstein, William. *Men and Memories 1900–22*. London: Faber, 1932.

Rothenstein, William. *Since Fifty: Men and Memories 1922–1938*. New York: Macmillan, 1940.

Said, Edward. *Joseph Conrad and the Fiction of Autobiography*. Cambridge, MA: Harvard University Press, 1966.

Saunders, Max. "A Life in Writing: Ford Madox Ford's Dispersed Autobiographies." *Antaeus*, 56 (Spring 1986), 125–42.

Saunders, Max. *Ford Madox Ford: A Dual Life*. 2 vols. Oxford: Oxford University Press, 1996.

Saunders, Max. "Reflections on Impressionist Autobiography: James, Conrad and Ford." In *Conrad, James, Ford, and Other Relations* in the series "Joseph Conrad: Eastern and Western Perspectives," ed. Wieslaw Krajka. Lublin/Columbia University Press, 2003.

Saunders, Max. *Self Impression: Life-Writing, Autobiografiction, and the Forms of Modern Literature*. Oxford: Oxford University Press, 2010.

Sayeau, Michael. *Against the Event: The Everyday and the Evolution of Modernist Narrative*. Oxford: Oxford University Press, 2013.

Sayre, Robert. *The Examined Self: Benjamin Franklin, Henry Adams, Henry James*. Princeton: Princeton University Press, 1964.

Seymour, Miranda. *A Ring of Conspirators: Henry James and his Literary Circle*. London: Hodder, 1988.

Schumaker, Wayne. *English Autobiography: Its Emergence, Materials and Forms*. Berkeley and Los Angeles: University of California Press, 1954.

Sebald, W. G. *The Rings of Saturn*. Trans. Michael Hulse. London: Harvill, 1999.

Sebald, W. G. *Vertigo*. Trans. Michael Hulse. Reprint. London: Vintage, 2002.

Sebald, W. G. *A Place in the Country*. Trans. Jo Catling. London: Hamish Hamilton, 2013.

Sherborne, Michael. *H. G. Wells: Another Kind of Life*. London: Peter Owen, 2010.

Sherry, Norman. *Conrad's Eastern World*. Cambridge: Cambridge University Press, 1966.

Sherry, Norman. *Conrad's Western World*. Cambridge: Cambridge University Press, 1971.

Sherry, Norman. *Conrad and His World*. London: Thames & Hudson, 1972.

Shields, David. *Reality Hunger: A Manifesto*. London: Hamish Hamilton, 2010.

Simon, Linda. *The Biography of Alice B. Toklas*. Garden City, NY: Doubleday, 1977.

Simon, Linda. *Gertrude Stein Remembered*. Lincoln: University of Nebraska Press, 1994.

Sitwell, Edith. *Selected Letters*. Ed. John Lehmann and Derek Parker. London: Macmillan, 1970.

Skinner, Paul, ed. *Ford Madox Ford's Literary Contacts*. International Ford Madox Ford Studies 6. Amsterdam/New York: Rodopi, 2007.

Smith, David C. *H. G. Wells: Desperately Mortal*. New Haven and London: Yale University Press, 1986.

Snitow, Ann Barr. *Ford Madox Ford and the Voice of Uncertainty*. Baton Rouge: Louisiana State University Press, 1984.

Sontag, Susan. *On Photography*. London: Allen Lane, 1978.

Sontag, Susan. *Where the Stress Falls*. 2002. Reprint. London: Vintage, 2003.

Sontag, Susan. *Reborn: Early Diaries, 1947–1963*. London: Hamish Hamilton, 2008.

Souhami, Diana. *Gertrude and Alice*. London: Weidenfeld & Nicolson, 1991.

Spengemann, William. *The Forms of Autobiography*. New Haven: Yale University Press, 1980.

Sprigge, Elizabeth. *Gertrude Stein: Her Life and Work*. London: Hamish Hamilton, 1957.

Stang, Sondra J., ed. *The Presence of Ford Madox Ford*. Philadelphia: University of Pennsylvania Press, 1981.

Stang, Sondra J. and Karen Cochran, eds. *The Correspondence of Ford Madox Ford and Stella Bowen*. Bloomington and Indianapolis: Indiana University Press, 1994.

Stanley, Liz. *The Auto/Biographical "I."* Manchester: Manchester University Press, 1992.

Stape, John. *The Several Lives of Joseph Conrad*. London: Heinemann, 2007.

Stein, Gertrude. *Geography and Plays*. Boston: Four Seas, 1922.

Stein, Gertrude. *The Autobiography of Alice B. Toklas*. London: The Bodley Head, 1933.

Stein, Gertrude. *Portraits and Prayers*. New York: Random House, 1934.

Stein, Gertrude. *Lectures in America*. New York: Random House, 1935.

Stein, Gertrude. *Narration*. Introduction by Thornton Wilder. Chicago: University of Chicago Press, 1935.

Stein, Gertrude. *The Geographical History of America*. 1936. Reprint. Ed. with an introduction by William Gass. Baltimore: Johns Hopkins University Press, 1995.

Stein, Gertrude. *Everybody's Autobiography*. London: Heinemann, 1938.

Stein, Gertrude. *Picasso*. London: Batsford, 1938.

Stein, Gertrude. *Paris France*. 1940. Reprint. New York: Liveright, 1970.

Stein, Gertrude. *Wars I Have Seen*. London: Batsford, 1945.

Stein, Gertrude. *Four in America*. 1947. Reprint. Books for Libraries, 1969.

Stein, Gertrude. *The Unpublished Writings of Gertrude Stein*. 8 vols. New Haven: Yale University Press, 1951–8.

Stein, Gertrude. *Stanzas in Meditation and Other Poems (1929–1933)*. Ed. Donald Sutherland. New Haven: Yale University Press, 1956. Volume 6 of the Yale edition of the *Unpublished Writings of Gertrude Stein*.

Stein, Gertrude. *Fernhurst, Q.E.D., and Other Early Writings*. 1971. Reprint, with an introduction by Leon Katz. New York: Liveright, 1983.

Stein, Gertrude. "A Transatlantic Interview." In *A Primer for the Gradual Understanding of Gertrude Stein*. Ed. Robert Bartlett Haas. Los Angeles: Black Sparrow Press, 1971.

Stein, Gertrude. *How Writing Is Written*. Volume II of the Previously Uncollected Writings of Gertrude Stein. Ed. Robert Bartlett Haas. Los Angeles: Black Sparrow Press, 1974.

Stein, Gertrude. *Reflection on the Atomic Bomb*. Volume 1 of the Previously Uncollected Writings of Gertrude Stein. Ed. Robert Bartlett Haas. Los Angeles: Black Sparrow Press, 1975.

Stein, Gertrude. *Blood on the Dining-Room Floor*. Reprint with introduction by Janet Hobhouse. London: Virago, 1985.

Stein, Gertrude. *The Letters of Gertrude Stein and Carl Van Vechten, 1913–1946*. Ed. Edward Burns. 2 vols. New York: Columbia University Press, 1986.

Stein, Gertrude. *The Letters of Gertrude Stein and Thornton Wilder*. Ed. Edward Burns and Ulla Dydo with William Rice. New Haven: Yale University Press, 1996.

Stein, Gertrude. *Writings*. 2 vols. New York: Library of America, 1998.

Steiner, Wendy. *Exact Resemblance to Exact Resemblance: The Literary Portraiture of Gertrude Stein*. New Haven: Yale University Press, 1978.

Strachey, Lytton. *Eminent Victorians*. London: Chatto & Windus, 1918.

Sturrock, John. "The New Model Autobiographer." *New Literary History*, 9 (1977), 51–63.

Sturrock, John. *The Language of Autobiography*. Cambridge: Cambridge University Press, 1993.

Sutherland, Donald. *Gertrude Stein: A Biography of her Work*. New Haven: Yale University Press, 1951.

Tanner, Tony. *Henry James and the Art of Nonfiction*. Athens: University of Georgia Press, 1995.

Thirlwell, Angela. *Into the Frame: The Four Loves of Ford Madox Brown*. London: Pimlico, 2010.

Tintner, Adeline R. "Autobiography as Fiction: The Usurping Consciousness as Hero of James's Memoirs." *Twentieth Century Literature*, 23 (1977), 242–4.

Toklas, Alice B. *What is Remembered*. London: Michael Joseph, 1963.

Toklas, Alice B. *Staying on Alone: Letters of Alice B. Toklas*. Ed. Edward Burns. New York: Liveright, 1973.

Vasari, Giorgio. *Lives of the Painters, Sculptors and Architects*. Trans. G. du C. de Vere. New York: Abrams, 1979.

Wagner, Geoffrey. *Wyndham Lewis: A Portrait of the Artist as the Enemy*. London: Routledge & Kegan Paul, 1957.

Wagner-Martin, Linda. *Favoured Strangers: Gertrude Stein and her Family*. New Brunswick: Rutgers University Press, 1995.

Watt, Ian. *Conrad in the Nineteenth Century*. London: Chatto & Windus, 1980.

Watts, Cedric. *Joseph Conrad: A Literary Life*. London: Macmillan, 1989.

Weintraub, Karl. *The Value of the Individual: Self and Circumstance in Autobiography*. Chicago: University of Chicago Press, 1978.

Wells, Frank, ed. *H. G. Wells: A Pictorial Biography*. London: Jupiter, 1977.

Wells, H. G. *The Time Machine*. 1895. Reprint. London: Penguin, 2005.

Wells, H. G. *The Island of Dr. Moreau*. 1896. Reprint. London: Penguin, 2005.

Wells, H. G. *The Invisible Man*. 1897. Reprint. London: Penguin, 2005.

Wells, H. G. *The War of the Worlds*. 1898. Reprint. London: Penguin, 2005.

Wells, H. G. *Love and Mr. Lewisham*. 1900. Reprint. London: Penguin, 2005.

Wells, H. G. *The First Men in the Moon*. 1901. Reprint. London: Penguin, 2005.

Wells, H. G. *Kipps*. 1905. Reprint. London: Penguin, 2005.

Wells, H. G. *Tono-Bungay*. 1909. Reprint. London: Penguin, 2005.

Wells, H. G. *The History of Mr. Polly*. 1910. Reprint. London: Penguin, 2005.

Wells, H. G. *The New Machiavelli*. 1911. Reprint. London: Penguin, 2005.

Wells, H. G. *Boon, The Mind of the Race, The Wild Asses of the Devil and The Last Trump*. Pseud. Reginald Bliss. London: Unwin, 1915.

Wells, H. G. *Russia in the Shadows*. London: Hodder, 1920.

Wells, H. G. *The Story of a Great Schoolmaster*. London: Chatto & Windus, 1924.

Wells, H. G. *The World of William Clissold*. 3 vols. London: Ernest Benn, 1926.

Wells, H. G. *The Bulpington of Blup*. London: Hutchinson, 1932.

Wells, H. G. *Experiment in Autobiography*. 2 vols. 1934. Reprint. London: Faber & Faber, 1984.

Wells, H. G. *The Anatomy of Frustration*. London: The Cresset Press, 1936.

Wells, H. G. *Apropos of Dolores*. London: Jonathan Cape, 1938.

Wells, H. G. *'42 to '44: A Contemporary Memoir*. London: Secker, 1944.

Wells, H. G. *The Happy Turning*. London: Heinemann, 1945.

Wells, H. G. *Mind at the End of its Tether*. London: Heinemann, 1945.

Wells, H. G. *H. G. Wells in Love*. Ed. G. P. Wells. London: Faber & Faber, 1984.

Wells, H. G. *The Correspondence of H. G. Wells*. Ed. David C. Smith. 4 vols. London: Pickering & Chatto, 1998.

West, Anthony. *H. G. Wells: Aspects of a Life*. London: Hutchinson, 1984.

West, Geoffrey. *H. G. Wells: A Sketch for a Portrait*. London: Howe, 1930.

West, Rebecca. *The Selected Letters of Rebecca West*. Ed. Bonnie Kime Scott. New Haven: Yale University Press, 2000.

Wharton, Edith. *The Decoration of Houses*. With Ogden Codman. New York: Scribner's, 1897.

Wharton, Edith. *Italian Villas and Their Gardens*. 1904. Reprint. New York: Da Capo, 1976.

Wharton, Edith. *The House of Mirth*. 1905. Reprint. New York: Penguin, 1985.

Wharton, Edith. *Italian Backgrounds*. 1905. Reprint: Hopewell, NJ: Ecco, 1998.

Wharton, Edith. *A Motor-Flight through France*. London: Macmillan, 1908.

Wharton, Edith. *Artemis to Actaeon and Other Verse*. New York: Scribner's, 1909.

Wharton, Edith. *Ethan Frome*. 1911. New York: Macmillan, 1987.

Wharton, Edith. *The Reef*. 1912. Reprint. New York: Penguin, 1994.

Wharton, Edith. *The Custom of the Country*. 1913. Reprint. New York: Penguin, 1987.

Wharton, Edith. *Fighting France: From Dunkerque to Belfort*. New York: Scribner's, 1915.

Wharton, Edith. *Summer*. 1917. Reprint. New York: Penguin, 1993.

Wharton, Edith. *French Ways and Their Meaning*. 1919. Reprint. Lee, MA: Berkshire House, 1997.

Wharton, Edith. *The Age of Innocence*. 1920. Reprint. New York: Penguin, 1985.

Wharton, Edith. *In Morocco*. 1920. Reprint. London: Century Hutchinson, 1984.

Wharton, Edith. *The Writing of Fiction*. New York: Scribner's, 1925.

Wharton, Edith. *Twelve Poems*. London: Riccardi, 1926.

Wharton, Edith. *Hudson River Bracketed*. New York: Appleton, 1929.

Wharton, Edith. *The Gods Arrive*. New York: Appleton, 1932.

Wharton, Edith. *A Backward Glance*. New York: Appleton-Century, 1934.

Wharton, Edith. "Terminus." First published in R. W. B. Lewis, *Edith Wharton: A Biography*. New York: Harper & Row, 1975.

Wharton, Edith. *The Letters of Edith Wharton*. Ed. R. W. B. Lewis and Nancy Lewis. London: Simon & Schuster, 1988.

Wharton, Edith. "The Fullness of Life." In *The Muse's Tragedy and Other Stories*. Ed. Candace Waid. New York: Signet, 1990.

Wharton, Edith. *Novellas and Other Writings*. New York: Library of America, 1990. Includes "Life & I."

Wharton, Edith. "'The Life Apart' (L'ame close)." First published in "Texts and Contexts of Edith Wharton's Love Diary." Ed. Kenneth M. Price and Phyllis McBride. *American Literature*, 66:4 (1994), 663–88.

Wharton, Edith. *The Uncollected Critical Writings*. Ed. Frederick Wegener. Princeton: Princeton University Press, 1996. Includes "A Little Girl's New York," 274–87.

Wharton, Edith. *The Correspondence of Edith Wharton and Louis Bromfield*. Ed. Daniel Bratton. Ann Arbor: Michigan State University Press, 2000.

White, Andrea. "Writing from Within: Autobiography and Immigrant Subjectivity in *The Mirror of the Sea*." In *Conrad in the Twenty-First Century*. Ed. Carola M. Kaplan, Peter Mallios, and Andrea White. New York: Routledge, 2005.

Wiesenfarth, Joseph. *Ford Madox Ford and the Regiment of Women*. Madison: University of Wisconsin Press, 2005.

Will, Barbara. *Unlikely Collaboration: Gertrude Stein, Bernard Faÿ, and the Vichy Dilemma*. New York: Columbia University Press, 2011.

Wineapple, Brenda. *Sister Brother: Gertrude and Leo Stein*. London: Bloomsbury, 1996.

Wolff, Cyntha Griffin. *A Feast of Words: The Triumph of Edith Wharton*. New York: Oxford University Press, 1977.

Woodall, Joanna, ed. *Portraiture*. Manchester: Manchester University Press, 1997.

Woolf, Virginia. *The Death of the Moth and Other Essays*. London: Hogarth Press, 1942.

Woolf, Virginia. *A Writer's Diary*. Ed. Leonard Woolf. London: Hogarth Press, 1953.

Woolf, Virginia. *Collected Essays*. Ed. Leonard Woolf. 4 vols. London: Chatto & Windus, 1966–7.

Woolf, Virginia. *The Letters of Virginia Woolf*. Ed. Nigel Nicolson and Joanne Trautmann. 6 vols. London: Hogarth Press, 1975–80.

Woolf, Virginia. *The Diary of Virginia Woolf*. Ed. Anne Olivier Bell and Andrew McNeillie. 5 vols. London: Hogarth Press, 1977–84.

Woolf, Virginia. *The Essays of Virginia Woolf*. Ed. Andrew McNeillie. 6 vols. London: Hogarth Press, 1986.

Woolf, Virginia. *Moments of Being*. Ed. Jeanne Schulkind. London: Pimlico, 2002.

Index

Note: Pictures are indicated in italics. Endnotes are indicated by "n" followed by note number.
Articles "a," "the" preceding titles are disregarded in the sorting. Ex.: *A Backward Glance* is sorted under "b."

Wells, H. G. 14–15, 22, 39, 43, 51, 60, 65,
69–70, 81, 107, 174
anecdotes about 83
on Conrad and privacy 57–8
on Conrad/Ford collaboration 12, 83
criticism of Conrad 134
criticism of Ford 83, 92, 127,
129–30, 135
criticism of James 123, 135
dealing with endings 144–5
death of loved ones 126–7
discussion of satire with Lewis 186–7
on global governance 235n47
on his childhood body 131
on his parents' marriage 131
interest in society 129
James's criticism of 123
Lewis's account of 197
love relationships 131, 132, 137–8,
139–44
love tribulations 138
and novelistic autobiography 121–2
on novel vs. autobiography 135
"picshuas" 132–3
portrait of Conrad 10
praise of Conrad 16
preface to Gissing's novel 125
psychology of his persona 127–8, 129,
130, 136
secrecy 130
short temper 122
in Stein's Autobiography 157
and truth-telling 127, 141
views on fate 215–16
West's biography of 126
on writing 145
Wells, Isabel (wife) 131, 132
death 126
Wells, Marjorie (daughter-in-law) 139
Wells Archive (University of Illinois) 145
West, Anthony 137
West, Geoffrey (Wells, G.) 126
West, Rebecca 129, 139, 190
Lewis's account of 204
on Vorticism 192
Wells's memories of 140–1
Wharton, Edith 5, 37, 41, 43, 44, 51, 94
affair with Fullerton 113–17
on the art of biography 97
childhood fears 98–9

compartmentalization in 111–12
death of loved ones 101
deflection in 103
disclaimer about truthfulness 102
final years 118
friendships' influence on 104–5
genesis of A Backward Glance 101–2
instructions on her death 118
meeting James 105–6
mimicry of James's circumlocutions 107
move to Paris 95
nicknames by James 106
omissions in 103–4, 109
portrait of James 106
praise of James's verbal memories 107–8
recalling James's depression 108–9
secrecy 99, 104, 105
selectivity 105
sexuality 99–100, 103
social life 109–11
war experiences 95, 111
writing habits 96
Wharton, Teddy 41, 101
omission of illness 109
What Maisie Knew (James) 49
When Blood is Their Argument (Ford) 79
Wilder, Thornton 167, 171–2
Will, Barbara 176
Wineapple, Brenda 238n13
The Wings of the Dove (James) 66
"The Winner Loses" (Stein) 171
Winthrop, Egerton 105
Wolff, Cynthia Griffin 94, 113
Woman Knitting (Lewis) 184
Woman With a Fan (Picasso) 153
Women & Men (Ford) 74
Woolf, Leonard 210
Woolf's suicide letter to 212
Woolf, Virginia 3, 4, 6
attempts at autobiography 209
autobiography as a creative holiday 214
diaries 209–10
first memories 211–12
on Lewis's satire 187
memories of her mother 215
present tense writing 210–11
sense of the past 212
suicide letter 212
writing as a coping mechanism 215
on writing biographies 213